Analysis Toolpak Tools (continued)	*Description*
ANOVA: Two-Factor Without Replication	Tests hypothesis that means of two or more samples measured on two factors are equal based on one sampling.
Correlation	Computes the correlation coefficient between two data sets.
Descriptive Statistics	Provides a summary of a variety of basic statistical measures.
Exponential Smoothing	Predicts a value based on the forecast for the prior period, adjusted for the error in that prior forecast.
F-test: Two-Sample for Variances	Performs a test of hypothesis for equality of variances between two populations.
Histogram	Creates a frequency distribution and graphical histogram for a set of data.
Moving Average	Projects forecast values based on the average value of the variable over a specific number of preceding periods.
Rank and Percentile	Computes the ordinal and percentage rank of each value in a data set.
Regression	Used to develop a model relating time series data to a set of variables assumed to influence the data.
Sampling	Creates a simple random sample with replacement or a systematic sample from a population.
t-test: Paired Two Sample for Means	Performs a paired *t*-test to test a hypothesis for equality of means between two populations for small samples.
t-test: Two-Sample Assuming Equal Variances	Performs a test of hypothesis for equality of means between two populations if the populations are assumed to have equal variances.
t-test: Two-Sample Assuming Unequal Variances	Performs a test of hypothesis for equality of means between two populations if the populations are assumed to have unequal variances.
z-test: Two-Sample for Means	Performs a test of hypothesis for equality of means between two populations for large samples.

Prentice Hall Statistics Add-In	*Description*
Binomial Probabilities	Computes binomial probabilities and histogram.
Box-and-Whisker Plot	Creates a box-and-whisker plot of a data set.
Confidence Intervals	Computes confidence intervals for means with σ known or unknown, proportions, and population total.
c-Sample Tests	Performs chi-square test of independence.
Exponential Probabilities	Computes exponential probabilities.
Normal Probabilities	Computes normal probabilities.
Normal Probability Plot	Generates a normal probability plot from a set of data.
One-Sample Tests	Performs hypothesis tests for means with σ known or unknown, and for proportions.
Poisson Probabilities	Computes Poisson probabilities and histogram.
Random Sample Generator	Generates a random sample without replacement.
Sample Size	Determines sample sizes for means and proportions.
Sampling Distribution Simulation	Generates a simulated sampling distribution from a uniform, standardized normal, or discrete population.
Stem-and-Leaf Display	Creates a stem-and-leaf display of a data set.
Two-Sample Tests	Performs *t*-test for difference in means; *F*-test for equality of variances; chi-square and *z*-tests for proportions.

To our wives, Beverly and Meri, for all their encouragement and understanding.

James R. Evans and David L. Olson

STATISTICS, DATA ANALYSIS, AND DECISION MODELING

James R. Evans

University of Cincinnati

David L. Olson

Texas A&M University

Prentice Hall
Upper Saddle River, NJ 07458

VP/Editorial Director: Jim Boyd
Editor-in-Chief: Natalie Anderson
Senior Editor: Tom Tucker
Editorial Assistant: Kerri Limpert
Senior Marketing Manager: Debbie Clare
Director of Production: Michael Weinstein
Production Manager: Gail Steier de Acevedo
Production Coordinator: Kelly Warsak
Permissions Coordinator: Monica Stipanov
Manufacturing Buyer: Natacha St. Hill Moore
Senior Manufacturing and Prepress Manager: Vincent Scelta
Cover Design: Bruce Kenselaar
Cover Photo: Kolea Baker Artists Representative, Inc.
Full Service Composition: BookMasters, Inc.

Library of Congress Cataloging-in-Publication Data

Evans, James R. (James Robert)
    Statistics, data analysis, and decision modeling / James R. Evans,
  David L. Olson.
      p. cm.
    Includes index.
    ISBN 0-13-020545-1
    1. Industrial management—Statistical methods.   2. Statistical
decision.   I. Olson, David Louis.   II. Title.
HD30.215.E93   1999
658.4′033—dc21   99-26628
                                             CIP

Prentice-Hall International (UK) Limited, London
Prentice-Hall of Australia Pty. Limited, Sydney
Prentice-Hall Canada Inc., Toronto
Prentice-Hall Hispanoamericana, S.A., Mexico
Prentice-Hall of India Private Limited, New Delhi
Prentice-Hall of Japan, Inc., Tokyo
Editora Prentice-Hall do Brasil, Ltda., Rio de Janeiro

Printed in the United States of America

10 9 8 7 6 5 4 3 2 1

Contents

PREFACE   xi

PART I

CHAPTER 1:   Data and Business Decisions   1

The Importance of Data Analysis and Decision Modeling   2

Types and Sources of Business Data   3

The Tracway database   6

Measurement and Statistics   10

Populations and samples   12

Decision Models   13

Using Microsoft Excel   14

Excel add-ins: PHStat, Crystal Ball, *and* TreePlan   15

Working with data   15

Summary   17

Questions and Problems   18

CHAPTER 2:   Displaying and Summarizing Data   19

Displaying Data with Charts and Graphs   20

Column and bar charts   23

Line charts   25

Pie charts   28

Area charts   29

Scatter diagrams   29

Summary of graphical display methods   30

Descriptive Statistics   30

Frequency distributions and histograms   32

Measures of central tendency   34

Measures of dispersion   36

Coefficient of variation   38

Measures of shape   38

Excel's descriptive statistics tool   38

Data profiles and proportions   41

v

Visual Display of Statistical Measures   43
   Box-and-whisker plots   43
   Stem-and-leaf displays   46

Statistical Relationships   48

Case Study: Using Descriptive Statistics for the Malcolm Baldrige
     National Quality Award   51

Summary   54

Questions and Problems   54

CHAPTER 3:   Random Variables and Probability Distributions   57

Basic Concepts   58
   Probability   58
   Random variables   59
   Probability distributions   59
   Expected value and variance of a random variable   62

Discrete Probability Distributions   63
   Bernoulli and binomial distributions   63
   Poisson distribution   65

Continuous Probability Distributions   66
   Uniform distribution   67
   Normal distribution   68
   Triangular distribution   71
   Exponential distribution   72
   Probability distributions in PHStat   *74*
   Other useful distributions   75

Random Sampling from Probability Distributions   78
   Random numbers   78
   Sampling from probability distributions   79
   Sampling from probability distributions in Excel   80
   Sampling distributions and sampling error   83

Summary   86

Questions and Problems   87

Appendix: Introduction to *Crystal Ball*   89
   Specifying input information   90
   Crystal Ball *output   94*

CHAPTER 4:   Sampling and Statistical Analysis for Decision Making   97

Statistical Sampling   98
   Sample design   99
   Sampling methods   100
   Errors in sampling   102
   Sampling from finite populations   103

Statistical Analysis of Sample Data   103

Estimation   103
   Point estimates   103
   Interval estimates   105

Confidence intervals for the mean   106
Confidence intervals for proportions   110
Confidence intervals and sample size   110

Hypothesis Testing   111
Hypothesis formulation   112
Significance level   113
Decision rules   114
Using p-*values*   116
Two-sample hypothesis tests for means   119
F-*test for testing variances*   119
Tests for proportions   122
Other hypothesis tests   124

ANOVA: Testing Differences of Several Means   125

Chi-Square Test for Independence   127

Summary   129

Questions and Problems   131

Appendix: Distribution Fitting   133
Distribution fitting with Crystal Ball   *137*

CHAPTER 5:   Statistical Quality Control   140

The Role of Statistics and Data Analysis in Quality Control   141

Statistical Process Control   142
Control charts   143
x̄- *and* R-*charts*   144
Analyzing control charts   148

Control Charts for Attributes   152

Statistical Issues in the Design of Control Charts   154

Process Capability Analysis   155

Summary   157

Questions and Problems   158

PART II

CHAPTER 6:   Regression   167

Simple Linear Regression   170
Least squares estimation   170

Measuring Variation about the Regression Line   173
Coefficient of determination and correlation coefficient   176
Standard error of the estimate and confidence bands   176

Regression as Analysis of Variance   178

Assumptions of Regression Analysis   181

Application of Regression Analysis to Investment Risk   182

Multiple Linear Regression   185
Interpreting results from multiple linear regression   187

Building Good Regression Models   188
    Using Adjusted R² to evaluate fit   *188*
    Correlation and multicollinearity   *189*
    Best subsets regression   *190*
Regression with Ordinal and Nominal Independent Variables   191
Regression Models with Nonlinear Terms   194
Summary   198
Questions and Problems   199

CHAPTER 7:   Forecasting   203
Qualitative and Judgmental Methods   204
    Historical analogy   *205*
    The Delphi method   *205*
    Applying the Delphi method   *206*
    Indicators and indexes   *208*
Statistical Forecasting Models   209
    Moving average models   *210*
    Error metrics and forecast accuracy   *212*
    Exponential smoothing models   *216*
    Incorporating trend and seasonality into exponential smoothing models   *217*
Regression Models   220
    Incorporating seasonality in regression models   *222*
The Practice of Forecasting   223
Summary   226
Questions and Problems   227
Appendix: *CB Predictor*   229

CHAPTER 8:   Selection Models and Risk Analysis   234
Decision Criteria and Selection   235
    Decisions involving a single alternative   *236*
    Sensitivity analysis   *237*
    Decisions involving mutually exclusive alternatives   *239*
    Decisions involving nonmutually exclusive alternatives   *241*
    Decisions involving uncertainty   *242*
Monte Carlo Simulation for Risk Analysis   249
Applications of Monte Carlo Simulation   253
    Project management   *253*
    Budget-constrained product selection   *257*
Case Study: Simulation and Risk Analysis in New Product Screening
    at Cinergy Corporation   259
Summary   263
Questions and Problems   263
Appendix: Additional *Crystal Ball* Options   271
    Correlated assumptions   *271*
    Freezing assumptions   *271*

Overlay charts   *272*
Trend charts   *272*
Sensitivity charts   *272*

CHAPTER 9:   Introduction to Optimization   276

Constrained Optimization   278

Types of Optimization Problems   279
  Linear optimization example: transportation problem   *280*
  Integer optimization example: project selection   *282*
  Nonlinear optimization example: hotel pricing   *283*

Spreadsheet Optimization   284
  Solving the optimal pricing problem   *285*

Solving Linear Optimization Models   286
  Interpreting Solver reports   *288*
  Difficulties with Solver   *290*

Solving Integer Optimization Models   291

Solving Nonlinear Optimization Models   292

Risk Analysis of Optimization Results   294

Combining Optimization and Simulation   296
  A portfolio allocation model   *296*
  Using OptQuest   *297*
  Interpreting results   *303*
  Adding a requirement   *303*

Summary   304

Questions and Problems   304

APPENDIX   315

Table A.1   The Standardized Normal Distribution   316

Table A.2   The Cumulative Standard Normal Distribution   317

Table A.3   Critical Values of *t*   319

Table A.4   Critical Values of *F*   321

INDEX   325

Preface

In recent years, we have seen two significant emerging trends in business schools. First, many schools are redesigning their programs around shorter, modular courses. Second, Microsoft Excel and other spreadsheet add-ins have become the principal tool for applications of quantitative methods. *Statistics, Data Analysis, and Decision Modeling* is written to meet the need for an introductory text that addresses both of these trends.

The purpose of this book is to provide a basic introduction to business statistics, focusing on practical applications of data analysis to business decision making. To support this purpose, we have integrated fundamental theory and practical applications in a spreadsheet environment. A unique feature of this book is the use of a comprehensive database (in the form of a Microsoft Excel workbook) for a fictitious company to illustrate techniques and methodology as well as to provide a source of problems and exercises in a unified business context. Spreadsheet add-ins, specifically *PHStat*—a collection of statistical tools that enhance the capabilities of Excel, published by Prentice Hall; the student version of *Crystal Ball*—the most popular commercial package for risk analysis; and *TreePlan*—a decision analysis add-in, are used for additional analysis capability.

The book consists of nine chapters.

- Chapter 1, *Data and Business Decisions,* describes the importance of, and types of data used in, business decision making. This chapter also provides the foundation for working with Excel and other add-ins, and introduces some fundamental concepts of measurement, sample data, and decision models.
- Chapter 2, *Displaying and Summarizing Data,* focuses on data visualization and descriptive statistics.
- Chapter 3, *Random Variables and Probability Distributions,* introduces basic concepts of probability distributions, random sampling, sampling distributions, and sampling error. *Crystal Ball* is introduced and used as a tool for simulating sampling distributions to gain insight into their nature. An appendix to the chapter provides a quasi-user's manual for *Crystal Ball.*
- Chapter 4, *Sampling and Statistical Analysis for Decision Making,* addresses sampling methods, statistical analysis of sample data, estimation, and hypothesis testing. It also provides an introduction to analysis of variance and an appendix describes distribution fitting using *Crystal Ball.*
- Chapter 5, *Statistical Quality Control,* develops some applications of statistical concepts presented in the previous chapters to the design and use of control charts and process capability studies.

- Chapter 6, *Regression,* introduces fundamental concepts and methods of both single and multiple regression.
- Chapter 7, *Forecasting,* discusses both qualitative and quantitative forecasting methods. These include statistical time series models and applications of regression analysis to forecasting.
- Chapter 8, *Selection Models and Risk Analysis,* is the first of two chapters that deal with decision models. In this chapter we describe criteria and approaches for selecting among decision alternatives, and illustrate Monte Carlo simulation with *Crystal Ball* for risk analysis.
- Chapter 9, *Introduction to Optimization,* introduces basic concepts of linear, integer, and nonlinear optimization models, spreadsheet formulations, and solution with Excel Solver. This chapter also illustrates how Monte Carlo simulation can provide additional insight about optimization results.

The first six or seven chapters can be used for a 5- or 6-week module for introductory statistics. For programs without a full follow-up course on management science, the full book can be used for a one-quarter or half-semester course that also provides an introduction to fundamental concepts of simulation, decision analysis, and optimization.

Throughout the book we have placed boxed "Notes" for Excel, *PHStat,* and *Crystal Ball* that provide procedural details of using specific functions, tools, or techniques. These provide key information for the student to apply the tools, but do not disrupt from the flow of the discussion.

The CD-ROM accompanying this book contains the database and other spreadsheet files used throughout the book, *PHStat,* the student version of *Crystal Ball,* and *TreePlan* software and documentation.

We would like to thank the following individuals who have provided reviews, suggestions, and guidance during the development of this book: Samir Barman, University of Oklahoma; James Cochran, University of Cincinnati; Lillian Fok, University of New Orleans; Soumen Ghosh, Georgia Institute of Technology; Jim Grayson, Augusta State University; Ina Markham, James Madison University; Tom McCullough, University of California at Berkeley; David Pentico, Duquesne University; Barbara Price, Georgia Southern University; Jeffrey Rummell, University of Connecticut at Storrs; and Barbara Russell, Saint Bonaventure University. Finally, we express our appreciation to our editor Tom Tucker, production coordinator Kelly Warsak, and the entire production staff at Prentice Hall for their dedication in developing and producing this book.

James R. Evans
David L. Olson

CHAPTER

1

Data and Business Decisions

Outline

The Importance of Data Analysis and Decision Modeling
Types and Sources of Business Data
   The Tracway Database
      Category I: Customer Satisfaction Measures
      Category II: Financial and Market Performance Measures
      Category III: Human Resource Measures
      Category IV: Supplier and Partner Performance Measures
      Category V: Organizational Effectiveness Measures
      Category VI: Quality Process Measures
Measurement and Statistics
   Populations and Samples
Decision Models
Using Microsoft Excel
   Excel Add-Ins: *PHStat* and *Crystal Ball*
   Working With Data
Summary
Questions and Problems

Managers often observe a problem and associate some prior actions or decisions to be the cause of the problem. For example, if a new advertising campaign happens to coincide with a drop in sales, some managers might drop the ad campaign quickly without any further analysis; if sales in some region fell from the previous year, the regional manager might blame her sales staff for not working hard. Clearly, it is dangerous to generalize on the basis of a single event or observation. A better approach would be to formulate a theory ("Certain ad campaigns positively affect sales") and test this theory in some way, either by collecting and analyzing some data ("Measure change in sales when advertising is adopted") or perhaps by developing a model of the situation that will explain the relationship between the variables ("When advertising is increased by 10 percent, sales increase by 15 percent"). Taking such a scientific approach can provide better insight into the nature of the relationships among the many factors contributing to the event and thus form the basis for better decisions. In contemporary business jargon, we often call this approach "management by fact" or "statistical thinking." However, few managers think in this fashion. They may lack the time to perform a thorough and objective analysis of data; in most cases, however, they simply do not know how to deal with data and information effectively.

Even when managers have good data and information, they may not use them effectively to make good decisions. The reasons for this include the inability to define appropriate decision alternatives, properly select from among alternatives to achieve a specific goal or objective, and identify the best alternative from among a seemingly endless number of choices. By knowing how to structure decision problems effectively into formal decision models, managers can apply useful mathematical and computer-based tools to assist them in making sound decisions.

Statistics, data analysis, and decision modeling are important tools for every contemporary manager. The purpose of this book is to introduce you to practical approaches for analyzing data, ways of using data effectively to make informed decisions, and approaches for developing, analyzing, and solving models of decision problems.

In this chapter we discuss the roles of data analysis and decision models in business, discuss how data are used in evaluating business performance, introduce some fundamental issues of statistics and measurement, and introduce spreadsheets as a support tool for data analysis and decision modeling. The key concepts that we will discuss are

- The scope of business performance data: customer satisfaction, financial and market, human resource, supplier and partner, and organizational effectiveness data;
- The role of statistics: using sample data to understand and draw inferences about populations and monitor the effectiveness of manufacturing and service processes;
- Common types of measurement scales: categorical, ordinal, interval, and ratio;
- Types of decision models that you will learn about in later chapters: regression models, forecasting models, selection models, simulation models, and optimization models; and
- Microsoft Excel and add-ins that are supplied with this book.

The Importance of Data Analysis and Decision Modeling

A phrase one often hears in many companies today is *In God we trust; all others use data.* Modern organizations truly manage by fact—they depend upon complete and accurate data for performance evaluation, improvement, and decision making. Businesses need many types of data, including customer, product and service performance, operations, market, competitive comparisons, supplier, employee-related, and cost and financial. *Analysis* refers to extracting larger meaning from data to support evaluation and decision making. One of the most important tools for analyzing data in business is **statistics,** which is the science of collecting, organizing, analyzing, interpreting, and presenting data. Through the analysis of data we derive *information*—an understanding of what the data tell us. Modern spreadsheet technology, such as Microsoft Excel, has made it quite easy to organize, analyze, and present data.

Statistics and other methods of data analysis help us to determine trends, projections, cause-and-effect relationships, and other significant meanings of data that might not be evident. For example, Sears Roebuck, Inc., provided a consulting group with 13 financial measures, hundreds of thousands of employee satisfaction data points, and millions of data points on customer satisfaction. Using advanced statistical tools, the analysts discovered that employee attitudes about their jobs and the company are key factors that predict their behavior with customers, which in turn predicts the likelihood of customer retention and recommendations, which in turn predicts financial performance. Sears can now predict that if a store increases its employee satisfaction score by five units, customer satisfaction scores will increase by two units, and revenue growth will beat the stores' national average by 0.5 percent.[1] Such an analysis can help managers to make decisions, for example, on improved human resource policies.

Data also provide key inputs to decision models. A **decision model** is a logical or mathematical representation of a problem or business situation. Decision models establish a relationship between actions that decision makers might take and results that they might expect, thereby allowing decision makers to predict what might happen based on the model assumptions. For instance, the manager of a grocery store might want to know how to best use price promotions, coupon programs, and advertising to increase sales. In the past, grocers have studied the relationship of sales volume to programs such as these by conducting controlled experiments to identify the relationship between actions and sales volumes.[2] That is, they implement different combinations of price promotions, coupon programs, and advertising (the decision variables) and then observe the sales that result. Using the data from these experiments and a statistical technique known as *regression analysis* (which we cover in chapter 5), we can develop a predictive model of sales as a function of the decision variables (price level, coupon usage, and advertising dollars). Such a regression model might look like the following:

$$Sales\ (\$) = a + b*Price + c*Coupons + d*Advertising + e*Price*Advertising$$

where *a, b, c, d,* and *e* are constants that are determined from the data. By setting levels for price, coupon usage, and advertising, the model estimates the level of sales that would result. The manager can use such a model to examine the effects that changes in these decisions would be expected to have on sales, and to identify effective pricing, promotion, and advertising strategies.

Part I of this book (chapters 1–5) focuses on fundamental issues of statistics and data analysis, along with a chapter on applications in quality control. Part II (chapters 6–9) introduces you to various types of decision models that rely on good data analysis.

Types and Sources of Business Data

Data and analysis support a variety of company purposes, such as planning, reviewing company performance, improving operations, and comparing company performance with competitors' or "best practices" benchmarks. Most organizations have traditionally focused on financial and market information, such as profit, sales volume, and market share. Today, however, many organizations create a "balanced scorecard" of measures that provide a comprehensive view of business performance. Such a scorecard is balanced by the interests of all stakeholders—customers, employees, stockholders, suppliers and partners, and the community—and allows organizations to focus on the critical success factors that lead to competitive advantage. Thus, a balanced scorecard often consists of five key categories:

1. *Customer satisfaction measures.* These include measures of customer satisfaction obtained from surveys as well as other indicators such as complaints.
2. *Financial and market performance measures.* Many types of financial performance measures are tracked. These might include return on investment, asset utilization,

---

[1]"Bringing Sears Into the New World," *Fortune*, October 13, 1997, 183–184.
[2]"Flanking in a Price War," *Interfaces* 19:2 (1989): 1–12.

operating margins, earnings per share, profitability, profit forecast reliability, liquidity, debt to equity ratio, and value added per employee. Market performance measures might include market share and business growth indexes.
3. *Human resource measures.* Examples of human resource measures are employee satisfaction, improvement suggestion rates, training effectiveness, absenteeism, and turnover.
4. *Supplier and partner performance measures.* These might include measures of quality, delivery, and price.
5. *Organizational effectiveness measures that support company strategy.* Appropriate measures might include quality indicators such as defects or field performance, productivity, cycle time, legal compliance, environmental improvements, rates of innovation, cost reductions, process yields, and shipment and document accuracy.

To illustrate how a balanced scorecard of performance measures is used in a business, we will discuss how Solectron Corporation, a two-time winner of the Malcolm Baldrige National Quality Award,[3] aligns their performance measures with their company goals and business processes. Solectron, based in Milpitas, California, is an independent provider of customized design and manufacturing services to electronics original equipment manufacturers (OEMs). In 1997, the company had 19 global locations, 20,000 employees, and annual revenues of $3.7 billion. Among Solectron's services are product design and development, electrical design, concurrent engineering, prototype build, component and packaging selection, printed circuit board assembly, and software and documentation packaging. Figure 1.1 shows how Solectron's performance measures link to their key business processes, business drivers, and company beliefs. These performance measures—an aggregation of raw data collected throughout the firm—are analyzed and evaluated by various managers as a basis for their business decisions. For example, the board of directors reviews customers, business, operational, human resource, and strategy data on a bimonthly basis; all managers review a comprehensive corporate scorecard quarterly; and site managers review more detailed performance data daily, weekly, and quarterly. Solectron focuses on timely and actionable information to address the needs of their stakeholders.

Data in the five categories we cited may come from a variety of sources: internal, external, and generated. Internal data might include accounting and financial data, sales, quality performance, employee productivity, turnover statistics, and so on. These data often are gathered using modern technology such as bar coding or automated transaction reporting. External data might include competitive performance data acquired from annual reports of other companies, Standard & Poor's (S&P) Compustat data sets, or industry trade associations; and government data from the Bureau of Commerce statistics (http://www.tcb-indicators.org/), the Bureau of the Census, the Bureau of Labor, and other cabinet departments. Other data must be generated through special efforts. For example, customer satisfaction data are often acquired by mail to telephone surveys, personal interviews, or focus groups; measures of supplier quality might be derived through laboratory experiments on raw materials purchased from suppliers. Except for leading-edge performers, most companies generally do a poor job of collecting relevant data and using it for decision making.

Data, whether gathered from internal, external, or generated sources, are usually maintained in a computer database. A well-designed computer database allows managers to easily access necessary data, obtain answers to specific queries, and link data to

[3]Adapted from Solectron's 1997 Malcolm Baldrige National Quality Award Application Summary. Solectron won the Baldrige Award in 1991 and 1997, becoming the first repeat winner.

Mission	Beliefs	Business Driver	Key Business Processes	Performance Measures
• Custom-integrated services • Worldwide responsiveness • Long-term partnerships • Ethical business practices	1. Customer First (stakeholder—Customer)	• Customer satisfaction	• Market and customer requirements determination • Annual customer survey • Customer satisfaction assurance process	• Overall evaluation of Solectron • Customer satisfaction index (CSI) • Customer return rate • Market share
	2. Respect for the Individual (stakeholder—Employee)	• Employee satisfaction	• Performance planning and evaluation • Training and development • Customer focus team deployment	• EOS • Absenteeism • Lost time per employee • Turnover
Vision Be the best and continuously improve.	3. Quality (stakeholders—Customer and Stockholder)	• Product quality • Process capability	• Continuous improvement • Benchmark industry performance • Hoshin planning	• Test and inspection yields • Manufacturing performance and delivery
	4. Supplier Partnership (stakeholder—Supplier)	• Supply quality and assurance	• Supply base management	• Supplier reject rates • # Strategic supplier relationships
	5. Business Ethics (all stakeholders)	• Customer confidence	• Ethical behavior • Understanding customer requirements and Solectron capabilities and then meeting commitments	• Customer likely to recommend Solectron • CSI
	6. Shareholder Value (stakeholder—Stockholder)	• Stockholder satisfaction	• Execute to the long-range plan (LRP) and annual operating plan (AOP) • EMS competitor analysis	• Revenue • PBT • ROA • EPS • PBT per employee
	7. Social Responsibility (stakeholder—Community)	• Environmental friendliness • Employee health and safety • Community involvement	• Environmental regulation compliance and proactive environmental action • Health and safety training, audits, and improvement • Proactive support for Solectron's communities	• Compliance • Recycling • Contributions • Involvement

FIGURE 1.1 Solectron's Information and Data

Source: Solectron 1997 Malcolm Baldrige National Quality Award Application Summary

decision models through a comprehensive decision support system. We will use a database for a fictitious company, Tracway International, Inc.,[4] as a basis for illustrating the use of statistical analysis and decision modeling approaches throughout this book.

THE TRACWAY DATABASE

To put the database in perspective, we will first provide some background about the company so that the applications of data analysis and decision modeling tools will be more meaningful. Tracway is a privately owned designer and producer of traditional lawn mowers used by home owners. Since home owners are more often using lawn cover or hiring lawn services (or in California and Arizona relying more on natural sand for their yards), the lawn mower market has not experienced high growth. In the past 10 years Tracway has added another key product, a medium-size diesel power lawn tractor (21–50 hp) with front and rear power take-offs (PTOs), Class I three-point hitches, four-wheel drive, power steering, and full hydraulics. This equipment is built primarily for a niche market consisting of large estates—including golf and country clubs, resorts, private estates, city parks, large commercial complexes, lawn care service providers, private home owners with five or more acres—and government (federal, state, and local) parks, building complexes, and military bases. The company is headquartered in St. Louis, Missouri, with manufacturing plants in St. Louis, Missouri; Greenwood, South Carolina; Camarillo, California; and Providence, Rhode Island.

In the United States, the focus of sales is on the Eastern Seaboard, California, the Southeast, and the south central states, which have the greatest concentration of estates. The market is cyclical, but the different products and regions balance some of this, with about 55 percent of total sales occurring in the spring and summer, about 25 percent in the fall, and about 20 percent in the winter. Outside the United States, Tracway has seen a declining European market, a growing South American market, and developing markets in the Pacific Rim and China. Annual sales are approximately $180 million.

Tracway provides most of the products to owner dealerships, which in turn sell directly to end users. The owner dealerships also function as maintenance and repair facilities for customers, including support for federal and foreign governments. Because of the importance of the dealerships to the company's success, steps are taken to ensure that they are successful. To minimize their inventory costs, the company guarantees delivery of replacement tractors for those sold within 5 working days and replacement equipment within 3 days for U.S. dealers. For dealers outside of the United States, replacement tractors are shipped within 48 hours and equipment within 24 hours of notification of sale. This approach has enabled the dealerships' inventory costs to be 57 percent below other dealers and demonstrates the commitment Tracway is making to dealers. Tracway also involves the dealers in the yearly planning process, new and upgrade design processes, pricing strategy, sales, and other meetings to fully integrate them into the business. When new products are designed, the dealers pilot use of the maintenance and support documentation for validation before finalization. Training of dealers in the operation and maintenance of new and modified tractors and equipment is always a top priority.

---

[4]This scenario was adapted from Gateway Estate Lawn Equipment Co. Case Study, used for the 1997 Malcolm Baldrige National Quality Award Examiner Training course. This material is in the public domain. The database, however, was developed by the authors.

Tracway employs 1,660 people worldwide. About half the workforce is based in St. Louis; the remainder is divided among the Camarillo, Greenwood, and Providence sites. Of the total workforce, 100 are classified as management, 1,150 as design and production, and the remainder as sales/administrative support.

Both end users and dealers are important customers for Tracway. Collection and analysis of end-user data showed that satisfaction with the products depends on high quality, easy attachment/dismount of implements, low maintenance, price, value, and service. For dealers, key requirements are high quality, parts and feature availability, rapid restock, discounts, and timeliness of support.

Tracway has several key suppliers: Mitsitsiu, Inc., the sole source of all diesel engines; LANTO Axles, Inc., which provides tractor axles; Schorst Fabrication, which provides subassemblies; Cuberillo, Inc., supplier of transmissions; and Specialty Machining, Inc., a supplier of precision machine parts.

To help manage this enterprise, Tracway collects a variety of data in each of the key categories noted earlier. These data, which are summarized in Table 1.1 and described in the following section, are stored in the form of a Microsoft Excel workbook (*Tracway.xls*) that is included on the CD-ROM accompanying this book. (The CD-ROM also contains other files for use in end-of-chapter problems.) All files are saved in Microsoft Excel 97 and 5.0/95 workbook format. Figure 1.2 shows the Excel screen for the Tracway database. Data for each of the key measures are stored in one of the worksheets. By clicking on any of the worksheet tabs, you may access the data. The navigation buttons allow you to move through the worksheets in the workbook (similar to moving through tracks on a compact disk!). A small red triangle in the upper right-hand corner of a cell indicates a comment. By positioning the cursor over that cell, you may

TABLE 1.1 Summary of Tracway Database

Measure	I Customer Satisfaction	II Finacial and Market Performance	III Human Resource	IV Supplier and Partner Performance	V Organizational Effectiveness	VI Quality Process
1	Dealer satisfaction	Mower unit sales	Employee satisfaction	On-time delivery	Engines	Blade weight
2	End-user satisfaction	Tractor unit sales	Employee success	Defects after delivery	Transmission costs	Mower test
3	Cross-sectional survey	Revenues	Blood pressure	Time-to-pay suppliers	Response time	Process capability
4	Survey recap	Pre-tax earnings		Tractor preparation	Stock	
5	Complaints	World mower unit sales		TracPrep samples		
6		World tractor unit sales				
7		World $ sold				
8		Mktshare mowers				
9		Mktshare tractors				
10		Mktshare combined				

FIGURE 1.2 Portion of Tracway Database in Microsoft Excel

	A	B	C	D	E	F	G	H	I	J	K
1	Dealer Satisfaction										
2											
3	*Survey Scale:*	0							Sample		
4	North America							Average	Size		
5	1996	1	0	2	13	22	1	3.82	50		
6	1997	0	0	2	14	20	14	3.92	50		
7	1998	1	1	1	6	36	15	4.00	60		
8	1999	1	2	6	13	38					
9	2000	2	3	5	15	44					
10											
11	South America										
12	1996	0	0	0	2	6	2	4.00	10		
13	1997	0	0	0	2	6	2	4.00	10		
14	1998	0	0	1	4	9	14	4.29	28		
15	1999	0	1	1	3	12	30	4.47	47		
16	2000	1	1	2	4	21	48	4.43	77		
17											
18	Europe										
19	1996	0	0	1	3	7	4	3.93	15		
20	1997	0	0	1	2	8	4	4.00	15		
21	1998	0	0	1	2	8	4	4.00	15		
22	1999	0	0	1	2	8	4	4.00	15		
23	2000								15		
24											
25	Pacific Rim										
26	1996								5		
27	1997								5		
28	1998								6		
29	1999	0		0	2	3	1	3.83	6		
30	2000	0	0	1	2	3	2	3.75	8		
31											
32	China										

Comment box: This worksheet provides dealer survey results of perceived Tracway product quality by year

Worksheet Tabs: I1 Dealer Satisfaction / I2 End-User Satisfaction / I3 Cross-Sectional Survey / I4 Survey Recap /

view the comment. The comments in the Tracway database describe the nature of the data on each worksheet. We will be using the Tracway database in many examples throughout this book.

Category I: Customer Satisfaction Measures

Quality is a key strategic factor for Tracway. Measures that Tracway uses to assess customer satisfaction are

- *I1 Dealer Satisfaction,* measured on a scale of 0–5 (0 = very poor, 1 = poor, 2 = mediocre, 3 = acceptable, 4 = excellent, and 5 = outstanding). Each year, dealers in each region are surveyed about Tracway product quality. The database contains data from cross-sectional surveys for the past 5 years.
- *I2 End-User Satisfaction,* measured on the same scale as dealers. Each year, 100 users from each region are surveyed about Tracway product quality. The database contains data for the past 5 years.
- *I3 Cross-Sectional Survey* is the complete survey data for the year 2000 for customer ratings of Tracway tractors. This worksheet contains 200 observations of customer ratings.
- *I4 Survey Recap* supplements the regular dealer and end-user product quality surveys with more detailed survey results about product quality, ease of use of Tracway products, the impact of price on purchasing decisions, and the level of service.
- *I5 Complaints* shows the number of complaints registered by all customers each month in each of Tracway's five regions (North America, South America, Europe, the Pacific, and China).

Category II: Financial and Market Performance Measures

Tracway measures a number of financial and market performance factors.

- *II1 Mower Unit Sales* and *II2 Tractor Unit Sales* provides Tracway sales by product by region on a monthly basis. Unit sales for each region are aggregated to obtain Tracway World Sales.
- *II3 Revenues* shows sales in dollars per month for each product (tractors and mowers) in each market region.
- *II4 Pre-Tax Earnings* provides pre-tax earnings, calculated as revenues minus production costs, as well as costs for overhead, dealer share, and tax and shipping. Return on revenue is calculated by dividing profit by revenue.
- The market within which Tracway operates is monitored monthly by region. Units sold are recorded in *II5 World Mower Unit Sales* and *II6 World Tractor Unit Sales*. These units are multiplied by Tracway sales prices to generate *II7 World $ Sold*, a regional calculation that is totaled by month in the World column.
- Tracway market share is calculated for each product and for total dollar sales. Market share by month by region is shown on worksheet *II8 Mktshare Mowers* and worksheet *II9 Mktshare Tractors*. Combined market share is calculated using Tracway sales prices, recorded by region by month on worksheet *II10 Mktshare Combined*.

Monthly data for all financial and market measures for the past 5 years are available.

Category III: Human Resource Measures

This group of data relates to measures of Tracway employees.

- *III1 Employee Satisfaction* provides data for the past 4 years of Tracway surveys of its employees to determine their overall satisfaction with their jobs with the same scale used for customers. Employees are surveyed quarterly; results are stratified by employee category: design and production, managerial and sales/administrative support.
- *III2 Employee Success* is cross-sectional data of a study of employee duration (length of hire) with Tracway. The 40 subjects were identified by reviewing hires from 10 years prior, and identifying those who were involved in managerial positions (either hired or promoted into management) at some time in this 10-year period.
- *III3 Blood Pressure* is a special survey conducted one time to compare managerial blood pressures in the North American region with that of Tracway managers in other regions.

Category IV: Supplier and Partner Performance Measures

This set of measures relates to relationships between Tracway and its partners, both suppliers and retailers.

- *IV1 On-Time Delivery* provides results for delivery-to-need date (1 day early or 0 days late), a critical measure to maintain the flow of the assembly lines. Tracway measures, on a monthly basis, the percent of shipments from each major supplier that meets the delivery-to-need date. Data for the past 5 years are available.
- *IV2 Defects After Delivery* shows the number of defects in supplier-provided material found in all shipments received from suppliers.

- *IV3 Time-to-Pay Suppliers* provides measurements in days from the time the invoice is received until the payment is sent.
- *IV4 Tractor Preparation* provides data consisting of tractor preparation costs from 570 dealers in the North American region for January 1996. *IV5 TracPrep Samples* provides random samples of these costs for each of the 60 months to support a study for the Tracway chief executive officer (CEO) to prepare for negotiations with North American dealers concerning shared expenses.

Category V: Organizational Effectiveness Measures

The following data are some measures of organizational effectiveness used in specific studies and analyses.

- *V1 Engines* gives 50 samples of the time required to produce a lawn mower engine using a new technology.
- *V2 Transmission Costs* shows the results of 30 samples each for three systems of producing Tracway tractor transmissions.
- *V3 Response Time* gives samples of the time taken by Tracway customer service personnel to respond to service calls.
- *V4 Stock* provides daily Tracway stock prices over a 6-month period.

Category VI: Quality Process Measures

This data includes three measures related to Tracway process quality.

- *VI1 Blade Weight* gives samples of mower blade weights, along with sample means and ranges.
- *VI2 Mower Test* gives 30 samples of 100 test results of mower functional performance after assembly.
- *VI3 Process Capability* gives samples of blade weights taken from a controlled process.

Measurement and Statistics

In reviewing the Tracway database, we can find two types of data: *discrete* and *continuous*. Discrete data, sometimes called **attributes data,** are numerical data that come from counting. For example, the dealer satisfaction data are discrete, since each observation is a whole number between 0 and 5. Another example of discrete data is the number of defects from suppliers. Continuous data, often called **variables data,** arise from a measurement process. Examples include costs, revenues, delivery times, production times, and so on.

Another way of classifying data is by its measurement scale. Failure to understand the differences in measurement scales can easily result in erroneous or misleading analysis. Data may be classified into four groups:

1. **Categorical (nominal) data,** which are sorted into categories according to specified characteristics. For example, customers might be classified by their geographical region as in the Tracway database (North America, South America, Europe, and Pacific); employees might be classified as managers, supervisors, and associates. The categories bear no quantitative relationship to one another, but usually an arbitrary number is assigned to each category to ease the process of managing the data and computing statistics. Categorical data are usually counted or expressed as percentages; statistics such as averages are difficult to interpret

and usually meaningless. Chapter 5 shows how categorical data can be included in regression analysis.

2. **Ordinal data,** which are ordered or ranked according to some relationship to one another. Examples include ranking regions according to sales levels each month and priorities assigned to jobs by a production scheduler. Ordinal data are more meaningful than categorical data because data in the different categories can be compared to one another according to some characteristic. However, like categorical data, averages are generally meaningless, because ordinal data have no fixed units of measurement. For instance, while a priority 1 job is higher than a priority 2 or 3 job, an average of job priorities would make little sense. In addition, meaningful numerical statements about differences between categories cannot be made.

3. **Interval data,** which are ordered, are characterized by a specified measure of the distance between observations but have no natural zero. A good example is temperature: Both Fahrenheit and Celsius scales represent a specified measure of distance—degrees—but have no natural zero. Thus we cannot say that 50 degrees is twice as hot as 25 degrees. Nevertheless, in contrast to ordinal data, interval data allow meaningful comparison of ranges, averages, and other statistics.

   In business, data from satisfaction rating scales, such as the one used for customer satisfaction in the Tracway database, are often considered to be interval data. Strictly speaking this is not correct, as the numerical "distance" between categories on the measurement scale, such as between *very poor* and *poor,* is meaningless. If respondents select their response on the basis of the category description, the data are ordinal. However, if respondents clearly understand that response categories are associated with the numerical measurement scale, then the data are interval. Usually this is a very tenuous assumption but, nevertheless, most users of survey data treat such data as interval, and we will make this assumption for the survey data in the Tracway database. You should remember, however, that care must be taken when collecting and interpreting survey data as interval data.

4. **Ratio data,** which have a natural zero. For example, sales dollars has an absolute zero (no sales activity at all). Knowing that the Seattle region sold $12,000,000 in March while the Tampa region sold $6,000,000 means that Seattle sold twice as much as Tampa. Most business and economic data fall into this category, and statistical methods are the most widely applicable. The sales and financial data in the Tracway database are ratio data.

This classification is hierarchical in that each level includes all of the information content of the one preceding it. For example, ratio information can be converted to any of the other types of data. Interval information can be converted to ordinal or categorical data, but cannot be converted to ratio data without the knowledge of the absolute zero point. Thus a ratio scale is the strongest form of measurement.

The managerial implications of this classification are in understanding the choice and validity of the statistical measures used. For example, it is much easier to state accurately that sales occurred in March (categorical data) than to state that sales increased relative to the prior month (ordinal data). Ordinal statements, in turn, are easier to state accurately than interval statements (sales increased by $50,000), or ratio statements (sales were $920,000 this month and $870,000 last month). On the other hand, a higher level of measurement is more useful to a manager because more complete statistical measures can be used to describe the data. Obtaining interval or ratio data can be more expensive, especially when surveying customers, but it may be needed for proper analysis. Thus, before data are collected, consideration must be given to the type of data needed.

POPULATIONS AND SAMPLES

Data that organizations collect can generally be classified into two categories: populations and samples. A **population** consists of all items of interest for a particular decision or investigation, for example, *all* married drivers over the age of 25. It is important to understand that a population can be anything we define it to be, such as all customers who have purchased from Tracway over the past year, or a set of potential users of Tracway's products, such as golf course superintendents. A company like Tracway probably keeps records of its customers, making it easy to retrieve data about the entire population of customers with prior purchases. However, it might be difficult to identify all golf course superintendents, even through professional trade associations.

A **sample** is a subset of a population. For example, a mailing list of superintendents belonging to a professional association would be a sample from the population of superintendents. A subset from this mailing list would also be a sample. Sampling is a desirable when complete information about a population is difficult or impossible to obtain. For example, it might be impossible to identify all golf course superintendents around the world, or it may be too expensive to send everyone on a mailing list a survey. In other situations, such as measuring the amount of stress needed to destroy an automotive tire, samples are necessary even though the entire population may be sitting in a warehouse.

In the Tracway database, a variety of sampling data is included. Dealer and customer survey data are obtained on a regular basis year after year. The data on the worksheet *Transmission Costs* involved physical experiments on equipment. Another example of sample data is provided by the worksheet *Employee Success,* where a convenience sample from personnel files was used.

We use samples to provide information about populations. We are all familiar with survey samples of voters prior to and during elections. A small subset of potential voters, if properly chosen on a statistical basis, can provide accurate estimates of the behavior of the voting population. Thus television network anchors can announce the winners of elections based on a small percentage of voters before all votes can be counted. Many businesses rely heavily on sampling. Producers of consumer products conduct small-scale market research surveys to evaluate consumer response to new products before full-scale production.

Statistics are summary measures of sample data used to draw inferences about population characteristics. You are familiar with a variety of statistics in daily life: baseball hitting averages, the Dow Jones Industrial Average, the Consumer Price Index, your average daily checking account balance, and many more. In business, statistical methods are used to present data in a concise and understandable fashion, estimate population characteristics, draw conclusions about populations from sample data, monitor quality, control processes, and develop useful decision models for prediction and forecasting. The collection, organization, and description of data is commonly called **descriptive statistics. Statistical inference** refers to the process of drawing conclusions about unknown characteristics of a population based on sample data. Finally, **predictive statistics**—developing predictions of future values based on historical data—is the third component of statistical methodology.

Decision Models

Decision models characterize the relationships between decision, or controllable, variables; uncontrollable inputs that capture the problem's environment; and outputs of interest to the decision maker. Spreadsheets are ideal vehicles for implementing decision models because of their versatility in managing data, evaluating different scenarios, and presenting results in a meaningful fashion. Figure 1.3 shows an example of a simple financial model expressed on an Excel spreadsheet. The model inputs are given in rows 4 through 8. The inputs are the base values in year 1 (column C) and inflation factors for subsequent years (column B). The key decision variables are the selling prices in each year. Model outputs are computed in the lower section of the spreadsheet. The formulas used to compute the outputs represent the "model." For example, the formulas used to compute the outputs for the first year are

$$\text{Total revenue: } C14 = C11*C8$$
$$\text{Cost of goods sold: } C15 = C4 + C5*C8$$
$$\text{Selling and administrative expenses: } C16 = C6 + C7*C8$$
$$\text{Profit before taxes: } C17 = C14 - C15 - C16$$
$$\text{Profit after taxes: } C18 = 0.52*C17$$

By substituting these formulas using a little algebra, we can express the final output in terms of the model inputs and decision variable as

$$\text{Profit after taxes: } C18 = 0.52*[C8*(C11 - C5 - C7) - C4 - C6]$$
$$= 0.52*[\text{unit sales}*(\text{selling price} - \text{unit cost of goods sold}$$
$$- \text{unit selling and administrative expenses})$$
$$- \text{fixed cost of goods sold} - \text{fixed selling and administrative expenses}]$$

With such a spreadsheet model, a manager may experiment with different assumptions, for example, changing the selling prices, inflation factors, or baseline values to answer a variety of "what if?" questions. In this way, the model can be used to analyze the effects

FIGURE 1.3 A Financial Decision Model

	A	B	C	D	E
1	**Profit Model**				
2		Inflation			
3	*Model Inputs and Assumptions*	factor	Year 1	Year 2	Year 3
4	Fixed cost of goods sold	3%	$ 100,000	$ 103,000	$ 106,090
5	Unit cost of goods sold	7%	$ 5.00	$ 5.35	$ 5.72
6	Fixed selling and administrative expenses	5%	$ 50,000	$ 52,500	$ 55,125
7	Unit selling and administrative expenses	7%	$ 2.00	$ 2.14	$ 2.29
8	Unit sales	15%	15,000	17,250	19,838
9					
10	*Decision Variables*				
11	Selling price		$ 20.00	$ 22.00	$ 25.00
12					
13	*Model Outputs*		Year 1	Year 2	Year 3
14	Total revenue		$ 300,000	$ 379,500	$ 495,938
15	Cost of goods sold		$ 175,000	$ 195,288	$ 219,650
16	Selling and administrative expenses		$ 80,000	$ 89,415	$ 100,549
17	Profit before taxes		$ 45,000	$ 94,798	$ 175,739
18	Profit after taxes		$ 23,400	$ 49,295	$ 91,384
19	*Cumulative profit*		*$ 23,400*	*$ 72,695*	*$ 164,079*

of uncertainty in inflation factors and sales levels, or to choose prices that meet certain cash flow or profitability requirements.

Decision models take many different forms. In Part II of this book, we introduce five generic types of decision models: *regression, forecasting, selection, simulation,* and *optimization.* We gave an example of a regression model for sales as a function of price, coupon usage, and advertising earlier in this chapter. The other types of decision models are briefly explained in the following paragraphs.

- **Forecasting models** support the important business need to analyze trends and predict the future using historical data. Forecasting models help managers estimate future sales levels, prices or costs, and economic indicators.
- **Selection models** assist a decision maker in comparing a small number of alternative options and seeking the best choice. Selection models might be used to choose where to build a new factory, how and when to expand capacity, or which new products to develop.
- **Simulation models** help in analyzing business decisions that involve significant uncertainty, for example, financial decisions for which future estimates of sales or costs are unknown with certainty, or models of manufacturing systems or other business processes in which jobs or customers arrive randomly. Simulation models help managers to gain a better understanding of the risks associated with decisions whose outcomes cannot be known for sure, and to assist them in choosing the best solution or systems design.
- **Optimization models** assist decision makers in identifying the best course of action to take, usually when faced with limited resources or other restrictions that must be satisfied. Such decision models have been very useful in problems such as product and process selection, operations scheduling, portfolio design, advertising planning, and many others.

Using Microsoft Excel

Spreadsheet software for personal computers has become an indispensable tool for business analysis, particularly for the manipulation of numerical data and the development and analysis of decision models. In this text, we will use Microsoft Excel to perform most calculations and analyses. We will assume that you are familiar with Excel and are competent with the following basic spreadsheet skills:

- Using windows, menus, and toolbars;
- Creating new files, opening existing files, and saving new files;
- Using workbooks and worksheets;
- Moving around the worksheet;
- Entering data;
- Building and editing formulas;
- Formatting a worksheet;
- Printing worksheets or selections;
- Using built-in functions;
- And most importantly, using Help files!

Other tools and procedures in Excel, such as creating graphs and charts, will be introduced as we need them throughout this book.

Microsoft Excel will provide most of the computational support required for the material in the book. Excel provides an add-in called the *Analysis Toolpak,* which contains a variety of tools for statistical computation. The *Analysis Toolpak* is not included in a standard Excel installation. To install it, select the *Add-Ins* option from the *Tools* menu. If *Analysis Toolpak* is not checked, simply check the box and click OK. You will not have to repeat this procedure when you run Excel in the future. If *Analysis Toolpak* does not appear in the list of add-ins, then you will have to run the Microsoft Excel setup procedure from your original distribution disk to make it available, choosing the "Custom" installation instead of "Typical."

EXCEL ADD-INS: *PHSTAT, CRYSTAL BALL,* AND *TREEPLAN*

Three other third-party add-ins available with this book provide additional capabilities and features not found in Excel. Prentice Hall's *PHStat* add-in provides useful statistical support that extends the capabilities of Excel. The Student Version of *Crystal Ball,* introduced in chapter 3, provides added ability to sample from probability distributions and perform risk-analysis simulations. *TreePlan* provides Excel support for decision trees. You should install these add-ins now on your computer. Refer to the installation procedures on the CD-ROM in the back of this book. When *PHStat* is loaded, Excel will display a new menu item—*PHStat*—on the menu bar as shown in Figure 1.4. *Crystal Ball* also creates new menu items, *Cell* and *Run,* as well as a new button bar. We will defer further discussion of *Crystal Ball* until chapter 3, and discuss *TreePlan* in chapter 8.

Throughout this book we will provide many "Notes" that describe how to use specific features of Microsoft Excel, *PHStat,* or *Crystal Ball.* These are introduced as needed to supplement examples and discussions of applications. It is important to read these notes and apply the procedures described in them in order to gain a working knowledge of the software features to which they refer.

WORKING WITH DATA

In many cases, data on Excel worksheets may not be in the proper form to use a statistical tool. Figure 1.5, for instance, shows the data from the Tracway worksheet *Defects After Delivery.* These data are conveniently sorted by month and year. Some tools in Excel's *Analysis Toolpak,* however, require that the data be listed in a single column

FIGURE 1.4 *PHStat* Menu

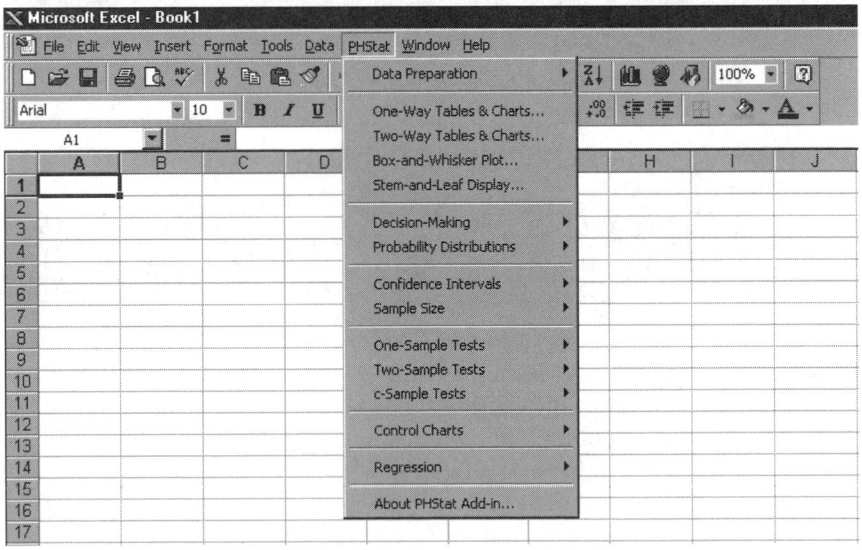

	A	B	C	D	E	F
1	Defects after delivery					
2						
3		1996	1997	1998	1999	2000
4	January	812	828	824	782	771
5	February	810	832	836	795	775
6	March	813	847	818	792	747
7	April	823	839	825	786	742
8	May	832	832	804	773	756
9	June	848	840	812	781	749
10	July	837	849	806	796	743
11	August	831	857	798	788	751
12	September	827	839	804	784	741
13	October	838	842	813	772	745
14	November	826	828	805	777	738
15	December	819	816	786	769	736

FIGURE 1.5 Worksheet *Defects After Delivery* in the Tracway Database

in the worksheet. As a user, you have two choices. You can manually move the data within the worksheet or you can use a *PHStat* utility from the *Data Preparation* option in the *PHStat* menu called *Stack Data* (see *PHStat Note: Using the Stack Data and Unstack Data Tools*). **To preserve the original database, we suggest that when you perform any analyses using the Tracway data, you copy the worksheet to a new blank workbook.** This can be done easily. Press the *Ctrl* and *A* keys simultaneously to select the entire worksheet, click the *Copy* button, then click the *New* button, and finally click *Paste* to place the worksheet in the new workbook.

PHStat Note: Using the Stack Data and Unstack Data Tools

From the *PHStat* menu, select *Data Preparation,* and then either *Stack Data* (to create a single column from multiple columns) or *Unstack Data* (to split a single column into multiple according to a grouping label). Figure 1.6 shows the dialog boxes that appear. To stack data in columns (with optional column labels) enter the range of the data in the *Unstacked Data Cell Range* box). If the first row of the range contains a label, check the box *First cells contain group labels.* These labels will appear in the first column of the stacked data to help you identify the data if appropriate.

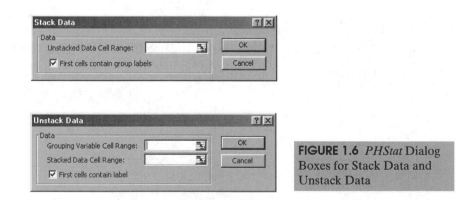

FIGURE 1.6 *PHStat* Dialog Boxes for Stack Data and Unstack Data

To unstack data in a single column and group them according to a set of labels in another column, enter the range of the column that contains the labels for the grouping variable in the *Grouping Variable Cell Range* box, and the range of the data in the *Stacked Data Cell Range* box. If the top row contains descriptive labels, check the *First cells contain label* box. This tool is useful when you wish to sort data into different groups.

	A	B	C	D	E	F
1	Defects after delivery					
2						
3		1996	1997	1998	1999	2000
4	January	812	828	824	782	771
5	February	810	832	836	795	775
6	March	813	847	818	792	747
7	April	823	839	825	786	742
8	May	832	832	804	773	756
9	June	848	840	812	781	749
10	July	837	849	806	796	743
11	August	831	857	798	788	751
12	September	827	839	804	784	741
13	October	838	842	813	772	745
14	November	826	828	805	777	738
15	December	819	816	786	769	736

Stack Data

Data
Unstacked Data Cell Range: $B$3:$F$15
☑ First cells contain group labels

OK   Cancel

FIGURE 1.7 *PHStat* Stack Data Application

	A	B	C
1	Group	Value	
2	1996	812	
3	1996	810	
4	1996	813	
5	1996	823	
6	1996	832	
7	1996	848	
8	1996	837	
9	1996	831	
10	1996	827	
11	1996	838	
12	1996	826	
13	1996	819	
14	1997	828	
15	1997	832	
16	1997	847	

FIGURE 1.8 Portion of the Worksheet "Stacked" for Defect Delivery Data

Figure 1.7 shows the use of the *Stack Data* tool in *PHStat* for the defect data. The tool creates a new worksheet called "Stacked" in your Excel workbook, a portion of which is shown in Figure 1.8. The column labeled "Group" shows the original column (year) from which the data came. If you apply the *Unstack Data* tool to Figure 1.8, you will put the data in its original form (although the month labels will not be included in the worksheet).

Summary

Data analysis and decision models provide managers with powerful tools to assist them in evaluating alternatives and understanding trade-offs in making decisions. This book is intended to develop your ability to analyze and use data for making business decisions, and to develop simple decision models for business problems. This chapter provided an overview of the types of data commonly used in business, the role of statistics in data analysis, and how data provide important inputs to decision models. Tools available to support this material include Microsoft Excel, *PHStat,* and *Crystal Ball.* The ability to properly analyze data depends on understanding differences among types of measurements, particularly categorical, ordinal, interval, and ratio scales. After reading the book, you should understand what kinds of sampling are appropriate, and how to deal with data obtained under various conditions.

Questions and Problems

1. The stock market undergoes occasional streaks upward, as well as plunges. If the Dow Jones Average were to drop 10 percent, how can understanding statistics suggest that it be a good idea to leave one's investment in stocks alone?

2. How can managers develop theories about the relationship between their actions and results?

3. Propose a managerial theory that relates customer satisfaction to company profits.

4. Explain the difference between data and information.

5. A company division corresponding to the geographic area of Washington state has had sales decrease 10 percent in the past year. An agency of Washington state reported that overall sales for this product declined 20 percent in this same year. Distinguish between data and information in this case.

6. A product manager is responsible for three products. Product A's sales increased 20 percent last quarter, Product B's sales increased 3 percent, and Product C's sales decreased 15 percent. What additional factors might be needed to assess product performances?

7. What is a decision model?

8. What sort of factors (variables) might be important in developing a decision model of the sales of an exclusive restaurant?

9. Critical success factors imply that some factors are more important than others to specific businesses. Critical success factors have been defined as "those measures on which the organization must perform well in order to survive." How does the concept of critical success factors fit with the concept of decision models?

10. Describe the concept of a balanced scorecard. Also describe how it relates to decision models.

11. Name measures that might be critical to customers, employees, stockholders, suppliers, and partners.

12. Read recent annual reports on selected Fortune 500 companies (most can be found on the World Wide Web) to determine what information these companies use for evaluating and analyzing their business performance. How prevalent is nonfinancial information?

13. Distinguish between external and internal data. Which of the two is most important to business decision making?

14. What sources do companies have for external data?

15. What is meant by "generating" data?

16. In the Tracway database, identify three internal factors measured, one external factor measured, and three generated factors.

17. What are the characteristics of nominal, or categorical, data?

18. What are the characteristics of ordinal data?

19. Describe the characteristics of interval data.

20. How can you identify ratio data?

21. What type of data are represented by the dealer satisfaction (worksheet I1) and user satisfaction (worksheet I2) data?

22. In the Tracway worksheet III2 (Employee Success), you will find data reporting whether or not employees had a college degree when hired. What type of data are these?

23. What type of data are the market share data for tractors given on the Tracway worksheet II9?

24. Describe the difference between a population and a sample.

25. Would surveying the first 100 customers of the day provide a useful sample of a retailing firm's client base?

26. Stack the tractor preparation costs on Tracway worksheet IV4, cells A3:F97, into one column.

C H A P T E R

2

Displaying and Summarizing Data

Outline

Displaying Data with Charts and Graphs
  Column and Bar Charts
  Line Charts
  Pie Charts
  Area Charts
  Scatter Diagrams
  Summary of Graphical Display Methods
Descriptive Statistics
  Frequency Distributions and Histograms
  Measures of Central Tendency
  Measures of Dispersion
  Coefficient of Variation
  Measures of Shape
  Excel's Descriptive Statistics Tool
  Data Profiles and Proportions
Visual Display of Statistical Measures
  Box-and-Whisker Plots
  Stem-and-Leaf Displays
Statistical Relationships
Case Study: Using Descriptive Statistics for the Malcolm Baldrige
  National Quality Award
Summary
Questions and Problems

In chapter 1 we discussed the role of data in modern organizations and described a typical database that might be maintained by a large manufacturer, Tracway International, Inc. In this chapter we discuss how to effectively display and summarize data for useful managerial information and insight. Because of the ease in which data can be generated and transmitted today, managers, supervisors, and even front-line workers can be overwhelmed. Hence, it is vital that critical data be displayed, aggregated, and summarized in as succinct a fashion as possible. Data visualization through various charts and plots provides simple communication vehicles that employees can easily understand. Statistical summaries, such as measures of central tendency, dispersion, and relationships among variables provide more precise quantitative information on which to base decisions. Spreadsheet software provides the capabilities to create visual displays and compute statistical measures. Our focus is on learning how to understand and incorporate these tools into making better decisions, as well as becoming proficient with the capabilities of Microsoft Excel.

The key concepts that we will discuss in this chapter are

- Visual data display: using line charts, bar charts, pie charts, area charts, scatter plots, box-and-whisker plots, and stem-and-leaf displays to understand data;
- Descriptive statistics: computing and understanding measures of central tendency (mean, median, mode), dispersion (range and variance), shape (skewness), fractiles (quartiles, deciles, and percentiles), and the coefficient of variation; and
- Statistical relationships: understanding linear relationships between two variables through correlation and covariance measures.

Displaying Data with Charts and Graphs

Henry Hudson recently joined the Tracway International, Inc., management team to oversee Tracway's production operations. Tracway originally produced lawn mowers, but a significant portion of sales volume over the past 10 years has come from the growing small tractor market. As we noted in chapter 1, Tracway sells their products worldwide, with sales regions including North America, South America, Europe, and the Pacific Rim. Three years ago a new region was opened to serve China, where a booming market for small tractors has been established. Tracway has always emphasized quality, and considers the quality they build into their products as their primary selling point. In the last 2 years Tracway has also emphasized the ease of use of their products.

Before digging into the details of operations, Henry wants to gain an overview of Tracway's overall business performance and market position. To effectively manage the production operation, Henry needs to understand the company's profit, market, and quality factors. To start, Henry wants to analyze company sales by product, region, and month; total dollar sales by region and month; market-share data; and quality-related survey data. These data are provided in the Tracway database introduced in chapter 1. We will use many worksheets from the Tracway database to illustrate the various concepts in this chapter. These include *Mower Unit Sales, Tractor Unit Sales, Pre-Tax Earnings, Revenues, Employee Success, Blood Pressure, Defects After Delivery,* and *Survey Recap.* Portions of these are shown in Figure 2.1 for your reference.

Tracway sells its mowers and tractors through independent dealers who receive 20 percent of the sales price for both products. This arrangement is the same in all five Tracway regions. Prices for Tracway products (wholesale, including intermediate dealer share) are given in Table 2.1. We will use this information for some calculations later in this chapter.

Raw data need to be converted into information to be interpreted by managers and employees. The easiest way to do this is to display the data visually using graphs and charts. For example, the sales of mowers and tractors are given in the Tracway database in the worksheets *Mower Unit Sales* and *Tractor Unit Sales.* The database includes monthly values of total world sales units and sales units segmented by region. With 5 years of monthly data, it is difficult to gain much understanding about Tracway sales

Mower Unit Sales

Month	World	NA	SA	Europe	Pacific	China
Jan-96	7020	6000	200	720	100	0
Feb-96	9280	7950	220	990	120	0
Mar-96	9780	8100	250	1320	110	0
Apr-96	11100	9050	280	1650	120	0
May-96	11930	9900	310	1590	130	0
Jun-96	12240	10200	300	1620	120	0
Jul-96	10740	8730	280	1590	140	0

Tractor Unit Sales

Month	World	NA	SA	Eur	Pac	China
Jan-96	1590	570	250	560	210	0
Feb-96	1710	610	270	600	230	0
Mar-96	1810	630	260	680	240	0
Apr-96	1860	680	270	650	260	0
May-96	1770	650	280	580	260	0
Jun-96	1740	600	270	590	280	0
Jul-96	1820	510	260	760	290	0

Pre-Tax Earnings

Month	Tractor	Mower	Production units Tractors	Mowers	Production Cost	Overhead	Revenue	Dealer 0.2	Tax&Ship 0.05	Profit	ROR
Jan-96	$1,750	$ 50	1590	7020	$ 3,133,500	$773,540	$ 5,472,000	$1,094,400	$ 273,600	$ 196,960	0.0360
Feb-96	$1,755	$ 50	1710	9280	$ 3,465,050	$773,540	$ 6,058,000	$1,211,600	$ 302,900	$ 304,910	0.0503
Mar-96	$1,763	$ 51	1810	9780	$ 3,689,810	$773,540	$ 6,408,000	$1,281,600	$ 320,400	$ 342,650	0.0535
Apr-96	$1,770	$ 51	1860	11100	$ 3,858,300	$773,540	$ 6,690,000	$1,338,000	$ 334,500	$ 385,660	0.0576
May-96	$1,778	$ 51	1770	11930	$ 3,755,490	$773,540	$ 6,503,000	$1,300,600	$ 325,150	$ 348,220	0.0535
Jun-96	$1,785	$ 51	1740	12240	$ 3,730,140	$773,540	$ 6,444,000	$1,288,800	$ 322,200	$ 329,320	0.0511
Jul-96	$1,792	$ 51	1820	10740	$ 3,809,180	$773,540	$ 6,534,000	$1,306,800	$ 326,700	$ 317,780	0.0486

Survey Recap

Region	Year	Dealer	Customer	Quality	Ease	Price	Service
NA	1996	3.82	3.98	3.8	3.1	3.3	3.5
NA	1997	3.92	4.04	3.9	3.3	3.2	3.7
NA	1998	4.00	4.03	4.2	3.4	3.5	4.0
NA	1999	4.05	4.08	4.5	4.0	3.6	4.1
NA	2000	4.11	4.12	4.6	4.3	3.7	4.3
SA	1996	4.00	4	4.1	2.8	3.1	3.8
SA	1997	4.00	3.95	4.1	2.9	3.2	3.8

Defects after delivery

	1996	1997	1998	1999	2000
January	812	828	824	782	771
February	810	832	836	795	775
March	813	847	818	792	747
April	823	839	825	786	742
May	832	832	804	773	756
June	848	840	812	781	749
July	837	849	806	796	743

Employee Success

Duration	Yrseducation	College gpa	Age	M/F	College Grad	Local
10	18	3.01	33	0	1	1
10	16	2.78	25	1	1	1
10	18	3.15	26	1	1	0
10	18	3.86	24	0	1	1
9.6	16	2.58	25	0	1	1
8.5	16	2.96	23	1	1	1
8.4	17	3.56	35	1	1	1

Blood Pressure

NA	Others
175	128
162	117
159	152
193	138
148	97
151	115
78	105

Revenues

Month	World	NA	SA	Eur	Pac	China
Jan-96	$ 5,472,000	$ 2,310,000	$ 770,000	$1,752,000	$ 640,000	$ -
Feb-96	$ 6,058,000	$ 2,625,000	$ 832,000	$1,899,000	$ 702,000	$ -
Mar-96	$ 6,408,000	$ 2,700,000	$ 805,000	$2,172,000	$ 731,000	$ -
Apr-96	$ 6,690,000	$ 2,945,000	$ 838,000	$2,115,000	$ 792,000	$ -
May-96	$ 6,503,000	$ 2,940,000	$ 871,000	$1,899,000	$ 793,000	$ -
Jun-96	$ 6,444,000	$ 2,820,000	$ 840,000	$1,932,000	$ 852,000	$ -
Jul-96	$ 6,534,000	$ 2,403,000	$ 808,000	$2,439,000	$ 884,000	$ -

FIGURE 2.1 Portions of the Tracway Database Used in This Chapter

simply by looking at the numbers. Of course, we could simplify the data by aggregating sales of each product by year as summarized in Table 2.2. From this information, we see that mower sales are relatively stable, while tractor sales are growing significantly. This information provides a good overview but hides a lot of detail, such as seasonal changes, that could significantly affect production plans.

TABLE 2.1	Tracway Product Prices	
Year	*Tractors*	*Mowers*
1996	$3,000	$100
1997	$3,100	$105
1998	$3,250	$110
1999	$3,400	$115
2000	$3,600	$125

TABLE 2.2	Tracway Sales by Product by Year	
Year	*Tractors Sold*	*Mowers Sold*
1996	20,840	110,520
1997	24,930	108,490
1998	29,530	109,270
1999	36,680	110,560
2000	46,120	109,930

Graphs and charts provide a convenient way to communicate information. Microsoft Excel offers a variety of options to express data visually. These include vertical and horizontal bar charts, line charts, pie charts, area charts, scatter plots, three-dimensional charts, and many other special types of charts. The Excel *Chart Wizard* (see *Excel Note: Using the Chart Wizard*) provides an easy way to create charts within your spreadsheet.

Excel Note: Using the *Chart Wizard*[1]

The Excel *Chart Wizard* is accessed from either the *Insert... Chart...* menu selection or by clicking on the Chart Wizard icon (the colored bar chart on the menu bar). The *Chart Wizard* guides you through four dialog boxes; the first is shown in Figure 2.2. The following steps outline the process of creating a chart:

1. Select the chart type from the list (e.g., *Bar*) and then click on the specific chart sub-type option. Click *Next* or press *Enter* to continue.

2. The second dialog box asks you to define the data to plot. You may enter the data range directly or highlight it in your spreadsheet with your mouse. You also need to define whether the data are stored by rows or columns. (Note: If the data you

wish to plot are not stored in contiguous columns, hold down the *Ctrl* key while selecting each block of data; then start the *Chart Wizard*.) The Series tab allows you to check and modify the names and values of the data series in your chart.

3. The third dialog box allows you specify details to customize the chart and make it easy to read and understand. You may specify titles for the chart and each axis, axis labels, style of gridlines, placement of the legend to describe the data series, data labels, and even a data table of values from which the chart is derived.

4. Finally, the last dialog box allows you to specify whether to place the chart as an object in an existing worksheet or as a new sheet in the workbook.

---

[1] In this and other Excel Notes in this book we provide some basic information about using key features in Excel. More detail can be found using Excel's Help files, and we encourage you to do so.

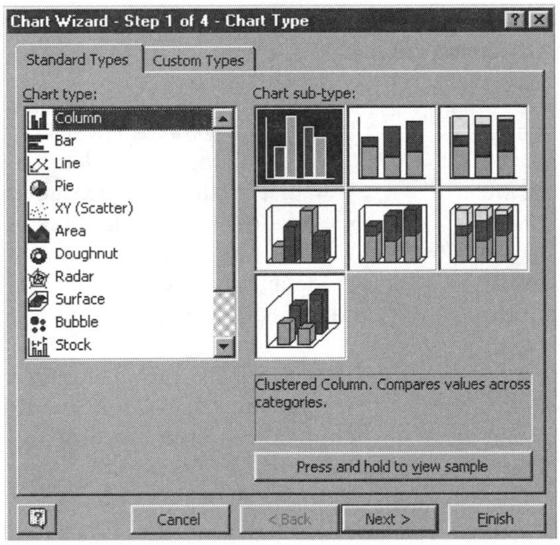

FIGURE 2.2 *Chart Wizard* Dialog Box

COLUMN AND BAR CHARTS

Excel distinguishes between vertical and horizontal bar charts, calling the former *column charts* and the latter *bar charts*. Figure 2.3 shows Tracway's sales history by product by month over the last 5 years on a column chart. The *Excel Note: Creating a Column Chart* describes the step-by-step procedure used to develop Figure 2.3. We generally will not guide you through every application, but will provide some guidance for new procedures as appropriate.

Column charts that include multiple data series provide a means of understanding the relative differences in the series. For example, Figure 2.3 shows that Tracway sells a

FIGURE 2.3 Column Chart for Tracway Sales by Product by Month

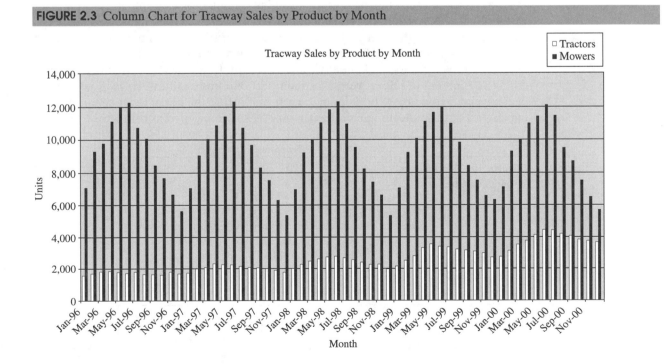

Excel Note: Creating a Column Chart

1. The first step is to access the data. In the Tracway database, tractor sales data (worldwide by month) are found in column B on the worksheet *Tractor Unit Sales,* and mower sales data (worldwide by month) are also in column B on the worksheet *Mower Unit Sales.* Column A lists the data labels (months). To graph these data together, we need to put them on the same sheet. Copy the data from cell B3 through B62 from worksheet *Tractor Unit Sales.* Using the *Paste Special* option from the *Edit* menu, place these data beginning in cell I3 on the *Mower Unit Sales* worksheet. To label tractors and mowers, replace the contents of cell B2 with "Mowers" and cell I2 with "Tractors."

2. The next step is to select the data to be plotted: cells A2 through B62. To include the tractor sales data, move the cursor to cell I2, press and hold the *Ctrl* key, and then select cells I2 through I62.

3. Access the *Chart Wizard* by clicking on the chart icon on the menu bar.

a. Use the default *Column chart type,* which should be *clustered column* style. Click *Next.*

b. The next dialog box is *Chart Source Data.* Since you selected the data you want to graph, you can see what the chart will look like in the viewing window. The *Columns* radio button is checked by default, because that is how the highlighted data was stored. If the chart looks correct, click *Next.*

c. The *Chart Options* dialog box appears next. Specify the Chart Title as "Tracway Sales by Product by Month," Category (X) Axis as "Month," and Value (Y) Axis as "Units." Click *Next.*

d. The last dialog box is *Chart Location.* You have the option of placing your chart on its own sheet or inserting it into the current sheet as an object. Either way, the chart can be copied to insert it in a Microsoft Word document or other applications.

---

large number of mowers in a very cyclical sales pattern without a noticeable trend. Tractors appear to have a much smaller cyclical sales behavior, while also exhibiting an upward trend. As tractors sell for much higher prices, this suggests larger revenue increases in the future.

Bar charts present information in a similar fashion. For example, Tracway's profit by month is calculated in the worksheet *Pre-Tax Earnings* in the Tracway database. We will assume that production is essentially a make-to-order environment (only minimal inventories are kept), thus the quantity sold is equal to the quantity produced. Overhead expenses are allocated equally to each month. Dealers selling Tracway products receive 20 percent of sales revenue for their part of doing business. Tracway pays 5 percent of revenues in taxes and shipping expenses. Profit is the net of revenue minus these expenses. For example, the profit for January 1996 is computed as follows:

		Tractors	*Mowers*	
January 1996 Revenue				$5,472,000
Production Costs				
	Unit Cost	$ 1,750	$ 50	
	Units Produced	1,590	7,020	
		$2,782,500	$351,000	($3,133,500)
Overhead				($773,540)
Dealer Return				($1,094,400)
Tax and Shipping				($273,600)
Profit				$196,960

The profit by product by year is shown in Table 2.3. The bar chart in Figure 2.4 displays the same information. However, it shows more clearly that the two products are

TABLE 2.3 Profit by Product by Year				
Year	*Tractor Profit*	*Percent of Revenue*	*Mower Profit*	*Percent of Revenue*
1996	$ 1,808,476	2.9	$1,246,014	11.3
1997	$ 2,674,309	3.5	$1,204,089	10.6
1998	$ 3,974,533	4.1	$1,226,497	10.2
1999	$11,802,463	9.5	$1,981,517	15.6
2000	$18,089,654	10.9	$2,549,603	18.6

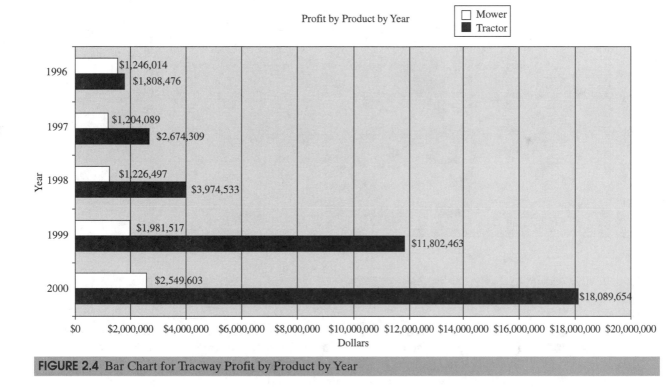

FIGURE 2.4 Bar Chart for Tracway Profit by Product by Year

in distinctively different phases of their life cycles. Mowers are a very mature product, with slight growth in profit, while tractors show a very strong growth in profit.

A *stacked column chart* (Figure 2.5) displays the same information more efficiently, although it can be more difficult to interpret. For instance, the relative contribution of each product to overall profit is very clear, but the magnitude of profit by product is lost. The contribution of tractors to Tracway profit is seen to be increasing (up to almost 90 percent in 2000), but the stacked bar chart does not reflect the magnitude of profit for each year. The ordinary bar chart in Figure 2.4 made the dollar value of profit by product by year much clearer.

LINE CHARTS

If too many different data series are plotted on column or bar charts, particularly for long periods of time, trends become more difficult to see visually. *Line charts,* however, provide a useful means for displaying data of this nature. For instance, a line chart showing Tracway's recent mower sales history by product and region over time is shown in

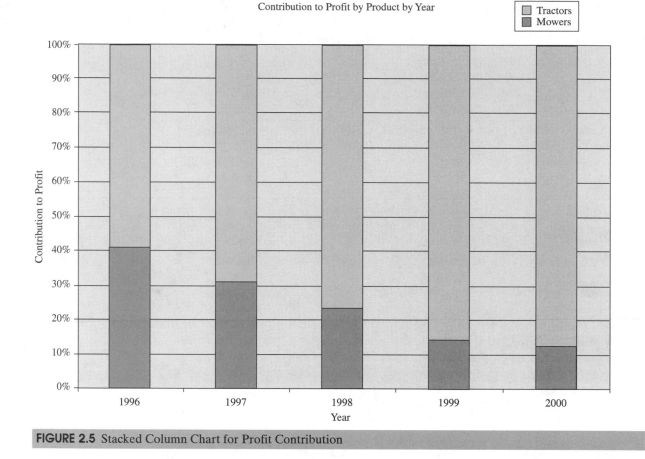

FIGURE 2.5 Stacked Column Chart for Profit Contribution

Figure 2.6. This chart shows that the North American region dominates mower sales (Tracway does not sell mowers in China). Both North American and European sales exhibit a seasonal pattern, as would be expected because of climatic conditions, but show no noticeable trend. European sales have a different cycle, with a longer annual peak sales period. Any trends for the South American and Pacific regions are not detectable, because unit sales in those regions are much smaller in scale than North American sales. This suggests that multiple data series in line charts can be difficult to interpret if the magnitude of the data values differs greatly. In this case, it would be advisable to create separate charts for the South American and Pacific regions.

Figure 2.7 shows a similar line chart for tractor sales. Tractor sales clearly show a growth trend in addition to seasonal changes. In the first of the 5 years displayed, North American and European regions had roughly the same sales volumes, with Europe actually having more sales of tractors. The South American and Pacific regions were both quite a bit smaller at that time. The North American region's sales of tractors experienced significant growth in the fourth and fifth years while European region sales dropped. South American sales climbed fairly steadily, without much of a cyclical pattern, to the point that tractor sales in the South American region exceeded that of the European region by the middle of the fourth year. Sales in the Pacific region have

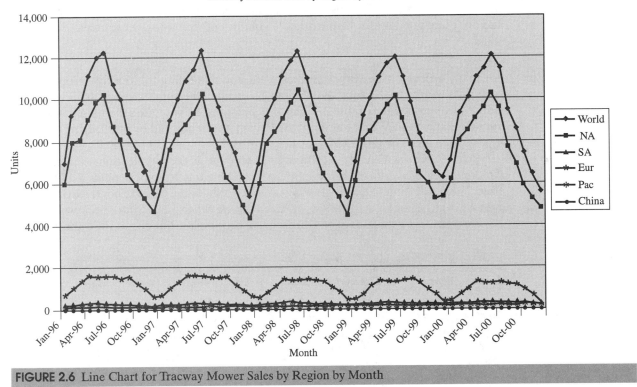

FIGURE 2.6 Line Chart for Tracway Mower Sales by Region by Month

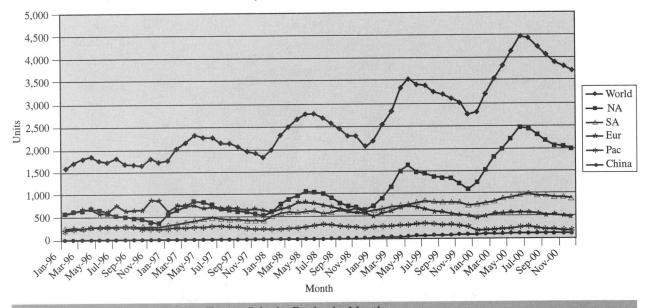

FIGURE 2.7 Line Chart for Tracway Tractor Sales by Region by Month

virtually declined to zero; however, the opening of the Chinese market in the third year shows promising growth. Thus we see that line charts help us identify cycles and trends, and are quite good at displaying relative volumes of multiple data sources.

PIE CHARTS

For many types of data, we are interested in understanding the relative proportion of each data source to the total. For example, consider the total revenue achieved by region and year, shown in Table 2.4. This was obtained by summing the data in the *Revenues* worksheet of the Tracway database (which was generated by multiplying units sold by the price given in Table 2.1).

Overall, we see a steady growth in sales revenue in the North American and South American regions while the European and Pacific regions are experiencing declining revenue. The new China region is growing rapidly. To show the relative contribution to revenue by each region for a specific operating year, we can use a *pie chart* as shown in Figure 2.8. Pie charts are useful for displaying relative proportion, but do not show the impact of

TABLE 2.4 Total Tracway Dollar Sales (in thousands) by Region by Year

Year	World	North America	South America	Europe	Pacific	China
1996	$ 73,572	$28,340	$10,133	$25,890	$ 9,209	$ 0
1997	$ 88,674	$34,375	$16,295	$27,560	$10,445	$ 0
1998	$107,992	$42,763	$24,228	$28,753	$11,371	$ 877
1999	$137,426	$62,758	$31,661	$26,674	$13,137	$3,196
2000	$179,773	$99,429	$39,688	$25,031	$10,189	$5,436

FIGURE 2.8 Pie Chart for Tracway Percentage of Revenue by Region in 2000

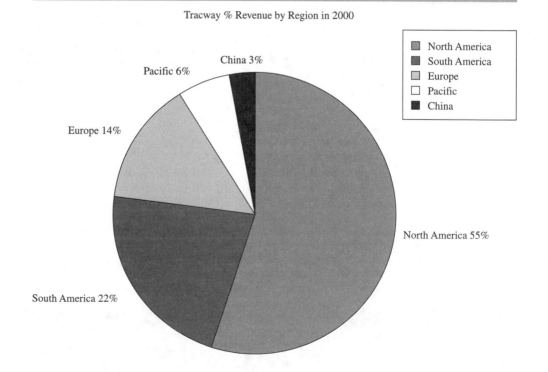

Tracway % Revenue by Region in 2000

time as well as line charts. In Figure 2.8, the high proportion due to North American sales is clearly evident, as are the relative proportions of South America and Europe.

AREA CHARTS

An *area chart* combines the features of a pie chart with those provided by line charts. For example, Figure 2.9 displays the monthly sales revenue by region by month. This chart shows not only the growing proportion of sales from the North American region but also its cyclical nature. Although the cyclical nature of the data by other regions is hard to detect, the overall cycle can easily be seen. Area charts present more information than pie or line charts alone, but suffer from the potential to clutter the observer's mind with too many details; thus they should be used with care.

SCATTER DIAGRAMS

Scatter diagrams show the relationship between two variables. For instance, Tracway management may be interested in the relationship of market share for tractors and market share for mowers in the North American region. If a strong relationship exists, we would expect that if one variable is large (or small), the other would also tend to be large (or small). A scatter diagram displays the value of one variable against the corresponding value of the other. To create a scatter diagram, we extract the data from the worksheets *Mower Unit Sales* and *Tractor Unit Sales* in the Tracway database, place them contiguously on a spreadsheet, and invoke the *Chart Wizard,* selecting *XY (scatter)* as the *Chart Type.*

Figure 2.10 shows a scatter diagram of the paired market share data. This scatter diagram shows little apparent relationship between the two market shares. The data

FIGURE 2.9 Area Chart for Tracway Revenue by Region by Month

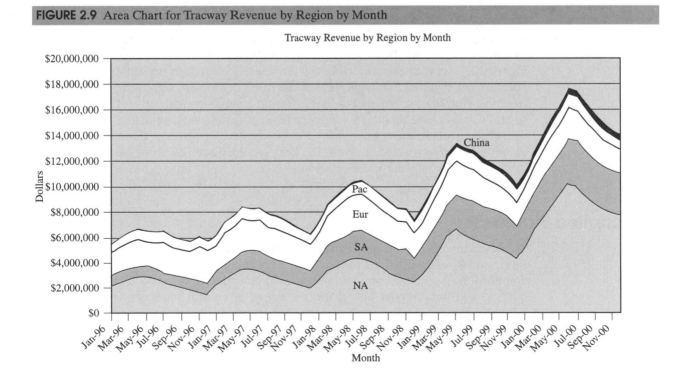

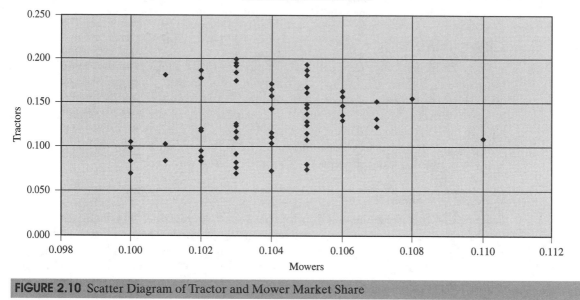

North American Market Share

FIGURE 2.10 Scatter Diagram of Tractor and Mower Market Share

do not appear to move together (that is, as one variable increases or decreases, the other does also). We will study models for understanding such relationships quantitatively in chapter 6.

SUMMARY OF GRAPHICAL DISPLAY METHODS

In summary, simply looking at tables of numbers often hides more than it informs. Graphical displays clearly make it easier to gain insights about the data. Thus graphs and charts are a means of converting raw data into useful managerial information. However, it can be easy to distort data by manipulating the scale on the chart. For example, Figure 2.11 shows South American tractor sales displayed on two different charts. As you can see, Figure 2.11b suggests that the trend is not very significant. (Check stock trends in your local newspaper—do they report changes consistently?) Creators of statistical displays have an ethical obligation to report data without deliberately trying to distort the truth. Another drawback of visual displays, however, is that they provide no *quantitative* summaries of the data. The next section discusses statistical measures useful in conveying information for decision making.

Descriptive Statistics

Statistical measures provide an effective and efficient way of obtaining meaningful information from data that are useful for making decisions. *Descriptive statistics* refers to a collection of quantitative measures and ways of describing data. This includes frequency distributions and histograms, measures of central tendency (mean, median, mode, midrange), and measures of dispersion (range, variance, standard deviation). Statistical support within Microsoft Excel can be accomplished in three ways:

South American Tractor Sales

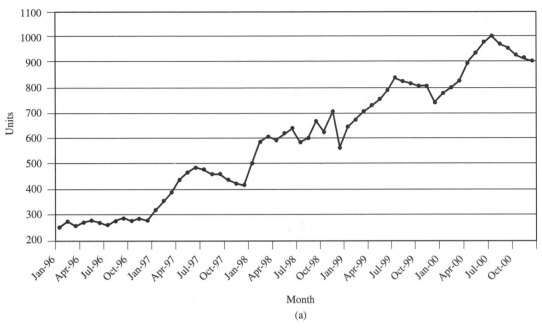

(a)

South American Tractor Sales

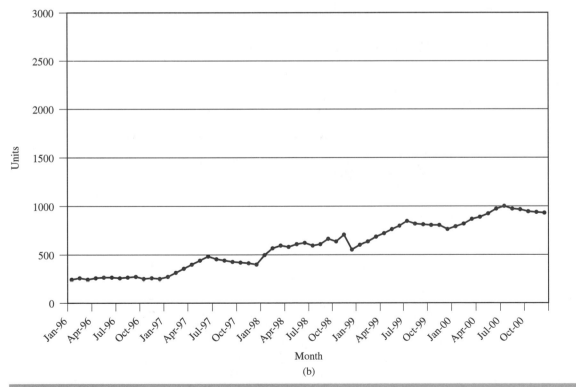

(b)

FIGURE 2.11 Two Charts of Identical Data

1. Using statistical functions that are entered in worksheet cells directly or embedded in formulas.
2. Using the Excel *Analysis Toolpak* add-in to perform more complex statistical computations, or
3. Using the Prentice Hall statistics add-in (*PHStat*) available with this book to perform analyses not designed into Excel.

Table 2.5 summarizes the descriptive statistics functions and tools available.

To illustrate the use of descriptive statistics, we will examine the results of a cross-sectional survey of Tracway managers (on the worksheet *Employee Success*) gathered from a study of the characteristics of employee retention. Figure 2.1 shows a portion of the worksheet, which includes information about college grade point average (GPA) (column C) and age at first employment with Tracway (column D). These data represent a sample from a much larger population of potential respondents (all Tracway employees).

FREQUENCY DISTRIBUTIONS AND HISTOGRAMS

Before computing any statistical measures, it is helpful to summarize the data in a **frequency distribution**—a tabular summary showing the frequency of observations in each of several nonoverlapping classes, or cells. A graphical depiction of a frequency distribution in the form of a column chart is called a **histogram.** Frequency distributions and histograms allow you to estimate key quantitative measures that characterize the data and visually understand the nature of the data. A frequency distribution and histogram of college grade points for the sample of 40 Tracway associates was created by using the *Analysis Toolpak* in Excel (see *Excel Note: Creating a Histogram*).

TABLE 2.5   Excel Statistical Functions and Tools

Excel Function	*Description*
AVERAGE(*data range*)	Computes the average value (arithmetic mean) of a set of data
MEDIAN(*data range*)	Computes the median (middle value) of a set of data
MODE(*data range*)	Computes the mode (most frequently occurring) of a set of data
VAR(*data range*)	Computes the variance of a set of data, assumed to be a sample
VARP(*data range*)	Computes the variance of a set of data, assumed to be an entire population
STDEV(*data range*)	Computes the standard deviation of a set of data, assumed to be a sample
STDEVP(*data range*)	Computes the standard deviation of a set of data, assumed to be an entire population
SKEW(*data range*)	Computes the skewness, a measures of the degree to which a distribution is not symmetric around its mean
PERCENTILE(*array, k*)	Computes the kth percentile of data in a range
QUARTILE(*array, quart*)	Computes the quartile of a distribution
CORREL(*array1,array2*)	Computes the correlation coefficient between two data sets

Analysis Toolpak Tools	*Description*
Descriptive Statistics	Provides a summary of a variety of basic statistical measures
Histogram	Creates a frequency distribution and graphical histogram for a set of data
Rank and Percentile	Computes the ordinal and percentage rank of each value in a data set
Correlation	Computes the correlation coefficient between two data sets

Prentice Hall Statistics Add-In	*Description*
Box-and-Whisker Plot	Creates a box-and-whisker plot of a data set
Stem-and-Leaf Display	Creates a stem-and-leaf display of a data set

Excel Note: Creating a Histogram

Access the *Histogram* tool by clicking on *Tools . . . Data Analysis* and selecting *Histogram* from the list. In the dialog box (Figure 2.12), specify the *Input Range* as C3:C43, which consists of the column label plus the 40 grade point ratios. Check the *Labels* box so that Excel knows that the range contains a label. If you do not specify a *Bin Range,* Excel will automatically determine cell ranges for the frequency distribution and histogram. Usually it is best to define the cell ranges by specifying the upper cell limits of each range in a column in your worksheet. (If you check the Data Labels box, be sure you include a column label such as "Bin" or "Upper Limit.") In our example, we specified the Bin Range as I3:I8, with cell values Upper Limit, 1.5, 2, 2.5, 3, and 3.5 in this range. Check the *Chart Output* box to create a histogram in addition to the frequency distribution.

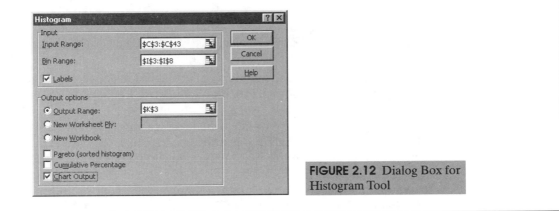

FIGURE 2.12 Dialog Box for Histogram Tool

Figure 2.13 shows the bin range, frequency distribution, and histogram. The frequency distribution is the table in the range K3:L9. *Upper limit* refers to the right boundary of each cell in which the data fall. For example, the first cell includes all data below 1.5; we see that no observations fall in this cell. The second cell includes all observations greater than or equal to 1.5 but less than 2; this cell has two observations, and so on. Although Excel does not provide the total, you can easily modify the spreadsheet to count the total number of observations and compute the fraction that fall within each interval—called the **relative frequency.** By summing all the relative frequencies at or below each upper limit, we have the **cumulative frequency.** The cumulative frequency represents the proportion of the sample that falls below the upper limit value. Note that relative frequencies must be between zero and one, and must add to one over all cells. This also means that the cumulative frequency for the last cell must equal one. We have done these computations in the following table.

Upper Limit	Frequency	Relative Frequency	Cumulative Frequency
1.5	0	0.000	0.000
2	2	0.050	0.050
2.5	4	0.100	0.150
3	19	0.475	0.625
3.5	11	0.275	0.900
4	4	0.100	1.000

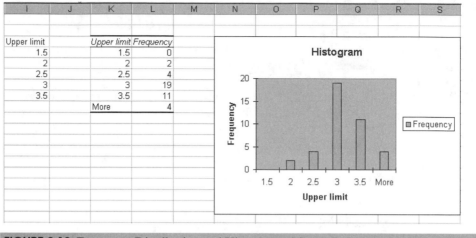

FIGURE 2.13 Frequency Distribution and Histogram of Grade Point Average

We see that nearly half of the grade point averages fell between 2.5 and 3, and that 37.5 percent of them were above 3. From the cumulative frequency column we see that only 15 percent fall below 2.5.

One important issue to consider when constructing frequency distributions and histograms is the number of cells to use. In general, you should use at least 5 but no more than 15. As we stated in the Excel Note, you should define the "Bin Range" yourself rather than let Excel do it for you. This allows you to control the number of cells and the endpoints. Sometimes you need to simply experiment to find the best number of cells that provide a useful picture of the data.

MEASURES OF CENTRAL TENDENCY

In viewing a histogram, you can generally tell approximately where the data are centered. Several measures quantify this "centering." The most common is the *average,* formally called the **arithmetic mean** (or simply the *mean*), which is the sum of the observations divided by the number of observations. We all use averages routinely in our lives, for example, to measure student accomplishment in a curriculum, to measure the scoring ability of sports figures, and as we show here, to measure performance in business. It is common practice in statistics to use Greek letters to represent population parameters and Roman letters to represent sample statistics. Thus, if a population consists of N observations $x_1, \ldots x_N$, the population mean, μ, is

$$\mu = \frac{\sum\limits_{i=1}^{N} x_i}{N}$$

The mean of a sample of n observations is

$$\overline{x} = \frac{\sum\limits_{i=1}^{n} x_i}{n}$$

For instance, the sum of the 40 grade point averages given on the worksheet *Employee Success* in the Tracway database is 117.37. The mean grade point average is therefore

$$\bar{x} = \frac{117.37}{40} = 2.93425$$

When data are summarized in a frequency distribution, rather than having to add the same numbers repeatedly, we may use the following formula to compute the mean:

$$\bar{x} = \frac{\sum_{i=1}^{n} f_i x_i}{n}$$

where f_i is the frequency of the observation x_i. This provides an exact value of the mean if the data are discrete. If the data are grouped into cells in a frequency distribution, we can use a modified version of this formula to estimate the mean by replacing x_i by a representative value for all the observations in each cell (such as the midpoint), $\hat{x}_i$. For the GPA example, if we use the midpoint of each cell as an estimate for all the observations in that cell, we would compute the mean GPA of the sample as follows:

GPA Range	Center ($\hat{x}_i$)	Frequency (f)	Product ($f\hat{x}_i$)
1.5–2.0	1.75	2	3.50
2.0–2.5	2.25	4	9.00
2.5–3.0	2.75	19	52.25
3.0–3.5	3.25	11	35.75
3.5–4.0	3.75	4	15.00
		40	115.5

Estimate of mean = 115.5/40 = 2.89

Note that this is not identical to the true mean of 2.93425. This is because we have not used the original data, but only five representative values. Although most statistics are simple concepts, they must be applied correctly, and we need to understand how they are computed to interpret them properly.

Another measure of central tendency is the **median**—the middle value when the data are arranged from smallest to largest. Thus half the observations would fall above the median and half below. For an odd number of observations, the median is the middle of the sorted numbers. For an even number of observations, the median is typically computed as the arithmetic mean of the two middle numbers. For the GPA example, we have 40 observations—an even number. We could use the *Data/Sort* option in Excel to rank order the grade point averages given in column C, and find that the 20th largest observation is 2.95, while the 21st largest observation is 2.96. The median is the average of these, 2.955. This is the same result we obtain by using the Excel function MEDIAN(C2:C41). As opposed to the mean, the median is not affected by extreme values or outliers, which tend to pull the value of the mean away from the center of the majority of the observations.

A third measure of central tendency is the **mode.** The mode is the observation that occurs most frequently. The mode is not affected by order, or differences in scale, but only by the count for each observation. The mode is more useful for data that consist of a relatively small number of unique values. In our example, the GPA data are continuous, and few values occur more than once. In this example we see that the following values occurred twice: 2.75, 2.86, 2.95, 2.96, 2.98, and 3.15. Thus all are modes of the distribution. When multiple modes exist, the Excel function MODE(C2:C41) returns the largest of these, in this case, 3.15.

Another measure of central tendency is the **midrange.** This is simply the average of the largest and smallest values in the data set. For the GPA data, the maximum value is 3.86 and the minimum value is 1.75. Thus the midrange is (3.86 + 1.75)/2 = 2.81. Caution must be exercised when using this statistic because extreme values easily distort the result.

All of these measures of central tendency provide estimates of a single value that in some fashion represents the entire distribution. In the GPA data, the mean of 2.93 and median of 2.955 were quite close, and accurately reflect the data. However, the mode is misleading because the data are continuous, and the midrange has substantial error because it only uses 2 of the 40 observations.

MEASURES OF DISPERSION

Dispersion refers to the degree of variation in the data; that is, the numerical spread (or compactness) of the data. For instance, the frequency distribution and histogram of the grade point averages in the Tracway sample clearly shows variation. Several statistical measures characterize dispersion: the *range, variance,* and *standard deviation.* The **range** is the simplest, and is computed as the difference between the maximum value and the minimum value in the data set. Although Excel does not provide a function for the range, it can be computed easily by the formula =MAX(*data range*) − MIN(*data range*). In the case of the grade point average data, the range is 3.86 − 1.75 = 2.11. This appears to be a rather wide range; however, there were only 2 observations below 2.0, and only 2 observations above 3.6. If we ignore these, we see that most of the data fall between 2.0 and 3.6. Rare observations that are radically different from the rest are called **outliers.** Outliers can dramatically affect the range. This demonstrates a problem with using the range: it uses only two pieces of data.

A more commonly used measure of dispersion is the **variance,** whose computation depends on *all* the data. The formula for the variance of a population is

$$\sigma^2 = \frac{\sum_{i=1}^{N}(x_i - \mu)^2}{N}$$

where x_i is the value of the *i*th item, N is the number of items in the population, and μ is the population mean. The variance of a set of sample data is calculated using the formula

$$s^2 = \frac{\sum_{i=1}^{n}(x_i - \bar{x})^2}{n - 1}$$

where n is the number of items in the sample, and $\bar{x}$ is the sample mean. It may seem peculiar to use a different "average" for populations and samples, but statisticians have shown that the sample variance provides a more accurate representation of the true population variance when computed in this way. Using the Excel function for the sample variance, VAR (*data range*), we obtain $s^2 = 0.207$ for the GPA data. (For populations, use the function VARP).

Another measure of dispersion is the **standard deviation,** which is defined as the square root of the variance. For a population, the standard deviation is computed as

$$\sigma = \sqrt{\frac{\sum_{i=1}^{N}(x_i - \mu)^2}{N}}$$

and for samples, it is

$$s = \sqrt{\frac{\sum_{i=1}^{n}(x_i - \bar{x})^2}{n - 1}}$$

Using the Excel function STDEV(*data range*), we find that $s = 0.455$ for the GPA data. The standard deviation is generally easier to interpret than the variance because its units of measure are the same as the units of the data. Thus, it can be more easily related to the mean or other statistics measured in the same units.

The standard deviation provides an indication of where the majority of data are clustered around the mean. For example, if we add and subtract one standard deviation from the mean of the GPA data, we obtain the interval [2.475, 3.385]. You may verify from the histogram that most of the data fall within this range. One of the most important results in statistics is that *almost all* of the data for any distribution fall within three standard deviations of the mean. For the GPA data, this range is [1.56, 4.30], and you can easily see this to be true.

The larger the standard deviation, the more the data are "spread out" from the mean. Thus, the standard deviation is a useful measure of *risk,* particularly in financial analysis. Figure 2.14 shows the distributions of potential returns of two investments. Both distributions have similar means, 6.66 percent and 6.39 percent. However, the standard deviations are quite different: 1.02 percent versus 2.79 percent. The first invest-

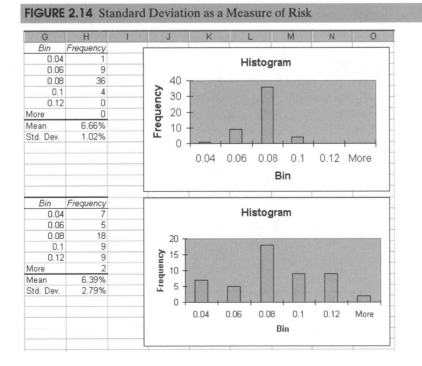

FIGURE 2.14 Standard Deviation as a Measure of Risk

ment has the smaller standard deviation; therefore little risk exists that the return will vary substantially from the mean. However, the larger standard deviation for the second investment implies that there is greater risk of achieving a significantly lower return, while at the same time, a greater potential exists of a higher return. This is easily seen by examining the histograms shown in Figure 2.14.

COEFFICIENT OF VARIATION

The **coefficient of variation** provides a relative measure of the dispersion in data relative to the mean, and is defined as

$$\text{Coefficient of Variation (CV)} = \sigma/\bar{x}$$

This statistic is useful when comparing the variability of two or more data sets when their scales differ. Sometimes the coefficient of variation is multiplied by 100 to express it as a percentage. For example, suppose that the standard deviation of a stock whose average price is $2 is $0.40, whereas the standard deviation of another stock whose average price is $80 is $6. You would expect the standard deviation of the $2 stock to be smaller; thus comparing standard deviations directly provides little information. However, looking at the CVs, $0.4/2 = 0.2$ or 20% versus $6/80 = 0.075$ or 7.5%, shows that the $2 stock shows much larger relative variation, indicating a higher relative level of risk.

MEASURES OF SHAPE

Histograms of sample data can take on a variety of different shapes. In Figure 2.13, we see that the distribution of grade point averages of Tracway employees has a distinct peak around the mean and median of roughly 2.9, and falls away in a similar fashion on both sides of the central value. Such a distribution is *symmetric.* Figure 2.15 shows a histogram for the age of the Tracway employees in the sample. This distribution is *skewed,* or asymmetrical; negatively skewed distributions tail off to the left; positively skewed distributions tail off to the right. The **coefficient of skewness,** which can be found using an Excel function in Table 2.5, measures the degree of asymmetry of a distribution around its mean. If the coefficient is positive, the distribution is positively skewed; if negative, it is negatively skewed. The closer the coefficient is to zero, the less the degree of skewness in the distribution. The skewness measure for GPAs is 1.41, indicating a positively skewed distribution reflecting the slightly heavier density to the left of the center in Figure 2.13. The skewness measure for the data in Figure 2.16 is –1.61, reflecting the more distinct negative skewness displayed by the histogram. A distribution whose coefficient of skewness is greater than 1 or less than –1 is generally regarded as highly skewed. A value between 0.5 and 1 or between –0.5 and –1 is moderately skewed. Coefficients between 0.5 and –0.5 indicate relative symmetry.

Comparing the measures of central tendency can also reveal information about the shape of a distribution. For example, in a perfectly symmetric distribution, the mean, median, and mode would all be the same. For the data in Figure 2.16, however, we find that the median = 4, mean = 4.11, and mode = 5. This clearly suggests a negatively skewed distribution.

EXCEL'S DESCRIPTIVE STATISTICS TOOL

Excel provides a useful tool for basic data analysis, which is available in the *Data Analysis Toolpak* from the *Tools* menu. The *Descriptive Statistics* tool provides a variety of statistical measures for one or more data sets: the mean, standard error, median, mode,

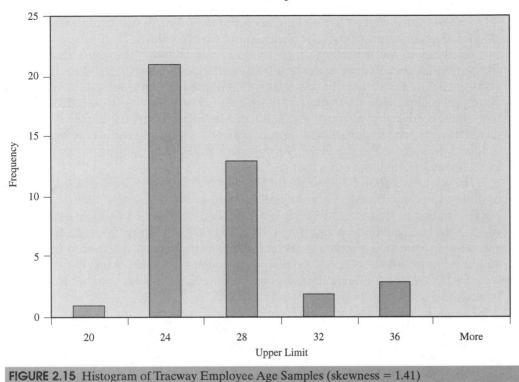

FIGURE 2.15 Histogram of Tracway Employee Age Samples (skewness = 1.41)

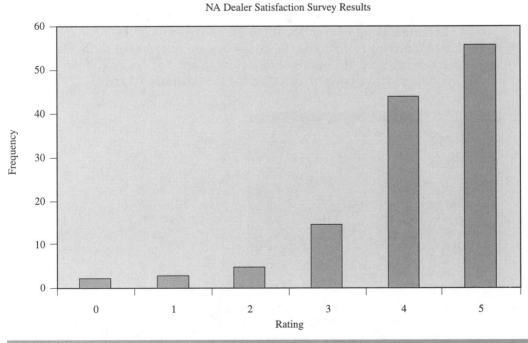

FIGURE 2.16 Histogram of North American Region Dealer Surveys, Year 2000 (skewness = −1.61)

standard deviation, sample variance, kurtosis, skewness, range, minimum, maximum, sum, count, kth largest and smallest values (for any value of k you specify), and the confidence level for the mean. We will discuss the standard error and confidence level in chapters 3 and 4, respectively, so you may ignore them for now.

To illustrate the use of this tool, let us revisit Tracway. Tracway's CEO, Mike Mortensen, is concerned about the health and welfare of his employees. Based upon his visits to each of the regions, he has gained the impression that associates in the North American region, while doing quite well, are under great pressure. To determine if business stress is adversely affecting the health of his North American managers, he contacted the personnel department, which obtained blood pressure readings for 20 randomly selected managers in the North American region, as well as 20 randomly selected managers from the other four regions.

The worksheet *Blood Pressure* in the Tracway database contains the blood pressure of these two groups in cells A3 through B23. If you select *Descriptive Statistics,* the dialog box shown in Figure 2.17 will appear. You need only enter the range of the data, which must be in a *single row or column.* If the data are in a matrix form, the tool treats each row or column as a separate data set, depending on which you specify. In this example, we have two samples, one in column A and the second in column B. Options selected in the *Descriptive Statistics* dialog box are summary statistics, and the 5th and 15th largest values. The results are shown in Figure 2.18.

Figure 2.18 shows that a rather large difference exists between the two means; the average blood pressure is 158 for the North American region, and about 120 for the other regions (in chapter 4 we will describe how to test for statistical significance of this difference). The median for North American managers is 160 compared to 116 for the other regions, and the mode is 175 in the North American group as opposed to 138 for the other regions. In addition, the dispersion within the North American group is larger than that of the other group, as demonstrated by the larger range and the larger variance. Finally, the North American region has a negatively skewed distribution, while the other group has almost no skewness at all. If you were Mike, what would you do next?

One important point to note about the use of the tools in the *Analysis Tookpak* versus Excel functions is that while functions dynamically change as the data in the spreadsheet are changed, the results of the tools are not. For example, if you compute the mean and standard deviation directly using the functions AVERAGE(*range*) and

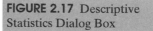

FIGURE 2.17 Descriptive Statistics Dialog Box

	A	B	C	D	E	F	G
1	Blood Pressure						
2							
3	NA	Others		*NA*		*Others*	
4	175	128					
5	162	117		Mean	158.2	Mean	119.5
6	159	152		Standard Error	5.33193	Standard Error	3.98715
7	193	138		Median	160.5	Median	116
8	148	97		Mode	175	Mode	138
9	151	115		Standard Deviation	23.84511	Standard Deviation	17.83108
10	78	105		Sample Variance	568.5895	Sample Variance	317.9474
11	176	113		Kurtosis	6.284795	Kurtosis	-1.07952
12	153	129		Skewness	-1.90519	Skewness	0.026551
13	148	141		Range	115	Range	63
14	171	137		Minimum	78	Minimum	89
15	183	89		Maximum	193	Maximum	152
16	162	106		Sum	3164	Sum	2390
17	149	137		Count	20	Count	20
18	181	115		Largest(5)	175	Largest(5)	137
19	175	95		Smallest(15)	175	Smallest(15)	137
20	139	106					
21	146	103					
22	152	129					
23	163	138					

FIGURE 2.18 Descriptive Statistics Results for Blood Pressure Data

STDEV(*range*), then changing the data in the range will automatically update these statistics. However, you would have to re-run the *Descriptive Statistics* tool to find new values after changing the data.

DATA PROFILES AND PROPORTIONS

Data profiles (or **fractiles**) describe the location and spread of data over its range. These measures include percentiles and quartiles. You are no doubt familiar with percentiles from standardized tests used for college or graduate school entrance examinations (SAT, ACT, GMAT, GRE, etc.). Percentiles specify the percentage of test takers who scored at or below the score of a particular individual. Specifically, the *kth percentile* is a value at or below which at least *k* percent of the observations lie. *Quartiles* divide the sorted data into four sets, representing the 25th percentile, 50th percentile, 75th percentile, and 100th percentile. Note that the median is actually the second quartile, with two-fourths of the data below the median, and two-fourths of the data above the median. One-fourth of the data is below the first quartile, and three-fourths of the data is below the third quartile. Similarly, *deciles* divide the data into 10 sets: the 10th, 20th, 30th percentiles, and so on.

In the previous example, comparing blood pressure readings of managers in the North American region with other Tracway managers is more clearly understood by using the *Rank and Percentile* tool from the Excel *Analysis Toolpak*. Figure 2.19 shows the dialog box for this tool, using the same blood pressure data. The *Rank and Percentile* tool sorts the data from highest to lowest, assigning the 100th percentile to the largest value and the 0 percentile to the smallest value. Intermediate values have percentiles in steps of $1/(n-1)$, where *n* is the number of observations. Figure 2.20 shows the result of using the *Rank and Percentile* tool. For instance, 100 percent of the rest of the North American sample falls below the sample with a blood pressure reading of 193. Eighteen of the remaining 19 observations, or 94.7 percent, fall below the subject with blood pressure of 183. Similarly, 17 of 19 observations, or 89.4 percent, fall below 181.

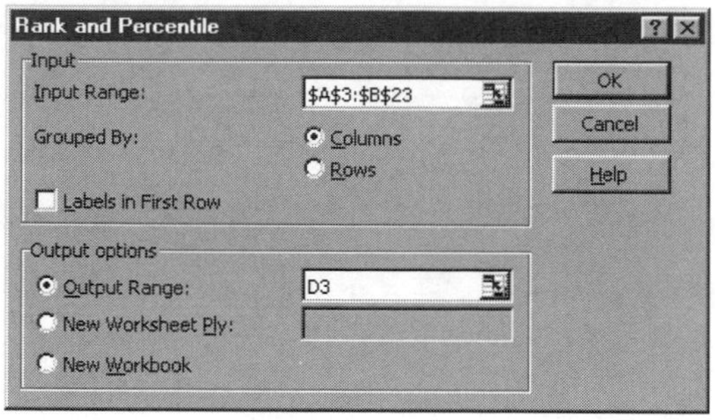

FIGURE 2.19 Rank and Percentile Dialog Box

	A	B	C	D	E	F	G	H	I	J	K
1		Blood Pressure									
2											
3	NA	Others		Point	NA	Rank	Percent	Point	Others	Rank	Percent
4	175	128		4	193	1	100.00%	3	152	1	100.00%
5	162	117		12	183	2	94.70%	10	141	2	94.70%
6	159	152		15	181	3	89.40%	4	138	3	84.20%
7	193	138		8	176	4	84.20%	20	138	3	84.20%
8	148	97		1	175	5	73.60%	11	137	5	73.60%
9	151	115		16	175	5	73.60%	14	137	5	73.60%
10	78	105		11	171	7	68.40%	9	129	7	63.10%
11	176	113		20	163	8	63.10%	19	129	7	63.10%
12	153	129		2	162	9	52.60%	1	128	9	57.80%
13	148	141		13	162	9	52.60%	2	117	10	52.60%
14	171	137		3	159	11	47.30%	6	115	11	42.10%
15	183	89		9	153	12	42.10%	15	115	11	42.10%
16	162	106		19	152	13	36.80%	8	113	13	36.80%
17	149	137		6	151	14	31.50%	13	106	14	26.30%
18	181	115		14	149	15	26.30%	17	106	14	26.30%
19	175	95		5	148	16	15.70%	7	105	16	21.00%
20	139	106		10	148	16	15.70%	18	103	17	15.70%
21	146	103		18	146	18	10.50%	5	97	18	10.50%
22	152	129		17	139	19	5.20%	16	95	19	5.20%
23	163	138		7	78	20	.00%	12	89	20	.00%

FIGURE 2.20 Rank and Percentile Results

Other fractiles can be calculated as well, based upon the sorted data obtained from the *Rank and Percentile* tool. Some of these are summarized as follows:

Quartiles	North America	Others
First Quartile	148.5	105.5
Second Quartile	160.5	116
Third Quartile	175	137

Deciles	North America	Others
1	142.5	96
2	148	104
3	150	106
4	152.5	114
5	160.5	116
6	162.5	128.5
7	173	133
8	175.5	137.5
9	182	139.5

Both quartiles and deciles provide a basis of comparison for the entire distribution of the two samples. Here the two data sets are clearly different. In general, deciles provide a more complete picture that may be more useful in distinguishing between samples.

A **proportion** is the fraction of data that has a certain characteristic. For example, in the *Overall Dealer Satisfaction* worksheet of the Tracway database, the proportion of the North American dealers who rated their satisfaction as a "5" in 1996 was $12/50 = 0.24$. Some attribute data have only two values. For example, in the worksheet *Mower Test,* we have samples of mower functional performance after assembly. The data are categorical, with values of Pass or Fail. For each sample, we may compute the proportion that pass the test by dividing the sum of the number that passed by the total in the sample.

Visual Display of Statistical Measures

Statisticians use other types of graphs to visually display the dispersion in a data set. Two useful tools are box-and-whisker plots and stem-and-leaf plots, both of which are available in the *PHStat* Excel add-in. When *PHStat* is installed, it opens a new menu item on the Excel menu bar called *Stat.* All procedures are accessed from this menu.

BOX-AND-WHISKER PLOTS

Box-and-whisker plots graphically display five key descriptive measures of a data set: the minimum, first quartile, median, third quartile, and maximum. Box-and-whisker plots can be created in Excel using *PHStat* (see *PHStat Note: Creating Box-and-Whisker Plots*).

PHStat Note: Creating Box-and-Whisker Plots

From the *PHStat* menu, select *Box-and-Whisker Plot.* The dialog box is shown in Figure 2.21. In the *Data Variable Cell Range* box, enter the range of the data; if the first cell contains a label, check the box below. For a single data set, check the *Single Group Variable* radio button. For multiple groups of data, check the appropriate button (see the *PHStat* note on stacked and unstacked data in chapter 1). In the *Output Options* section, you may enter a title for the chart. Checking the *Five-Number Summary* box will provide a worksheet with the minimum, first quartile, median, third quartile, and maximum values of the data set(s).

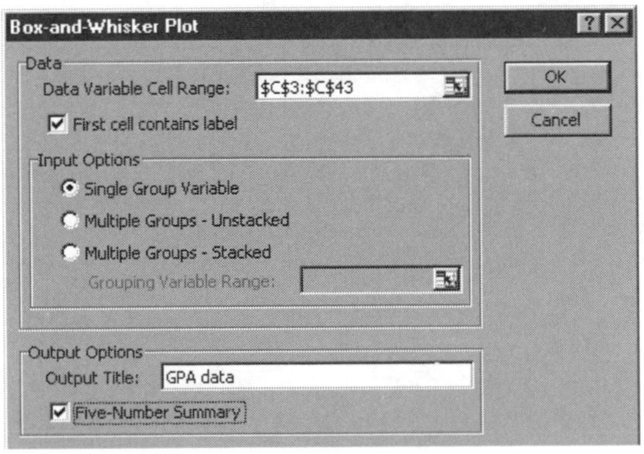

FIGURE 2.21 *PHStat* Dialog Box for Box-and-Whisker Plot

The box-and-whisker plot and summary statistics for the GPA data used earlier in this chapter is shown in Figure 2.22. The dashed lines represent the minimum and maximum values in the data set; the box encloses the first and third quartile points, which means that at least half the sample data fall within the box. The line inside the quartile box represents the median. We saw from the histogram that these data are relatively symmetric. The box-and-whisker plot shows this also, as the median line is in the center of the box and the whiskers—the lines between the median and the dashed minimum and maximum values that represent the range of the data—are approximately the same length.

Figure 2.23 displays a box-and-whisker plot for the age data, which was highly skewed. Here the median line is *not* centered on the box, and the top whisker is much

FIGURE 2.22 Box-and-Whisker Plot and Summary Statistics of GPA Data

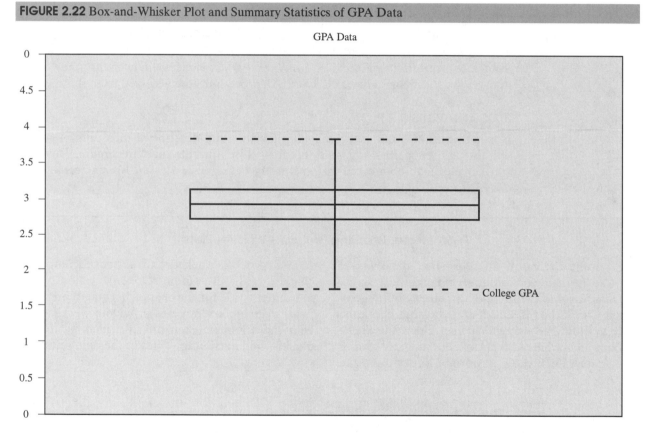

GPA Data

College GPA

	A	B
1	GPA data	
2		
3	Five-number Summary	
4	Minimum	1.75
5	First Quartile	2.75
6	Median	2.955
7	Third Quartile	3.15
8	Maximum	3.86

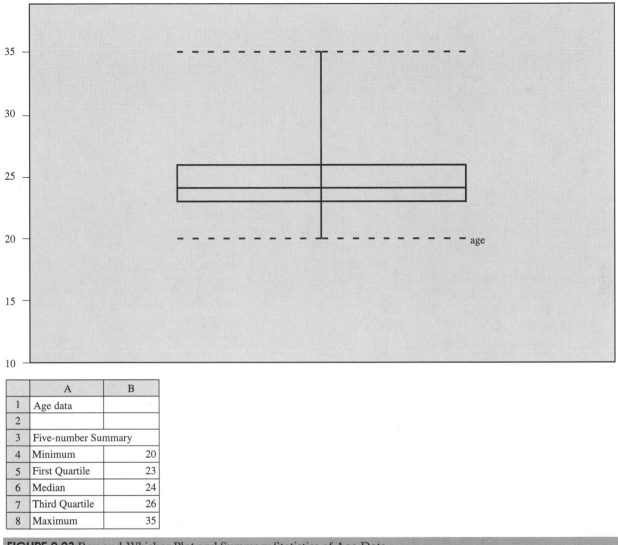

	A	B
1	Age data	
2		
3	Five-number Summary	
4	Minimum	20
5	First Quartile	23
6	Median	24
7	Third Quartile	26
8	Maximum	35

FIGURE 2.23 Box-and-Whisker Plot and Summary Statistics of Age Data

larger than the bottom one. These are characteristic of positively skewed data. Finally, Figure 2.24 shows a box-and-whisker plot for the data in the Tracway worksheet *Defects After Delivery*. You can see that the data for each year differ in symmetry, although the range is relatively constant. Overall, the number of defects is decreasing over time. Figure 2.25 shows the summary statistics for these plots. Box-and-whisker plots that have very large whiskers help identify outliers in data sets.

The difference between the first and third quartiles, $Q_3 - Q_1$, which is represented by the box in a box-and-whisker plot, is often called the **interquartile range,** or the **midspread.** This includes only the middle 50 percent of the data, and therefore is not influenced by extreme values. Thus it is sometimes used as an alternative measure of dispersion from the standard deviation.

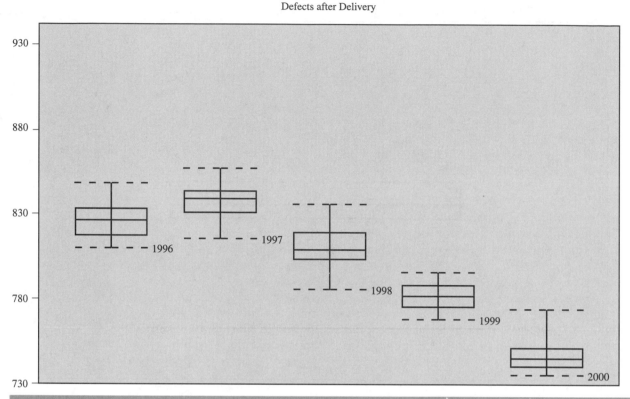

FIGURE 2.24 Box-and-Whisker Plot of Defects After Delivery

	A	B	C	D	E	F
1	Defects after delivery					
2						
3	Five-number Summary					
4		1996	1997	1998	1999	2000
5	Minimum	810	816	786	769	736
6	First Quartile	817.5	831	804	776	741.75
7	Median	826.5	839	809	783	746
8	Third Quartile	833.25	843.25	819.5	789	752.25
9	Maximum	848	857	836	796	775

FIGURE 2.25 Summary Statistics for Box-and-Whisker Plot of Defects After Delivery Data

STEM-AND-LEAF DISPLAYS

Another useful tool in visual displaying data is a stem-and-leaf display. The technique behind the stem-and-leaf display is to sort the data into equally dispersed cells. The stem represents the largest digit of the data series. The leaves are the second digit. Figure 2.26 shows a stem-and-leaf display for the GPA data (see *PHStat Note: Creating Stem-and-Leaf Displays*). In this data set, values ranged between 1.75 and 3.86; thus the stem values are 1.0, 2.0, and 3.0. Then for each of these stem values, the second digit for each of the observations is displayed. Note that there are 2 observations below 2.0: 1.75 and 1.84. Therefore, the leaves on the stem value of 1 are 7 and 8. The high number of zeros after the 3 indicates the large number of values between 3.0 and 3.1.

Figure 2.27 gives the stem-and-leaf display for the age data. Here we used the first two digits for the stem, and zeros are used to indicate the number of observations falling within each cell. Turned sideways, this looks like an ordinary histogram. The highly skewed nature of this data set is clearly evident.

	A	B	C	D	E	F	G	H
1				Stem and leaf				
2				for College gpa				
3				Stem unit: 1				
4								
5	Statistics			1	7 8			
6	Sample Size	40		2	1 4 5 5 6 6 7 7 7 8 8 8 8 8 9 9			
7	Mean	2.93425		3	0 0 0 0 0 0 0 0 1 1 1 1 1 2 4 4 5 5 6 6 8 9			
8	Median	2.955						
9	Std. Deviation	0.455338						
10	Minimum	1.75						
11	Maximum	3.86						

FIGURE 2.26 Stem-and-Leaf Display of GPA Data

	A	B	C	D	E	F
1				Stem and leaf		
2				for age		
3				Stem unit: 1		
4						
5	Statistics			20	0	
6	Sample Size	40		21	0 0	
7	Mean	25.15		22	0 0 0	
8	Median	24		23	0 0 0 0 0 0 0 0 0 0	
9	Std. Deviation	3.562986		24	0 0 0 0 0 0 0	
10	Minimum	20		25	0 0 0 0 0 0	
11	Maximum	35		26	0 0 0 0	
12				27	0	
13				28	0 0	
14				29		
15				30		
16				31		
17				32	0 0	
18				33	0	
19				34	0	
20				35	0	

FIGURE 2.27 Stem-and-Leaf Display of Age Data

PHStat Note: Creating Stem-and-Leaf Displays

From the *PHStat* menu, select *Stem-and-Leaf Display*. The dialog box is shown in Figure 2.28. Enter the range of the data in the first box, checking the *First cell contains label* box if appropriate. You may have the tool automatically calculate the stem unit, or you may specify it as a power of 10.

For example, if the numbers are large, say in the range of 800 to 900, then you might wish to specify the stem unit as 10 so that the stem values are 80, 81, 82, and so on, and leaves are the third digits. The stem-and-leaf display also provides summary statistics if the box is checked.

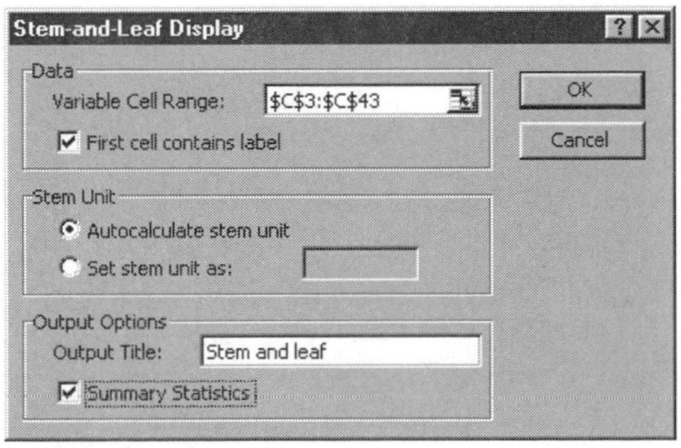

Stem-and-Leaf Display [?] [X]

Data
Variable Cell Range: $C$3:$C$43
☑ First cell contains label

OK
Cancel

Stem Unit
⦿ Autocalculate stem unit
○ Set stem unit as:

Output Options
Output Title: Stem and leaf
☑ Summary Statistics

FIGURE 2.28 *PHStat* Dialog Box for Stem-and-Leaf Display

Visual displays such as box-and-whisker plots and stem-and-leaf displays give more complete pictures of data sets. They are highly useful tools in exploring the characteristics of data before computing other statistical measures.

Statistical Relationships

Tracway uses an in-depth survey to identify the perception of their products by their customers. Four variables expected to be important in customer buying decisions are product quality, ease of use of the product, product price, and customer service. Aggregated data are available, providing average ratings by region by year on each of these measures in Table 2.6 (from the worksheet *Survey Recap* in the Tracway database). It is reasonable to think that perceptions of quality, use, price, and service would be closely related to customer satisfaction, some perhaps more so than others. Understanding such relationships is extremely important in making good business decisions because although companies cannot directly control factors such as sales or customer satisfaction, they *can* control the factors that influence these external measures. When a company understands how these factors impact key measures of business performance, it can make better decisions. Thus it is helpful to have statistical tools for measuring these relationships.

Two variables have a strong statistical relationship with one another if they appear to move together. For example, attendance at baseball games is often closely related to

TABLE 2.6   Quality Survey Data

| Region | Year | Dealer | Customer | Survey Averages by Factor | | | |
				Quality	Ease	Price	Service
NA	1996	3.82	3.98	3.8	3.1	3.3	3.5
NA	1997	3.92	4.04	3.9	3.3	3.2	3.7
NA	1998	4.00	4.03	4.2	3.4	3.5	4.0
NA	1999	4.05	4.08	4.5	4.0	3.6	4.1
NA	2000	4.11	4.12	4.6	4.3	3.7	4.3
SA	1996	4.00	4.00	4.1	2.8	3.1	3.8
SA	1997	4.00	3.95	4.1	2.9	3.2	3.8
SA	1998	4.29	3.99	4.2	3.2	3.2	3.9
SA	1999	4.47	4.00	4.2	3.7	3.4	4.1
SA	2000	4.43	4.02	4.3	3.9	3.5	4.2
Eur	1996	3.93	3.97	3.5	3.2	3.8	3.4
Eur	1997	4.00	3.99	3.6	3.4	3.7	3.5
Eur	1998	4.00	4.03	3.6	3.5	3.9	3.7
Eur	1999	4.00	4.09	3.8	4.2	4.0	3.8
Eur	2000	4.00	4.14	4.1	4.3	3.9	3.9
Pac	1996	3.20	3.92	3.8	3.0	3.5	3.9
Pac	1997	3.40	3.95	4.0	3.1	3.6	3.9
Pac	1998	3.67	4.00	4.1	3.3	3.4	4.0
Pac	1999	3.83	4.06	4.3	3.6	3.7	4.2
Pac	2000	3.75	4.07	4.4	3.9	3.6	4.3
China	1998	3.00	3.87	3.3	3.1	2.8	2.7
China	1999	2.50	3.89	3.5	3.8	3.1	2.8
China	2000	3.40	3.91	3.8	4.1	3.0	2.6

the win percentage of the team, and ice cream sales likely have a strong relationship with daily temperature. In these cases, you might suspect a definite cause-and-effect relationship. Sometimes, a statistical relationship exists even though one is not caused by the other. For example, the *New York Times* reported a strong relationship between the golf handicaps of corporate CEOs and their companies' stock market performance over three years. CEOs that were better-than-average golfers were likely to delivery above-average returns to shareholders.[2] You must be cautious in drawing inferences about causal relationships based solely on statistical relationships. On the other hand, you might want to spend more time out on the course!

Correlation is a measure of the strength of linear relationship between two variables, X and Y, and is measured by the (population) **correlation coefficient:**

$$\rho_{x,y} = \frac{\text{cov}(X,Y)}{\sigma_x \sigma_y}$$

The numerator is called the **covariance,** and is the average of the products of deviations of each observation from its respective mean:

$$\text{cov}(X,Y) = \frac{\sum_{i=1}^{N}(x_i - \mu_x)(y_i - \mu_y)}{N}$$

Similarly, the sample correlation coefficient is computed as

$$r = \frac{\sum_{i=1}^{n}(x_i - \bar{x})(y_i - \bar{y})}{(n-1)s_x s_y}$$

Correlation coefficients will range from –1 to +1. A correlation of 0 indicates that the two variables have no linear relationship to each other. Thus, if one changes, we can not reasonably predict what the other variable might do. A correlation coefficient of +1 indicates a perfect positive relationship; as one variable increases, the other will also increase. A correlation coefficient of –1 also shows a perfect relationship, except that as one variable increases, the other decreases. In economics, for example, a perfectly price-elastic product has a correlation between price and sales of –1; as price increases, sales decrease, and vice versa.

Using the *Correlation* tool (see *Excel Note: Using the Correlation Tool*) and the data in the worksheet *Survey Recap* in the Tracway database, the correlation between average customer ratings and average ratings of perceived product quality is computed to be 0.650. This positive correlation suggests that as customer rating goes up, the quality rating also tends to go up (but not all of the time). The scatter diagram in Figure 2.29 confirms this observation visually.

Tracway can use correlation to identify the apparent roles that quality, ease of use, price, and service have played in dealer and customer satisfaction. We could also correlate each variable to time to help understand trends. By using the *Correlation* tool for each pair of variables, we can construct the correlation matrix in Table 2.7. Note that the correlation of each variable with itself is automatically 1.0.

The correlation of 0.887 between Ease and Year shows that a strong positive trend over time exists. Tracway instituted a modification to their products in 1999 that made

---

[2] Adam Bryant, "CEOs' golf games linked to companies' performance," *The Cincinnati Enquirer,* June 7, 1998, E1.

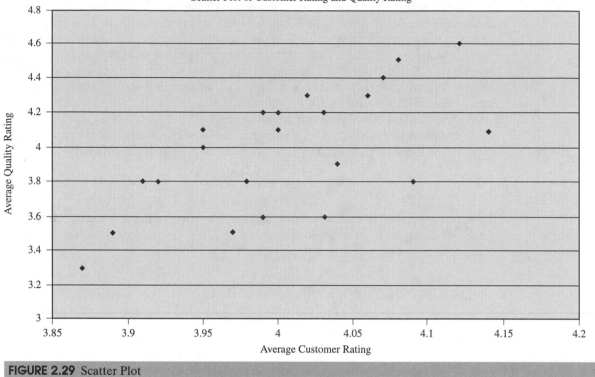

FIGURE 2.29 Scatter Plot

Excel Note: Using the Correlation Tool

Select the *Correlation* tool from the *Tools/Data Analysis* menu option. The dialog box is shown in Figure 2.30. You need only input the range of the data and specify whether the data are grouped by rows or columns (most applications will be grouped by columns), and whether the first row contains data labels. Output options are standard as in other tools we have discussed. The output of this tool is a matrix giving the correlation between each pair of variables.

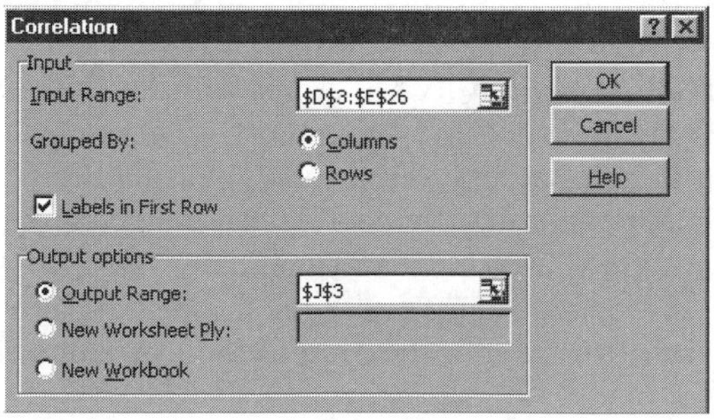

FIGURE 2.30 Correlation Dialog Box

TABLE 2.7 Correlation Matrix

	Year	Dealer	Customer	Quality	Ease	Price	Service
Year	1.0	0.109	0.431	0.441	0.887	0.173	0.151
Dealer		1.0	0.647	0.564	0.150	0.413	0.662
Customer			1.0	0.650	0.578	0.697	0.720
Quality				1.0	0.344	0.215	0.814
Ease					1.0	0.427	0.134
Price						1.0	0.551
Service							1.0

their equipment easier to use, and this had a positive impact on satisfaction. The other variables all have positive trends, meaning that as time goes by, ratings have tended to rise. However, some variables have risen faster than others. Customer satisfaction and product quality ratings are fairly high in their increases. Dealer satisfaction is only slightly higher with time.

The correlation matrix can also be used to identify those factors that seem to have the greatest relationship with dealer and customer satisfaction. For example, improved service has the highest correlation with dealer satisfaction, followed by product quality. Price and ease of use have smaller correlations to dealer ratings. Customer ratings are also all positively related to product features. All four are very close in value, with service having the highest correlation with positive customer rating. The conclusion that Tracway management might reach is that the company is emphasizing appropriate product features for customers, and that dealers, who must be kept happy in order to stay in business, are more concerned with quality and service features.

Case Study: Using Descriptive Statistics For The Malcolm Baldrige National Quality Award

This case study shows how descriptive statistics are used in the process of evaluating companies for the Malcolm Baldrige National Quality Award. The Malcolm Baldrige National Quality Award recognizes U.S. companies that excel in quality management practice and performance. The Award is a public-private partnership, funded primarily through a private foundation, and administered through the National Institute of Standards and Technology (NIST) in cooperation with the American Society for Quality (ASQ). It was created to

- Help stimulate American companies to improve quality and productivity for the pride of recognition while obtaining a competitive edge through increased profits;
- Recognize the achievements of those companies that improve the quality of their goods and services and provide an example to others;
- Establish guidelines and criteria that can be used by business, industrial, governmental, and other enterprises in evaluating their own quality improvement efforts; and
- Provide specific guidance for other American enterprises that wish to learn how to manage for high quality by making available detailed information on how winning enterprises were able to change their cultures and achieve eminence.

The award examination is based upon a rigorous set of criteria, called the *Criteria for Performance Excellence,* which consist of seven major categories:

Leadership
Strategic Planning
Customer and Market Focus
Information and Analysis
Human Resource Focus
Process Management
Business Results

Each category consists of several items that focus on major requirements on which businesses should focus. For example, the three items in the Process Management category are 6.1—Product and Service Processes, 6.2—Support Processes, and 6.3—Supplier and Partnering Processes. Each item, in turn, consists of a small number of areas to address, which seek specific information on approaches used to ensure and improve competitive performance, the deployment of these approaches, or results obtained from such deployment. A single free copy of the criteria can be obtained from NIST by contacting the Malcolm Baldrige National Quality Award, National Institute of Standards and Technology, Route 270 & Quince Orchard Road, Administration Building, Room A537, Gaithersburg, MD 20899, (301) 975-2036, FAX (301) 948-3716, or by visiting the Web site (http://www.quality.nist.gov/).

Applicants submit a 50-page document that describes their management practices and business results that respond to the criteria. The evaluation of applicants for the Award is conducted by a volunteer board of examiners selected by NIST. In the first stage, each application is reviewed by a team of examiners. They evaluate the applicant's response to each criteria item, listing major strengths and opportunities for improvement relative to the criteria. Based on these comments, a score from 0 to 100 in increments of 10 is given to each item. Scores for each examination item are computed by multiplying the examiner's score by the maximum point value that can be earned for that item, which varies by item. These point values weight the importance of each item in the criteria. The scores are reviewed by a panel of nine judges without knowledge of the specific companies. The higher-scoring applications enter a *consensus stage* in which a selected group of examiners, via telephone conferencing, discuss variations in individual assessments and scores, and arrive at consensus comments and scores for each item. The panel of judges then reviews the scores and selects the highest-scoring applicants for site visits. At this point, a team of seven examiners visits the company for about 3 days to verify information contained in the written application and resolve issues that are unclear. The judges use the site visit reports to recommend award recipients.

The consensus stage is an extremely important step of the process. It is designed to smooth out variations in examiners' scores, which inevitably arise because of different perceptions of the applicants' responses relative to the criteria, and provide useful feedback to the applicants. Statistics and data analysis tools are used to provide a summary of the examiners' scoring profiles and to schedule the order of discussion based on the variation in the scores and the point values of the items. Specifically, the standard deviation of each item's scores is multiplied by the point value to arrive at a weighted standard deviation. The discussion priorities of the items is based on these weighted standard deviations. Thus items having higher point values as well as larger variation among examiners will be discussed earlier in the consensus call, so that sufficient time can be allotted to their discussion and important items not be affected by fatigue during the conference call (which may last up to 5 hours or more).

Figures 2.31 through 2.33 illustrate a hypothetical example (all data and calculations may be found in the Excel workbook *baldrige.xls*). The distribution of examiner scores is shown in Figure 2.31. The weighted score is obtained by adding the product of the maximum point column entry times the examiner score for that item divided by 100. Thus each examiner score is the percentage of the maximum points awarded for that item. The box-and-whisker plot in Figure 2.32 shows the variation among item scores in a graphical fashion. On item 7.1, the examiners were very consistent, with most examiners assigning a score of 70, Examiner 1 a score of 60, and Examiner 5 a score of 80.

FIGURE 2.31 Examiner Scores for Hypothetical Baldrige Consensus Analysis

	A	B	C	D	E	F	G	H	I	J
1	Item	Maximum	Examiner	Examiner	Examiner	Examiner	Examiner	Examiner	Examiner	Examiner
2		Points	1	2	3	4	5	6	7	8
3	1.1	80	80	80	50	60	60	70	70	50
4	1.2	30	30	50	30	40	40	60	60	50
5	2.1	40	50	70	50	50	40	60	70	40
6	2.2	40	30	40	50	50	60	30	30	50
7	3.1	40	30	60	40	60	50	30	50	30
8	3.2	40	30	50	60	60	60	50	30	60
9	4.1	25	40	70	50	60	40	30	20	50
10	4.2	15	30	20	40	40	30	30	10	30
11	4.3	40	20	20	30	50	30	30	20	30
12	5.1	40	70	50	60	40	40	60	60	50
13	5.2	30	50	30	40	40	30	50	50	50
14	5.3	30	50	20	40	40	70	40	40	20
15	6.1	60	50	60	50	50	50	40	30	40
16	6.2	20	30	40	30	50	40	30	20	30
17	6.3	20	20	30	30	40	20	10	10	30
18	7.1	125	60	70	70	70	80	70	70	70
19	7.2	125	50	60	70	50	70	50	70	70
20	7.3	50	50	40	50	50	70	30	30	50
21	7.4	25	40	50	50	50	50	40	20	60
22	7.5	125	60	80	70	60	70	40	60	70
23	Weighted score		497	575.5	549.5	539.5	581	474	505.5	535.5

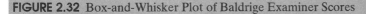

FIGURE 2.32 Box-and-Whisker Plot of Baldrige Examiner Scores

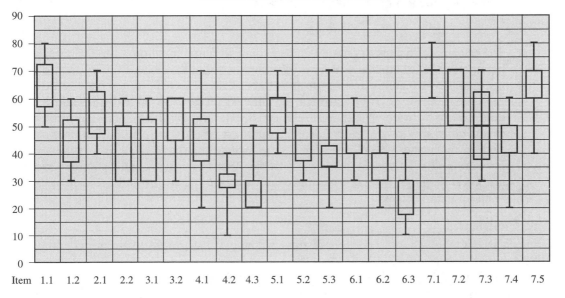

Box-and-Whisker Plot of Examiner Scores

	A	B	C	D	E	F	G	H
1	Item	Maximum	Average	Median		Standard	Weighted	
2		Points	Score	Score	Range	Deviation	Std. Dev.	Rank
3	7.5	125	63.8	65	30	11.9	1484.7	1
4	7.2	125	61.3	65	20	9.9	1238.8	2
5	1.1	80	65.0	65	30	12.0	956.2	3
6	7.1	125	70.0	70	10	5.3	668.2	4
7	7.3	50	46.3	50	20	13.0	651.2	5
8	6.1	60	46.3	50	20	9.2	549.7	6
9	3.2	40	50.0	55	30	13.1	523.7	7
10	3.1	40	43.8	45	0	13.0	521.0	8
11	5.3	30	40.0	40	30	16.0	481.1	9
12	2.1	40	53.8	50	10	11.9	475.1	10
13	2.2	40	42.5	45	20	11.6	466.0	11
14	5.1	40	53.8	55	30	10.6	424.3	12
15	4.1	25	45.0	45	30	16.0	400.9	13
16	4.3	40	28.8	30	10	9.9	396.4	14
17	1.2	30	45.0	45	20	12.0	358.6	15
18	7.4	25	45.0	50	40	12.0	298.8	16
19	5.2	30	42.5	45	20	8.9	265.9	17
20	6.3	20	23.8	25	20	10.6	212.1	18
21	6.2	20	33.8	30	10	9.2	183.2	19
22	4.2	15	28.8	30	20	9.9	148.7	20
23	Weighted Score		453.2	470.3				

FIGURE 2.33 Statistical Analysis and Weighted Ranks of Consensus Scores

The greatest range of scores awarded was for item 4.1, with Examiner 7 assigning a score of 20, and Examiner 2 giving a score of 70. Item 7.2 had less range, but more variance, as examiners for the most part assigned a score of either 50 or 70. In Figure 2.33, we show the key statistics of the distribution, including the averages, medians, ranges, and standard deviations. The weighted standard deviation is used to establish the ranking of each item (using the Excel function RANK). As shown, the data are sorted according to these rankings using the Sort command in the Data menu.

The Baldrige scoring example demonstrates the value of statistical tools, not only to provide a basis for ranking but also to examine specifics as to why a company was ranked wherever it was ranked. The analysis provided by the box-and-whisker plot, as well as the basic data in Figure 2.33, show where examiners differed the most and which items had the most impact in company ratings.

Summary

The purpose of data is to provide management with understanding and insight. The reporting system of most any organization can provide a large quantity of data to management; however, interpreting the data is not as easy. This chapter has introduced some fundamental graphical and statistical techniques that can be used to display and explore data. Charts provide visual interpretation of data and excellent communication vehicles in business. However, numerical measures are needed to quantify characteristics of data to make meaningful decisions. These include measures of central tendency, dispersion, and relationship between variables. Further insight can be obtained from graphical displays of such quantitative information using box-and-whisker plots and stem-and-leaf displays.

Questions and Problems

1. How can a cost accountant or financial analyst use graphs to aid in understanding firm operations?
2. What do descriptive statistics provide managers that detailed data does not?

3. Create a line chart for Tracway profit before overhead for the South American region by month. Obtain unit sales from the *Mower Unit Sales* and *Tractor Unit Sales* worksheets, revenues from the *Revenues* worksheet, and unit costs from the *Pre-Tax Earnings* worksheet. Also include costs for dealer share (20 percent of revenue) and shipping (5 percent of revenue).

4. What is the rate of return before overhead, defined as profit divided by cost, for the South American region in the year 2000? Define rate of return as profit over cost. (Generate needed data from the worksheets as given in Problem 3.)

5. Graph the South American region profit by year with a bar chart for the years 1996 through 2000.

6. What is the annual increase in contribution to profit before overhead on the part of the South American region for the years 1997/1996 through 2000/1999?

7. Develop pie charts using data from the *Mower Unit Sales* worksheet showing the percentage of sales in the years 1996 and 2000 by region for mowers.

8. Develop an area chart from the *Mower Unit Sales* worksheet to display mower unit sales by region monthly over the period 1996 through 2000.

9. Develop a scatter diagram using data from the *End-User Satisfaction* worksheet that displays user satisfaction by region over time.

10. Compare the mean, median, and mode of the number of days Tracway takes to pay invoices, found on the *Time to Pay Supplier* worksheet. Explain the meaning of the results and evaluate the implications.

11. Compare the mean, median, and mode of blood pressure for the North American region managers and other managers given in the *Blood Pressure* worksheet. Explain the meaning of the results and evaluate the implications.

12. Compare the mean, median, and mode of the costs of the current and alternative processes to build transmissions given in the *Transmission Costs* worksheet. Explain the meaning of the results and evaluate the implications.

13. Compare the range and standard deviation of blood pressure for North American region managers and other managers given in the *Blood Pressure* worksheet. Explain the meaning of the results and evaluate the implications.

14. Compare the range and standard deviation of the costs of the current and alternative processes to build transmissions given in the *Transmission Costs* worksheet. Explain the meaning of the results and evaluate the implications.

15. Review the skewness and kurtosis of the number of days Tracway takes to pay invoices, found in the *Time to Pay Supplier* worksheet. Explain the meaning of the results you obtain and evaluate the implications.

16. Compare the skewness and kurtosis of blood pressure for the North American region managers and other managers given in the *Blood Pressure* worksheet. Explain the meaning of the results you obtain and evaluate the implications.

17. Compare the skewness and kurtosis of the costs of the current and alternative processes to build transmissions given in the *Transmission Costs* worksheet. Explain the meaning of the results you obtain and evaluate the implications.

18. Develop profiles (quartiles, deciles) of the number of days Tracway takes to pay invoices, found in the *Time to Pay Supplier* worksheet.

19. Develop profiles (quartiles, deciles) of blood pressure for the North American region managers and other managers given in the *Blood Pressure* worksheet.

20. Develop profiles (quartiles, deciles) of the costs of the current and alternative processes to build transmissions given in the *Transmission Costs* worksheet.

21. Construct and interpret a box-and-whisker plot for the number of days Tracway takes to pay invoices, found in the *Time to Pay Supplier* worksheet.

22. Construct and interpret a box-and-whisker plot for the costs to build transmissions given in the *Transmission Costs* worksheet.

23. Construct and interpret a stem-and-leaf display for the *Time to Pay Supplier* worksheet data.

24. Construct and interpret a stem-and-leaf display for Tracway manager blood pressure, using data on the *Blood Pressure* worksheet.
25. Construct and interpret stem-and-leaf displays for the three transmission systems given in the *Transmission Costs* worksheet.
26. Find the correlation between the S&P 500 and Tracway stock price using data in the *Stock* worksheet. What does this tell you?
27. Find the correlation matrix for duration with the company and the other variables for which data are given on worksheet *Employee Success*. Interpret the results.
28. Why would the correlation between the North American region managers and other Tracway managers based on the data as given on the *Blood Pressure* worksheet have no meaning?

PART I

CHAPTER 3

Random Variables and Probability Distributions

Outline

Basic Concepts
    Probability
    Random Variables
    Probability Distributions
    Expected Value and Variance of a Random Variable
Discrete Probability Distributions
    Bernoulli and Binomial Distributions
    Poisson Distribution
Continuous Probability Distributions
    Uniform Distribution
    Normal Distribution
    Triangular Distribution
    Exponential Distribution
    Probability Distributions in *PHStat*
    Other Useful Distributions
Random Sampling From Probability Distributions
    Random Numbers
    Sampling from Probability Distributions
    Sampling from Probability Distributions in Excel
Sampling Distributions and Sampling Error
Summary
Questions and Problems
Appendix: Introduction to *Crystal Ball*
    Specifying Input Information
    Crystal Ball Output

Most business decisions involve some elements of uncertainty. For example, in models of manufacturing operations the job arrival times, job types, processing times, times between machine breakdowns, and repair times all involve uncertainty. Similarly, a

57

model that predicts the future return of an investment portfolio requires a variety of uncertain assumptions about economic conditions and market behavior. Specifying the nature of such assumptions is a key modeling task that relies on fundamental knowledge of random variables and probability distributions—the subject of this chapter. Random variables and probability distributions are also important in applying statistics to analyze sample data from business processes, because sample data are usually assumed to stem from some underlying probability distribution. Thus we will also examine characteristics of sampling distributions in this chapter and introduce simulation as a tool for understanding them and errors associated with sampling. The key concepts and tools that we will study are

- The notion of probability, and the calculation of joint, marginal, and conditional probabilities;
- Random variables, including their definition and calculations of expected value and variance;
- Probability distributions: discrete and continuous distributions, and their applications in probability modeling;
- Simulation techniques for random sampling from probability distributions, the concept of random numbers, and an introduction to the Excel add-in, *Crystal Ball;* and
- Sampling distributions and sampling error.

Basic Concepts

In this section we define and illustrate the fundamental concepts of probability, random variables, and probability distributions. Many of these concepts are similar to the ideas we developed in chapter 2. Here, however, the focus is on theoretical models rather than on sample data.

PROBABILITY

The notion of probability is used every day, from casino gambling to weather forecasts to stock market predictions. **Probability** is the likelihood that an event will occur. We can think of an event as the outcome of some experiment such as rolling dice, observing the weather, or watching the stock market. The outcomes might be sum of the dice, the weather for the next day, or the value of the Dow Jones industrial average (DJIA) at the end of the next year. Whatever the outcomes, two conditions must hold. First, the probability associated with any outcome must be between 0 and 1. Second, the sum of the probabilities over all possible outcomes must be 1.

Probability may be viewed in one of three ways. First, if the process that generates the event is known, probabilities can be determined from theoretical arguments; this is the *classical definition* of probability. For example, if we count the possible outcomes associated with rolling two dice, we can easily determine that out of 36 possible outcomes, one will be the number 2, six will be the number 7, and so on. Thus the probability of rolling a 7 is 6/36 = 1/6. The second approach to probability, called the *relative frequency definition,* is based on empirical data. For example, a meteorologist knows that on 10 days when certain weather conditions have been observed, it has rained the next day 8 times. Thus the probability of rain the next day would be specified as 0.8, or 80 percent. Finally, the *subjective method* of probability is based on judgment, as financial analysts might do in predicting a 75 percent chance that the DJIA will increase 10 percent over the next year.

RANDOM VARIABLES

A **random variable** is a numerical description of the outcome of an experiment. Random variables are usually denoted by capital letters, such as X or Y; specific values of random variables are denoted by lowercase letters. Some "experiments," such as rolling dice or observing the value of the DJIA, naturally have numerical outcomes; for others, such as the weather, we might have to associate some arbitrary numerical value to the outcomes, such as $0 = $ sunny, $1 = $ cloudy, $2 = $ rain, and so on. Random variables may be *discrete* or *continuous*. For example, the outcome of rolling dice, the weather for the next day, and the number of customers who respond to a telemarketing campaign are discrete random variables; the value of the DJIA, the time to repair a failed machine, and the return on an investment are continuous. A discrete random variable can have only a countable number of outcomes. For the experiment of rolling two dice, the possible outcomes are the numbers 2 through 12. For a telemarketing campaign, the outcomes are nonnegative integers up to the number of customers contacted.

PROBABILITY DISTRIBUTIONS

A **probability distribution** is a characterization of the possible values that a random variable may assume along with the probability of assuming these values. For a discrete random variable X, the probability of each discrete outcome x_i is characterized by a **probability mass function, $p(x)$.** A probability mass function has the properties that the probability of each outcome must be between 0 and 1, and the sum of all probabilities must add to 1; that is

$$0 \le p(x_i) \le 1$$

$$\sum_i p(x_i) = 1$$

For example, the weekly demand of a slow-moving product might have the following probability mass function (here, $x_1 = 0, x_2 = 1$, and so on):

Demand, x	Probability, p(x)
0	0.1
1	0.2
2	0.4
3	0.3
4 or more	0

A **cumulative distribution function,** $P(x)$, specifies the probability that the random variable will assume a value less than or equal to a specified value, x. In the previous example, the cumulative distribution function is

Demand, x	Cumulative Probability, P(x)
0	0.1
1	0.3
2	0.7
3 or more	1.0

Many situations involve two or more random variables. For example, the number of weekly mortgage applications at a bank and the interest rate are random variables. Over several months when interest rates remained relatively stable, the bank observed the following data, which show the frequency of applications during weeks with given interest rates:

| | \multicolumn{5}{c}{Number of Applications} |
Interest rate	5	6	7	8	Total
7.0%	3	4	6	2	15
7.5%	2	4	3	1	10
8.0%	3	1	1	0	5
Total	8	9	10	3	30

By dividing the number in each cell by the total number of applications (30), we construct a **joint probability distribution** for the two random variables (note that calculations are rounded to three decimal places):

| | \multicolumn{5}{c}{Number of Applications} |
Interest Rate	5	6	7	8	Total
7.0%	0.100	0.133	0.200	0.067	0.500
7.5%	0.067	0.133	0.100	0.033	0.333
8.0%	0.100	0.033	0.033	0	0.167
Total	0.267	0.300	0.333	0.100	1.000

Thus the joint probability of having an interest rate of 7.0 percent and five applications in a particular week is 0.10. The probabilities in the last row and column are called **marginal probabilities,** and represent the probability associated with each random variable alone. For instance, the probability of five applications during a week is 0.267. Two discrete random variables X and Y are **independent** if the joint probability for any values x and y equals the product of the marginal probabilities; that is, $p(x, y) = p(x)p(y)$. In this example it is easy to see that the interest rate and number of applications are *not* independent, because the probability of a rate of 7.0 percent and five applications, 0.100, is not the product of the marginal probabilities, $0.500 \times 0.267 = 0.1335$. It is important to realize that you cannot multiply two probabilities together to obtain the joint probability unless the random variables are independent.

We can also compute **conditional probabilities,** which are the probabilities of the occurrence of one event, given that another event is known to have occurred. For example, suppose we know that the interest rate is 7.5 percent. What is the probability of receiving five applications when this is known? From the first table, we see that of the 10 weeks observed when the interest rate is 7.5 percent, 2 had five applications. Thus the conditional probability is 0.20. We can find this from the joint and marginal probabilities by dividing the joint probability by the marginal probability. In general,

$$p(x|y) = p(x, y)/p(y)$$

where $p(x|y)$ is read as "probability of x given y." Thus the probability of receiving five applications, given an interest rate is 7.5 percent, is $0.067/0.333 = 0.20$; similarly, the probability of receiving six applications, given an interest rate of 7.5 percent, is 0.133/0.333 = 0.40. This formula provides additional insight into the notion of independent random variables. Note that

$$p(x, y) = p(x|y)p(y)$$

But we stated earlier that if X and Y are independent, then $p(x,y) = p(x)p(y)$ for all values x and y, or by substitution, $p(x) = p(x|y)$. This simply says that the probability of the random variable X does not depend on the value of Y. The symmetric statement is also true for independence: $p(y) = p(y|x)$, meaning that the probability of the random variable Y does not depend on the value of X.

A continuous random variable assumes outcomes over a continuous range of real numbers. Examples of continuous random variables include the daily temperature, the time to complete a task, and a company's quarterly earnings. Sometimes the distinction between a discrete and continuous random variable is not clear. For example, stock prices are recorded in increments of one-eighth. Technically, this is discrete; however, for practical purposes of building and analyzing decision models, it is easier to consider stock prices as continuous random variables.

The probabilities of various outcomes of continuous random variables are characterized by a **probability density function, $f(x)$.** A density function has the properties that $f(x) \geq 0$ for all values of x, and that the total area under the function is 1. The cumulative distribution function is denoted $F(x)$. The probability that the random variable will assume a value between a and b is given by the area under the function between a and b. As an illustration, Figure 3.1 shows a triangular distribution. Using simple geometry, it is easy to see that the total area under the curve is 1.0. Figure 3.2 shows the probability that X is greater than 4.7. Using similar triangles (0.3/0.5 = h/2), we see that the height of the function at $x = 4.7$ is 1.2. Therefore, the area of the triangle to the right of 4.7 is ½ (height)(base) = ½ (1.2)(0.3) = 0.18. If we know the explicit expression for the cumulative distribution function, $F(x)$, the probability that x is between a and b is equal to the difference of the cumulative distribution function evaluated at these two points, namely, $F(b) - F(a)$.

You probably see the analogy between probability distributions and the frequency distributions we studied in chapter 2. The key difference is that a frequency distribution

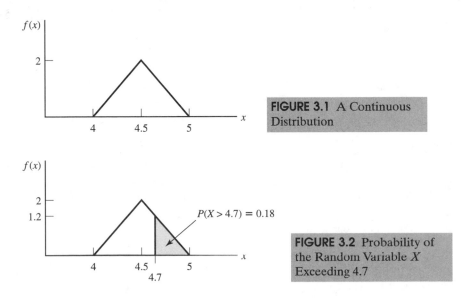

FIGURE 3.1 A Continuous Distribution

FIGURE 3.2 Probability of the Random Variable X Exceeding 4.7

characterizes *sample data,* whereas a probability distribution is a theoretical model of all possible values that a random variable may assume. An important application of sample frequency distributions is in gaining insight into the nature of the underlying probability distribution of the population from which the sample came.

A working knowledge of theoretical probability distributions is important for several reasons. First, it can help you to understand the underlying process that generates sample data. We will investigate the relationship between distributions and samples later in this chapter. Second, many phenomena in business and nature follow some theoretical distribution, and therefore are useful in building decision models. Finally, working with distributions is essential in computing probabilities of outcomes to assess risk and make decisions. Table 3.1 summarizes most of the important Excel functions that relate to this topic.

EXPECTED VALUE AND VARIANCE OF A RANDOM VARIABLE

The **expected value** of a random variable corresponds to the notion of the mean, or average, for a data set. For a discrete random variable X, the expected value is the weighted average of all possible outcomes, where the weights are the probabilities:

$$E[X] = \sum_{i=1}^{\infty} x_i \, p(x_i)$$

TABLE 3.1 Probability Distribution Support for Excel

Excel Function	*Description*
BINOMDIST(*number_s, trials, probability_s, cumulative*)	Returns the individual term binomial distribution.
POISSON(*x, mean, cumulative*)	Returns the Poisson distribution.
NORMDIST(*x, mean, standard_deviation, cumulative*)	Returns the normal cumulative distribution for the specified mean and standard deviation.
NORMSDIST(*z*)	Returns the standard normal cumulative distribution (mean = 0, standard deviation = 1).
STANDARDIZE(*x, mean, standard_deviation*)	Returns a normalized value for a distribution characterized by a mean and standard deviation.
EXPONDIST(*x, lambda, cumulative*)	Returns the exponential distribution.
LOGNORMDIST(*x, mean, standard_deviation*)	Returns the cumulative lognormal distribution of *x*, where ln(*x*) is normally distributed with parameters mean and standard deviation.
BETADIST(*x, alpha, beta, A, B*)	Returns the cumulative beta density function.
GAMMADIST(*x, alpha, beta, cumulative*)	Returns the gamma distribution.
WEIBULL(*x, alpha, beta, cumulative*)	Returns the Weibull distribution.

Prentice Hall Statistics Add-In	*Description*
Binomial Probabilities	Computes binomial probabilities and histogram.
Poisson Probabilities	Computes Poisson probabilities and histogram.
Normal Probabilities	Computes normal probabilities.
Exponential Probabilities	Computes exponential probabilities.
Sampling Distribution Simulation	Generates a simulated sampling distribution from a uniform, standardized normal, or discrete population.

In the slow-moving product demand example, the expected value is

$$E[X] = 0(0.1) + 1(0.2) + 2(0.4) + 3(0.3) = 1.9$$

This means that, over the long run, the average demand is 1.9. The definition of expected value of a continuous random variable is similar; however, it relies on notions of calculus, so we will not discuss it in this book.

The **variance** of a random variable X is defined as

$$\text{Var}[X] = \sum_{j=1}^{\infty} (x_j - E[X])^2 p(x_j)$$

For the previous example, the variance is

$$\text{Var}[X] = (0 - 1.9)^2 (0.1) + (1 - 1.9)^2 (0.2) + (2 - 1.9)^2 (0.4) + (3 - 1.9)^2 (0.3)$$
$$= 0.89$$

The variance is often denoted as σ_x^2. Similar to our discussion in chapter 2, the variance measures the uncertainty of the random variable; the higher the variance, the higher the uncertainty of the outcome. Although variances are easier to work with mathematically, we usually measure the variability of a random variable by the **standard deviation, σ_x,** which is simply the square root of the variance:

$$\sigma_x = \sqrt{\sum_{j=1}^{\infty} (x_j - E[X])^2 p(x_j)}$$

The standard deviation for the product demand example is $\sqrt{.89} = .943$. The standard deviation, σ_x, is expressed in the same units as the random variable, and thus is a more meaningful measure than the variance. The standard deviation is a measure of risk, and therefore is a critical concept in financial modeling.

It is important to understand that the expected value, variance, and standard deviation of random variables are not sample statistics like the mean, sample variance, and sample standard deviation we introduced in chapter 2. Rather, they are measures associated with the population of all possible outcomes of the random variable.

Discrete Probability Distributions

Three useful discrete distributions are the Bernoulli, binomial, and Poisson distributions.

BERNOULLI AND BINOMIAL DISTRIBUTIONS

The *Bernoulli distribution* characterizes a random variable with two possible outcomes with constant probabilities of occurrence. Typically, these outcomes represent "success" ($x = 1$) or "failure" ($x = 0$). The probability mass function is

$$p(x) = p \qquad \text{if } x = 1$$
$$= 1 - p \quad \text{if } x = 0$$

where p represents the probability of success. A Bernoulli distribution might be used to model whether an individual responds positively to a telemarketing promotion. For example, if you estimate that 3 percent of customers contacted will make a purchase, the probability distribution that describes whether or not an individual makes a purchase is

$$p(x) = 0.03 \quad \text{if } x = \text{"purchase"}$$
$$= 0.97 \quad \text{if } x = \text{"not purchase"}$$

The *binomial distribution* models n independent replications of a Bernoulli trial with probability p of success on each trial. The random variable x represents the number of successes in these n trials. The probability mass function is

$$p(x) = \binom{n}{x} p^x (1-p)^{n-x} \quad \text{for } x = 0, 1, 2, \ldots, n$$
$$0 \text{ otherwise}$$

The notation $\binom{n}{x}$ represents the number of ways of choosing x distinct items from a group of n items, and is computed as

$$\binom{n}{x} = \frac{n!}{x!(n-x)!}$$

where $n!$ (n factorial) $= n(n-1)(n-2)\ldots(2)(1)$, and $0! = 1$.

The expected value of the binomial distribution is np, and the variance is $np(1-p)$. A binomial distribution might be used to model the results of sampling inspection in a production operation or the effects of drug research on a sample of patients. For example, if the probability that any individual will react positively to a new drug is 0.8, then the probability distribution that x individuals will react positively out of a sample of 10 is

$$p(x) = \binom{10}{x} (0.8)^x (0.2)^{10-x} \quad \text{for } x = 0, 1, 2, \ldots, 10$$
$$0 \text{ otherwise}$$

If $x = 4$, for example, we have

$$p(4) = \binom{10}{4} (0.8)^4 (0.2)^{10-4} = \frac{10!}{4!6!}(0.4096)(0.000064) = 0.005505$$

Binomial probabilities are cumbersome to compute by hand, but can be computed in Excel using the function BINOMDIST(*number_s, trials, probability_s, cumulative*). See *Excel Note: Using the Excel Paste Function Button* for some tips. Figure 3.3 shows the results of using this function to compute the distribution for this example. The probability that four individuals will react positively is 0.005505, for example. You should verify that the sum of the probabilities is 1.0 because all possible outcomes are shown in this

	A	B	C	D	E	F	G
1	**Binomial Probabilities**						
2	n	10					
3	p	0.8					
4							
5	**x**	**p(x)**					
6	0	0.000000	←	=BINOMDIST(A6,$B$2,$B$3,FALSE)			
7	1	0.000004					
8	2	0.000074					
9	3	0.000786					
10	4	0.005505					
11	5	0.026424					
12	6	0.088080					
13	7	0.201327					
14	8	0.301990					
15	9	0.268435					
16	10	0.107374					

FIGURE 3.3 Computing Binomial Probabilities Using the Excel Function BINOMDIST

distribution. The probability that *at least* four individuals will react positively can be found by subtracting the probability of 3 or less from 1:

$$P(X \geq 4) = 1 - 0.000000 - 0.000004 - 0.000074 - 0.000786 = 0.999136.$$

POISSON DISTRIBUTION

The Poisson distribution is a discrete distribution used to model the number of occurrences in some unit of measure; for example, the number of events occurring in an interval of time, the number of items demanded per customer from an inventory, or the number of errors per line of software code. The Poisson distribution assumes no limit

---

Excel Note: Using the Excel Paste Function Button

Any of the Excel functions in Table 3.1 can be accessed by clicking the Paste Function button (f_x) on the toolbar. This is particularly useful if you are not sure of what to enter for the arguments. Figure 3.4 shows the dialog box from which you may select the function you wish to use, in this case, the binomial distribution function. Once this is selected, the dialog box in Figure 3.5 appears. When you click in any empty cell, a description of the argument is shown. Thus if you are not sure what to enter for the *cumulative* argument, the explanation in Figure 3.5 will help you. For further information, you could click the Help button in the lower left-hand corner.

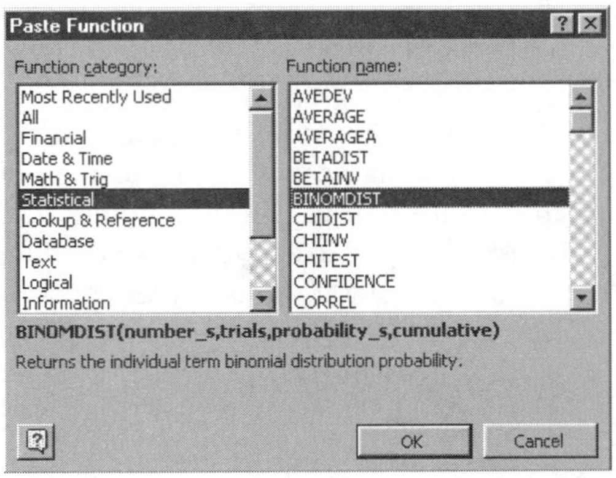

FIGURE 3.4 Paste Function Dialog Box

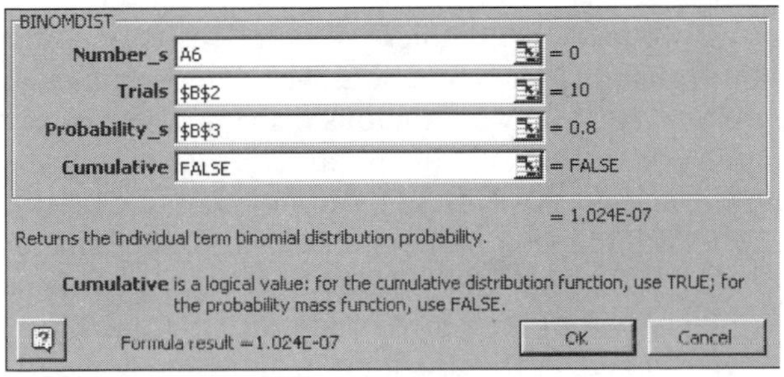

FIGURE 3.5 Binomial Distribution Function Dialog Box

	A	B	C	D	E	F
1	Poisson Distribution					
2	Mean	12				
3						
4	x	p(x)				
5	1	0.00007	← =POISSON(A5,$B$2,FALSE)			
6	2	0.00044				
7	3	0.00177				
8	4	0.00531				
9	5	0.01274				
10	6	0.02548				
11	7	0.04368				
12	8	0.06552				
13	9	0.08736				
14	10	0.10484				
15	11	0.11437				
16	12	0.11437				

FIGURE 3.6 Computing Poisson Probabilities Using the Excel Function POISSON

on the number of occurrences, that occurrences are independent, and that the average number is constant. The probability mass function is

$$p(x) = \frac{e^{-\lambda}\lambda^x}{x!} \quad \text{for } x = 0, 1, 2, \ldots$$
$$= 0 \text{ otherwise}$$

where the mean number of occurrence in the defined unit of measure is λ. The expected value of the Poisson distribution is λ and the variance also is equal to λ.

For example, suppose the average number of customers arriving at an ATM during lunch hour is $\lambda = 12$ customers per hour. The probability that exactly x customers will arrive during the hour is

$$p(x) = \frac{e^{-12}\,12^x}{x!} \quad \text{for } x = 0, 1, 2, \ldots$$
$$= 0 \text{ otherwise}$$

Poisson probabilities are cumbersome to compute by hand. Many books have tables, but probabilities can easily be computed in Excel using the function POISSON(*x, mean, cumulative*). Figure 3.6 shows the results of using this function to compute the distribution for this example. Thus the probability of exactly one arrival during the lunch hour is 0.00007, the probability of two arrivals is 0.00044, and so on. Because the possible values of a Poisson random variable is infinite, we have not shown the complete distribution in Figure 3.6. For large values of x, however, $p(x)$ will be 0, at least for reasonable numbers of decimal places.

Continuous Probability Distributions

Continuous probability distributions are defined by their density functions; discrete distributions are defined by probability mass functions. The density and mass functions depend on one or more *parameters*. Many continuous distributions can assume different shapes and sizes, depending on the value of the parameters. There are three basic types of parameters. A **shape parameter** controls the basic shape of the distribution. For certain distributions, changing the shape parameter will cause major changes in the form of the distribution. For others, the changes will be less severe. A **scale parameter** controls the unit of measurement within the range of the distribution. Changing the scale parameter either contracts or expands the distribution along the horizontal axis. Finally, a **location parameter** specifies the location of the distribution relative to zero on the horizontal axis. The location parameter may be the midpoint or the lower endpoint of the range of the distribution. Not all distributions will have all three parameters; some may have more than one shape parameter. Understanding the effects of these parameters is important in selecting distributions as inputs to decision models.

In this section we review some of the more common types of probability distributions used in decision modeling; discuss how shape, scale, and location parameters affect the distributions; and describe typical situations for which each distribution often applies.

UNIFORM DISTRIBUTION

The uniform distribution characterizes a random variable for which all outcomes between some minimum and maximum value are equally likely. For a uniform distribution with a minimum value a and a maximum value b, the density function is

$$f(x) = \frac{1}{b-a} \quad \text{if } a \leq x \leq b$$

and is shown in Figure 3.7. The distribution function is

$$
\begin{aligned}
F(x) &= 0 && \text{if } x < a \\
&= \frac{x-a}{b-a} && \text{if } a \leq x \leq b \\
&= 1 && \text{if } b < x
\end{aligned}
$$

The mean of the uniform distribution is $(a+b)/2$, and the variance is $(b-a)^2/12$. Note that a is a location parameter since it controls the location of the distribution along the horizontal axis. The difference, $b-a$, is a scale parameter. Increasing $b-a$ elongates the distribution; decreasing $b-a$ compresses it. There is no shape parameter since any uniform distribution is flat. The uniform distribution is often used when little knowledge about a random variable is available; the parameters a and b are chosen judgmentally to reflect a modeler's best guess about the range of the random variable. Although Excel does not provide a function to compute uniform probabilities, the formula is simple enough to incorporate into a spreadsheet.

With continuous distributions, it makes sense to compute only probabilities of intervals. For example, suppose that sales revenue for a Tracway product varies uniformly each week between $1,000 and $2,000. Then the probability that sales revenue will be less than $1,300 is

$$F(1,300) = \frac{1,300 - 1,000}{2,000 - 1,000} = 0.3$$

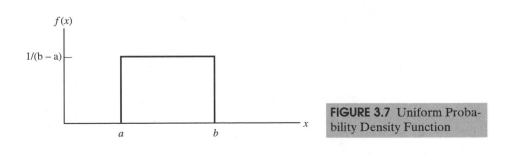

FIGURE 3.7 Uniform Probability Density Function

This is shown in Figure 3.8 as the area under the distribution to the left of $x = 1,300$. Similarly, the probability that revenue will be between \$1,500 and \$1,700 is $F(1,700) - F(1,500) = 0.7 - 0.5 = 0.2$.

In general, if we know the cumulative distribution for any random variable X, the probability that X will be between a and b is computed as the difference between the cumulative distribution evaluated at b and at a:

$$P(a \le X \le b) = F(b) - F(a)$$

NORMAL DISTRIBUTION

The *normal distribution* is described by the familiar bell-shaped curve. The normal distribution is symmetric, and has the property that the median equals the mean. Thus half the area falls above the mean and half below it. Although the range of x is unbounded, meaning that the tails of the distribution extend to negative and positive infinity, most of the density is close to the mean. It is characterized by two parameters: the mean, μ (the location parameter), and the variance, σ^2 (the scale parameter). Thus as μ changes, the location of the distribution on the x-axis also changes, and as σ^2 is decreased or increased, the distribution becomes narrower or wider, respectively.

The normal distribution is observed in many natural phenomena. Errors of various types, such as deviation from specifications of machined items, often are normally distributed. Thus the normal distribution finds extensive applications in quality control. Processing times in some service systems also follow a normal distribution. Another useful application is that the distribution of the averages of random variables having *any* distribution tends to be normal as the number of random variables increases.

The probability density function for the normal distribution is

$$f(x) = \frac{e^{\frac{-(x-\mu)^2}{2\sigma^2}}}{\sqrt{2\pi\sigma^2}}$$

however, the distribution function cannot be expressed mathematically, only numerically. Figure 3.9 provides a sketch of the **standard normal distribution,** with $\mu = 0$ and $\sigma = 1$. The standard normal distribution is provided in the appendix at the end of this book in two forms. Table A.1 is a table of areas from 0 to z; Table A.2 is a table of the cumulative probabilities from negative infinity to z. In both cases, z represents the number of standard deviations from the mean of zero.

Any normal distribution with an arbitrary mean μ and standard deviation σ may be transformed to a standard normal distribution by applying the following formula:

$$z = \frac{x - \mu}{\sigma}$$

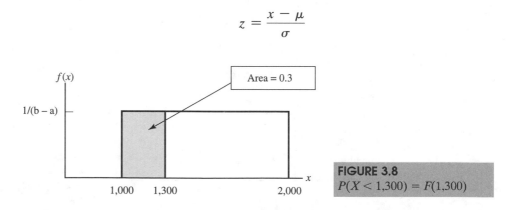

FIGURE 3.8
$P(X < 1,300) = F(1,300)$

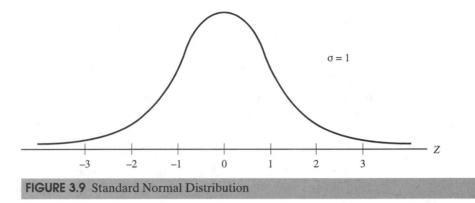

FIGURE 3.9 Standard Normal Distribution

This is particularly useful when solving problems involving normal distributions. For example, suppose the distribution of customer demand is normal with a mean of 750 units/month and a standard deviation of 100 units/month. Figure 3.10(a) shows the probability that demand will exceed 900 units as the area under the normal distribution. To find this probability using the tables in the appendix, we transform this into a standard normal distribution by finding the z-value that corresponds to $x = 900$ (Figure 3.10b):

$$z = \frac{900 - 750}{100} = 1.5$$

FIGURE 3.10 Computing $P(\text{demand} > 900)$

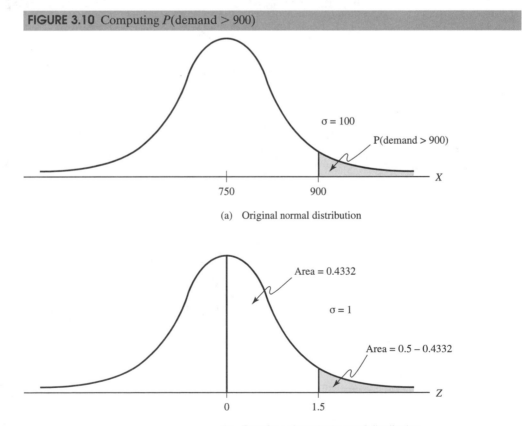

(a)   Original normal distribution

(b)   Transformed standard normal distribution

From Table A.1, the area between 0 and 1.5 is 0.4332; thus the area from 1.5 to infinity is $0.5 - 0.4332 = 0.0668$. Alternatively, from Table A.2, the cumulative probability for $z = 1.5$ is 0.9332. Therefore, the probability that z exceeds 0.9332 (equivalently, the probability that x exceeds 900) is $1 - 0.9332 = 0.0668$.

Probabilities for negative values of z are found by symmetry of the distribution. For instance, suppose we want to find $P(X > 700)$ (see Figure 3.11a). Transforming this into a standard normal distribution yields the z-value

$$z = \frac{700 - 750}{100} = -0.5$$

From Table A.1 in the appendix, a z-value of -0.5 corresponds to an area of 0.1915. To find the probability we seek, we must add this to 0.5 and obtain 0.6915. Alternatively, from Table A.2 we find the cumulative probability for $z = +0.5$ as 0.6915. From Figure 3.11b, we see that this is precisely the probability we wanted to compute.

Another common calculation involving the normal distribution is to find the value of x corresponding to a specified probability. For the same example of customer demand, suppose we wish to find the level of demand that will be exceeded only 10 percent of the time. This is illustrated in Figure 3.12. An upper tail probability of 0.10 is equivalent to a cumulative probability of 0.90. From Table A.2 in the appendix, we see that $z = 1.28$. This means that

$$z = \frac{x - 750}{100} = 1.28$$

FIGURE 3.11 Computing $P(\text{demand} > 700)$

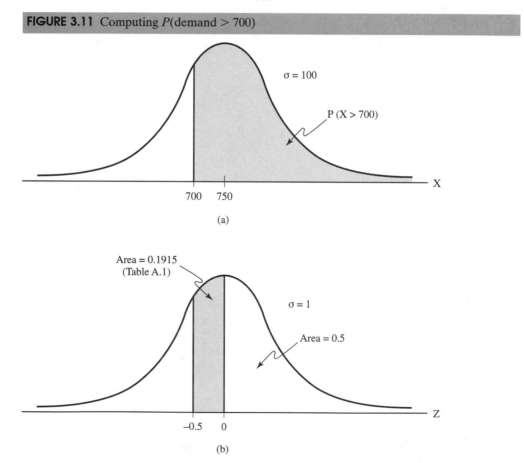

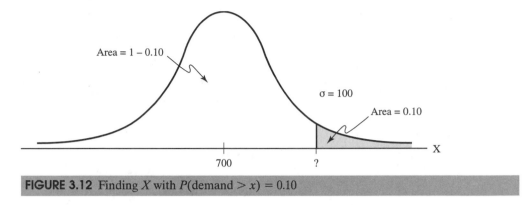

FIGURE 3.12 Finding X with $P(\text{demand} > x) = 0.10$

or $x = 878$. Which table you use is a matter of preference. To use them correctly, however, you should always draw a picture!

Two Excel functions are used to compute normal probabilities: NORMDIST(x, *mean, standard_deviation, cumulative*), and NORMSDIST(z). NORMSDIST(z) generates the same values as Table A.2 in the appendix at the end of the book. Figure 3.13 shows the application of NORMDIST. For the cumulative distribution, the last argument of the function, *cumulative,* must be set to *TRUE.* The Excel function STANDARDIZE(x, *mean, standard_deviation*) can be used to compute z-values within a spreadsheet; this function essentially computes z-values using the formula $z = (x - \text{mean})/\text{standard deviation}$. Thus STANDARDIZE($700, 750, 100$) $= -0.5$ as in the example in Figure 3.11.

TRIANGULAR DISTRIBUTION

The triangular distribution is defined by three parameters: the minimum a, maximum b, and most likely, c. Outcomes near the most likely value have a higher chance of occurring than those at the extremes. By varying the position of the most likely value relative to the extremes, the triangular distribution can be symmetric or skewed in either direction as shown in Figure 3.14. The probability density function is given by

$$
\begin{aligned}
f(x) &= \frac{2(x - a)}{(b - a)(c - a)} \qquad \text{if } a \leq x \leq c \\
&= \frac{2(b - x)}{(b - a)(b - c)} \qquad \text{if } c < x \leq b \\
&= 0 \text{ otherwise}
\end{aligned}
$$

	A	B	C	D	E	F	G
1	**Normal Distribution**						
2	Mean	750					
3	Std. Dev.	100					
4							
5		**Cumulative**					
6	x	**Probability**					
7	300	0.0000					
8	400	0.0002					
9	500	0.0062					
10	600	0.0668					
11	700	0.3085					
12	800	0.6915					
13	900	0.9332	◄	=NORMDIST(A13,$B$2,$B$3,TRUE)			
14	1000	0.9938					
15	1100	0.9998					

FIGURE 3.13 Computing Normal Probabilities Using the Excel Function NORMDIST

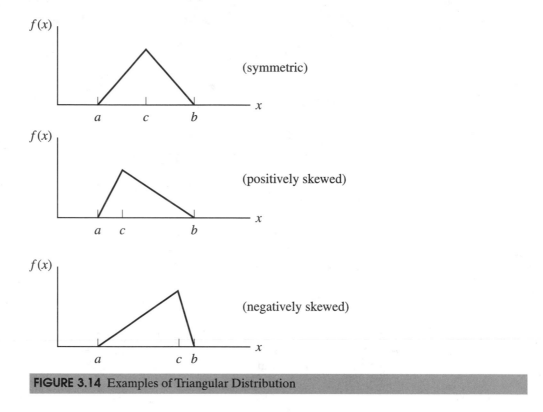

FIGURE 3.14 Examples of Triangular Distribution

From Figure 3.14, you can see that a is the location parameter, $(b - a)$ is the scale parameter, and c is the shape parameter. The distribution function is

$$
\begin{aligned}
F(x) &= 0 && \text{if } x < a \\
&= \frac{(x - a)^2}{(b - a)(c - a)} && \text{if } a \leq x \leq c \\
&= 1 - \frac{(b - x)^2}{(b - a)(b - c)} && \text{if } c < x \leq b \\
&&& \text{if } b < x
\end{aligned}
$$

The mean is computed as $(a + b + c)/3$ and the variance is $(a^2 + b^2 + c^2 - ab - ac - bc)/18$.

The triangular distribution is often used as a rough approximation of other distributions, such as the normal distribution, or in the absence of more complete data. Because it depends on three simple parameters and can assume a variety of shapes—for example, it can be skewed in either direction by changing the value of c—it is very flexible in modeling a wide variety of assumptions. One drawback, however, is that it is bounded, thereby eliminating the possibility of extreme outlying values that might possibly occur. Excel does not have a function to return triangular probabilities, but the formulas can easily be used in a spreadsheet.

EXPONENTIAL DISTRIBUTION

The exponential distribution models events that recur randomly over time. Thus it is often used to model the time between customer arrivals to a service system and the time to failure of machines, light bulbs, and other mechanical or electrical components. A key property of the exponential distribution is that it is *memoryless;* that is, the current time has no effect on future outcomes. For example, the length of time until a machine failure has the same distribution no matter how long the machine has been running.

The exponential distribution has the density function

$$f(x) = \lambda e^{-\lambda x}, \; x \geq 0$$

and distribution function

$$F(x) = 1 - e^{-\lambda x}, \; x \geq 0$$

The mean of the exponential distribution $= 1/\lambda$ and the variance $= (1/\lambda)^2 = (\text{mean})^2$. The exponential distribution has no shape or location parameters; λ is the scale parameter. Figure 3.15 provides a sketch of the exponential distribution. The exponential distribution has the property that it is bounded below by 0, has its greatest density at 0, and the density declines as x increases.

To illustrate the exponential distribution, suppose that the mean time to failure of a critical component of Tracway's engines is 8,000 hours. The probability that the engine will fail before x hours is given by the cumulative exponential distribution. Thus the probability of failing before 5,000 hours is

$$F(5,000) = 1 - e^{-(1/8000)(5000)} = 1 - e^{-5/8} = 0.465$$

The Excel function EXPONDIST(*x, lambda, cumulative*) can be used to compute exponential probabilities. Figure 3.16 shows the cumulative distribution for this example. Note that the mean is *not* the same as the parameter lambda; thus in the Excel function, lambda is set equal to the reciprocal of the mean.

The exponential distribution has an important relationship with the Poisson: if X has a Poisson distribution, then $1/X$ has an exponential distribution. For example, if the *number of arrivals* to a bank is Poisson distributed, then the *time between arrivals* is exponential.

FIGURE 3.15 The Exponential Distribution ($\mu = 1$)

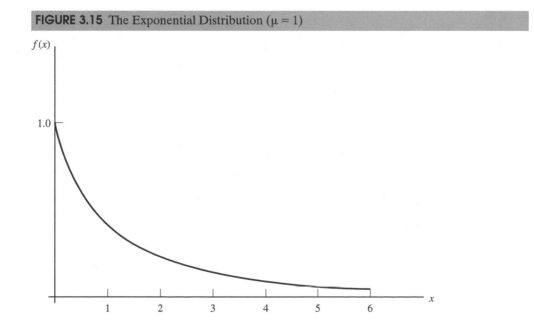

	A	B	C	D	E	F
1	Exponential Distribution					
2						
3	Mean	8000				
4						
5		Cumulative				
6	x	Probability				
7	1000	0.118		=EXPONDIST(A7,1/$B$3,TRUE)		
8	2000	0.221				
9	3000	0.313				
10	4000	0.393				
11	5000	0.465				
12	6000	0.528				
13	7000	0.583				
14	8000	0.632				
15	9000	0.675				
16	10000	0.713				
17	11000	0.747				
18	12000	0.777				
19	13000	0.803				
20	14000	0.826				
21	15000	0.847				

FIGURE 3.16 Computing Exponential Probabilities Using the Excel Function EXPONDIST

PROBABILITY DISTRIBUTIONS IN *PHSTAT*

PHStat has several routines for generating probabilities of distributions we have discussed. This allows you to compute probabilities without requiring you to develop a detailed worksheet in Excel. The distributions available are

- Normal,
- Binomial,
- Exponential, and
- Poisson.

The accompanying *PHStat Note* describes the binomial option; other probabilities can be generated in a similar fashion.

PHStat Note: Generating Binomial Probabilities

From the *PHStat* menu, select *Probability Distributions* and then *Binomial. . . .* The dialog box in Figure 3.17 prompts you for the distribution's parameters and range of outputs desired. By checking the boxes for *Cumulative Probabilities* and *Histogram,* the routine provides additional information as shown in Figure 3.18, specifically columns D through G, and the histogram of the probability distribution for the range specified.

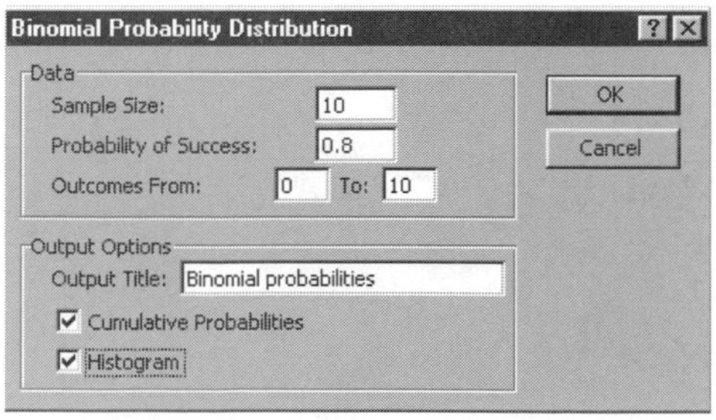

FIGURE 3.17 Binomial Probability Distribution Dialog Box in *PHStat*

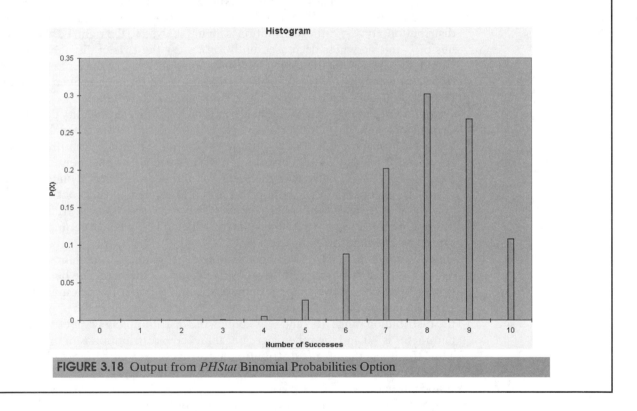

	A	B	C	D	E	F	G
1	Binomial probabilities						
2							
3	Sample size	10					
4	Probability of success	0.8					
5	Mean	8					
6	Variance	1.6					
7	Standard deviation	1.264911					
8							
9	Binomial Probabilities Table						
10		X	P(X)	P(<=X)	P(<X)	P(>X)	P(>=X)
11		0	1.02E-07	1.02E-07	0	1	1
12		1	4.1E-06	4.2E-06	1.02E-07	0.999996	1
13		2	7.37E-05	7.79E-05	4.2E-06	0.999922	0.999996
14		3	0.000786	0.000864	7.79E-05	0.999136	0.999922
15		4	0.005505	0.006369	0.000864	0.993631	0.999136
16		5	0.026424	0.032793	0.006369	0.967207	0.993631
17		6	0.08808	0.120874	0.032793	0.879126	0.967207
18		7	0.201327	0.3222	0.120874	0.6778	0.879126
19		8	0.30199	0.62419	0.3222	0.37581	0.6778
20		9	0.268435	0.892626	0.62419	0.107374	0.37581
21		10	0.107374	1	0.892626	0	0.107374

FIGURE 3.18 Output from *PHStat* Binomial Probabilities Option

OTHER USEFUL DISTRIBUTIONS

Many other probability distributions find application in decision modeling, especially those distributions that assume a wide variety of shapes. Such distributions provide much flexibility in representing empirical data that may be available. We provide a brief description of these distributions; further details may be found in more advanced texts on probability and statistics.

- *Lognormal Distribution* If the natural logarithm of a random variable X is normal, then X has a lognormal distribution. Because the lognormal distribution is positively skewed and bounded below by zero, it finds applications in modeling phenomena that have low probabilities of large values and cannot have negative values, such as the time to complete a task. Other common examples include stock prices and real estate prices. The lognormal distribution is also often used for "spiked" service times; that is, when the probability of zero is very low but the most likely value is just greater than zero.

- *Gamma Distribution* The gamma distribution is a family of distributions defined by a shape parameter α, a scale parameter β, and a location parameter L. L is the lower limit of the random variable x; that is, the gamma distribution is defined for $x > $ L. The gamma distribution is often used to model the time to complete a task, such as customer service or machine repair. It is used to measure the time between the occurrence of events when the event process is not completely random. It also finds application in inventory control and insurance risk theory.

    A special case of the gamma distribution when $\alpha = 1$ and L $= 0$ is called the *Erlang distribution*. The Erlang distribution also can be viewed as the sum of k independent and identically distributed exponential random variables. The mean is k/λ and the variance is k/λ^2. When $k = 1$, the Erlang is identical to the exponential distribution. For $k = 2$, the distribution is highly skewed to the right. For larger values of k, this skewness decreases, until for $k = 20$, the Erlang distribution looks similar to a normal distribution. One common application of the Erlang distribution is for modeling the time to complete a task when it can be broken down into independent tasks, each of which has an exponential distribution.

- *Weibull Distribution* The Weibull distribution is another probability distribution capable of taking on a number of different shapes defined by a the scale parameter α and a shape parameter β. Both α and β must be greater than zero. When L $= 0$ and $\beta = 1$, the Weibull distribution is the same as the exponential distribution with $\lambda = 1/\alpha$. By choosing the scale parameter L different from 0, you can model an exponential distribution that has a lower bound different from zero. When $\beta = 3.25$, the Weibull approximates the normal distribution. Weibull distributions are often used to model results from life and fatigue tests, equipment failure times, and times to complete a task.

- *Beta Distribution* One of the most flexible distributions for modeling variation over a fixed interval from zero to a positive value s is the beta. The beta distribution is a function of two shape parameters, α and β both of which must be positive. The parameter s is the scale parameter. Note that s defines the upper limit of the distribution range. If α and β are equal, the distribution is symmetric. If either parameter is 1.0 and the other is greater than 1, the distribution is in the shape of a "J." If α is less than β, the distribution is positively skewed; otherwise it is negatively skewed. These properties can help you to select appropriate values for the shape parameters.

- *Geometric Distribution* The geometric distribution is a sequence of Bernoulli trials that describes the number of trials until the first success. An example is the number of parts manufactured until a defect occurs, assuming that the probability of a defect is constant for each trial.

- *Negative Binomial Distribution* Similar to the geometric distribution, the negative binomial distribution models the distribution of the number of trials until the rth success, for example, the number of sales calls needed to sell 10 orders.

FIGURE 3.19 Shapes of Some Probability Distributions

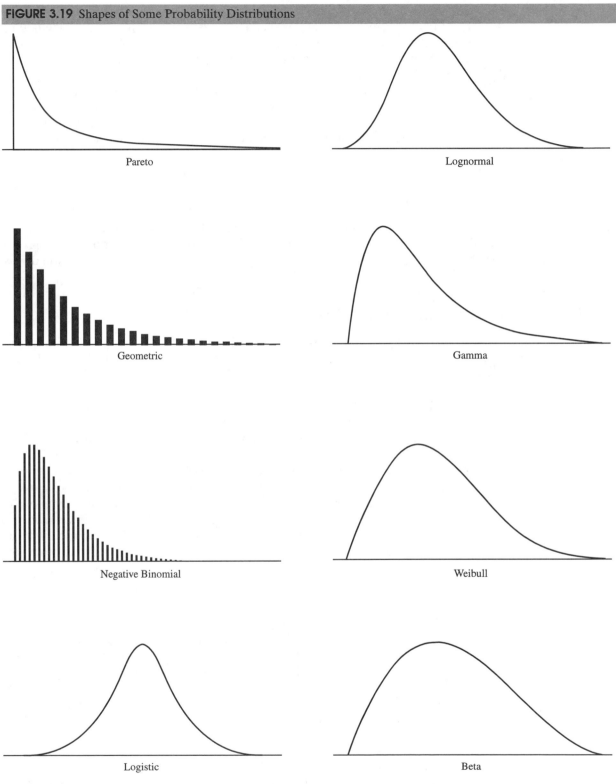

Pareto

Lognormal

Geometric

Gamma

Negative Binomial

Weibull

Logistic

Beta

- *Hypergeometric Distribution*   The hypergeometric distribution is similar to the binomial distribution, except that it applies to sampling without replacement. It is often used in quality control inspection applications.
- *Logistic Distribution*   The logistic distribution is commonly used to describe the growth of a population over time.
- *Pareto Distribution*   The Pareto distribution describes phenomena in which a small proportion of items accounts for a large proportion of some characteristic. For example, a small number of cities constitute a large proportion of the population. Other examples include the size of companies, personal incomes, and stock price fluctuations.
- *Extreme Value Distribution*   The extreme value distribution describes the largest value of a response over a period of time, such as rainfall, earthquakes, and breaking strengths of materials.

Figure 3.19 is a graphical summary of some of the distributions we have discussed. Understanding the shapes of these distributions makes it easier to select an appropriate distribution for a decision modeling application. In the next chapter, we will discuss fitting an appropriate distribution to sample data.

Random Sampling from Probability Distributions

Many decision models contain random variables. To analyze these models with spreadsheets, we will need to generate outcomes from many different types of probability distributions, such as discrete, normal, exponential, or Poisson distributions. Sometimes physical processes can be used to generate random outcomes from specific distributions. For example, rolling a die is a physical experiment that randomly generates a number from a discrete probability distribution that is uniformly distributed between 1 and 6. Other experiments include spinning a roulette wheel, drawing from a deck of shuffled cards, or selecting numbered balls from a cage as is done for state lotteries. Clearly, these approaches cannot be used for most practical problems. **Simulation** involves sampling from probability distributions. Although we will discuss the use of simulation for analyzing risk in decision problems in chapter 7, the ability to simulate outcomes from probability distributions will greatly help in understanding important statistical issues involving sample data. We will describe the fundamental concepts of sampling from probability distributions so that you will understand how this is accomplished in Excel and other software programs, and then use them to gain insight about sampling distributions.

RANDOM NUMBERS

The basis for generating samples from probability distributions is a *random number*. In simulation, a **random number** is defined as one that is *uniformly distributed between 0 and 1*. Technically speaking, computers cannot generate true random numbers since they must use a predictable algorithm. However, the algorithms are designed to generate a stream of numbers that *appear* to be random. In Excel, we may generate a random number within any cell using the function RAND( ). This function has no arguments; therefore, nothing should be placed within the parentheses. Table 3.2 shows a table of 100 random numbers generated in Excel. You should be aware that, unless the automatic recalculation feature is suppressed, whenever any cell in the spreadsheet is modified the values in any cell containing the RAND( ) function will change. Automatic recalculation can be changed to manual in the *Tools/Options/Calculation* menu. Under manual recalculation mode, the worksheet is recalculated only when the F9 key is pressed.

TABLE 3.2	One Hundred Random Numbers								
0.007120	0.215576	0.386009	0.201736	0.45799	0.127602	0.387275	0.639298	0.757161	0.285388
0.714281	0.165519	0.768911	0.687736	0.466579	0.481117	0.260391	0.508433	0.528617	0.755016
0.226987	0.454259	0.487024	0.269659	0.531411	0.197874	0.527788	0.613126	0.716988	0.747900
0.339398	0.434496	0.398474	0.622505	0.829964	0.288727	0.801157	0.373983	0.095900	0.041084
0.692488	0.137445	0.054401	0.483937	0.954835	0.643596	0.970131	0.864186	0.384474	0.134890
0.962794	0.808060	0.169243	0.347993	0.848285	0.216635	0.779147	0.216837	0.768370	0.371613
0.824428	0.919011	0.820195	0.345563	0.989111	0.269649	0.43317	0.36907	0.845632	0.158662
0.428903	0.470202	0.064646	0.100007	0.379286	0.183176	0.180715	0.008793	0.569902	0.218078
0.951334	0.258192	0.916104	0.271980	0.330697	0.989264	0.770787	0.107717	0.102653	0.366096
0.635494	0.395185	0.320618	0.003049	0.153551	0.231191	0.73785	0.633932	0.056315	0.281744

SAMPLING FROM PROBABILITY DISTRIBUTIONS

Sampling from discrete probability distributions is rather easy. We will illustrate this process using the example of a discrete probability distribution for demand introduced earlier in this chapter. The cumulative distribution follows; we need to randomly draw a sample from it.

Demand, x	Cumulative Probability, P(x)
0	0.1
1	0.3
2	0.7
3 or more	1.0

Two properties of discrete probability distributions that allow us to use random numbers to generate samples are (1) the probability of any outcome is always between 0 and 1, and (2) the sum of the probabilities of all outcomes adds to 1. We can therefore break up the range from 0 to 1 into intervals that correspond to the probabilities of discrete outcomes. Any random number, then, must fall within one of these intervals. For instance, the interval from 0 up to but not including 0.1 would correspond to the outcome $x = 0$; the interval from 0.1 up to but not including 0.3 corresponds to $x = 1$; and so on. (For consistency, we do not include the upper limit of an interval in the interval to prevent overlap.) This is summarized as follows:

Interval	Demand, x
0.0 to 0.1	0
0.1 to 0.3	1
0.3 to 0.7	2
0.7 to 1.0	3

To generate an outcome from this distribution, all we need to do is to select a random number and determine the interval into which it falls. Suppose we use the first column in Table 3.2. The first random number is 0.00712. This falls in the first interval; thus the first sample outcome is $x = 0$. The second random number is 0.714281. This number falls in the last interval, generating a sample outcome of $x = 3$. If this is done repeatedly, the frequency of occurrence of each outcome should be proportional to the random number range because random numbers are uniformly distributed. We can easily use this approach to generate outcomes from any discrete distribution.

This approach of generating random numbers and transforming them into outcomes from a probability distribution may be used to sample from most any distribution. A generated value from a probability distribution is called a **random variate.** For example, it is quite easy to transform a random number into a random variate from an arbitrary uniform distribution with parameters a and b. Consider the formula

$$U = a + (b - a)*R$$

where R is some random number. Note that when $R = 0$, $U = a$, and when $R = 1$, $U = b$. For any other value of R between 0 and 1, $(b - a)*R$ represents the same proportion of the interval (a, b) as R does of the interval $(0, 1)$. Thus all real numbers between a and b can occur. Because R is uniformly distributed, so also is U. However, it is certainly not obvious how to generate random variates from other distributions such as a normal or exponential. We will not describe the technical details of how this is done, but rather just describe the capabilities available in Excel.

SAMPLING FROM PROBABILITY DISTRIBUTIONS IN EXCEL

Excel allows you to generate random variates from discrete distributions and certain others using the *Random Number Generation* option in the *Analysis Toolpak* (see *Excel Note: Sampling from Probability Distributions*). However, one disadvantage with using the *Random Number Generation* tool is that you must repeat the process to generate a new set of sample values; pressing the F9 key will not change the values.

Excel has several functions that may be used to generate random variates. The most common ones are

- NORMINV(*probability, mean, standard_deviation*)—normal distribution,
- NORMSINV(*probability*)—standard normal distribution, and
- LOGINV(*probability, mean, standard_deviation*)—lognormal distribution where $\ln(x)$ has the specified mean and standard deviation.

Some advanced distributions are

- BETAINV(*probability, alpha, beta, A, B*)—beta distribution, and
- GAMMAINV(*probability, alpha, beta*)—gamma distribution.

To use these, simply enter RAND( ) in place of *probability* in the function. For example, NORMINV(RAND( ), 5, 2) will generate random variates from a normal distribution with mean 5 and standard deviation 2. Each time the worksheet is recalculated (for instance, when the F9 key is pressed) a new random number and hence a new random variate are generated. These functions may be embedded in cell formulas and will generate new values whenever the worksheet is recalculated.

PHStat also includes the ability to generate samples from a uniform (0,1) distribution, standard normal distribution, and an arbitrary discrete distribution (see *PHStat Note: Sampling Distributions Simulation*). As with the Excel Random Number Generation tool, this *PHStat* tool generates the samples "off-line;" that is, they cannot be embedded directly into other cell formulas.

The capabilities of Excel and *PHStat* for sampling from probability distributions are rather limited. However, this book includes a student version of *Crystal Ball,* an Excel add-in designed to facilitate the process of simulating spreadsheet models. *Crystal*

Excel Note: Sampling from Probability Distributions

From the main toolbar, select *Tools/Data Analysis/ Random Number Generation*. The Random Number Generation dialog box shown in Figure 3.20 appears. You may select from seven distributions: uniform, normal, Bernoulli, binomial, Poisson, patterned, or discrete. (The patterned distribution is characterized by a lower and upper bound, a step, a repetition rate for values, and a repetition rate for the sequence.) You are asked to specify the upper-left cell reference of the output table that will store the outcomes, the number of variables (columns of values you want generated), the number of random numbers (the number of data points you want generated for each variable), and the type of distribution. The default distribution is the discrete distribution, which we illustrate. To use the discrete distribution, the spreadsheet must contain a table with two columns: the left column containing the outcomes, and the right column containing the probabilities associated with the outcomes (which must sum to 1.0). Figure 3.21 shows an example. The outcomes generated are found in cells C3 through C12.

The dialog box in Figure 3.20 also allows you the option of specifying a *random number seed*. A random number seed is a value from which a stream of random numbers is generated. By specifying the same seed, you can produce the same random numbers at a later time. This is desirable when we wish to reproduce an identical sequence of "random" events in a simulation in order to test the effects of different policies or decision variables under the same circumstances.

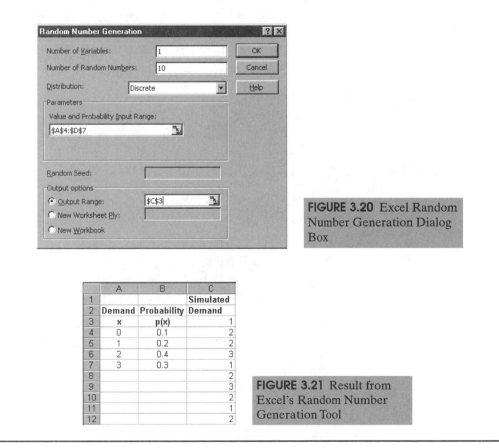

FIGURE 3.20 Excel Random Number Generation Dialog Box

	A	B	C
1			Simulated
2	Demand	Probability	Demand
3	x	p(x)	1
4	0	0.1	2
5	1	0.2	2
6	2	0.4	3
7	3	0.3	1
8			2
9			3
10			2
11			1
12			2

FIGURE 3.21 Result from Excel's Random Number Generation Tool

PHStat Note: Sampling Distributions Simulation

From the *PHStat* menu, select *Probability Distributions,* then *Sampling Distributions Simulation.* The dialog box shown in Figure 3.22 appears. You must enter the number of samples to be generated, the sample size, and the type of distribution (uniform, standardized normal, or discrete). If you select the discrete distribution, you also need to enter the range in a worksheet that contains the probability mass function. You may also opt for a histogram as part of the output. The procedure creates a new worksheet with the sample output in columns, along with the mean of each sample, overall mean, and standard error (to be discussed shortly). An example for the standardized normal distribution is shown in Figure 3.23.

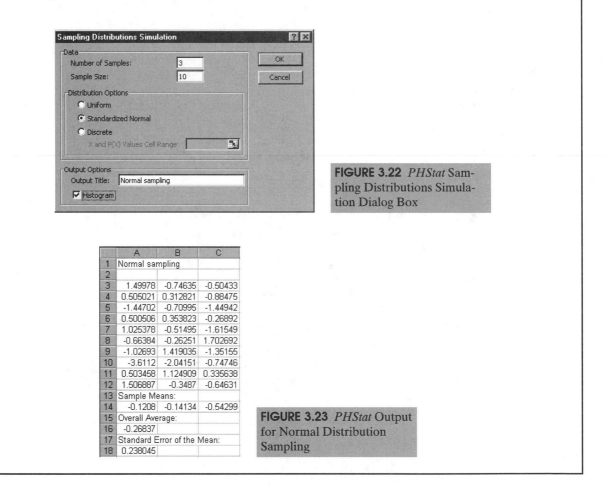

FIGURE 3.22 *PHStat* Sampling Distributions Simulation Dialog Box

FIGURE 3.23 *PHStat* Output for Normal Distribution Sampling

Ball provides functions for all of the distributions described in this chapter that can be entered directly into cell formulas in a spreadsheet: uniform, normal, triangular, binomial, Poisson, geometric, hypergeometric, lognormal, exponential, Weibull, beta, gamma, logistic, Pareto, extreme value, and negative binomial, as well as user-defined custom distributions. These are listed in Table 3.3. For example, to generate a sample from a uniform distribution between 10 and 20, you would enter the formula

$$= \text{CB.UNIFORM}(10,20)$$

TABLE 3.3   Probability Distribution Functions Available in *Crystal Ball*
CB.BETA(*Alpha, Beta, Scale*)
CB.BINOMIAL(*Probability, Trials*)
CB.CUSTOM(*Cell range*)
CB.EXPONENTIAL(*Rate*)
CB.EXTREMEVALUE(*Mode, Scale*) (for maximum)
CB.EXTREMEVALUE2(*Mode, Scale*) (for minimum)
CB.GAMMA(*Location, Scale, Shape*)
CB.GEOMETRIC(*Probability*)
CB.HYPERGEOMETRIC(*Probability, Trials, Population*)
CB.LOGNORMAL(*Mean, Standard Deviation*)
CB.NEGBINOMIAL(*Probability, Trials*)
CB.NORMAL(*Mean, Standard Deviation*)
CB.PARETO(*Location, Shape*)
CB.POISSON(*Rate*)
CB.TRIANGULAR(*Minimum, Likeliest, Maximum*)
CB.UNIFORM(*Minimum, Maximum*)
CB.WEIBULL(*Location, Scale, Shape*)

into the appropriate cell. This is much more flexible than using either the Excel *Random Number Generation* tool or the *PHStat Sampling Distribution Simulation* tool.

The appendix to this chapter describes some of the basic capabilities of *Crystal Ball* that relate to probability distributions (further capabilities will be described in chapter 7). We suggest that you read this now so that you may better understand the use of *Crystal Ball* in the remainder of this chapter.

SAMPLING DISTRIBUTIONS AND SAMPLING ERROR

Whenever we collect data, we are essentially taking a sample from some generally unknown probability distribution. Usually the goal is to estimate a population parameter, such as the mean. An important statistical question is: How good is the estimate obtained from the sample? Let us perform an experiment using *Crystal Ball*. We will generate samples from a normal distribution with mean 10 and standard deviation 1.0 using the spreadsheet model in Figure 3.24 (see *Crystal Ball Note: Sampling from a Normal Distribution*). Figure 3.25 shows one sample of size 50, and Figure 3.26 shows one sample of size 500. Notice that as the sample size gets larger, the frequency distribution begins to assume the shape of the normal distribution.

More revealing, however, are the results for 10 independent samples of each size shown in Figure 3.27. Each of the observations represents the mean of a sample. Two things are evident. First, the average of the 10 sample means for $n = 500$ is closer to the true mean of 10.0 than the average of the sample means for $n = 50$. Second, the standard deviation of the sample means for $n = 500$ is much smaller, indicating that they vary less from the true population mean than those for $n = 50$. In other words, samples of size 500 have less *sampling error* than samples of size 50.

The means of multiple samples of a fixed size n from some population will form a distribution, which we call the **sampling distribution of the mean.** The sampling distribution of the mean characterizes the population of means of *all possible samples* of a given size. (In Figure 3.27 we have 10 samples from the sampling distribution of the mean for each sample size.) From our experiment, we saw that as the sample size

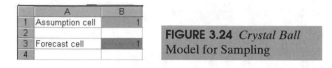

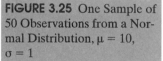

FIGURE 3.24 *Crystal Ball* Model for Sampling

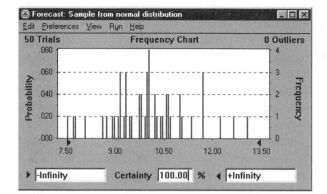

FIGURE 3.25 One Sample of 50 Observations from a Normal Distribution, $\mu = 10$, $\sigma = 1$

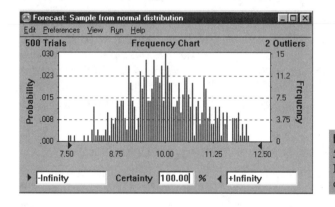

FIGURE 3.26 One Sample of 500 Observations from a Normal Distribution, $\mu = 10$, $\sigma = 1$

Crystal Ball Note: Sampling from a Normal Distribution

An **assumption cell** is a value cell in a spreadsheet model that has been defined as a probability distribution. The cell must contain a simple constant and no formula. In Figure 3.24, cell B1 is an assumption cell. (In the student version of *Crystal Ball,* only the following distributions may be used for assumption cells: uniform, normal, triangular, Poisson, exponential, and user-defined custom.) To define this cell as a normal distribution, first click in it, select *Define Assumption* from the *Cell* menu, choose the normal distribution from the distribution gallery, and specify the mean as 10 and the standard deviation as 1.0. Click OK to return to the spreadsheet.

A **forecast cell** is a formula cell whose values we want to track during a simulation. Forecast cells refer either directly or indirectly to assumption cells. In Figure 3.24, cell B3 has the formula =B1 because all we wish to do is capture the samples drawn from the normal distribution assumption cell. Define cell B3 as a forecast cell by first clicking in it, choosing *Define Forecast* from the *Cell* menu, entering a name for the forecast cell ("Sample from normal distribution"), and then clicking OK. Choose *Run Preferences* in the *Run* menu, select *Trials,* and specify either 50 or 500 to run the experiment.

D	E	F
Trial	n = 50	n = 500
1	9.6470	9.9246
2	10.0206	9.9800
3	10.3006	10.0658
4	9.9079	10.0909
5	9.9043	10.1273
6	10.1973	9.9552
7	10.3475	9.9375
8	10.0586	10.0801
9	9.9604	9.9748
10	9.8590	10.0327
Mean	10.02031	10.01688
Std. Dev.	0.214332	0.071559

FIGURE 3.27 Results of Sampling Experiment

increases, the variance of the sampling distribution decreased. This suggests that the estimates we obtain from larger sample sizes provide greater accuracy in estimating the true population mean. The standard deviation of the sampling distribution of the mean is called the **standard error of the mean** and is computed as

$$\text{Standard error of the mean} = \sigma/\sqrt{n}$$

where σ is the standard deviation of the distribution of individual observations and n is the sample size. From this formula, we see that as n increases, the standard error decreases, just as our experiment demonstrated.

We may estimate the standard error of the mean by dividing the sample standard deviation (because the true population parameter is unknown) by the square root of n. Figure 3.28 shows the statistics from the last experiment with $n = 500$. We see that the sample standard deviation of the 500 samples is 1.02. Therefore, the standard error of the mean is estimated to be $1.02/\sqrt{500} = 0.0456$, or 0.05, which is given on the last line of the chart. The "standard deviations" in row 12 of Figure 3.27 are different estimates of the standard error—not based on the preceding formula, but based on a limited number of means from each sampling distribution. Because we had only 10 values, the accuracy is not very good.

What about the shape of the sampling distribution of the mean? Statisticians have shown that if the population is normal, then the sampling distribution of the mean will also be normal for any sample size, and that the mean of the sampling distribution will be the same as that of the population. Furthermore, the **central limit theorem,** one of the most important practical results in statistics, states that if the sample size is large enough, the sampling distribution of the mean can be approximated by a normal distribution, *regardless* of the shape of the population distribution. We can illustrate this easily with a simple experiment in Excel (we invite you to try this). Copy the RAND( )

Forecast: Sample from normal distribution

Edit Preferences View Run Help

Cell B3 **Statistics**

Statistic	Value
Trials	500
Mean	9.99
Median	10.00
Mode	---
Standard Deviation	1.02
Variance	1.04
Skewness	-0.09
Kurtosis	3.14
Coeff. of Variability	0.10
Range Minimum	6.81
Range Maximum	13.05
Range Width	6.24
Mean Std. Error	0.05

FIGURE 3.28 *Crystal Ball* Statistics Report Summary

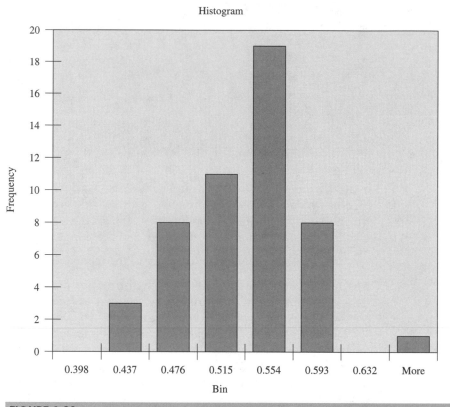

FIGURE 3.29 Distribution of 50 Sample Means from a Uniform Distribution

function into a matrix of 30 rows by 50 columns. This represents 50 samples of size $n = 30$. Compute the mean of each column, and construct a histogram of the 50 means. Figure 3.29 shows one result. Although the distribution of the individual values is uniform, the distribution of the sample means looks more like a normal distribution. As the sample size and the number of samples increase, the distribution will become closer in shape to a normal distribution.

Understanding the standard error of the mean and characteristics of the sampling distribution is important for designing sampling experiments and performing various statistical tests. We address these issues in other chapters.

Summary

Probability distributions characterize the theoretical outcomes of random variables—numerical values of the outcomes of some experiment. Probability distributions form the basis for drawing inferences and conclusions about sample data and for building useful decision models that incorporate uncertainty and risk. Probability distributions can be discrete or continuous, depending on the application. Useful discrete distributions include the binomial and Poisson; useful continuous distributions are the uniform, normal, triangular, and exponential.

Excel, *PHStat,* and *Crystal Ball* provide the capability to generate random samples from various probability distributions. Simulated samples not only provide important insights into the nature of sample data, but will also be useful inputs to decision models that assess risk in chapter 7.

The key to understanding sample data is that any statistic, such as the mean, computed from sample data is subject to error. The error associated with sample means can be quantified by the standard error of the mean. Larger sample sizes provide smaller standard errors, and thus more accurate estimates of population means.

Questions and Problems

1. Provide several examples of random events in everyday life.
2. If you observe that each application in a student registration process takes a constant time as opposed to a random time, what could you say about the behavior of each system, and what would you be able to measure or predict?
3. Explain the difference between a discrete random variable and a continuous random variable.
4. Explain the difference between a discrete probability mass function and the probability distribution of a continuous random variable.
5. Sketch a typical cumulative distribution function for a discrete and a continuous random variable. What are the characteristics of each?
6. Why would the number of arrivals per minute at a fast-food service facility not be independent with respect to the time of day?
7. Do stocks traded on the New York Stock Exchange vary independently?
8. Calculate the expected value and variance of the following discrete data, assuming that the data are a population.

Value	Frequency
0	56
1	28
2	12
3	3
4	0
5	1

9. If the following discrete data were obtained by sampling, calculate the expected value and variance.

Value	Frequency
0	56
1	28
2	12
3	3
4	0
5	1

10. Describe the relationship of the standard deviation to the variance. Discuss the dimensions of each.
11. A major application of data mining in marketing is determining the attrition of customers. If the probability of a long-distance carrier's customer leaving for another carrier from one month to the next is 0.2, and the carrier currently has 10,000 customers, what would be the expected value of retained customers, what would be the standard deviation, and what distribution would apply?

12. If a long-distance carrier conducted a telemarketing campaign to generate new clients, and the probability of successfully gaining a new customer was 0.02, what would be the probability that contacting 100 potential customers would result in 0, 1, 2, 3, or 4 successes? Identify both the probability density function and cumulative density function. (Use Excel's BINOMDIST function.)

13. A telephone call center consists of people placing marketing calls to customers with a probability of success of 0.01. Each person can place 120 calls per hour. The manager is very harsh on those who do not get a successful call each hour. Calculate the probability that 0, 1, or 2 successes would be obtained each hour.

14. A financial consultant has an average of six customers arrive each day. The consultant's overhead requires that at least five customers arrive in order that fees cover expenses. Identify the probabilities of zero through four customers arriving in a given day.

15. Calculate the average cost of producing a Tracway transmission under the current system using the data in the Tracway worksheet *Transmission Costs*. Plot a histogram of these data, and judge whether or not assuming a normal distribution would be appropriate. What evidence does the histogram provide to judge whether or not these data are normally distributed?

16. Assuming that the data in the Tracway worksheet *Transmission Costs* are normally distributed, what is the probability that the current cost to Tracway of producing a transmission would exceed $300?

17. Tracway is considering an alternative system to produce transmissions; these data are also found in the Tracway worksheet *Transmission Costs*. Is this data likely to be normally distributed?

18. Using the data in the Tracway worksheet *Transmission Costs* and assuming a normal distribution, what is the probability that a transmission produced by Alternative A would cost $300 or more?

19. Tracway is considering a second alternative system to produce transmissions (found in the Tracway worksheet *Transmission Costs*). Is this data likely to be normally distributed?

20. Using the data in the Tracway worksheet *Transmission Costs* and assuming a normal distribution, what is the probability that a transmission produced by Alternative B would cost $300 or more?

21. Identify the minimum, median, and maximum values for the costs of the three systems using the data on the *Transmission Costs* worksheet of the Tracway database, as well as the probability of costing $300 or more. Assuming that the data are distributed following the triangular distribution, estimate the expected value, standard deviation, and probability that cost will exceed $300.

22. For the time to produce a mower engine (worksheet *Engines* in the Tracway database), plot a histogram of the data. Use bin limits of 50, 54, 58, 62, and 66 seconds. What distribution seems likely?

23. Given the assumption that the mower engine data in the Tracway worksheet *Engines* (after subtracting the minimum) is exponentially distributed, estimate the mean and standard deviation.

24. Generate 20 normally distributed random variates from a distribution with a mean of 50 and a standard deviation of 10. Sort these numbers and compare the sample mean and variance with the input parameters.

25. Generate a set of 200 random numbers and place these in cells A1 through A200. In Excel or *PHStat,* convert these to exponentially distributed random numbers with a mean of 50 by entering the formula below in the next column to the right (cell B1) of the uniform numbers

$$=-50*LN(1-A1)$$

Copy this formula down through all 200 cells through cell B200. Compare the mean and standard deviation obtained in problem 24.

26. Generate 50 exponentially distributed random variates with a mean of 25, and copy these to some column (column C) using the *Paste Special* option in Excel and clicking the *Values* radio button. Then sort column C. Generate 50 normally distributed random variates with the same mean of 25 and a standard deviation of 6. Use the same procedure to paste these normally distributed numbers next to the exponentially distributed numbers (column D). Comment on the difference.

27. Generate 20 groups of 5 uniformly distributed numbers, and calculate the mean of each group. Identify the mean and variance of all 100 numbers, as well as the mean and variance of the 20 means. Compare the variance of the means with the standard error of the mean of the 100 numbers.

28. Generate 30 groups of 6 random numbers, and calculate the mean of each of the 30 groups. Identify the mean and variance of all 180 numbers, as well as the mean and variance of the 30 means. Compare the variance of the means with the standard error of the mean of the 180 numbers.

29. Generate three data sets of normally distributed random variates, all with a mean of 80 and a standard deviation of 5. Let data set 1 to be 50 groups of 5, data set 2 be 50 groups of 10, and data set 3 be 50 groups of 30. Calculate the mean of each group. Compare the average of the means for each set, as well as their variances. What can you conclude?

Appendix: Introduction to *Crystal Ball*

Crystal Ball is a spreadsheet add-in that was developed and is published by Decisioneering, Inc.[1] *Crystal Ball* allows you to define cells in spreadsheets as random variables with specified distributions, draw samples from these distributions, evaluate the spreadsheet formulas using the sample data, and collect extensive statistical information about the distribution of one or more output cells of interest. This process is often called **Monte Carlo simulation.** Such information is useful in analyzing risks associated with decisions, as we will explore further in chapter 7.

To use *Crystal Ball,* we must perform the following steps:

1. Develop the spreadsheet model,
2. Define assumptions for probabilistic variables,
3. Define the forecast cells—that is, the output variables of interest,
4. Set the number of replications,
5. Run the simulation, and
6. Interpret the results.

To illustrate this process, we will use the simple financial decision model spreadsheet that we introduced in Figure 1.3.

We have modified the spreadsheet in Figure 1.3 slightly by including a three-year total profit in cell E21 as is shown in Figure 3A.1; this will be the output variable (forecast) in which we are interested. We will assume that the probabilistic variables in this model are the inflation factors for all costs and expenses, the unit sales in the first year, and the rate of sales growth. The product manager has identified the following judgmental estimates for the distributions of these variables:

a. Inflation factor for fixed cost of goods sold: uniform between 2% and 4%
b. Inflation factor for per unit cost of goods sold: uniform between 5% and 9%
c. Inflation factor for fixed selling and administrative expense: triangular with minimum = 3%, most likely = 5% and maximum = 6%

[1] The student version of *Crystal Ball* distributed with this book has some restrictions and limitations as compared with the full-featured version. These will be described in chapter 4.

	A	B	C	D	E	F
1	**Profit Model**					
2		*Inflation*				
3	***Model Inputs and Assumptions***	*factor*	*Year 1*	*Year 2*	*Year 3*	
4	Fixed cost of goods sold	3%	$ 100,000	$ 103,000	$ 106,090	
5	Unit cost of goods sold	7%	$ 5.00	$ 5.35	$ 5.72	
6	Fixed selling and administrative expenses	5%	$ 50,000	$ 52,500	$ 55,125	
7	Unit selling and administrative expenses	7%	$ 2.00	$ 2.14	$ 2.29	
8	Unit sales	15%	15,000	17,250	19,838	
9						
10	***Decision Variables***					
11	Selling price		$ 20.00	$ 22.00	$ 25.00	
12						
13	***Model Outputs***		*Year 1*	*Year 2*	*Year 3*	
14	Total revenue		$ 300,000	$ 379,500	$ 495,938	
15	Cost of goods sold		$ 175,000	$ 195,288	$ 219,650	
16	Selling and administrative expenses		$ 80,000	$ 89,415	$ 100,549	
17	Profit before taxes		$ 45,000	$ 94,798	$ 175,739	
18	Profit after taxes		$ 23,400	$ 49,295	$ 91,384	
19	***Cumulative profit***		***$ 23,400***	***$ 72,695***	***$ 164,079***	
20						
21				***Total Profit***	***$ 260,174***	

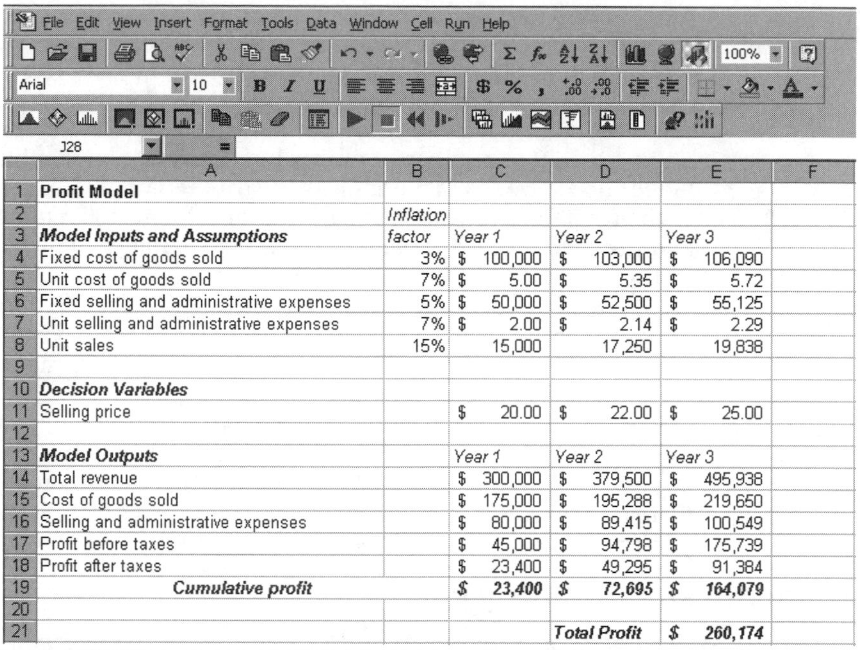

FIGURE 3A.1 Modified Profit Model Spreadsheet

d. Inflation factor for per unit selling and administrative expense: triangular with minimum = 4%, most likely = 7% and maximum = 9%
e. Sales in year 1: normal with mean 15,000 and standard deviation = 1,000
f. Inflation factor for sales growth rate: triangular with minimum = 5%, most likely = 15%, and maximum = 20%

If *Crystal Ball* is installed properly, it can be invoked from the *Tools/Add-ins* menu in Excel. In Figure 3A.1, the Excel screen after *Crystal Ball* is started includes two new menu items: *Cell* and *Run.* In addition, a button bar just above the spreadsheet provides shortcut commands for *Crystal Ball* instead of pointing to the *Cell* or *Run* menus.

SPECIFYING INPUT INFORMATION

The first step in using *Crystal Ball* is to define the probability distributions for input variables; the cells in the spreadsheet corresponding to these variables are called *assumption cells.*[2] To define them, first select a cell or range of cells. From the *Cell* menu, select *Define Assumption. Crystal Ball* displays a gallery of probability distributions from which to choose and prompts you for the parameters. For example, let us define the distribution for the inflation factor for fixed cost of goods sold. First click in cell B4. Then select *Cell/Define Assumption. Crystal Ball* displays the distribution gallery shown in Figure 3A.2.[3] Since we assume that this variable has a uniform distribution, we click on the uniform distribution and then the OK button. A dialog box is then displayed. You need enter only the minimum value and maximum value of the distribution. Clicking "Enter" fixes these values and rescales the picture to allow you to see what the distri-

[2] The student version of *Crystal Ball* is limited to a maximum of six assumption cells.
[3] The distribution gallery in student version of *Crystal Ball* is limited to the following probability distributions: normal, triangular, uniform, Poisson, exponential, and custom.

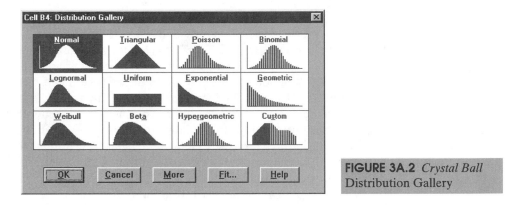

FIGURE 3A.2 *Crystal Ball* Distribution Gallery

bution looks like (this feature is quite useful for flexible families of distributions such as the gamma or beta discussed in this chapter). The result for the example is shown in Figure 3A.3. Clicking "OK" accepts your choice and returns to the main screen. You may change the appearance of assumption cells in the spreadsheet (for example, color or shading) using the *Cell Preferences* option in the *Cell* menu.

We repeat this process for each of the probabilistic assumptions in the model. Figure 3A.4 shows the dialog box for the normal distribution assumption for Year 1 sales.

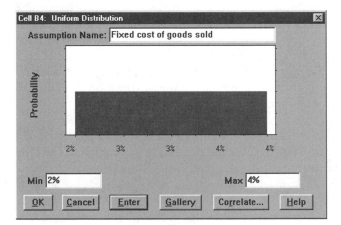

FIGURE 3A.3 Uniform Distribution Assumption Dialog Box

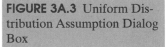

FIGURE 3A.4 Normal Distribution Assumption Dialog Box

Enter the mean and standard deviation in the boxes provided. Clicking "Enter" redraws the figure to the specifications provided; clicking "OK" accepts the assumption and returns to the main screen. In Figure 3A.4 you may notice two small black triangles and one open diamond just below the horizontal axis. These are called "grabbers" because you may click and hold the left mouse button on them and move them to modify the distribution. For the normal distribution shown, moving the left or right triangle grabber will create a truncated distribution. You should experiment with moving the grabbers for other distributions to see how they work. For distributions like the triangular, the grabbers allow you to easily change the truncation and most likely value.

After all assumptions are defined, you must define one or more *forecast cells* that define the output variables of interest.[4] Click in cell E19, which represents three-year profit, then select *Define Forecast* from the *Cell* menu. The *Define Forecast* dialog box is shown in Figure 3A.5. If *Display Window Automatically* is checked, you will see the output distribution being built as the simulation is replicated by *Crystal Ball*. You may define several forecast cells as appropriate.

Next, select the *Run Preferences* item from the *Run* menu. The dialog box, shown in Figure 3A.6, allows you to choose the number of trials (replications) and select other options such as controlling the random number generation process.[5] We chose 1,000 replications.

If you click the *Sampling* button, another dialog box opens (Figure 3A.7), and you may choose between two sampling methods: Monte Carlo or Latin Hypercube. Monte Carlo sampling generates random variates randomly over the entire range of possible values. With Latin Hypercube sampling, an assumption's probability distribution is divided into intervals of equal probability, and *Crystal Ball* generates an assumption value for each interval. The number of intervals is determined by the *Minimum Sample Size* option in the *Run Preferences* dialog box. Latin Hypercube sampling is more precise because it samples the entire range of the distribution in a more consistent manner. However, it requires additional memory requirements.

If you select the *Options* button, another dialog box opens (Figure 3A.8) and you may choose to have the assumption cells retain their original values or the estimated means from sampling after the simulation is completed. The latter option is useful if you wish to perform additional spreadsheet calculations using the estimated means after the simulation is completed (we will see an example of this in the next chapter).

Finally, select *Run* from the *Run* menu and watch *Crystal Ball* go to work! The *Run* menu also provides options to stop a simulation in progress, continue, and reset values

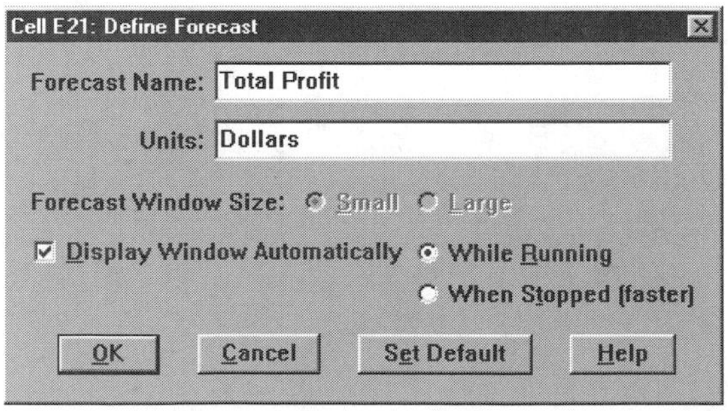

FIGURE 3A.5 Define Forecast Dialog Box

---

[4] The student version of *Crystal Ball* is limited to a maximum of six forecast cells.
[5] The maximum number of trials in the student version of *Crystal Ball* is limited to 1,000.

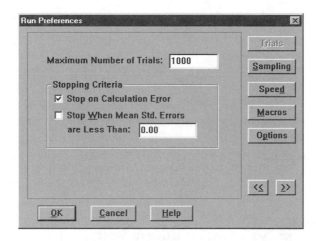

FIGURE 3A.6 Run Preferences Dialog Box

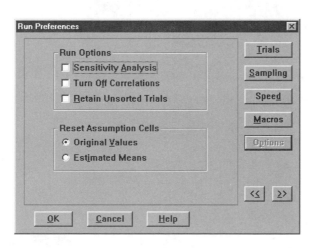

FIGURE 3A.7 Sampling Preferences Options

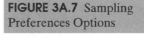

FIGURE 3A.8 Other Run Preferences Options

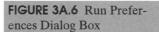

(that is, clear statistics and results). It is important to clear statistics if you need to rerun a simulation.

CRYSTAL BALL OUTPUT

The principal output reports provided by *Crystal Ball* are the *forecast chart, percentiles summary,* and *statistics summary.* Figure 3A.9 shows the forecast chart for the three-year profit after 1,000 replications. The forecast chart is a histogram of the outcome variable that includes all values within 2.6 standard deviations of the mean, which represents approximately 99 percent of the data. (This may be changed in the *Preferences/ Choose Display Range* menu.) The number of outliers is shown in the upper right corner of the chart. For this example, we have three data points outside 2.6 standard deviations of the mean. Just below the horizontal axis at the extremes of the distribution are two small triangles, called *end-point grabbers*. The range values of the variable at these positions are given in the boxes at the bottom left and right corners of the chart. The percentage of data values between the grabbers is displayed in the "Certainty" level box at the lower center of the chart.

Questions involving risk can be answered by manipulating the end-point grabbers or by changing the range and certainty values in the boxes. Several options exist.

1. You may move an end-point grabber by clicking and holding the left mouse button on the grabber and moving it. As you do, the distribution outside of the middle range changes color, the range value corresponding to the grabber changes to reflect its current position, and the certainty level changes to reflect the new percentage between the grabbers. Figure 3A.10 shows the result of moving the left

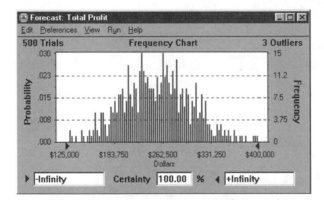

FIGURE 3A.9 *Crystal Ball* Forecast Chart

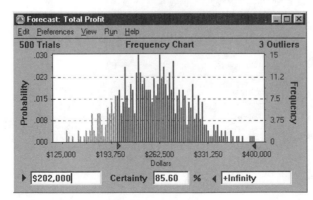

FIGURE 3A.10 Moving Left End-Point Grabber in the Forecast Chart

grabber to the value $202,000. The dark portion of the histogram represents 85.60 percent of the distribution (as given in the Certainty box).

2. You may type specific values in the range boxes. When you do, the grabbers automatically move to the appropriate positions and the certainty level changes to reflect the new percentage of values between the range values. For example, suppose you want to determine the percentage of values between $150,000 and $300,000. If you enter these numbers in the range boxes, the grabbers will automatically move to those positions, the portion of the histogram outside of these values will lighten, and the certainty level will change to reflect the percentage of the distribution between these values.

3. You may specify a certainty level. If the end-point grabbers are free (as indicated by a black color), the certainty range will be centered around the mean (or median as specified in the *Preferences/Statistics* menu option). For example, Figure 3A.11 shows the result of changing the certainty level to 90 percent. The range centered about the mean is from $172,848 through $333,020. You may anchor an end-point grabber by clicking on it. When anchored, the grabber will be a lighter color. (To free an anchored grabber, click anywhere in the chart area.) If a grabber is anchored and you specify a certainty level, the free grabber moves to a position corresponding to this level. Finally, you may cross over the grabbers to determine certainty levels for the ends of the distribution.

The forecast chart may be customized to change its appearance through the *Preferences/Chart Preferences* dialog box. The chart may be displayed as an area, outline, or column (bar) chart; and may be displayed as a frequency distribution (the default), cumulative distribution, or reverse cumulative distribution. The number of groups determines the granularity of the chart; a smaller number of groups provides less detail. The number format may be changed in the *Preferences/Format Preferences* dialog box.

The Percentiles report can be displayed from the *View* menu. An example is shown in Figure 3A.12. For example, we see that the chance that the total profit will not exceed $212,463 is only 20 percent. From the *View* menu you may also select a statistics report. This report, shown in Figure 3A.13, provides a summary of key descriptive statistical measures. The mean standard error defines the standard deviation for the sampling distribution of the mean, based on the run of 1,000 samples, and can be used to construct confidence intervals as we will describe in the next chapter.

Customized reports can be created from the *Run* menu by choosing *Create Report*. This option allows you to select a summary of assumptions and output information that we described. These are created in a separate Excel worksheet and may be printed.

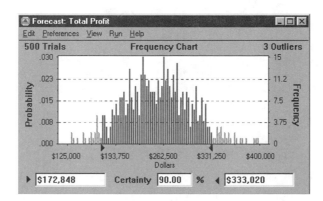

FIGURE 3A.11 90 Percent Certainty Level

Forecast: Total Profit

Edit Preferences View Run Help

Cell E21   **Percentiles**

Percentile	Dollars
0%	$103,897
10%	$193,084
20%	$212,463
30%	$227,657
40%	$240,385
50%	$254,646
60%	$267,523
70%	$281,195
80%	$296,004
90%	$318,645
100%	$397,914

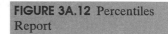

FIGURE 3A.12 Percentiles Report

Forecast: Total Profit

Edit Preferences View Run Help

Cell E21   **Statistics**

Statistic	Value
Trials	500
Mean	$254,642
Median	$254,646
Mode	---
Standard Deviation	$49,979
Variance	$2,497,915,696
Skewness	0.02
Kurtosis	2.99
Coeff. of Variability	0.20
Range Minimum	$103,897
Range Maximum	$397,914
Range Width	$294,017
Mean Std. Error	$2,235.14

FIGURE 3A.13 Statistics Report

References

Berk, K. N. & Carey, P., *Data Analysis with Microsoft Excel 5.0 for Windows,* Cambridge, MA: Course Technology, Inc., 1995.

Decisioneering, Inc., *Crystal Ball Version 4.0 User Manual.*

Evans, M., Hastings, N., and Peacock, B., *Statistical Distributions,* 2nd ed., New York: John Wiley & Sons, Inc., 1993.

Law, A. M. & Kelton, W. D., *Simulation Modeling & Analysis,* 2nd ed., McGraw-Hill, 1991.

Middleton, M. R., *Data Analysis Using Microsoft Excel 5.0,* Belmont, CA: Duxbury Press, 1995.

PART I

CHAPTER

4

Sampling and Statistical Analysis for Decision Making

Outline

Statistical Sampling
    Sample Design
    Sampling Methods
    Errors in Sampling
    Sampling from Finite Populations
Statistical Analysis of Sample Data
Estimation
    Point Estimates
    Interval Estimates
    Confidence Intervals for the Mean
    Confidence Intervals for Proportions
    Confidence Intervals and Sample Size
Hypothesis Testing
    Hypothesis Formulation
    Significance Level
    Decision Rules
    Using p-values
    Two-Sample Hypothesis Tests for Means
    F-Test for Testing Variances
    Tests for Proportions
    Other Hypothesis Tests
ANOVA: Testing Differences of Several Means
Chi-Square Test for Independence
Summary
Questions and Problems
Appendix: Distribution Fitting
    Distribution Fitting with *Crystal Ball*

In chapters 1–3, we discussed the use of data and sampling for managing and decision making, introduced methods for data visualization and descriptive statistics, and gained an understanding of some important probability distributions used in statistics and decision modeling. These topics focused on how to view data to gain better understanding and insight. However, managers need to go further than simply understanding what data tell; they need to be able to *draw conclusions* about the data to make effective decisions. Sampling methods and statistical analysis of data provide the tools for doing this.

In this chapter we focus on using statistics to estimate important population parameters and make inferences about sample data. The key concepts and tools that we will present are

- Statistical sampling, including sample design, simple random sampling, and other sampling schemes; sampling error; and sample size determination;
- Estimation, focusing on point estimates, interval estimates, and confidence intervals;
- Principles of hypothesis testing, and examples of hypothesis tests for means, variances, and proportions;
- An introduction to analysis of variance (ANOVA), which also will be used in later chapters; and
- The chi-square test for independence.

The appendix to this chapter discusses distribution fitting, particularly using *Crystal Ball*.

Statistical Sampling

Sampling approaches play an important role in providing information for making business decisions. Sampling is a valuable tool in many business decisions, because in most situations the population is generally too large to deal with effectively or practically; it may be impossible or too expensive to obtain all the data in the population. Thus we collect sample data in order to draw conclusions about unknown populations.

We will use five worksheets from the Tracway database to demonstrate some of the decisions that can be addressed through sampling. Portions of these are shown in Figure 4.1 for your reference. The worksheet *Transmission Costs* consists of sample costs

	A	B	C
1	Transmission costs		
2			
3	Current	Process A	Process B
4	$ 242	$ 242	$ 292
5	$ 176	$ 275	$ 321
6	$ 286	$ 199	$ 314
7	$ 269	$ 219	$ 242
8	$ 327	$ 273	$ 278
9	$ 264	$ 265	$ 300
10	$ 296	$ 435	$ 301

	A	B
1	TracPrep Samples	
2		
3	$ 83.67	
4	$ 64.87	
5	$ 96.03	
6	$ 91.22	
7	$ 107.56	
8	$ 89.81	
9	$ 98.80	
10	$ 109.45	

FIGURE 4.1 Portions of the Tracway Database Used in this Chapter

	A	B
1	Response time	
2		
3	1.69	
4	0.97	
5	3.44	
6	2.76	
7	5.07	
8	2.56	
9	3.83	
10	5.34	

	A	B	C	D	E	F
1	On-Time Delivery					
2						
3	Month	Percent	Sample size		Year	Total Deliveries
4	Jan-96	98.4%	1086		1996	14149
5	Feb-96	98.1%	1101		1997	15144
6	Mar-96	98.3%	1108		1998	16101
7	Apr-96	98.6%	1216		1999	16517
8	May-96	98.7%	1183		2000	16986
9	Jun-96	98.6%	1176			
10	Jul-96	98.6%	1198			

	A	B	C	D	E	F	G
1	Employee Success						
2							
3	Duration	Yrseducation	College gpa	Age	M/F	College Grad	Local
4	10	18	3.01	33	0	1	1
5	10	16	2.78	25	1	1	1
6	10	18	3.15	26	1	1	0
7	10	18	3.86	24	0	1	1
8	9.6	16	2.58	25	0	1	1
9	8.5	16	2.96	23	1	1	1
10	8.4	17	3.56	35	1	1	1

FIGURE 4.1 (*continued*)

for producing tractor transmissions with three alternative machinery systems. This data set will be used to demonstrate statistical estimation and testing hypotheses about means and variances. The data set in the *TracPrep Samples* worksheet is used to demonstrate calculations of required sample size. The data set in the *Response Time* worksheet will be used to demonstrate hypothesis testing of single mean estimates. The worksheet *On-Time Delivery* will be used to demonstrate estimation of proportions. Finally, the data set in the *Employee Success* worksheet will be used to demonstrate chi-square tests for independence.

SAMPLE DESIGN

The first step in sampling is to design an effective sampling plan that will yield representative samples of the populations under study. A **sampling plan** is a description of the approach that will be used to obtain samples from a population prior to any data collection activity. A sampling plan states the objectives of the sampling activity, the target population, the population *frame* (the list from which the sample is selected), the method of sampling, the operational procedures for collecting the data, and the statistical tools that will be used to analyze the data. The objectives of a sampling study might be to estimate key parameters of a population, such as a mean, proportion, or standard deviation of dealer preparation costs, or it might be to determine if significant differences exist between two populations, such as the costs of different systems to produce tractor transmissions.

The ideal frame is a complete list of all members of the target population, for example, the data available on the worksheet *TracPrep Samples* for January 1996 in the North American region. However, a frame may not be the same as the target population. In the worksheet *Transmission Costs,* the frame is a set of samples from an infinite population generated from physical testing. As another example, the target population might be all potential users of Tracway products, which might be impossible to identify—at least in a cost-effective manner—whereas a practical frame might be a list of golf course superintendents and lawn service providers. Understanding how well the frame represents the target population helps us to understand how representative the actual sample is of the target population, and hence the validity of any statistical conclusions drawn from the sample.

SAMPLING METHODS

Sampling methods can be *subjective* or *probabilistic*. Subjective methods include **judgment sampling,** in which expert judgment is used to select the sample (survey the "best" customers); and **convenience sampling,** in which samples are selected based on the ease in which the data can be collected (survey all customers I happen to visit this month). Probabilistic sampling involves selecting the items in the sample using some random procedure. **Simple random sampling** involves selecting items in a sample so that each has an equal chance of being selected. Simple random samples may be selected with or without replacement. *Sampling with replacement* means that once an item is selected, it is returned to the frame and has the same probability of being selected again. *Sampling without replacement* means that once an item is selected, it is removed from the frame and cannot be selected more than once.

If the population data are stored in a database, simple random samples generally can be obtained easily by generating random numbers as we discussed in chapter 3. For example, suppose that a database consists of 400,000 customers and we wish to sample 250. The Excel function RAND( ) or the Analysis tool *Random Number Generation* (described in chapter 3) can be used to generate 250 random numbers. This does not, however, guarantee that all numbers are unique. Thus if you wish to sample without replacement, you must search for any duplicates, discard them, and replace them with new random numbers. If the data are available on an Excel worksheet, the Analysis Tool *Sampling* allows you to select a simple random sample or a systematic sample from a list in an Excel spreadsheet (see *Excel Note: Using the Sampling Tool*). This sampling tool generates random samples with replacement. *PHStat* provides a tool to generate a random sample without replacement, guaranteeing that each item in the sample will be unique (see *PHStat Note: Using the Random Sample Generator*).

Other methods of sampling include the following:

- **Systematic sampling** is a sampling plan that selects items periodically from the population. For example, to sample 250 names from a list of 400,000, every 1,600th name could be selected. If the first item is selected randomly among the first 1,600, then a probabilistic sample results. This approach can be used for telephone sampling when supported by an automatic dialer programmed to dial numbers in a systematic manner. However, systematic sampling is not the same as simple random sampling because, for any sample, every item in the population does not have an equal chance of being selected. In some situations, this approach can induce significant bias if the population has some underlying pattern. For example, sampling orders received every 7 days may not yield a representative sample if customers tend to send orders on certain days every week.

- **Stratified sampling** applies to populations that are divided into natural subsets (strata), and allocates the appropriate proportion of samples to each stratum. For example, a large city may be divided into political districts called wards. Each ward has a different number of citizens. A stratified sample would choose a sample of individuals in each ward proportionate to its size. This approach ensures that each stratum is weighted by its size relative to the population, and can provide better results than simple random sampling if the items in each stratum are not homogeneous. However, issues of cost or significance of certain strata might make a disproportionate sample more useful. For example, the ethnic or racial mix of each ward might be significantly different, making it difficult for a stratified sample to obtain the desired information.
- **Cluster sampling** is based on dividing a population into subgroups (clusters) and taking a simple random sample of the clusters. The items within each cluster become the members of the sample. For example, a company like Tracway might segment its customers into many smaller geographical regions. If each region can be assumed to be representative of the population, then a sampling of clusters would represent the entire population.

Excel Note: Using the Sampling Tool

Assume that we wish to sample from a population of 100 observations located in cells A1 through A100 on a worksheet. From the *Tools* menu, select *Data Analysis* and then *Sampling*. The dialog box shown in Figure 4.2 appears.

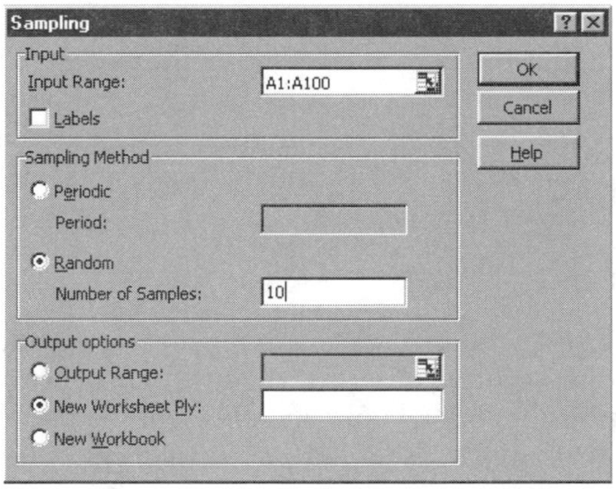

FIGURE 4.2 Dialog Box for Excel Sampling Tool

In the *Input Range* box, you specify the data range from which the sample will be taken. The *Labels* box can be checked if the first row is a data set label. There are two options for sampling. Sampling can be *Periodic,* and you will be prompted for the *Period,* which is the interval between sample observations from the beginning of the data set. For example, if a period of 5 is used, observations 5, 10, 15, and so on will be selected as samples. Sampling can also be *Random,* and you will be prompted for the *Number of Samples*. Excel will then randomly select this number of samples (with replacement) from the specified data set.

PHStat Note: Using the Random Sample Generator

This tool can be used to generate a random list of integers between 1 and a specified population size or to randomly select values from a population on a worksheet without replacement. From the *PHStat* menu, select *Data Preparation* and then *Random Sample Generator*. Figure 4.3 shows the dialog box that appears. Enter the sample size desired in

the *Sample Size* box. Click the first radio button if you want a list of random integers, and enter the population size in the box below this option. Click the second radio button to select a sample from data on a worksheet. The range of the data must be entered in the *Values Cell Range* box (check *First cell contains labels* if appropriate).

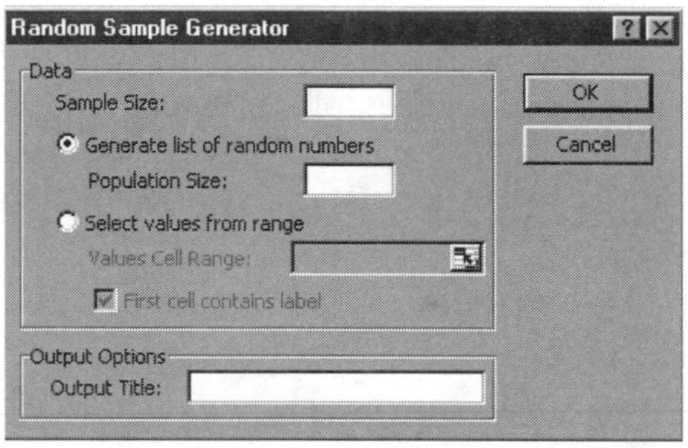

FIGURE 4.3 *PHStat* Random Sample Generator Dialog Box

These alternative sampling methods have some advantages if used appropriately. Systematic sampling is useful when a population is large and it is difficult to search through a database to find items that correspond to random numbers. When items in strata are relatively homogeneous, the strata will have low variances, and thus stratified sampling can use relatively smaller sample sizes than simple random sampling to obtain similar results. Cluster sampling provides good results if the elements of each cluster are heterogeneous and the clusters are representative of the entire population. Although cluster sampling generally requires larger sample sizes than other methods, total costs may be reduced in some applications, such as when interviewers must visit homes and need remain only within the clusters.

ERRORS IN SAMPLING

The purpose of sampling is to obtain statistics that estimate population parameters. Sample design can lead to two sources of errors. The first type of error, *nonsampling error,* occurs when the sample does not adequately represent the target population. This is generally a result of poor sample design, such as using a systematic sample when a simple random sample would have been more appropriate. *Sampling (statistical) error* occurs because samples are only a subset of the total population. We observed sampling error with the simulation experiments in chapter 3. Sampling error is inherent in any sampling process; although it can be minimized, it cannot be totally avoided.

Sampling error depends on the size of the sample relative to the population. Thus determining the number of observations to take is essentially a statistical issue that is based on the accuracy of the estimates needed to draw a useful conclusion. We discuss this later in this chapter. However, from a practical standpoint, one must also consider the cost of sampling and sometimes make a trade-off between cost and the information that is obtained.

SAMPLING FROM FINITE POPULATIONS

In most practical applications, such as survey research, samples are drawn from finite populations without replacement. However, proper application of statistical theory—for example, the central limit theorem and the calculation of the standard error that we discussed in chapter 3—assumes that samples are selected with replacement. When the sample size, n, is less than about 5 percent of the population size, N, the difference is insignificant. However, when the sample is larger than this, a correction factor should be used in computing the standard error when sampling without replacement. Specifically, the standard error should be multiplied by

$$\sqrt{\frac{N-n}{N-1}}$$

Thus the standard error of the mean would be

$$\sigma_{\bar{x}} = \frac{\sigma}{\sqrt{n}} \sqrt{\frac{N-n}{N-1}}$$

Statistical Analysis of Sample Data

Sample data provide the basis for many useful analyses to support decision making. These include *estimation* of population parameters and development of *confidence intervals* for population parameters, which provide an interval estimate of the parameter along with a probability that the interval correctly estimates the true population parameter. Statistical sampling also provides a means to compare alternative decisions or processes. For example, to evaluate existing and proposed production processes for producing transmission systems, Tracway might use sampling to estimate the average cost and variance of each process. If the proposed process has the lowest average cost, it generally would be preferred. However, because of sampling error, the process with the lowest average cost might not be significantly better than the alternative. *Hypothesis testing* is a tool that allows you to draw valid statistical conclusions about the value of population parameters or differences between them.

A variety of support is available in Microsoft Excel to perform statistical analyses. This includes standard Excel functions, the *Analysis Toolpak,* and the *Prentice Hall Statistics* add-in available with this book. Table 4.1 summarizes these options; we will illustrate many of them in this chapter.

Estimation

Estimation involves assessing the value of a population parameter using sample data. **Point estimates** are single numbers used to estimate the population parameter. However, because of sampling error, it is unlikely that a point estimate will equal the true population parameter. **Interval estimates** provide a means of assessing sampling error and provide a range of values within which the population parameter is believed to be.

POINT ESTIMATES

The most common point estimates are the descriptive statistical measures described in chapter 2 and summarized in Table 4.2. They are used to estimate the population parameters, also listed in Table 4.2.

Suppose that we performed an experiment in which we repeatedly sampled from a population and computed a point estimate for a population parameter (similar to the

TABLE 4.1 Statistical Analysis Support in Excel

Excel Function	*Description*
CONFIDENCE(*alpha, standard_dev,size*)	Returns the confidence interval for a population mean.
CHITEST(*actual_range, expected_range*)	Returns the test for independence; the value of the chi-square distribution and the appropriate degrees of freedom.
TTEST(*array1, array2, tails, type*)	Returns the probability associated with a *t*-test.
ZTEST(*array, x, sigma*)	Returns the two-tailed *p*-value of a *z*-test.

Analysis Toolpak Tools	*Description*
Sampling	Creates a simple random sample with replacement or a systematic sample from a population.
t-test: Paired Two Sample For Means	Performs a paired *t*-test to test a hypothesis for equality of means between two populations for small samples.
t-test: Two-Sample Assuming Equal Variances	Performs a test of hypothesis for equality of means between two populations if the populations are assumed to have equal variances.
t-test: Two-Sample Assuming Unequal Variances	Performs a test of hypothesis for equality of means between two populations if the populations are assumed to have unequal variances.
z-test: Two-Sample for Means	Performs a test of hypothesis for equality of means between two populations for large samples.
F-test: Two-Sample for Variances	Performs a test of hypothesis for equality of variances between two populations.
ANOVA: Single Factor	Tests hypothesis that means of two or more samples measured on one factor are equal.
ANOVA: Two-Factor With Replication	Tests hypothesis that means of two or more samples measured on two factors are equal, more than one sample per group.
ANOVA: Two-Factor Without Replication	Tests hypothesis that means of two or more samples measured on two factors are equal based on one sampling.

Prentice Hall Statistics Add-In	*Description*
Random Sample Generator	Generates a random sample without replacement.
Confidence Intervals	Computes confidence intervals for means with σ known or unknown, proportions, and population total.
Sample Size	Determines sample sizes for means and proportions.
One-Sample Tests	Performs hypothesis tests for means with σ known or unknown, and for proportions.
Two-Sample Tests	Performs *t*-test for difference in means; *F*-test for equality of variances; chi-square and *z*-tests for proportions.
c-Sample Tests	Performs chi-square test of independence.
Normal probability plot	Generates a normal probability plot from a set of data.

TABLE 4.2 Common Point Estimates

Point Estimate	*Population Parameter*
Sample mean, $\bar{x}$	Population mean, μ
Sample variance, s^2	Population variance, σ^2
Sample standard deviation, s	Population standard deviation, σ
Sample proportion, p	Population proportion, π

Crystal Ball experiment in chapter 3). Each individual point estimate will vary from the population parameter; however, we hope that the average (expected value) of all possible point estimates equals the population parameter. If the expected value of an estimator equals the population parameter it is intended to estimate, the estimator is said to be **unbiased.** If this is not true, the estimator is called **biased.** A biased estimator might consistently underestimate the parameter it is intended to estimate. Clearly, we would like estimators to be unbiased. Fortunately, all the estimators in Table 4.2 are unbiased, and therefore are meaningful for making decisions involving the population parameter. In particular, you may recall a difference in calculating the sample variance versus the population variance. Recall that the sample variance is computed by the formula

$$s^2 = \frac{\sum_{i=1}^{n} (x_i - \bar{x})^2}{n - 1}$$

whereas the population variance is computed by

$$\sigma^2 = \frac{\sum_{i=1}^{N} (x_i - \mu)^2}{N}$$

Statisticians have shown that the denominator $n - 1$ used in computing s^2 is necessary to provide an unbiased estimator of σ^2. If we simply divided by the number of observations, the estimator would tend to underestimate the true variance.

To illustrate some important issues regarding point estimation, Tracway might wish to obtain point estimates of the mean cost for the three processes (the current system, Alternative A, and Alternative B) it is considering for producing tractor transmissions. The worksheet *Transmission Costs* in the Tracway database provides 30 observations from each process. Point estimates for the mean, variance, and standard deviation are as follows:

Process	Sample Mean	Sample Variance	Sample Standard Deviation
Current	$289.60	2,061.1 ($^{2})	$45.40
Alternative A	$285.50	4,217.6 ($^{2})	$64.94
Alternative B	$298.43	435.4 ($^{2})	$20.87

These point estimates indicate that Alternative A is slightly less expensive than the current system, but has a higher variance. Alternative B has a smaller variance than the other two; however, it also has the highest average value. Thus it is not clear how to interpret these values and make an informed decision. Interval estimates, which we discuss next, provide more useful information than point estimates alone.

INTERVAL ESTIMATES

An interval estimate provides a range within which we believe the true population parameter falls. A **confidence interval (CI)** is an interval estimate that also specifies the likelihood that the interval contains the population parameter. This probability is called the *level of confidence,* and is usually expressed as a percentage. For example, we might state that "a 90 percent CI for the mean is 10 ± 2." The value 10 is the point estimate calculated from the sample data, and 2 can be thought of as a margin for error. Thus the interval estimate is [8, 12]. The level of confidence, denoted by $1 - \alpha$, is 0.90. This means that, based on the sample data, the probability that the confidence interval contains the true population parameter is 0.90. Equivalently, the value of α represents the probability that a confidence interval will *not* include the true population parameter. Commonly used confidence levels are 90, 95, and 99 percent; the higher the confidence level, the more assurance we have that the interval contains the population parameter. As the confidence level increases, the confidence interval becomes larger.

CONFIDENCE INTERVALS FOR THE MEAN

We stated that the sample mean, $\bar{x}$, is a point estimate for the population mean μ. We can use the central limit theorem (see chapter 3) to quantify the sampling error in $\bar{x}$. Recall that the central limit theorem states that no matter what the underlying population, the distribution of sample means is approximately normal with mean μ and standard deviation $\sigma_{\bar{x}} = \sigma/\sqrt{n}$. The value of α represents the proportion of sample means expected to be outside the confidence interval. Therefore, $100(1 - \alpha)$ percent of sample means (for all possible samples of size n) would fall within $\mu \pm z_{\alpha/2}(\sigma/\sqrt{n})$. This is illustrated in Figure 4.4.

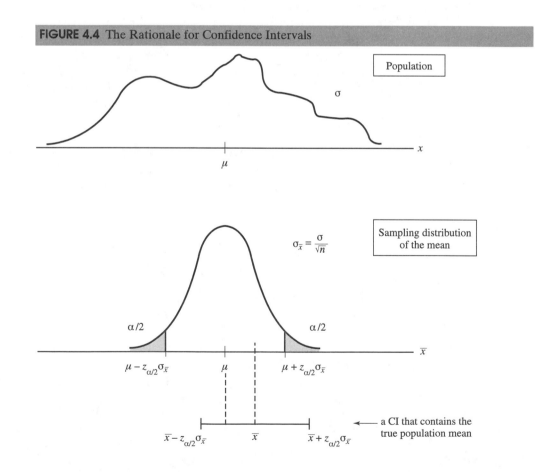

FIGURE 4.4 The Rationale for Confidence Intervals

Because we do not know μ but estimate it by $\bar{x}$, a $100(1 - \alpha)$ percent confidence interval for the population mean μ is

$$\bar{x} \pm z_{a/2} \left(\sigma/\sqrt{n} \right)$$

From Figure 4.4, note that whenever the sample mean falls within the interval $\mu \pm z_{\alpha/2}(\sigma/\sqrt{n})$, the confidence interval will contain the true population mean; however, if $\bar{x}$ falls in one of the tails, the confidence interval will not contain the true mean. Thus the CI will contain the true population mean $100(1 - \alpha)$ percent of the time. The value $z_{\alpha/2}$ may be found from a standard normal table (Table A.1 in the appendix at the end of the book), or may be computed in Excel using the function NORMSINV$(1 - \alpha/2)$. For the most common confidence levels used, we have

Confidence Level	$z_{\alpha/2}$
90%	1.645
95%	1.96
99%	2.575

The confidence interval we developed, however, assumes that we know the standard deviation. When the standard deviation is unknown, as would almost always be the case, we need to use the **t-distribution** to compute a confidence interval. The t-distribution is actually a family of probability distributions with a shape similar to the standard normal distribution. Different t-distributions are distinguished by an additional parameter, **degrees of freedom (df).** The t-distribution has a larger variance than the standard normal, but as the number of degrees of freedom increases, it converges to the standard normal distribution (see Figure 4.5). When sample sizes get to be as large as 120, the distributions are virtually identical; even for sample sizes as low as 30 to 35, it becomes difficult to distinguish between the two. Thus for large sample sizes, many people use z-values to establish confidence intervals even when the standard deviation is unknown. We must point out, however, that for any sample size, the *true* distribution of the sample mean is the t-distribution, so when in doubt, use the t.

FIGURE 4.5 Convergence of t-Distribution to the Normal Distribution

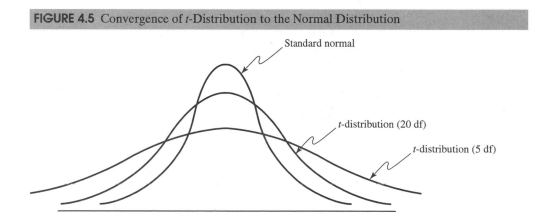

The concept of degrees of freedom can be puzzling. It can best be explained by examining the formula for the sample variance:

$$s^2 = \frac{\sum_{i=1}^{n} (x_i - \bar{x})^2}{n - 1}$$

Note that to compute s^2 we need to first compute the mean, $\bar{x}$. If we know the value of the mean, then we need only know $n - 1$ distinct observations; the nth is completely determined. The number of sample values that are free to vary defines the number of degrees of freedom; in general, df equals the number of sample values minus the number of estimated parameters. Because the sample variance uses one estimated parameter, the mean, the t-distribution used in confidence interval calculations has $n - 1$ degrees of freedom. Because the t-distribution explicitly accounts for the effect of the sample size in estimating the population variance, it is the proper one to use for any sample size. However, for large samples the difference between t- and z-values is very small.

Using the t-distribution, a $100(1 - \alpha)$ percent confidence interval for the population mean μ is

$$\bar{x} \pm t_{\alpha/2, n-1} \left(s/\sqrt{n}\right)$$

where $t_{\alpha/2, n-1}$ is the value from the t-distribution with $n - 1$ degrees of freedom giving an upper-tail probability of $\alpha/2$. We may find t-values in Table A.3 in the appendix at the end of the book or by using the Excel function TINV(*probability, degrees of freedom*). However, take careful note that "probability" in the function TINV refers to the probability in *both* tails of the distribution. Thus $t_{\alpha/2, n-1}$ in Table A.3 is equivalent to TINV(α, df).

In the Tracway example, suppose we wish to find a 99 percent CI for the mean of each transmission system process. A 99 percent CI corresponds to $1 - \alpha = 0.99$. Thus $\alpha/2 = 0.005$. Using the t-distribution, we find that $t_{.005, 29} = 2.7564$, yielding a 99 percent CI for the mean of

$$289.6 \pm 2.7564(45.4/\sqrt{30}) = 289.6 \pm 22.85 \text{ or } [266.75, 312.45]$$

This means that there is a 0.99 probability that a sample of size 30 has a sampling error of \$22.85 or less. Thus if we chose 100 samples of size 30 and computed a confidence interval for each of them, we would expect 99 of the confidence intervals to contain the true population mean. Stated less formally, we are 99 percent confident that the true population mean falls between \$266.65 and \$312.35.

Because we have a sample size of 30, let us compare this confidence interval to that using a normal distribution. From Table A.1, or using the function NORMSINV(.995) in Excel, we find $z = 2.576$. Thus a 99 percent CI for the mean of the current process using the normal distribution would be

$$289.6 \pm 2.576(45.4/\sqrt{30}) = 289.6 \pm 21.4 \text{ or } [268.2, 311.0]$$

This confidence interval is close to that found using the t-distribution, but is slightly smaller (the width is 93.65 percent of the correct CI).

Now suppose that we used only the first 25 samples (having a sample mean of \$286.84 and a sample standard deviation of 48.96). Using the t-distribution in Table A.3 or the Excel function TINV(0.01, 24), we have $t_{.005, 24} = 2.7969$, and the confidence interval is

$$286.84 \pm 2.7969(48.96/\sqrt{25}) = 286.84 \pm 27.39 \text{ or } [259.45, 314.23]$$

However, using the normal distribution results in the confidence interval

$$286.64 \pm 2.576(48.96/\sqrt{25}) = 286.64 \pm 25.22 \text{ or } [261.42, 311.86]$$

The ratio of the width of this CI to that of the *t*-distribution is now 92.07 percent. Thus as the sample size gets smaller, the errors in using z instead of *t* magnify.

PHStat provides tools for computing confidence intervals for the mean, with the standard deviation either known or unknown (see *PHStat Note: Confidence Intervals for the Mean*).

PHStat Note: Confidence Intervals for the Mean

From the *PHStat* menu, select *Confidence Intervals,* and then *Estimate for the mean, sigma known . . .* , or *Estimate for the mean, sigma unknown. . . .* The dialog box for the case when sigma is unknown is shown in Figure 4.6. First enter the confidence level. If you know the sample statistics (as we have entered for the Tracway example), click the radio button *Sample Statistics Known,* and enter them in the appropriate boxes. Otherwise, you may have the tool compute the sample statistics by specifying the range of the data in the second option. If the sample came from a finite population, we suggest that you check the box for *Finite Population Correction* in Output Options and enter the population size. This adjusts the standard error using the finite population correction factor discussed earlier in this chapter. Figure 4.7 shows the output yielding the same results for the Tracway example we discussed.

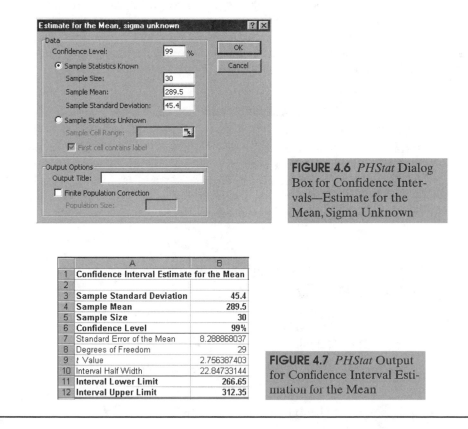

FIGURE 4.6 *PHStat* Dialog Box for Confidence Intervals—Estimate for the Mean, Sigma Unknown

	A	B
1	Confidence Interval Estimate for the Mean	
2		
3	Sample Standard Deviation	45.4
4	Sample Mean	289.5
5	Sample Size	30
6	Confidence Level	99%
7	Standard Error of the Mean	8.288868037
8	Degrees of Freedom	29
9	t Value	2.756387403
10	Interval Half Width	22.84733144
11	Interval Lower Limit	266.65
12	Interval Upper Limit	312.35

FIGURE 4.7 *PHStat* Output for Confidence Interval Estimation for the Mean

CONFIDENCE INTERVALS FOR PROPORTIONS

For categorical variables having only two possible outcomes, such as good or bad, male or female, and so on, we are usually interested in the proportion of observations in a sample that have a certain characteristic. An unbiased estimator of a population proportion π is the sample statistic $p = x/n$, where x is the number in the sample having the desired characteristic, and n is the sample size. If we are sampling with replacement from a finite population, the sampling distribution of π follows the binomial distribution with mean $n\pi$ and variance $\pi(1 - \pi)/n$. Thus the standard error of the proportion is $\sqrt{\pi(1 - \pi)/n}$. When $n\pi$ and $n(1 - \pi)$ are at least 5, the sampling distribution approaches the normal distribution. Therefore, under these conditions, we may use z-values to determine the range of sampling error for a specified confidence level. A $100(1 - \alpha)$ confidence interval for the proportion is

$$p \pm z_{\alpha/2} \sqrt{\frac{p(1 - p)}{n}}$$

For example, if a sample of 1,000 voters found that 51 percent voted for a particular candidate ($p = 0.51$) in a two-candidate race, then a 90 percent confidence interval ($\alpha/2 = .05$) for the population proportion would be

$$0.51 \pm 1.645 \sqrt{\frac{0.51 \times 0.49}{1,000}} = 0.51 \pm 0.026$$

If the sample represented the overall voting population, we are 90 percent confident that the true proportion of the vote in favor of the candidate falls between 0.484 and 0.536. Because of this uncertainty of the sample data, even though the *point estimate* indicates a majority vote, the candidate might lose because the true population proportion might be less than 0.50! *PHStat* provides a simple tool for finding confidence intervals for proportions in the *Confidence Intervals* option.

CONFIDENCE INTERVALS AND SAMPLE SIZE

In all the formulas for confidence intervals, the sample size plays a critical role in determining the width of the confidence interval. If we have already collected the data, we may be constrained by the amount of data available. However, if we are planning a sampling study, we could determine the appropriate sample size needed to estimate the population parameter within a specified level of precision. For example, consider the large sample confidence interval for the mean with an unknown population variance:

$$\bar{x} \pm z_{\alpha/2} \, (s/\sqrt{n})$$

Suppose we want the width of the confidence interval on either side of the mean to be at most E. In other words,

$$E \geq z_{\alpha/2} \, (s/\sqrt{n})$$

Solving for n, we find

$$n \geq (z_{\alpha/2})^2 \, (s^2)/E^2$$

Of course, we do not know s^2 since we have not yet collected any data. A common sense approach would be to take an initial sample to estimate s^2. If $z_{\alpha/2}(s/\sqrt{n}) \leq E$, then we clearly have achieved our goal. If not, we can use s^2 to determine n using the previous formula and collect additional data as needed. Note that if s^2 changes significantly, we still might not have achieved the desired precision and might have to repeat the process. Usually, however, this will be unnecessary.

As an example, consider the problem of estimating Tracway dealer preparation costs in the North American region. The worksheet *TracPrep Samples* in the Tracway database shows the means of 60 monthly samples of 50 costs each for tractor preparation in the North American region over the period January 1996 through December 2000. Although these costs are recorded in chronological order, Tracway feels that it is reasonable to treat them as independent; thus a periodic sampling plan was selected, because there is no reason to expect that periodic observations would be different from the others. We used the Excel *Sampling* tool with a period of 11 to obtain the desired 50 observations. (This process actually yielded 51 observations, the last of which was discarded.) The mean cost over all 60 months is estimated as $99.51 with a sample standard deviation of 15.87. If management wanted a 95 percent confidence interval with an error of no more than $E = \$1$, the sample size required is

$$n \geq (1.96)^2(15.87)^2/(1)^2 = 967.5$$

This tight a confidence interval is clearly expensive, requiring almost one thousand samples. Given this information, management decided that a 95 percent confidence interval with an error of no more than $5 would suffice. The required sample size is

$$n \geq (1.96)^2(15.87)^2/(5)^2 = 38.70$$

or about 39. In practice a round number such as 50 might be used, which will provide an error of less than $5. The Excel function CONFIDENCE(.95,15.87,50) finds the confidence interval of (95.11, 103.91) with an actual maximum error of $4.40 with 95 percent confidence.

In a similar fashion we can compute the sample size required to achieve a desired confidence interval half-width for a proportion by solving the following equation for n:

$$E \geq z_{\alpha/2} \sqrt{\frac{p(1-p)}{n}}$$

This yields

$$n \geq \frac{(z_{\alpha/2})^2\, p(1-p)}{E^2}$$

PHStat provides a tool for computing sample sizes for estimating both means and proportions (see *PHStat Note: Determining Sample Size*).

Hypothesis Testing

Hypothesis testing involves drawing inferences about two contrasting propositions (hypotheses) relating to the value of a population parameter, and using sample data to make a decision about which hypothesis can be supported. For example, we had previously developed point estimates for the costs of the current process for producing tractor transmissions along with two alternatives. The estimated cost for the current system is $289.60 per transmission, while the estimated cost for Alternative A was $285.50. This

PHStat Note: Determining Sample Size

From the *PHStat* menu, select *Sample Size,* and then either *Determination for the Mean* or *Determination for the Proportion*. The dialog box for the mean is shown in Figure 4.8. You need to enter the standard deviation, sampling error desired, and confidence level. The output options also al-low you to incorporate a finite population correction factor. The tool creates a new worksheet with the results for the Tracway example shown in Figure 4.9. The tool for the proportion sample size is similar.

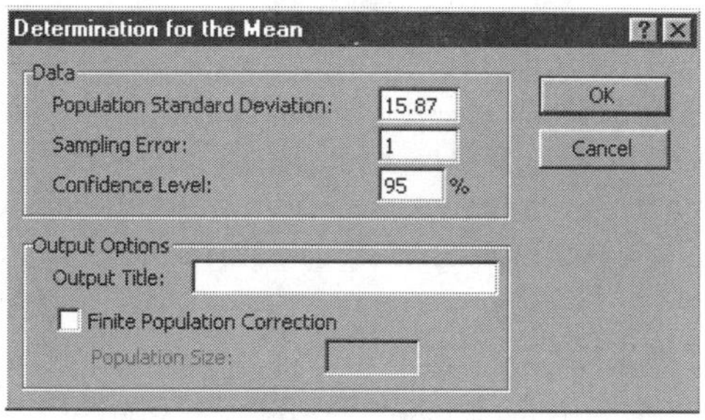

FIGURE 4.8 *PHStat* Dialog Box for Sample Size Determination for the Mean

	A	B
1	Sample Size Determination	
2		
3	Population Standard Deviation	15.87
4	Sampling Error	1
5	Confidence Level	95%
6	Z Value	-1.95996108
7	Calculated Sample Size	967.4950448
8	Sample Size Needed	968

FIGURE 4.9 *PHStat* Results for Sample Size Determination

suggests that Alternative A is less expensive. However, because both cost estimates were based on samples and involve sampling error, we cannot be completely certain that Alternative A is clearly superior. Hypothesis testing can be used to determine whether the mean costs of both systems are equal or not in a statistical sense. This involves

1. Formulating the hypotheses to test,
2. Selecting a *level of significance,* which defines the risk of incorrectly concluding that the assumed hypothesis is correct,
3. Determining a decision rule on which to base a conclusion,
4. Collecting data and calculating a test statistic, and
5. Applying the decision rule to the test statistic and drawing a conclusion.

HYPOTHESIS FORMULATION

Hypothesis testing begins by defining two alternative, mutually exclusive, propositions. The first is called the **null hypothesis,** denoted by H_0, which represents a theory or statement about the status quo that is accepted as correct. The second is called the **alternative hypothesis,** denoted by H_1, which must be true if we conclude that the null hypothesis is false. For example, past data might indicate that the mean time to respond to customer service calls is 4.5 hours. A manager might suspect that the time has changed because of new technology that was recently installed. Therefore, the null hypothesis would be

$$H_0: \text{mean response time} = 4.5 \text{ hours}$$
$$H_1: \text{mean response time} \neq 4.5 \text{ hours}$$

Clearly, if we conclude that H_0 is false, H_1 must be true. A different set of hypotheses for this scenario might be

$$H_0: \text{mean response time} \geq 4.5 \text{ hours}$$
$$H_1: \text{mean response time} < 4.5 \text{ hours}$$

Again, note that either one or the other hypothesis must be true.

These examples considered hypotheses about a single population parameter, and are called *one-sample hypothesis tests*. We could also formulate hypotheses about the parameters of two populations, called *two-sample tests*. For instance, in the Tracway example, we might define the null hypothesis to be

$$H_0: \text{Mean cost of the current process} = \text{mean cost of Alternative A}$$
$$H_1: \text{Mean cost of the current process} \neq \text{mean cost of Alternative A}$$

or

$$H_0: \text{Mean cost of the current process} \leq \text{mean cost of Alternative A}$$
$$H_1: \text{Mean cost of the current process} > \text{mean cost of Alternative A}$$

Hypothesis testing always assumes that H_0 is true, and sample evidence is obtained to determine whether H_1 is more likely to be true. Because the sample evidence can provide only a conclusion about H_1, we cannot statistically "prove" that H_0 is true; we can only fail to reject it. Thus if we cannot reject the null hypothesis, we have shown only that there is insufficient evidence to conclude that it is not true. However, rejecting the null hypothesis does provide proof in a statistical sense that the null hypothesis is not true, and that the alternative hypothesis is therefore correct. For instance, in the previous example, if the null hypothesis that the mean cost of the current process $\leq$ mean cost of Alternative A is rejected, this would provide significant statistical evidence that Alternative A is less expensive than the current process.

SIGNIFICANCE LEVEL

Hypothesis testing can result in four outcomes:

1. The null hypothesis is actually true, and the test correctly fails to reject it.
2. The null hypothesis is actually false, and the hypothesis test correctly reaches this conclusion.
3. The null hypothesis is actually true, but the hypothesis test incorrectly rejects it (called **Type I error**).
4. The null hypothesis is actually false, but the hypothesis test incorrectly fails to reject it (called **Type II error**).

The probability of making a Type I error is generally denoted by α and is called the **level of significance** of the test. This probability is essentially the risk that you can afford to take in making the incorrect conclusion that the alternative hypothesis is true when in fact the null hypothesis is true. The **confidence coefficient** is $1 - \alpha$, which is the probability of correctly failing to reject the null hypothesis. For a confidence coefficient of 0.95, we mean that at least 95 out of 100 samples support the null hypothesis rather than the alternative hypothesis. Commonly used levels for α are 0.10, 0.05, and 0.01, resulting in confidence levels of 0.90, 0.95, and 0.99, respectively.

The probability of a Type II error is denoted by β. Unlike α, this cannot be specified in advance, but depends on the true value of the (unknown) population parameter. To see this, suppose that our hypotheses are

$$H_0: \text{mean response time} = 4.5 \text{ hours}$$
$$H_1: \text{mean response time} \neq 4.5 \text{ hours}$$

Then if the true mean response is, say, 6.0, we would expect to have a much lower probability of incorrectly concluding that the null hypothesis is true than when the true mean response is 4.6, for example. In the first case, the sample mean would very likely be far from the hypothesized value of 4.5, leading us to reject H_0. In the second case, however, even though the true mean is not 4.5, we would have a much higher probability of failing to reject H_0 because small differences would be attributed to sampling error. The value $1 - \beta$ is called the **power of the test** and represents the probability of correctly rejecting the null hypothesis when it is indeed false. Generally, as α decreases, β increases, so the decision maker must consider the trade-offs of these risks. If the power of the test is deemed to be too small, it can be increased by taking larger samples. Larger samples enable us to detect small differences between the sample statistics and population parameters with more accuracy. However, a larger sample size incurs higher costs, putting more meaning to the adage "You can't get something for nothing." Table 4.3 summarizes this discussion.

DECISION RULES

The decision to reject or fail to reject a null hypothesis is based on computing a test statistic that is a function of the mean, variance, or proportion from sample data, and comparing it to the hypothesized sampling distribution of the test statistic. The sampling distribution is usually the normal distribution, *t*-distribution, or some other well-known distribution. The sampling distribution is divided into two parts, a *rejection region* and a *non-rejection region*. If the null hypothesis is true, it is unlikely that the test statistic will fall into the rejection region. Thus if the test statistic falls in the rejection region, we reject the null hypothesis; otherwise we fail to reject it. The probability of falling in the rejection region if H_0 is true is the probability of a Type I error, α.

The rejection region generally occurs in the tails of the sampling distribution of the test statistic. For tests in which the alternative hypothesis is accepted if the test statistic is either significantly high or low, for example,

$$H_0: \text{mean response time} = 4.5 \text{ hours}$$
$$H_1: \text{mean response time} \neq 4.5 \text{ hours}$$

the rejection region will occur in *both* the upper and lower tail of the distribution (see Figure 4.10a). This is called a **two-tailed** test of hypothesis. Because the probability that the test statistic falls into the rejection region, given that H_0 is true, is α, the area within each tail must be $\alpha/2$.

TABLE 4.3 Error Types in Hypothesis Testing

	Test Rejects H_0	*Test Fails to Reject H_0*
Alternative hypothesis (H_1) is true	Correct	Type II error
Null hypothesis (H_0) is true	Type I error	Correct

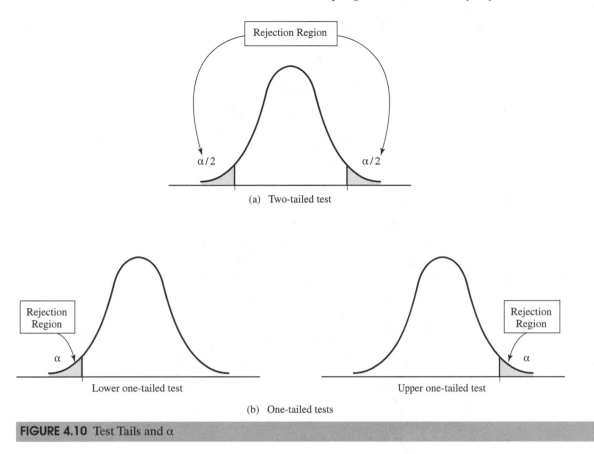

FIGURE 4.10 Test Tails and α

The other type of hypothesis, which specifies a direction of relationship such as

H_0: mean response time $\geq$ 4.5 hours

H_1: mean response time $<$ 4.5 hours

is a **one-tailed** test of hypothesis. In this case, the rejection region occurs in one tail of the distribution (see Figure 4.10b). Determining the correct tail of the distribution to use as the rejection region for a one-tailed test is easy. If H_1 is stated as "$<$," the rejection region is in the lower tail; if H_1 is stated as "$>$," the rejection region is in the upper tail. The rejection region is defined by a *critical value* of the test statistic. Lower-tail critical values are negative; upper-tail critical values are positive. Both Excel and *PHStat* have tools for conducting various types of hypothesis tests (as summarized in Table 4.1). We will illustrate several of them in this section.

We will illustrate these hypothesis tests using the worksheet *Response Time* in the Tracway database. This worksheet contains 50 observations of the time (in hours) taken by Tracway personnel to respond to customer requests for service. Tracway management would like to ensure that the average response time is no more than 4.5 hours, as part of their strategy of providing a high level of service to customers. The average service time for these 50 observations is 3.85 hours, with a standard deviation of 1.73 hours. Although this mean appears to be well below the standard of 4.5 hours, we cannot state definitively that the company is meeting its goal because of possible sampling error. Thus we would like to disprove the hypothesis that mean response time is greater than or equal to 4.5 hours, so as to provide statistical evidence that the mean response time is less than 4.5 hours.

Thus we will test the hypotheses:

H_0: mean response time $\geq$ 4.5 hours
H_1: mean response time $<$ 4.5 hours

This is a one-tailed, one-sample test for the mean with an unknown standard deviation. The test statistic is

$$t = \frac{\bar{x} - \mu_0}{s/\sqrt{n}}$$

Because the rejection region is in the lower tail, the decision rule is to reject H_0 if $t <$ $-t_{n-1,\alpha}$. Note that the critical value is negative because this is a lower one-tailed test. The rationale for this rule is simple. Notice that if the sample mean is much larger than $\mu_0 = 4.5$, then the value of t will be a large positive number and it is unlikely that we would reject the null hypothesis. If, however, the true mean response time is less than 4.5, then the sample mean will most likely be less than 4.5, and the value of t will be negative. If it is "negative enough;" that is, if it falls in the lower tail of the t-distribution with a 0.05 level of significance, then we would reject H_0. The value of the sample statistic t is -2.653 and the critical value is $-t_{49,.05} = -1.6766$. Therefore, we would reject H_0, suggesting that the mean response time is indeed less than 4.5 hours. *PHStat* provides a routine for conducting t-tests (see *PHStat Note: Testing Hypotheses for the Mean, Sigma Unknown*).

To illustrate a two-tailed one-sample test for the mean with an unknown standard deviation, let us test the hypotheses

H_0: mean response time $=$ 4.5 hours
H_1: mean response time $\neq$ 4.5 hours

for a significance level of 0.95. The test statistic is the same as in the previous case but the decision rule is to reject H_0 if $|t| > t_{n-1,\alpha/2}$; in other words, if the test statistic value falls below the negative critical value or above the positive critical value. Computing the value of t, we obtain

$$t = \frac{\bar{x} - \mu_0}{s/\sqrt{n}} = \frac{3.85 - 4.5}{1.73/\sqrt{50}} = -\frac{0.65}{0.244659} = -2.657$$

Thus the absolute value of t is 2.657. Because $t_{49,.025} = 2.0096$, we reject the null hypothesis that the mean is 4.5 hours. Figure 4.12 verifies the conclusion we reached.

We may conduct many other tests of hypotheses; several common ones are summarized in Table 4.4. The basic principles are the same; the major difference lies in the test statistic and decision rule used. In subsequent sections we will illustrate other specific types of hypothesis tests.

USING *p*-VALUES

An alternative approach to comparing a test statistic to a critical value in hypothesis testing is to find the probability of obtaining a test statistic value equal to or more

PHStat Note: Testing Hypotheses for the Mean, Sigma Unknown

From the *PHStat* menu, select *One-Sample Tests,* then *t-Test for the Mean, Sigma Unknown.* The dialog box, shown in Figure 4.11, first asks you to input the value of the null hypothesis and significance level. Similar to the confidence interval tools, you can either specify the sample statistics or let the tool compute them from the data. The sample statistics have been entered for the Tracway example in Figure 4.11. Under Test Options, you may choose among a two-tailed test, upper-tail test, or lower-tail test. Figure 4.12 shows the output provided by this tool. Key statistics are computed as well as the conclusion of the test.

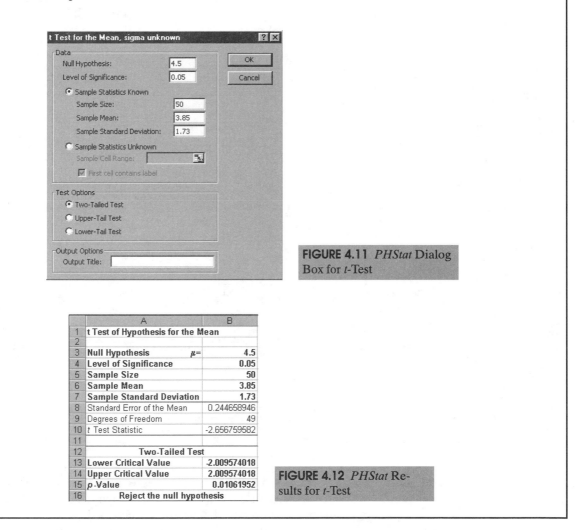

FIGURE 4.11 *PHStat* Dialog Box for *t*-Test

	A	B
1	t Test of Hypothesis for the Mean	
2		
3	Null Hypothesis $\mu=$	4.5
4	Level of Significance	0.05
5	Sample Size	50
6	Sample Mean	3.85
7	Sample Standard Deviation	1.73
8	Standard Error of the Mean	0.244658946
9	Degrees of Freedom	49
10	t Test Statistic	-2.656759582
11		
12	Two-Tailed Test	
13	Lower Critical Value	-2.009574018
14	Upper Critical Value	2.009574018
15	p-Value	0.01061952
16	Reject the null hypothesis	

FIGURE 4.12 *PHStat* Results for *t*-Test

extreme than that obtained from the sample data when the null hypothesis is true. This probability is commonly called a ***p*-value.** For example, first consider the two-tailed test for the mean response time. The *t* statistic for the hypothesis test is 2.653. What is the probability of obtaining a test statistic either greater than 2.653 or less than −2.653? Using the Excel function TDIST (*x, degrees_freedom, tails*), with $x = 2.653$,

TABLE 4.4 Common Types of Hypothesis Tests

Type of Test	*Hypotheses Tested*	*Test Statistic*	*Decision Rule*
One-sample test for mean (two-tailed), σ known	$H_0: \mu = \mu_0$ $H_1: \mu \neq \mu_0$	$z = \dfrac{\bar{x} - \mu_0}{\sigma/\sqrt{n}}$	Reject H_0 if $z < -z_{\alpha/2}$ or $z > z_{\alpha/2}$
One-sample test for means (two-tailed), σ unknown	$H_0: \mu = \mu_0$ $H_1: \mu \neq \mu_0$	$t = \dfrac{\bar{x} - \mu_0}{s/\sqrt{n}}$	Reject H_0 if $t < -t_{n-1,\alpha/2}$ or $t > t_{n-1,\alpha/2}$
One-sample test for mean (lower one-tailed), σ known	$H_0: \mu \geq \mu_0$ $H_1: \mu < \mu_0$	$z = \dfrac{\bar{x} - \mu_0}{\sigma/\sqrt{n}}$	Reject H_0 if $z < -z_\alpha$
One-sample test for mean (upper one-tailed), σ known	$H_0: \mu \leq \mu_0$ $H_1: \mu > \mu_0$	$z = \dfrac{\bar{x} - \mu_0}{\sigma/\sqrt{n}}$	Reject H_0 if $z > z_\alpha$
One-sample test for mean (lower one-tailed), σ unknown	$H_0: \mu \geq \mu_0$ $H_1: \mu < \mu_0$	$t = \dfrac{\bar{x} - \mu_0}{s/\sqrt{n}}$	Reject H_0 if $t < -t_{n-1,\alpha}$
One-sample test for mean (upper one-tailed), σ unknown	$H_0: \mu \leq \mu_0$ $H_1: \mu > \mu_0$	$t = \dfrac{\bar{x} - \mu_0}{s/\sqrt{n}}$	Reject H_0 if $t > t_{n-1,\alpha}$
Two-sample test for means (two-tailed), σ known	$H_0: \mu_1 - \mu_2 = 0$ $H_1: \mu_1 - \mu_2 \neq 0$	$z = \dfrac{\bar{x}_1 - \bar{x}_2}{\sqrt{\sigma_1^2/n_1 + \sigma_2^2/n_2}}$	Reject H_0 if $z < z_{\alpha/2}$ or $z > z_{\alpha/2}$
Two-sample test for means (two-tailed), σ unknown, assumed equal	$H_0: \mu_1 - \mu_2 = 0$ $H_1: \mu_1 - \mu_2 \neq 0$	$t = \dfrac{\bar{x}_1 - \bar{x}_2}{\sqrt{\dfrac{(n_1 - 1)s_1^2 + (n_2 - 1)s_2^2}{n_1 + n_2 - 2}\left(\dfrac{n_1 + n_2}{n_1 n_2}\right)}}$	Reject H_0 if $t < t_{\mathrm{df},\alpha/2}$ or $t > t_{\mathrm{df},\alpha/2}$ $\mathrm{df} = n_1 + n_2 - 2$
One-sample test for proportion (two-sided)	$H_0: \pi = \pi_0$ $H_1: \pi \neq \pi_0$	$z = \dfrac{p - \pi_0}{\sqrt{\pi_0(1 - \pi_0)/n}}$	Reject H_0 if $z < -z_{\alpha/2}$ or $z > z_{\alpha/2}$

degrees_freedom $= 49$, and tails $= 2$ (because this is a two-tailed test), we find this probability to be 0.0107. Because we used a level of significance $\alpha = 0.05$, we reject the null hypothesis. In other words, there is only about a 1 percent chance that the *t*-value would be this large if the null hypothesis were true. For the one-tailed test, we find TDIST(2.653,49,1) $= 0.0054$. (Note that when using the TDIST function, you need to use a positive value for *x*. Although our *t*-value is negative, the distribution is symmetric, so it makes no difference.) Using a significance level of 0.05, a 0.0054 probability would lead us to reject H_0.

TWO-SAMPLE HYPOTHESIS TESTS FOR MEANS

Hypothesis testing finds wide applicability in comparing two populations. For example, in the Tracway situation we described earlier, we might want to test the hypotheses

H_0: Mean cost of the current process $=$ mean cost of Alternative A
H_1: Mean cost of the current process $\neq$ mean cost of Alternative A

If we cannot reject the null hypothesis, then even though the means seem to differ, this difference would most likely be due to sampling error.

A critical issue in determining the appropriate test to apply is whether we may assume that the variances of the two populations are equal. To identify statistically whether or not two variances are equal, we could use the *F*-test described in the next section. If there is strong evidence that the population variances are or can be assumed to be equal, we may compute the test statistic using the appropriate formula in Table 4.4, the *PHStat* tool *Two-Sample Tests/t-Test for Differences in Two Means,* or the Excel tool *t-Test: Two-Sample Assuming Equal Variances.* Even if the population variances are equal, sample variances will generally not be. The test summarized in Table 4.4 *pools,* or combines, the variances to estimate a common variance for both populations.

The mathematics for the test when the variances are unequal is too complex to describe, and few basic statistics texts deal with this case. However, we may use the Excel tool *t-Test: Two-Sample Assuming Unequal Variances,* which is explained in *Excel Note: Using the Two-Sample t-Test with Unequal Variances,* to test the hypothesis. We use the data on the worksheet *Transmission Costs,* located in cells A4:A33 for the current process and cells B4:B33 for Alternative A, from the Tracway database. Each sample consists of 30 observations, and we will set the probability of a Type I error to 0.05. This is a two-tailed test, because we are testing the null hypothesis that the two means are equal against the alternative hypothesis that they are not.

Figure 4.14 shows the results. The computed *t* statistic is 0.2834 while the critical value for the two-tailed test is 2.006645. Therefore, we cannot reject the null hypothesis that the means are equal. Alternatively, we could examine the *p*-value of 0.778 and note that it is much larger than the level of significance of 0.05, again reaching the same conclusion. Note that failing to reject the null hypothesis is not the same as rejecting the alternative hypothesis. This simply says that, given a confidence level of 0.95, the *t*-test was unable to indicate a significant difference in the mean costs of the two systems.

We could also test the hypotheses

H_0: Mean cost of the current process $\leq$ mean cost of Alternative A
H_1: Mean cost of the current process $>$ mean cost of Alternative A

Rejecting H_0 would provide statistical evidence that Alternative A is superior to the current process. We leave the interpretation of the one-tailed test results from Figure 4.14 to you as an exercise.

F-TEST FOR TESTING VARIANCES

As we have seen, Excel supports two different *t*-tests, one assuming equal variances, and the other assuming unequal variances. We can test for equality of variances between two populations using the *F-test.* To use this test, we must assume that both samples are

120 CHAPTER 4 *Sampling and Statistical Analysis for Decision Making*

Excel Note: Using the Two Sample *t*-Test with Unequal Variances

From the main menu bar, select *Tools,* followed by *Data Analysis,* and *t-Test: Two-Sample Assuming Unequal Variances.* The dialog box shown in Figure 4.13 appears. We enter the ranges for each variable and a value for the significance level, or Alpha (α) *level,* as it is called in Excel. The default is 0.05. If you leave the box *Hypothesized Mean* *Difference* blank, the test is just for equality of means. The tool allows you to specify a value d to test the hypothesis $H_0: \mu_1 - \mu_2 = d$. In the results for this tool, you will notice that the degrees of freedom are different than the degrees of freedom for the equal-variance case because they are based on a different calculation.

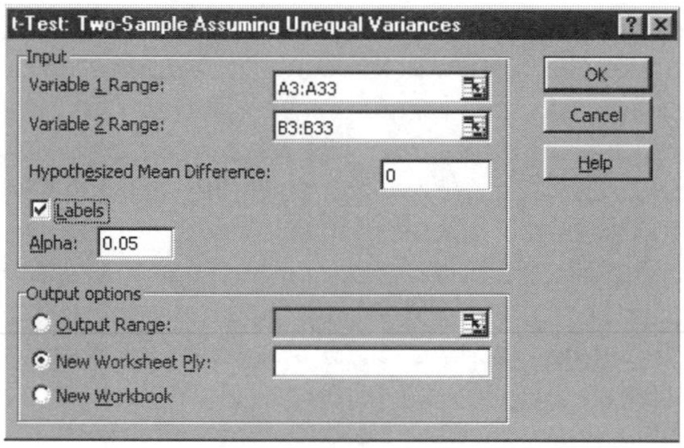

FIGURE 4.13 Excel Dialog Box for Two-Sample *t*-Test Assuming Unequal Variance

Something else to pay close attention to when using Excel is the fact that it reports critical values and *p*-values for both one- and two-tailed tests. This might be a bit confusing. Actually, Excel computes the proper results for either case; you need only compare the *t* statistic to the critical value or the *p*-value to the significance level for the type of test you are conducting. You need to remember, however, that if the significance level is, for example, 0.05, the area of the rejection region in each tail for a two-tailed test is 0.025 (as we showed in Figure 4.10). You will note that the critical value for the two-tailed test in Figure 4.12 is larger than that for the one-tailed test because of this fact; the rejection region is further from the mean. Similarly, the *p*-value is twice as large as that for a one-tailed test, because it accounts for the probability of obtaining a result higher than the positive value of the test statistic and lower than its negative value.

E	F	G
t-Test: Two-Sample Assuming Unequal Variances		
	Current	Process A
Mean	289.6	285.5
Variance	2061.145	4217.638
Observations	30	30
Hypothesized Mean Difference	0	
df	52	
t Stat	0.283405	
P(T<=t) one-tail	0.388996	
t Critical one-tail	1.674689	
P(T<=t) two-tail	0.777992	
t Critical two-tail	2.006645	

FIGURE 4.14 Results of *t*-Test Comparing Current Process and Alternative A

drawn from normal populations. The *F*-test statistic is the ratio of the variances of the two samples:

$$F = \frac{S_1^2}{S_2^2}$$

This statistic is compared to a critical value from the *F*-distribution for a given confidence level. Like the *t*-distribution, the *F*-distribution is characterized by degrees of freedom. However, the *F*-statistic has *two* values of degrees of freedom—one for the sample variance in the numerator, and the other for the sample variance in the denominator. In both cases, the number of degrees of freedom is equal to the respective sample size minus 1. The *F*-test can be applied using the *Data Analysis Toolpak* in Excel (see *Excel Note: Using the F-Test for Equality of Variances Tool*) or the *PHStat* tool found in the menu by choosing *Two-Sample Tests/F-Test for Differences in Two Variances*.

To illustrate the *F*-test, we will use the Tracway transmission data. We can test for the equality of variances of all three pairs of processes, resulting in three distinct hypotheses tests. First, we can test the hypothesis that the variance of the current system is equal to the variance of Alternative A:

$$H_0: \sigma_{current}^2 = \sigma_{Alternative\ A}^2$$
$$H_1: \sigma_{current}^2 \neq \sigma_{Alternative\ A}^2$$

The hypotheses for testing the current system against Alternative B and Alternative A against Alternative B are similar.

Excel Note: Using the *F*-Test for Equality of Variances Tool

From the main menu bar, select *Tools,* followed by *Data Analysis,* and *F-Test Two-Sample for Variances.* The dialog box shown in Figure 4.15 will appear. We specify the *Variable 1 Range* and the *Variable 2 Range* for both data sets and a value for the significance level, α. The Excel output provides only a one-tailed test, however. If a two-tailed test is desired, as you would want to test for equality of variances, use $\alpha/2$ for the significance level. If the variance of variable 1 is greater than the variance of variable 2, the output will specify the upper tail; otherwise, you obtain the lower tail information. If you want to compute the critical values for both tails, you will need to run the test twice, reversing the orders of the *Variable 1 Range* and the *Variable 2 Range* data; however, the *p*-values would be the same. If you are running a two-tailed test, be cautious to compare the *p*-value with $\alpha/2$, which you should have specified as the significance level.

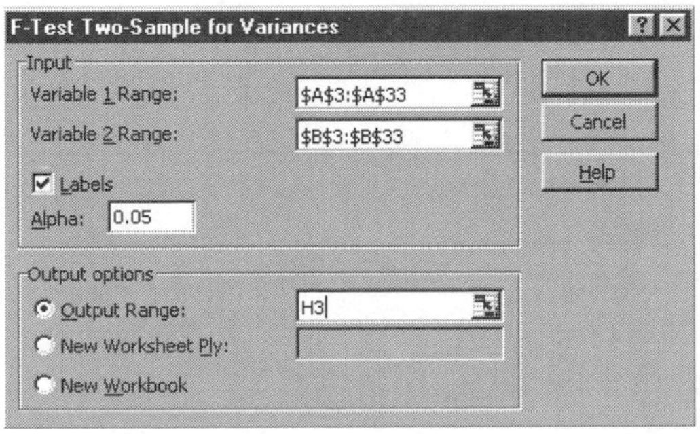

FIGURE 4.15 Excel Dialog Box for *F*-Test for Equality of Variances

The results of these three tests, using a significance level of 0.05, are shown in Figure 4.16. We see that we cannot reject the null hypothesis of equality of variance for the current process with Alternative A since the *F*-ratio (no matter how it is computed—either as the ratio of the variance of the current system to Alternative A or Alternative A to the current system) falls between the critical values of 0.475964 and 2.100997. Alternatively, the *p*-value is greater than the significance level we chose. Had we performed the *F*-test first, we should have used the *t*-test assuming equality of variances for testing the difference in means of the current process versus Alternative A.

Note that the test rejects the null hypotheses for comparing the current system against Alternative B and Alternative A against Alternative B. Thus we can conclude that the variance of Alternative B is significantly different from the variances of the current system and Alternative A.

TESTS FOR PROPORTIONS

Many important business measures, such as market share or the proportion of deliveries received on time, are expressed as proportions. Table 4.5 shows the proportion of on-time deliveries from suppliers. This information is derived from the Tracway database worksheet *On-Time Delivery*. In 1996, Tracway set a company goal of achieving at least a 99 percent on-time delivery rate. The data suggest that the proportion of on-time deliveries has improved modestly each year. We might wish to test a hypothesis that the proportion of on-time deliveries in the last year is 0.99 or less against the alternative that it is greater than 0.99:

$$\text{H}_0: p_{2000} \leq 0.99$$
$$\text{H}_1: p_{2000} > 0.99$$

If proportions can be assumed to be independent, and this is probably the case for such data, we can also test for differences in proportions, for example

$$\text{H}_0: p_{1996} - p_{2000} = 0$$
$$\text{H}_1: p_{1996} - p_{2000} \neq 0$$

FIGURE 4.16 *F*-Test Results Comparing the Variances of the Three Transmission Processes

H	I	J	K	L	M	N	O	P
F-Test Two-Sample for Variances			F-Test Two-Sample for Variances			F-Test Two-Sample for Variances		
	Current	Process A		Current	Process B		Process A	Process B
Mean	289.6	285.5	Mean	289.6	298.4333	Mean	285.5	298.4333
Variance	2061.145	4217.638	Variance	2061.145	435.3575	Variance	4217.638	435.3575
Observations	30	30	Observations	30	30	Observations	30	30
df	29	29	df	29	29	df	29	29
F	0.488696		F	4.734373		F	9.687758	
P(F<=f) one-tail	0.029265		P(F<=f) one-tail	3.63E-05		P(F<=f) one-tail	1.38E-08	
F Critical one-tail	0.475964		F Critical one-tail	2.100997		F Critical one-tail	2.100997	
F-Test Two-Sample for Variances			F-Test Two-Sample for Variances			F-Test Two-Sample for Variances		
	Process A	Current		Process B	Current		Process B	Process A
Mean	285.5	289.6	Mean	298.4333	289.6	Mean	298.4333	285.5
Variance	4217.638	2061.145	Variance	435.3575	2061.145	Variance	435.3575	4217.638
Observations	30	30	Observations	30	30	Observations	30	30
df	29	29	df	29	29	df	29	29
F	2.04626		F	0.211221		F	0.103223	
P(F<=f) one-tail	0.029265		P(F<=f) one-tail	3.63E-05		P(F<=f) one-tail	1.38E-08	
F Critical one-tail	2.100997		F Critical one-tail	0.475964		F Critical one-tail	0.475964	

TABLE 4.5	Tracway Supplier On-Time Delivery Proportions by Year
Year	Proportion of Supplier Deliveries On-Time
1996	0.985
1997	0.987
1998	0.988
1999	0.990
2000	0.992

For both cases, the hypothesis test is based on the *z* statistic as shown in Table 4.4. We will illustrate these hypothesis tests using the *PHStat* tools (see *PHStat Note: z-Tests for Proportions*). Figure 4.17 shows the results for the hypothesis that the proportion of on-time deliveries in the year 2000 is no greater than 0.99. We reject the null hypothesis, and the very small *p*-value shows that it is highly unlikely that the hypothesis would be true. Figure 4.18 shows the results of the second set of hypotheses, namely, that the proportions for 1996 and 2000 are equal. Again we see that the hypothesis is rejected, with an extremely small *p*-value.

An important observation is that a significant difference (and a very small *p*-value) is almost always going to be identified if sample size is large enough. Here, the sample

	A	B
1	Z Test of Hypothesis for the Proportion	
2		
3	Null Hypothesis *p*=	0.99
4	Level of Significance	0.05
5	Number of Successes	16850
6	Sample Size	16986
7	Sample Proportion	0.991993406
8	Standard Error	0.000763435
9	Z Test Statistic	2.611101755
10		
11	Upper-Tail Test	
12	Upper Critical Value	1.644853
13	*p*-Value	0.004512587
14	Reject the null hypothesis	

FIGURE 4.17 *PHStat* Results for One-Sample Test of a Proportion

	A	B
1	Z Test for Differences in Two Proportions	
2		
3	Hypothesized Difference	0
4	Level of Significance	0.05
5	Group 1	
6	Number of Successes	13937
7	Sample Size	14149
8	Group 2	
9	Number of Successes	16850
10	Sample Size	16986
11	Group 1 Proportion	0.985016609
12	Group 2 Proportion	0.991993406
13	Difference in Two Proportions	-0.006976797
14	Average Proportion	0.988822868
15	Z Test Statistic	-5.830632529
16		
17	Two-Tailed Test	
18	Lower Critical Value	-1.959961082
19	Upper Critical Value	1.959961082
20	*p*-Value	5.53932E-09
21	Reject the null hypothesis	

FIGURE 4.18 *PHStat* Results for Two-Sample Test of Equality of Proportions

PHStat Note: z-Tests for Proportions

PHStat provides two tools for testing hypotheses regarding proportions. Tests involving a single proportion can be found by selecting the menu item *One-Sample Tests* and choosing *z-Test for the Proportion,* and tests involving two proportions can be found by selecting the menu item *Two-Sample Tests* and choosing *z-Test for Differences* *in Two Proportions.* Figure 4.19 shows the dialog boxes for these two options. The tool requires you to enter the value for the null hypothesis, significance level, sample sizes, number of successes, and the type of test. Note that you cannot enter the proportion alone, because the test depends on the sample size.

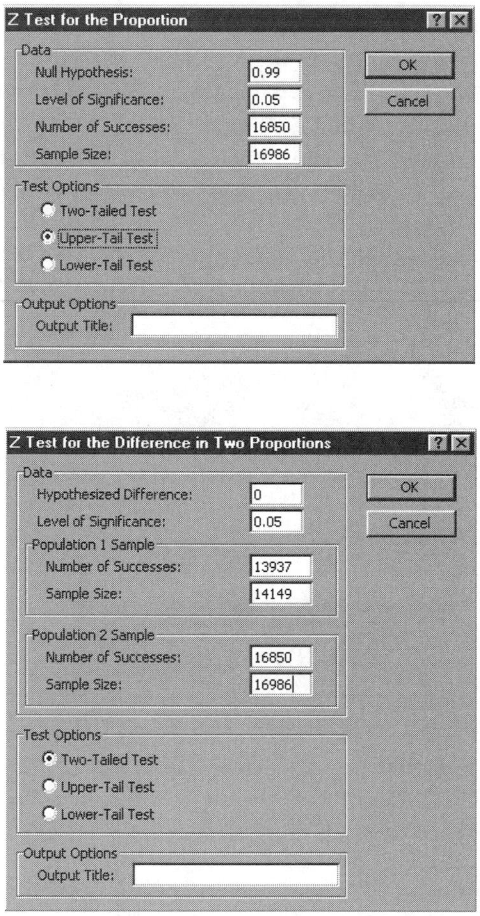

FIGURE 4.19 *PHStat* Dialog Boxes for z-Tests for Proportions

size is very large, so significant differences were almost inevitable. Had the sample sizes been much smaller, we might not have rejected both null hypotheses based on the data.

OTHER HYPOTHESIS TESTS

Excel has a variety of other hypothesis testing tools available as summarized in Table 4.1. The approach and methodology are similar; what is important to know is which test to use. One principal drawback of most of these tests is that normality of the data is assumed. If the data are not normal, we might be able to transform the data or use a non-parametric statistics test such as the Wilcoxon test. We refer you to more comprehensive texts on statistics, such as Levine, et al., (1997) for further information.

ANOVA: Testing Differences of Several Means

To this point, we have discussed hypothesis tests that compare a population parameter to a constant value, or compare the means or proportions of two different populations. Often, we would like to compare the means of several different groups to determine if all are equal, or if any are significantly different from the rest. For example, in the Tracway transmission example, we have data on three types of processes. (In statistical terminology, the process is called a **factor,** and we have three categorical levels of this factor—the current system, Alternative A, and Alternative B.) Thus it would appear that we will have to perform three different pair tests to establish whether any significant differences exist among them. As the number of populations increases, you can easily see that the number of pair tests grows large very quickly. Fortunately, other statistical tools exist that eliminate the need for such a tedious approach. **Analysis of Variance (ANOVA)** provides a tool for doing this.

ANOVA requires assumptions that the m groups or factor levels being studied represent populations whose outcome measures are randomly and independently obtained, are normally distributed, and have equal variances. The principle behind ANOVA is to compare ratios of variances of the different levels. The null hypothesis is that if the factor level varies, the means of all outcomes are equal; the alternative hypothesis is that at least one mean differs:

$$H_0: \mu_1 = \mu_2 = ... = \mu_m$$

H_1: at least one mean is different from the others

We will assume that sample j has n_j observations. ANOVA examines the variation among and within the m groups or levels. Specifically, the total variation in the data is expressed as the variation among groups plus the variation within groups:

$$SST = SSB + SSW$$

where SST = total variation in the data
SSB = variation between groups
SSW = variation within groups

We compute these terms using the following formulas:

$$SST = \sum_{j=1}^{n} \sum_{i=1}^{n_j} (X_{ij} - \overline{\overline{X}})^2$$

$$SSB = \sum_{j=1}^{n} n_j (\overline{X}_j - \overline{\overline{X}})^2$$

$$SSW = \sum_{j=1}^{n} \sum_{i=1}^{n_j} (X_{ij} - \overline{X}_j)^2$$

where $\overline{\overline{X}}$ = overall or grand mean
X_{ij} = ith observation in group j
$\overline{X}_j$ = sample mean of group j

From these formulas, you can see that each term is a "sum of squares" of elements of the data; hence the notation "SST," which can be thought of as the "Sum of Squares

Total"; SSB is the "Sum of Squares Between" groups; and SSW is the "Sum of Squares Within" groups. By dividing these sums of squares by their respective degrees of freedom, we obtain three variances, or *mean squares:*

$$MSB = SSB/(m-1)$$
$$MSW = SSW/(n-m)$$
$$MST = SST/(n-1)$$

where n is the total number of observations and m is the number of factors.

Because the mean squares are variances, we can use the F-test to determine whether the mean square between groups is significantly larger than the mean square within groups using the F statistic

$$F = MSB/MSW$$

This statistic follows an F-distribution with $m-1$ and $n-m$ degrees of freedom. Therefore, if F is larger than the critical value from the F-distribution, we reject H_0.

ANOVA derives its name from the fact that we are analyzing variances in the data. If the null hypothesis is true, then $\overline{X} = \overline{X}_j$ and, consequently, the within-group variation should equal the total variation and the F statistic ideally will be zero (examine the previous formulas). If the means among groups are different, then MSB will not be zero and the F statistic will be large. If it is large enough based on the level of significance chosen, we can conclude that the alternate hypothesis is true. However, ANOVA does not provide any information about which mean(s) would be different.

We use the data on the worksheet *Transmission Costs* from the Tracway database and the Excel ANOVA tool (see *Excel Note: Using the ANOVA Analysis Tool*) to illustrate ANOVA. Specifically, we will test the null hypothesis that the means of all three systems are equal against the alternative hypothesis that at least one of the means differs. The Excel output is given in Figure 4.20. The output report begins with a summary report of key statistics for each group.

The ANOVA section reports the details of the hypothesis test. There are 90 observations in total and we need to estimate the overall mean to compute SST; thus SST has 89 degrees of freedom. Similarly, to compute SSB we need to estimate the mean of each group; thus SSB has 2 degrees of freedom. This leaves 87 degrees of freedom for SSW. Using this information, the mean squares are computed. For example, $MSB = 2,621.089/2 = 1,310.544$, and $MSW = 194,710.1/87 = 2,238.047$. The F-ratio is $MSB/MSW = 1,310.544/2,238.047 = 0.586$. Since this is smaller than the critical value of the F-distribution of 3.101 for an α of 0.05, we fail to reject the null hypothesis. The

FIGURE 4.20 ANOVA Results for Transmission Processes

	A	B	C	D	E	F	G
1	Anova: Single Factor						
2							
3	SUMMARY						
4	*Groups*	*Count*	*Sum*	*Average*	*Variance*		
5	Current	30	8688	289.6	2061.145		
6	Process A	30	8565	285.5	4217.638		
7	Process B	30	8953	298.4333	435.3575		
8							
9							
10	ANOVA						
11	*Source of Variation*	*SS*	*df*	*MS*	*F*	*P-value*	*F crit*
12	Between Groups	2621.089	2	1310.544	0.585575	0.558965	3.101292
13	Within Groups	194710.1	87	2238.047			
14							
15	Total	197331.2	89				

Excel Note: Using the ANOVA Analysis Tool

To use ANOVA to test for difference in sample means, select the *Tools* menu, then *Data Analysis,* and then *Anova: Single Factor*. This displays the dialog box shown in Figure 4.21. You need only specify the input range of the data, and whether it is stored in rows or columns (that is, whether each factor level or group is a row or column in the range). You must also specify the level of significance (*Alpha*) and the output options. The tool computes the sums of squares, mean squares, *F* statistic, critical value, and *p*-value.

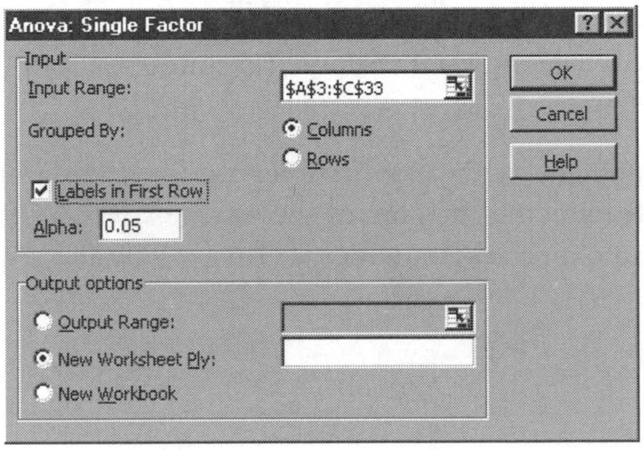

FIGURE 4.21 Excel Dialog Box for Single-Factor ANOVA Test

p-value of α reported by Excel is 0.559, which leads us to the same conclusion. This means that we cannot conclude that the three means are significantly different. This supports the decision to keep the current system for producing tractor transmissions. Even though Alternative A appears to improve costs over the current system, we have insufficient evidence to ensure that the population of Alternative A costs was superior to the population of current system costs.

Chi-Square Test for Independence

A common problem is to determine whether two categorical variables are independent; that is, they exhibit no relationship between them. For example, a consumer study might collect data on preferences of three different soft drinks for both male and female high school students. The objective of the study might be to determine if soft drink preferences are independent of gender. Independence would mean that the preferences would be essentially the same no matter if the individual is male or female. On the other hand, if males have different preferences than females, the variables would be dependent. As another example, a company such as Tracway collects categorical data on its customer satisfaction survey each month. The company might like to determine if category responses are independent of time.

Such situations can be analyzed using a contingency table and the chi-square test for independence. A **contingency table** is a matrix of *r* rows and *c* columns that shows the value of two categorical variables together. As an example, Tracway surveyed its managerial employees who were initially hired 10 years ago. These data are given on the worksheet *Employee Success* in the Tracway database. This survey included the time these 40 people stayed with Tracway, as well as their GPA from college. A contingency table for these data is given in Table 4.6. GPAs are classified as either 3.0 or higher or

TABLE 4.6   Contingency Table for Chi-Square Test

	≤ *4 Years*	*4–7 Years*	*Over 7 Years*
GPA 3.0 or higher	7	4	5
GPA under 3.0	7	8	9

below 3.0, and the career time with Tracway is divided into three categories. Each cell in the table shows the number of managers that fall into each combination of categories. A hypothesis to test might be that the length of time a management employee stayed with Tracway is independent of their college GPA. The hypotheses can be expressed as

H_0: the two categorical variables are independent

H_1: the two categorical variables are dependent

We can use the frequencies in the contingency table to compute a test statistic, called a **chi-square statistic,** which is the sum of the squares of the differences between observed frequency, f_0, and expected frequency, f_e, divided by the expected frequency in each cell:

$$\chi^2 = \sum \frac{(f_o - f_e)^2}{f_e}$$

The expected frequency is what would be expected if the null hypothesis is true. For example, of 40 observations, 16, or 40 percent, had GPAs of 3.0 or higher. If GPA and length of time with Tracway are indeed independent, we would expect that 40 percent of the total number of observations within each category would also have GPAs of 3.0 or higher. Thus the expected number in the first cell of the first column would be $14(.4) = 5.6$. The closer the actual counts are to the expected counts, the smaller will be the value of the chi-square statistic. We compare this statistic for a specified level of significance α to the critical value from a chi-square distribution with $(r-1)(c-1)$ degrees of freedom. If the test statistic exceeds the critical value, we reject H_0. For this example, we will choose $\alpha = .05$. The calculations are shown in Table 4.7, and the chi-

TABLE 4.7   Chi-Square Calculation For Tracway Tenure vs. GPA

Actual	≤ *4 Years*	*4–7 Years*	*7 or More Years*	
GPA ≥ 3.0	7	4	5	
GPA < 3.0	7	8	9	
Expected				
GPA ≥ 3.0	5.6	4.8	5.6	
GPA < 3.0	8.4	7.2	8.4	
Difference Squared				
GPA ≥ 3.0	1.96	0.64	0.36	
GPA < 3.0	1.96	0.64	0.36	
Difference Squared/Expected				
GPA ≥ 3.0	0.35	0.133	0.064	Total
GPA < 3.0	0.233	0.089	0.043	0.913

square statistic is computed as 0.913. We could find the critical value in a table, or use the chi-square tool in the *PHStat* add-in (see *PHStat Note: Chi-Square Test for Independence*). Figure 4.22 shows the results of the *PHStat* tool. Because the chi-square statistic is smaller than the critical value of 5.99, we cannot reject the null hypothesis.

We may also use p-values to draw our conclusion. The number of degrees of freedom is $(c-1)(r-1) = (3-1)(2-1) = 2$. Using the Excel function CHIDIST(*statistic, degrees_freedom*) with "statistic" = 0.913 and 2 degrees of freedom, we obtain a probability of 0.633. (This value is also computed by the *PHStat* tool as shown in Figure 4.22.) Because this exceeds the level of significance of 0.05, we cannot reject the null hypothesis. Excel also includes the function CHITEST(*actual_range,expected_range*), which will return the probability of a Type I error. In this example, entering the actual range (observed values) and expected range (expected values) from the spreadsheet, Excel returns a probability of 0.633, the same as before.

Summary

This chapter discussed statistical sampling, statistical estimation, hypothesis testing, and (in the appendix) distribution fitting. Accurate, unbiased measurement is necessary for valid statistical inferences. Sampling theory helps the process of gathering good data. Generally, samples should be gathered in such a way that every target population member has an equal chance of selection, although other types of sampling are often necessary. Because of sampling error, point estimates alone generally are not sufficient. Thus confidence intervals provide a means of quantifying the sampling error in the estimate. As sample sizes increase, confidence intervals decrease, providing more accurate estimates.

Hypothesis testing is the process of drawing inferences about population parameters. The approach involves formulating an appropriate hypothesis, selecting a level of significance, determining a decision rule, collecting data, calculating a test statistic, and applying the decision rule to the test statistic to draw a conclusion. Many different types

FIGURE 4.22 *PHStat* Results for Chi-Square Test

	A	B	C	D	E	F	G
1	**Chi-Square Test**						
2							
3	**Observed Frequencies:**				**Column variable**		
4			**Row variable**	**<=4 years**	**4-7 years**	**> 7 years**	**Total**
5			**GPA >= 3.0**	7	4	5	16
6			**GPA < 3.0**	7	8	9	24
7			**Total**	14	12	14	40
8							
9	**Expected Frequencies:**				**Column variable**		
10			**Row variable**	**<=4 years**	**4-7 years**	**> 7 years**	**Total**
11			**GPA >= 3.0**	5.6	4.8	5.6	16
12			**GPA < 3.0**	8.4	7.2	8.4	24
13			**Total**	14	12	14	40
14							
15							
16	**Level of Significance**	**0.05**					
17	Number of Rows	2					
18	Number of Columns	3					
19	Degrees of Freedom	2					
20	**Critical Value**	**5.991476**					
21	**Chi-Square Test Statistic**	**0.912698**					
22	***p*-Value**	**0.633593**					
23	**Do not reject the null hypothesis**						

PHStat Note: Chi-Square Test for Independence

From the *PHStat* menu, select *Chi-Square Test.* In the dialog box shown in Figure 4.23, enter the significance level and the number of rows and columns in the contingency table. *PHStat* then creates a worksheet, shown in Figure 4.24, in which you need to enter the values for the contingency table in the Observed Frequencies section. You may also replace the row and column headings (R1, R2, C1, etc.) with the labels for your specific problem. After you complete the table, the calculations are performed automatically.

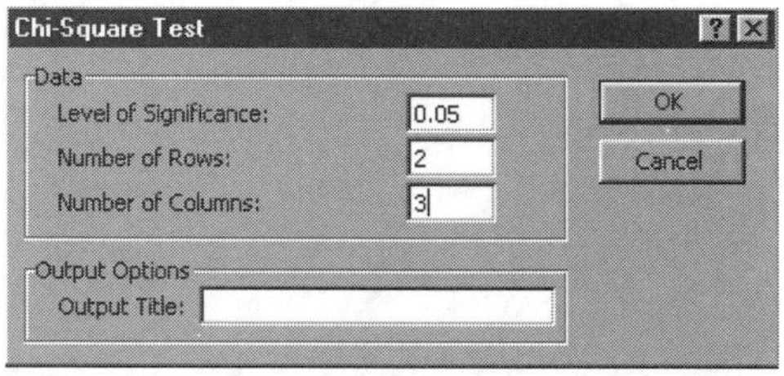

FIGURE 4.23 *PHStat* Dialog Box for Chi-Square Test

	A	B	C	D	E	F	G
1	**Chi-Square Test**						
2							
3	**Observed Frequencies:**				**Column variable**		
4			**Row variable**	**C1**	**C2**	**C3**	**Total**
5			**R1**				0
6			**R2**				0
7			**Total**	0	0	0	0
8							
9	**Expected Frequencies:**				**Column variable**		
10			**Row variable**	**C1**	**C2**	**C3**	**Total**
11			**R1**	#DIV/0!	#DIV/0!	#DIV/0!	#DIV/0!
12			**R2**	#DIV/0!	#DIV/0!	#DIV/0!	#DIV/0!
13			**Total**	#DIV/0!	#DIV/0!	#DIV/0!	#DIV/0!
14	#DIV/0!						
15							
16	**Level of Significance**	**0.05**					
17	Number of Rows	-0.5					
18	Number of Columns	0					
19	Degrees of Freedom	1.5					
20	**Critical Value**	**3.841455**					
21	**Chi-Square Test Statistic**	**#DIV/0!**					
22	***p*-Value**	**#DIV/0!**					
23	**#DIV/0!**						

FIGURE 4.24 *PHStat* Worksheet for Chi-Square Test

of hypothesis tests were discussed, including tests for means, proportions, and independence, as well as extensions to analysis of variance and distribution fitting. Thus hypothesis testing can be used for a wide variety of applications.

Each of the tests requires assumptions. The *t*-tests, ANOVA, and *F*-tests require that the data being analyzed be normally distributed. If this assumption is not appropriate, nonparametric techniques often provide a useful alternative to draw statistical inferences. Conover (1980) is an excellent reference for nonparametric testing.

Questions and Problems

1. Define a sampling plan. What is the purpose of using a sampling plan?
2. Describe an ideal population frame.
3. Explain the common types of subjective sampling methods, and identify their distinguishing characteristic.
4. Describe the key characteristics of random sampling.
5. What issues of bias might one need to consider when using systematic or stratified sampling?
6. The *Tractor Prep* worksheet in the Tracway database includes 570 costs of preparing tractors for sale. Generate 50 samples using random sampling from this set. Compare the mean and variance of this sample with that of 50 periodic samples with a period of 10.
7. The *Cross-Sectional Survey* worksheet in the Tracway database provides 200 observations on four variables (ratings on quality, ease, price, and service). Generate 30 random samples from each column, and compare the mean for each rating with the average of each column from the worksheet *Survey Recap*. What might explain any systematic difference?
8. The worksheet *Stock* in the Tracway database provides 126 observations ranging from June 30, 2000, through December 29, 2000, for S&P (column B), Tracway stock (column C), percent change in S&P (column D), and percent change in Tracway stock (column E). Take a periodic sample with period 4 from column C, Tracway stock. Calculate the mean and variance of these 32 observations. Take a random sample of 32 observations, and calculate the mean and variance. Compare the two different sample means and variances.
9. Compare nonsampling error with sampling error.
10. If a random sample of 600 is taken from a population of 1,000 members, and a mean of 36.0 with a standard deviation of 10.0 is obtained, what is the standard error of the mean?
11. The worksheet *Employee Success* in the Tracway database provides 40 samples of Tracway employees on a number of variables. Develop 90 percent confidence intervals for the mean time with the company for those with college GPAs greater than or equal to 3.0 and those with GPAs less than 3.0, and compare.
12. Using the *Employee Success* worksheet in the Tracway database, develop 90 percent confidence intervals for female and male employees and compare.
13. Using the *Employee Success* worksheet in the Tracway database, develop 90 percent confidence intervals for employees without college degrees and employees with college degrees, and compare.
14. Using the *Employee Success* worksheet in the Tracway database, develop 90 percent confidence intervals for employees from the local area and employees from outside the local area, and compare.
15. If there are 24 observations in a sample (the number of observations with GPA below 3 in problem 11), and the *t*-distribution is used, how many degrees of freedom are there?
16. Construct the 80, 90, and 95 percent confidence intervals for a company's market share, given an average market share of 0.2 based on 50 samples.
17. If, based on 500 samples, a political candidate finds that 245 people would vote for him in a two-person race, what is the 90 percent confidence interval for his expected proportion of the vote?
18. If, based on 100 samples, a political candidate found that 39 people would vote for her in a two-person race, what is the 95 percent confidence interval for her expected proportion of the vote?

19. A political pollster wants to be 98 percent sure of the outcome of a local election, where preliminary sampling indicates that the mean vote for the supported candidate is 0.51. How many samples are needed to attain this confidence level?

20. A political pollster wants to be 90 percent sure of the outcome of a local election, where preliminary sampling indicates that the mean vote for the supported candidate is 0.55. Estimate the required sample size to reach a conclusion at this level of confidence.

21. Trade associations such as the United Dairy Farmers Association frequently conduct surveys to identify characteristics of their membership.[1] If this organization conducted a survey to estimate the annual per-capita consumption of milk, and wanted to be 95 percent confident that the estimate was no more than 0.5 gallons away from the actual average, what sample size is needed? Past data has indicated that the standard deviation is approximately four gallons.

22. A manufacturer conducted a survey among 400 randomly selected target market households in the test market for its new disposable diapers.[2] The objective of the survey was to determine the trial rate for its new brand. If the sample trial rate was 20 percent, what would the 95 percent confidence limits be?

23. If a manufacturer conducted a survey from 400 randomly selected target market households, and wanted to be 95 percent confident that the difference between the sample estimate and the actual trial rate for their new product was no more than 4 percent, what sample size would be needed? (Assume the proportion obtained was 0.5, which would be the worst case.)[3]

24. Discuss the different forms of hypotheses that one may test. How should the null hypothesis be stated relative to the alternative hypothesis?

25. Test the hypothesis that the Tracway cost of tractor preparation is less than $100 per tractor using the sample data on the worksheet *Tractor Prep* in the Tracway database. Then test the hypothesis that preparation cost per tractor is less than $130 per tractor at the 5 percent alpha limit.

26. Test the hypothesis that Tracway management employees with college degrees will stay with Tracway at least three years after hire, based upon the sample data on the worksheet *Employee Success* in the Tracway database. Use an alpha level of 5 percent.

27. The worksheet *Employee Success* in the Tracway database provides 40 samples of Tracway employees on a number of variables. Test the hypothesis that those with GPAs greater than or equal to 3.0 stay with Tracway longer than those with GPAs below 3.0 at a confidence level of 90 percent.

28. Using data on the worksheet *Employee Success* in the Tracway database, test the hypothesis that there is no difference between the time male and female managers stay with Tracway at the 95 percent level of confidence.

29. Using the data on the worksheet *Employee Success* in the Tracway database, test the hypothesis that employees from the local area stay with Tracway longer than employees from outside the local area, testing at the 90 percent level of confidence.

30. Discuss Type I and Type II errors in the context of the hypotheses tested in problem 30.

31. The worksheet *Blood Pressure* in the Tracway database provides data on the blood pressure of North American regional managers and other regional managers. Test for difference in variance of these two sets using a confidence level of 0.05 for alpha. The hypothesis is that variance 1 = variance 2.

32. The worksheet *Employee Success* in the Tracway database provides 40 samples of Tracway employees on a number of variables. Use ANOVA to test the hypothesis

[1] Adapted from Crask, Fox, and Stout, *Marketing Research: Principles & Applications* (Prentice Hall, 1995), 240.
[2] Ibid., 241.
[3] Ibid.

that those with GPAs greater than or equal to 3.0 stay with Tracway longer than those with GPAs below 3.0 with an alpha level of 0.05.
33. Using the data on the worksheet *Employee Success* in the Tracway database, use ANOVA to test for differences in the average time that employees from the local area stay with Tracway compared with employees from outside the local area, testing at an alpha of 0.1.
34. Use the *PHStat* chi-square test to determine if the time with Tracway is independent of gender.

The following problems depend on the material in the appendix to this chapter.
35. Use *Crystal Ball* to test for the best distribution fit for the costs of each of the three systems (current, A, and B) to produce transmissions on the worksheet *Transmission Costs* in the Tracway database. Use the chi-square option, and identify the three distributions *Crystal Ball* identifies as having the best fit.
36. Use *Crystal Ball* to test for the best distribution fit for the time to produce a mower engine (worksheet *Engines* in the Tracway database).

Appendix: Distribution Fitting

In many decision models, empirical data may be available, either in historical records or collected through special efforts. For example, maintenance records might provide data on machine failure rates and repair times, or observers might collect data on service times in a bank or post office. Consider, for example, the sample data in Table 4A.1. We might take these data and create an empirical distribution by developing a histogram as shown in Figure 4A.1. If these data represent an important variable in a decision model, we might wish to attempt to fit a theoretical distribution to the data to verify goodness-of-fit statistically. We would then use this theoretical distribution in our model analysis.

To select an appropriate theoretical distribution, we might begin by examining a histogram of the data to look for the distinctive shapes of particular distributions. This is why we studied different distributions in chapter 3. For example, normal data is symmetric, with a peak in the middle. Exponential data is very positively skewed, with no negative values. Various forms of the gamma, Weibull, or beta distributions could be used for distributions that do not seem to fit one of the other common forms. This approach is not, of course, always accurate or valid, and sometimes it can be difficult to apply, especially if sample sizes are small. However, it may narrow the search to a few potential distributions.

The histogram in Figure 4A.1 does not provide much insight into the nature of the distribution. It clearly does not appear to be exponential. We might suspect uniform; however, the distribution does appear to be somewhat clustered toward the center,

TABLE 4A.1	A Sample of 30 Observations	
5.076808	5.050842	6.398492
4.895876	5.300643	4.615494
6.778780	6.236305	6.091197
6.909572	6.829625	6.121048
6.474918	4.524959	4.927547
7.607923	4.913438	6.651687
6.699065	4.965261	5.968593
6.019929	5.505035	4.147587
5.249301	5.170052	5.468820
4.653011	4.132489	6.241657

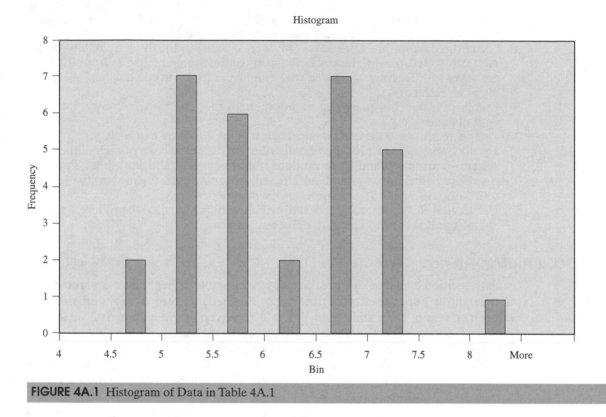

FIGURE 4A.1 Histogram of Data in Table 4A.1

suggesting that a normal distribution might be more appropriate. We can easily be fooled by the variation that arises from small sample sizes. Thus we should gather more information.

Summary statistics can provide additional clues about the nature of a distribution. The mean, median, standard deviation, and coefficient of variation (the standard deviation divided by the mean) often provide clues about the nature of the distribution. For example, normally distributed data tend to have a fairly low coefficient of variation; however, this may not be true if the mean is small. For normally distributed data, we would also expect the median and mean to be approximately the same. For exponentially distributed data, however, the median will be less than the mean. Also, we would expect the mean to be about equal to the standard deviation. We could also look at the skewness index. Normal data is not skewed, whereas lognormal and exponential data are positively skewed.

Table 4A.2 shows some summary statistics for the sample data. The coefficient of variation, 0.161, is rather low. The skewness index, 0.173, likewise is quite low, indicating that the distribution is basically symmetric. The mean and median are very close. All this suggests that the sample might have been drawn from a normal distribution, despite the fact that the histogram does not look very "normal" (perhaps due to such a small sample size).

A visual way to attempt to verify whether a set of data fits a particular distribution is to construct a *probability plot*. A probability plot transforms the cumulative probability scale (vertical axis) so that the graph of the cumulative distribution will be a straight line. This is illustrated in Figure 4A.2 for a standard normal distribution. A probability plot allows us to check the validity of the assumed distribution. The closer the points are to a straight line, the better the fit to the assumed distribution. A normal prob-

TABLE 4A.2	Summary Statistics for Sample Data in Table 4A.1
mean	5.65420
median	5.48693
minimum	4.13249
maximum	7.60792
standard deviation	0.91019
coeff of variation	0.16098
skewness index	0.17339

ability plot of the sample data in Table 4A.1 generated by *PHStat* (see *PHStat Note: Normal Probability Plot*) is shown in Figure 4A.3. Although the data appear to follow a relatively straight line, there is some systematic nonlinearity to the data, suggesting that a normal distribution may not fit very well.

The examination of histograms and summary statistics might provide some hypotheses; however, these should be verified in a more formal manner. *Goodness-of-fit tests* provide statistical evidence to test hypotheses about the *nature* of the distribution. The most commonly used goodness-of-fit test is the chi-square (χ^2) test. The chi-square goodness-of-fit tests test the hypothesis

H_0: the sample data come from a specified distribution (e.g. normal)

against the alternative hypothesis

H_1: the sample data do not come from the specified distribution

With this test you can disprove the fit of a particular distribution, but cannot statistically *prove* that data come from the distribution. The hypothesized distribution is partitioned

FIGURE 4A.2 Constructing a Normal Probability Plot Scale

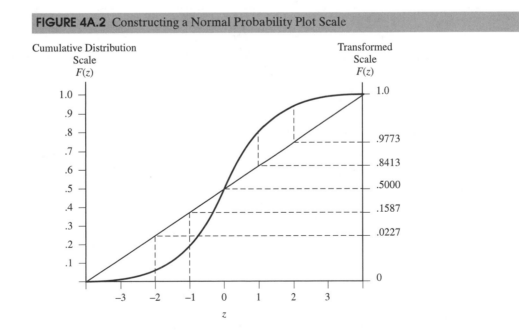

Normal Probability Plot

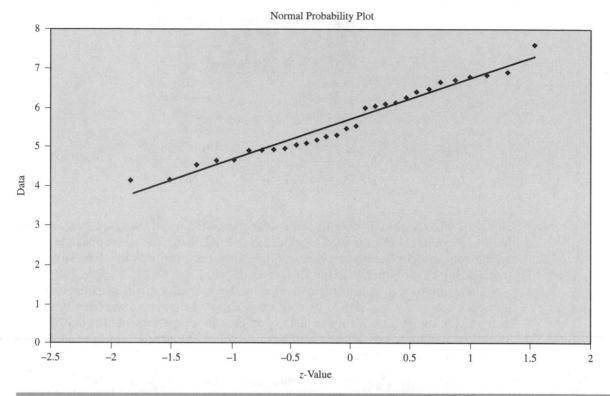

FIGURE 4A.3 Normal Probability Plot from *PHStat*
(Note: The straight line was added by clicking on one of the points to select the data series and then clicking the right mouse button. Select *Add Trendline* to fit a straight line to the data. This will be discussed further in the next chapter.)

PHStat Note: Normal Probability Plot

From the *PHStat* menu, select *Probability Distributions* and then *Normal Probability Plot*. In the dialog box, you need to specify the range of the data. The tool creates the plot on a new worksheet as well as an additional worksheet with the calculations used to construct the chart.

---

into cells like a frequency distribution, and we need to compute the expected number of observations that would fall into each cell, if indeed the null hypothesis is true. The test statistic is computed in the same way as in the test for independence in contingency tables, by summing the squares of the differences between the observed and expected frequencies divided by the expected frequency. Finding the expected frequencies often requires some advanced knowledge of working with probability distributions, so we will not show the detailed calculations, especially because these can be performed within *Crystal Ball*. Other tests are available, such as the Kolmogorov-Smirnov test and the Anderson-Darling test, which is similar to the Kolmogorov-Smirnov test except that it places more weight on the tail observations. The *Crystal Ball* Help option provides some technical details of these tests.

DISTRIBUTION FITTING WITH *CRYSTAL BALL*

Crystal Ball provides a very useful and powerful data-fitting capability. We will illustrate this capability using the data given in Table 4A.1. Figure 4A.4 shows the Excel screen after *Crystal Ball* has been loaded. Two new menu items appear on the main menu bar: *Cell* and *Run*. (The third line of buttons also provide shortcuts to invoke *Crystal Ball* menu commands.)

To invoke the distribution fitting capability, select *Cell* from the main menu, and then select *Define Assumption. . . .* The *Crystal Ball* distribution gallery (Figure 3A.2 in the appendix to chapter 3) is displayed. Click *Fit*. The first of two dialog boxes, shown in Figure 4A.5, is displayed. If the data are in the front-most spreadsheet, select *Active Worksheet* (*Crystal Ball* also allows fitting data from a separate text file), and enter the range of the data in the box to the right. Clicking *Next* displays the second dialog box, shown in Figure 4A.6. You may select all continuous distributions in the distribution gallery[4], any subset, or just the normal distribution. You must also select the type of test; in this example, we selected the Kolmogorov-Smirnov test. Check the box *Show Comparison Chart and Goodness-of-Fit Statistics* to display comparative results.

Crystal Ball then fits each of the continuous distributions available in the distribution gallery to the data set. It rank orders them by the Kolmogorov-Smirnov test score. The best-fitting distribution is then displayed in a Comparison Chart window with distribution parameters and goodness-of-fit scores, as shown in Figure 4A.7. You may select the *Prefs* button to customize the chart display type; in Figure 4A.7 we used a cumulative distribution instead of the frequency distribution because of the small sample size. A Kolmogorov-Smirnov value of less than 0.03 indicates a close fit. Since the value is 0.1091, the fit is not particularly good. By clicking the *Next Distribution*

FIGURE 4A.4 Excel Screen with *Crystal Ball* Add-in

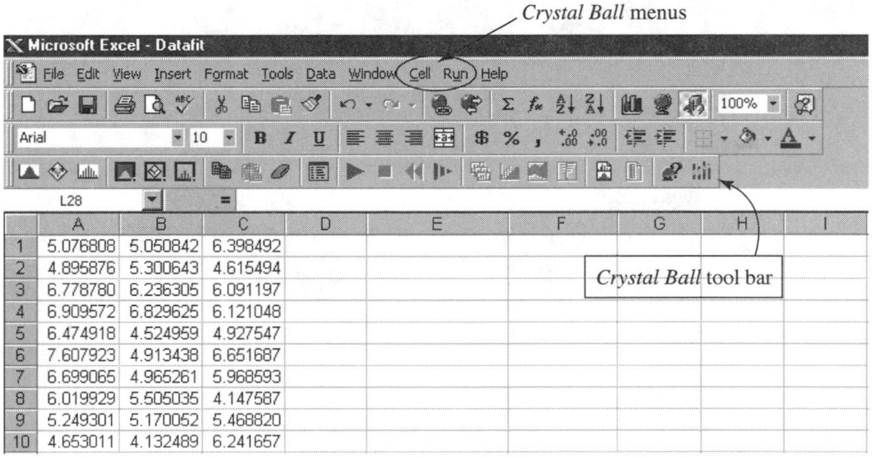

---

[4] The student version of *Crystal Ball* has a limited number of available distributions.

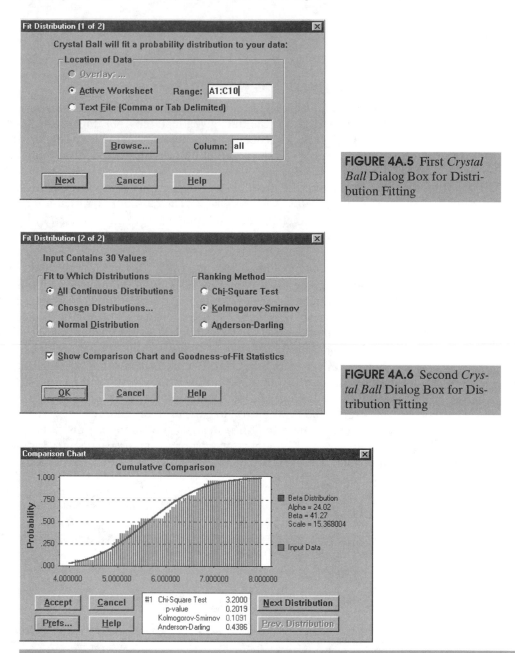

FIGURE 4A.5 First *Crystal Ball* Dialog Box for Distribution Fitting

FIGURE 4A.6 Second *Crystal Ball* Dialog Box for Distribution Fitting

FIGURE 4A.7 Cumulative Distribution Comparison Chart

button, the comparison charts for other distributions can be displayed. Table 4A.3 summarizes the results.

What may be surprising is that the data set in Table 4A.1 was actually generated in Excel *from a normal distribution* with a mean of 6 and a standard deviation of 1! With small sample sizes, it may be difficult to obtain a good fit because of sampling error as this example shows. Thus for practical decision models, it is important to try to obtain a large, representative, sample of data.

TABLE 4A.3 Summary of Distribution Fitting Results					
Distribution	*Parameter Values*	χ^2	*p*	*K - S*	*A - D*
Beta	$\alpha = 24.02, \beta = 41.27$, scale $= 15.37$	3.20	.2019	.1091	.4386
Logistic	mean $= 5.64$, scale $= 0.54$	6.80	.0786	.1165	.5565
Triangular	min $= 3.79$, mode $= 4.93$, max $= 8.23$	2.80	.2466	.1173	.3183
Normal	mean $= 5.65$, std $= 0.91$	4.80	.1870	.1178	.4720
Weibull	loc $= 3.68$, scale $= 2.22$, shape $= 2.29$	5.20	.0743	.1215	.3836
Lognormal	mean $= 5.65$, std $= 0.91$	5.20	.1577	.1289	.4749
Gamma	loc $= 2.48$, scale $= .26$, shape $= 12.08$	5.20	.0743	.1327	.4622
Extreme value	mode $= 5.22$, scale $= 0.79$	7.20	.0658	.1462	.4799
Uniform	min $= 4.01$, max $= 7.73$	9.20	.0267	.1863	1.2744
Pareto	loc $= 4.09$, shape $= 3.21$	20.00	.0002	.2723	2.8450
Exponential	rate $= 0.17$	85.60	.0000	.5066	9.4629

References

Davis, D. and Cosenza, R. M., *Business Research for Decision Making*, Boston: Kent Publishing Company, 1985.

Conover, W. J., *Practical Nonparametric Statistics*, 2nd ed., New York: John Wiley and Sons, 1980.

Harnett, D. L. and Horrell, J. F., *Data, Statistics, and Decision Models with Excel,* New York: John Wiley & Sons, Inc., 1998.

Levine, David M., Berenson, Mark L., and Stephan, David, *Statistics for Managers Using Microsoft Excel,* Upper Saddle River, NJ: Prentice Hall, 1999.

Stevens, S. S., "On the theory of scales of measurement," *Science,* 103, June 7, 1946, 677–680.

5

Statistical Quality Control

Outline

The Role of Statistics and Data Analysis in Quality Control
Statistical Process Control
    Control Charts
    $\bar{x}$- and R-charts
    Analyzing Control Charts
Control Charts for Attributes
Statistical Issues in the Design of Control Charts
Process Capability Analysis
Summary
Questions and Problems

An important application of statistics and data analysis in both manufacturing and service operations is in the area of *quality control*. Quality control methods help employees monitor production operations to ensure that output conforms to specifications. This is important in manufactured goods because product performance depends on achieving design tolerances. It is also vital to service operations to ensure that customers receive error-free, consistent service.

Why is quality control necessary? The principal reason is that no two outputs from any production process are exactly alike. If you measure any quality characteristic—such as the diameters of machined parts, the amount of liquid in a bottle, or the number of errors in processing orders at a distribution center—you will discover some variation. Variation is the result of many small differences in those factors that comprise a process: people, machines, materials, methods, and measurement systems. Taken together, they are called **common causes of variation.**

Other causes of variation occur sporadically, and can be identified and either eliminated or at least explained. For example, when a tool wears down, it can be replaced; when a machine falls out of adjustment, it can be reset; or when a bad lot of material is discovered, it can be returned to the supplier. Such examples are called **special causes of variation.** Special causes of variation cause the distribution of process output to change over time. Using statistical tools, we can identify when they occur and take appropriate action, thus preventing unnecessary quality problems. Equally important is knowing when to leave the process alone and not react to common causes over which we have no control.

In this chapter we introduce basic ideas of *statistical process control* and *process capability analysis*—two important tools in helping to achieve quality. The key concepts that we will describe are

- the statistical basis and the application of control charts for monitoring both attributes and variables data,
- rules for determining when data signal the need for change, and
- the use of statistics for measuring the capability of a process to meet specifications.

The applications of statistics to quality control are far more extensive than we can present; additional information may be found in the material in the references section.

The Role of Statistics and Data Analysis in Quality Control

We can learn a lot about the common causes of variation in a process and their effect on quality by studying process output. For example, suppose that Tracway manufactures an important machined bearing for its engines. Key questions to ask might include: What is the average dimension? How much variability occurs in the output of the process? What does the distribution look like? What proportion of product that does not conform to design specifications can we expect to produce? These are fundamental questions that can be addressed with statistics.

The role of statistics is to provide tools to analyze data collected from a process, and to enable employees to make informed decisions when the process needs short-term corrective action or long-term improvements. Statistical methods have been used for quality control since the 1920s when they were pioneered at Western Electric Company. They became a mainstay of Japanese manufacturing in the early 1950s; however, they did not become widely used in the United States until the quality management movement of the 1980s, led by pioneers such as W. Edwards Deming and Joseph M. Juran, both of whom were instrumental in the adoption of these methods in Japan. Since then, statistical quality control has been shown to be a proven means of improving customer satisfaction and reducing costs in many industries.

To illustrate the applications of statistics to quality control, we will use three worksheets from the Tracway database: *Blade Weight,* which provides sample data from a manufacturing process; *Mower Test,* which gives samples of functional performance test results; and *Process Capability,* which contains additional sample data of mower blade weights. Portions of these worksheets are illustrated in Figure 5.1 for your reference.

FIGURE 5.1 Portions of Worksheets in the Tracway Database Used in This Chapter

	A	B	C	D	E	F	G	H	I
1	Blade Weight								
2									
3	Sample			Observations				Sample mean	Sample range
4	1	4.88	4.75	4.97	4.93	5.05		4.916	0.30
5	2	4.92	4.99	5.06	4.88	4.97		4.964	0.18
6	3	5.02	5.00	5.06	4.88	4.96		4.984	0.18
7	4	4.97	4.91	5.04	4.81	4.96		4.938	0.23
8	5	5.00	5.18	4.87	5.16	4.99		5.040	0.31
9	6	4.99	4.95	5.00	5.03	5.04		5.002	0.09
10	7	4.86	4.63	5.03	4.87	4.91		4.860	0.40

	A	B	C	D	E	F	G
1	Mower Test						
2							
3	Sample						
4	1	2	3	4	5	6	7
5	Pass	Fail	Pass	Pass	Pass	Pass	Pass
6	Pass	Fail	Pass	Pass	Pass	Pass	Pass
7	Pass	Pass	Pass	Pass	Pass	Pass	Pass
8	Pass	Pass	Pass	Pass	Pass	Pass	Pass
9	Pass	Pass	Pass	Pass	Pass	Pass	Pass
10	Pass	Pass	Pass	Pass	Pass	Pass	Pass

	A	B	C
1	Process Capability		
2			
3	5.21		
4	5.02		
5	4.9		
6	5		
7	5.16		
8	5.03		
9	4.96		
10	5.04		

FIGURE 5.1 (*continued*)

Statistical Process Control

In chapter 1 we defined two types of data: attributes and variables. Data that come from counting are called *attributes data.* Examples of attributes data are the number of defective pieces in a shipment of components, the number of errors on an invoice, and the percentage of customers rating service a 6 or 7 on a 7-point satisfaction scale. Data that come from measurements along a continuous scale are called *variables data.* Examples of variables data are the inside diameter of a drilled hole, the weight of a carton, and the time between order and delivery. This distinction is important because different statistical process control tools must be used for each type of data.

When a process operates under ideal conditions, variation in the distribution of output is due to common causes. When only common causes are present, the process is said to be **in control.** A controlled process is stable and predictable to the extent that we can predict the likelihood that future output will fall within some range once we know the probability distribution of outcomes. Special causes, however, cause the distribution to change. The change may be a shift in the mean, an increase or decrease in the variance, or a change in shape. Clearly, if we cannot predict how the distribution may change, then we cannot compute the probability that future output will fall within some range. When special causes are present, the process is said to be **out of control** and needs to be corrected to bring it back to a stable state. **Statistical process control (SPC)** provides a means of identifying special causes as well as telling us when the process is in control and should be left alone. Control charts were first used by Dr. Walter Shewhart at Bell Laboratories in the 1920s (they are sometimes called Shewhart charts). Dr. Shewhart was the first person to make a distinction between common causes of variation and special causes of variation.

SPC consists of the following:

1. Selecting a sample of observations from a production or service process;
2. Measuring one or more quality characteristics;
3. Recording the data;
4. Making a few calculations;

5. Plotting key statistics on a *control chart;*
6. Examining the chart to determine if any unusual patterns, called **out-of-control conditions,** can be identified; and
7. Determining the cause of out-of-control conditions and taking corrective action.

When data are collected, it is important to clearly record the data, the time the data were collected, the measuring instruments that were used, who collected the data, and any other important information such as lot numbers, machine numbers, and the like. By having a record of such information, we can trace the source of quality problems more easily.

CONTROL CHARTS

A **run chart** is a line chart in which the independent variable is time and the dependent variable is the value of some sample statistic, such as the mean, range, or proportion. A **control chart** is a run chart that has two additional horizontal lines, called control limits, as illustrated in Figure 5.2. Control limits are chosen statistically so that there is a high probability (usually greater than 0.99) that sample statistics will fall randomly within the limits *if the process is in control.*

To understand the statistical basis for control charts, let us assume that we are dealing with a variables measurement that is normally distributed with a mean μ and standard deviation σ. If the process is stable, or in control, then each individual measurement will stem from this distribution. In high-volume production processes, it is generally difficult, if not impossible, to measure each individual output, so we take samples at periodic intervals. For samples of a fixed size, n, we know from chapter 3 that the sampling distribution will be normal with mean μ and standard deviation (standard error) $\sigma_{\bar{x}} = \sigma/\sqrt{n}$. We would expect that about 99.7 percent of sample means will lie within three standard errors of the mean, or between $\mu - 3\sigma_{\bar{x}}$ and $\mu + 3\sigma_{\bar{x}}$, provided the process remains in control. These values become the theoretical control limits for a control chart to monitor the centering of a process using the sample mean. Of course,

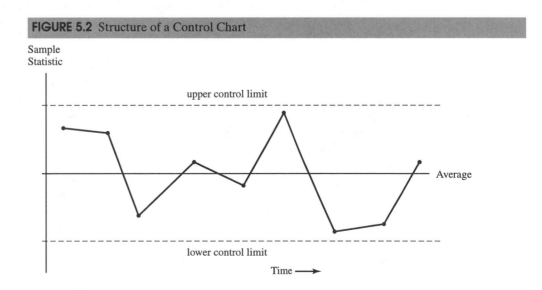

FIGURE 5.2 Structure of a Control Chart

we do not know the true population parameters, so we estimate them by the sample mean and sample standard deviation. Thus the actual control limits would be

$$\text{Lower control limit: } \bar{x} - 3s_{\bar{x}}$$
$$\text{Upper control limit: } \bar{x} + 3s_{\bar{x}}$$

In general, control limits are established as plus or minus three standard deviations from the mean of the sampling distribution of the statistic we plot on the chart. Statisticians have devised various formulas for computing these limits in a practical manner that is easy for shop floor workers to understand and use. However, the theory is based on understanding the sampling distribution of the statistic we measure.

There are many different types of control charts. We will introduce two types of control charts in this chapter: $\bar{x}$- and R-charts for variables data, and p-charts for attributes data. Discussions of other types of charts may be found in the publications in the references section.

$\bar{x}$- AND R-CHARTS

The $\bar{x}$-**chart** monitors the centering of process output for variables data over time by plotting the mean of each sample. In manufacturing, for example, the permissible variation in a dimension is usually stated by a **nominal specification** (target value) and some **tolerance,** for example, $0.025 \pm .003$. The nominal is 0.025 and the tolerance is $\pm .003$. The $\bar{x}$-chart is used to keep a process centered on the target. The R-**chart,** or range chart, monitors the variability in the data as measured by the range of each sample. Thus the R-chart monitors the uniformity or consistency of the process. The smaller the value of R, the more uniform is the process. Any increase in the average range is undesirable; this would mean that the variation is getting larger. However, decreases in variability signifies improvement. We could use the standard deviation of each sample instead of the range to provide a more accurate characterization of variability; however, for small samples (around 8 or less), little differences will be apparent. Also, if the calculations are done manually by a worker on the shop floor, R-charts are much easier to apply.

The basic procedure for constructing and using any control chart is to first gather at least 25–30 samples of data with a fixed sample size n from a production process, measure the quality characteristic of interest, and record the data. We will illustrate the construction of a control chart using the worksheet *Blade Weight* in the Tracway database. This worksheet shows 30 samples of mower blade weights from Tracway's manufacturing process. Each sample consists of five individual observations. In column H we calculate the mean of each sample, and in column I, the range. Once we have done this for each sample, we compute the average mean, $\bar{\bar{x}} = 4.992$, and the average range, $\overline{R} = .162$. Figures 5.3 and 5.4 show plots of the sample means and ranges. Although we observe variation in the data, we cannot yet determine whether this variation is due to some assignable cause or is simply due to chance.

The final step to complete the control charts is to compute control limits. As we explained earlier, control limits are boundaries within which the process is operating in statistical control. Control limits are based on past performance and tell us what values we can expect for $\bar{x}$ or R as long as the process remains stable. If a point falls outside the control limits or if some unusual pattern occurs, then we should be suspicious of a special cause. The upper control limit for the R-chart is given by the formula

$$\text{UCL}_R = D_4 \overline{R}$$

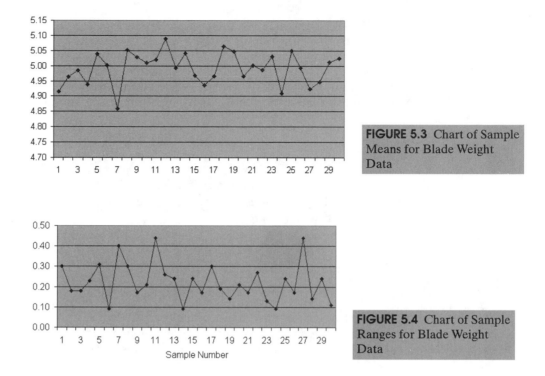

FIGURE 5.3 Chart of Sample Means for Blade Weight Data

FIGURE 5.4 Chart of Sample Ranges for Blade Weight Data

and the lower control limit for the *R*-chart is given by the formula

$$\text{LCL}_R = D_3 \overline{R}$$

D_3 and D_4 are constants that depend on the sample size and are found in Table 5.1. The theory is a bit complicated, but suffice it to say that these constants have been

TABLE 5.1	Control Chart Factors		
Sample size	A_2	D_3	D_4
2	1.880	0	3.267
3	1.023	0	2.574
4	.729	0	2.282
5	.577	0	2.114
6	.483	0	2.004
7	.419	.076	1.924
8	.373	.136	1.864
9	.337	.184	1.816
10	.308	.223	1.777
11	.285	.256	1.744
12	.266	.283	1.717
13	.249	.307	1.693
14	.235	.328	1.672
15	.223	.347	1.653

determined from the sampling distribution of R so that, for example, $D_4\overline{R} = \overline{R} + 3s_R$ as we had described earlier.

Since the sample size is five, $D_4 = 2.114$. Therefore, the upper control limit for the example is $2.114(0.162) = 0.342$. In this example, D_3 for a sample size of five is 0, so the lower control limit is 0. We then draw and label these control limits on the chart.

For the $\overline{x}$-chart, the control limits are given by the formulas

$$\mathrm{UCL}_{\overline{x}} = \overline{\overline{x}} + A_2\overline{R}$$
$$\mathrm{LCL}_{\overline{x}} = \overline{\overline{x}} - A_2\overline{R}$$

Again, the constant A_2 is determined so that $A_2\,\overline{R}$ is equivalent to three standard errors in the sampling distribution of the mean. For a sample size of five, $A_2 = 0.577$. Therefore, the control limits are

$$\mathrm{UCL}_{\overline{x}} = 4.992 + (.577)(.162) = 5.085$$
$$\mathrm{LCL}_{\overline{x}} = 4.992 - (.577)(.162) = 4.899$$

We could draw these control limits on the charts to complete the process. *PHStat* includes a routine for constructing $\overline{x}$- and R-charts (see *PHStat Note:* $\overline{x}$- *and* R-*charts*). The charts generated by this routine are shown in Figures 5.5 and 5.6. The next step is to analyzed the charts to determine the state of statistical control.

FIGURE 5.5 *PHStat R*-chart for Blade Weight Data

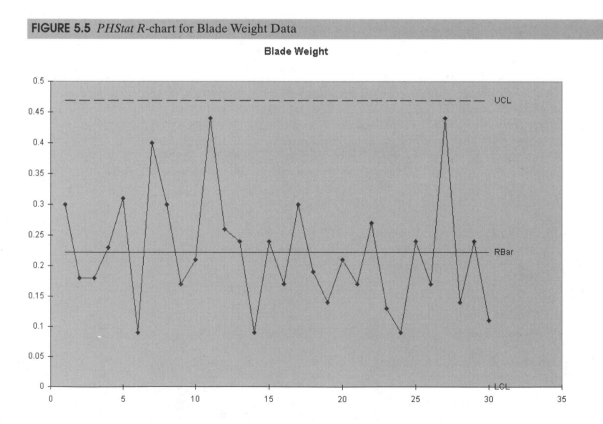

Blade Weight

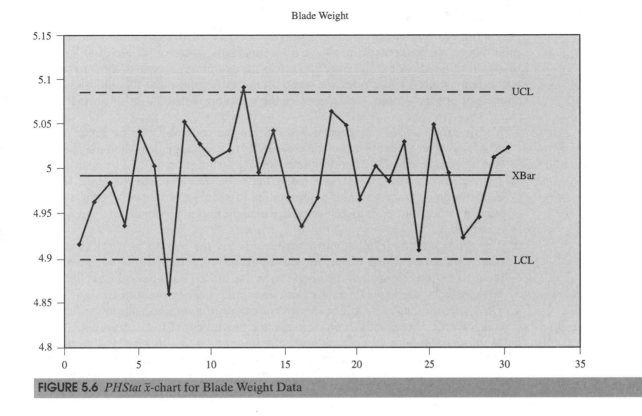

Blade Weight

FIGURE 5.6 *PHStat* $\bar{x}$-chart for Blade Weight Data

PHStat Note: $\bar{x}$- and *R*-charts

From the *PHStat* menu, select *Control Charts,* followed by *R and Xbar Charts*. The dialog box that appears is shown in Figure 5.7. Your worksheet must have already calculated the sample means and ranges. The cell ranges for these data are entered in the appropriate boxes. You must also provide the sample size in the Data section, and have the option of selecting only the *R*-chart or both the $\bar{x}$- and *R*-charts. *PHStat* will create several worksheets for calculations and the charts.

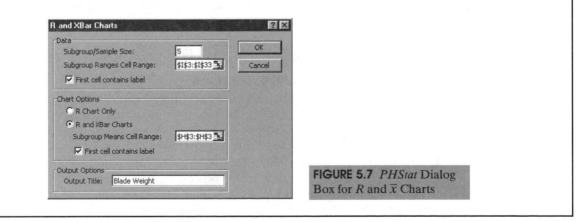

FIGURE 5.7 *PHStat* Dialog Box for *R* and $\bar{x}$ Charts

ANALYZING CONTROL CHARTS

When a process is in statistical control, the points on a control chart should fluctuate at random between the control limits, and no recognizable patterns should exist. The following checklist provides a set of general rules for examining a control chart to see if a process is in control. These rules are based on the assumption that the underlying distribution of process output—and therefore the sampling distribution—is normal.

1. *No points are outside the control limits.* Since the control limits are set at three standard errors from the mean, the probability of this happening when the process is in control is only 0.0027 under the normality assumption.
2. *The number of points above and below the center line is about the same.* If the distribution is symmetric, as is a normal distribution, we would expect this to occur. If the distribution is highly skewed, we might find a disproportionate amount on one side.
3. *The points seem to fall randomly above and below the center line.* If the distribution is stable, we would expect the same chances of getting a sample above the mean as below. However, if the distribution has shifted during the data collection process, we would expect a nonrandom distribution of sample statistics.
4. *There are no steady upward or downward trends of points moving toward either control limit.* These would indicate a gradual movement of the distribution.
5. *Most points, but not all, are near the center line; only a few are close to the control limits.* For a normal distribution, about 68 percent of observations fall within one standard deviation of the mean. If, for example, we see a high proportion of points near the limits, we might suspect that the data came from two distinct distributions (visualize an inverted normal distribution).

For the Tracway data, we see that $\bar{x}$-chart has two points outside the control limits. Thus we would probably conclude that these are due to some special cause. However, we should review the information to verify this; that is why it is important to keep good records of data, including the time at which each sample was taken and the process conditions at that time (who was running the process, where the material came from, etc.). Most of the time it is easy to identify a logical cause. A common reason for a point falling outside a control limit is an error in the calculation of the sample values of $\bar{x}$ or R. Other possible causes are a sudden power surge, a broken tool, a measurement error, or an incomplete or omitted operation in the process. Once in a while, however, these outlying points are a normal part of the process and occur simply by chance. When special causes are identified, these data should be deleted from the analysis, and new control limits should be computed.

The most common types of other out-of-control conditions are summarized next.

Sudden Shift in the Process Average

When an unusual number of consecutive points fall on one side of the center line (see Figure 5.8), it usually indicates that the process average has suddenly shifted. Typically, this is the result of an external influence that has affected the process; this would be a special cause. In both the $\bar{x}$- and R-charts, possible causes might be a new operator, a new inspector, a new machine setting, or a change in the setup or method.

In the R-chart, if the shift is up, the process has become less uniform. Typical causes are carelessness of operators, poor or inadequate maintenance, or possibly a fixture in need of repair. If the shift is down, uniformity of the process has improved. This might be the result of improved workmanship or better machines or materials.

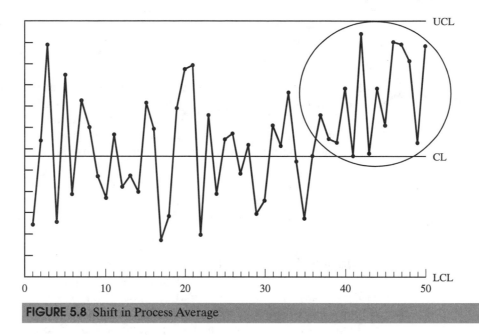

FIGURE 5.8 Shift in Process Average

Cycles

Cycles are short, repeated patterns in the chart, having alternate high peaks and low valleys (see Figure 5.9). These are the result of causes that come and go on a regular basis. In the $\bar{x}$-chart, cycles may be the result of operator rotation or fatigue at the end of a shift, different gauges used by different inspectors, seasonal effects such as temperature or humidity, or differences between day and night shifts. In the *R*-chart, cycles can

FIGURE 5.9 Cycles

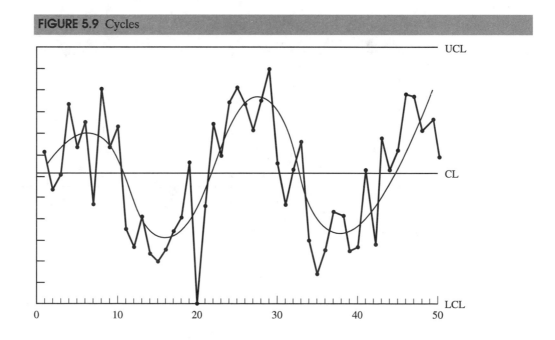

occur from maintenance schedules, rotation of fixtures or gauges, differences between shifts, or operator fatigue.

Trends

A trend is the result of some cause that gradually affects the quality characteristics of the product and causes the points on a control chart to gradually move up or down from the center line (see Figure 5.10). As a new group of operators gain experience on the job, for example, or as maintenance of equipment improves over time, a trend may occur. In the $\bar{x}$-chart, trends may be the result of improving operator skills, dirt or chip buildup in fixtures, tool wear, changes in temperature or humidity, or aging of equipment. In the R-chart, an increasing trend may be due to a gradual decline in material quality, operator fatigue, gradual loosening of a fixture or a tool, or dulling of a tool. A decreasing trend often is the result of improved operator skill, improved work methods, better materials, or improved or more frequent maintenance.

Hugging the Center Line

Hugging the center line occurs when nearly all the points fall close to the center line (see Figure 5.11). In the control chart, it appears that the control limits are too wide. A common cause of this occurrence is when the sample is taken by selecting one item systematically from each of several machines, spindles, operators, and so on. A simple example will illustrate this. Suppose that one machine produces parts whose diameters average 7.508 with variation of only a few thousandths; a second machine produces parts whose diameters average 7.502, again with only a small variation. Taken together, you can see that the range of variation would probably be between 7.500 and 7.510, and average about 7.505. Now suppose that we sample one part from each machine and compute a sample average to plot on an $\bar{x}$-chart. The sample averages will consistently be around 7.505, since one will always be high and the second will always be low. Even though there is a large variation in the parts taken as whole, the sample averages will not reflect this. In such a case, it would be more appropriate to construct a control chart for each machine, spindle, operator, and so on.

FIGURE 5.10 Gradual Trend

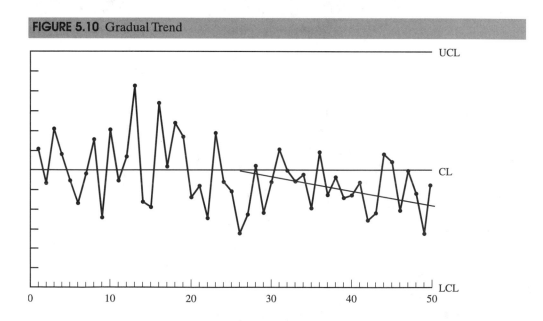

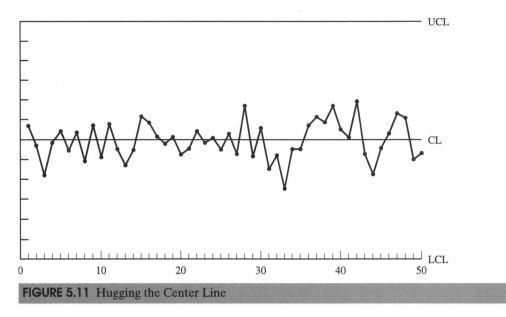

FIGURE 5.11 Hugging the Center Line

An often overlooked cause for this pattern is miscalculation of the control limits, perhaps by using the wrong factor from the table or misplacing the decimal point in the computations.

Hugging the Control Limits

This pattern appears when many points are near the control limits with very few in between (see Figure 5.12). It is often called a mixture, and is actually a combination of two different patterns on the same chart. A mixture can be split into two separate patterns, as Figure 5.13 illustrates. A mixture pattern can result when different lots of material are used in one process, or when parts are produced by different machines but fed into a common inspection group.

FIGURE 5.12 Hugging Control Limits

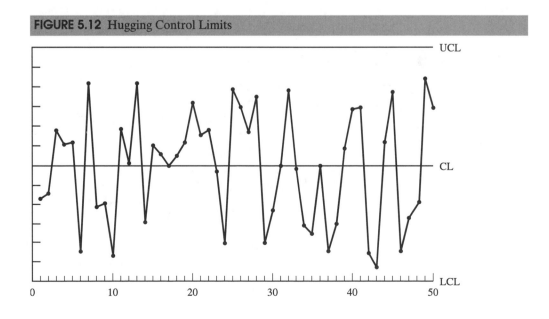

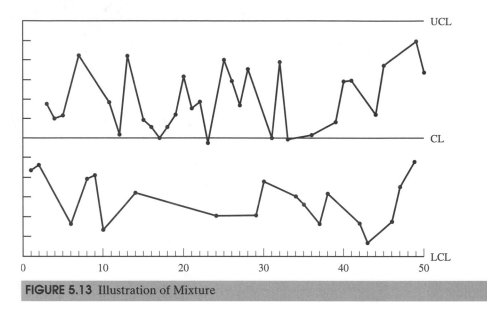

FIGURE 5.13 Illustration of Mixture

Quality control practitioners advocate simple rules, based on sound statistical principles, for operationalizing these concepts. For example, if 8 consecutive points fall on one side of the center line, then you can conclude that the mean has shifted. Why? If the distribution is symmetric, then the probability that the next sample falls above or below the mean is 0.5. Because samples are independent, the probability that 8 consecutive samples will fall on one side of the mean is $(0.5)^8 = 0.0039$—a highly unlikely occurrence. Another rule often used to detect a shift is finding 10 of 11 consecutive points on one side of the center line. The probability of this occurring can be found using the binomial distribution

$$p(10) = \binom{11}{10}(0.5)^{10}(0.5)^1 = 0.00537$$

These examples show the value of statistics and data analysis in common production operations.

Control Charts for Attributes

Attributes data assume only two values such as good or bad, present or absent, acceptable or not acceptable, and so on. Attributes data cannot be measured, only counted. The most common control chart for attributes data is the *p*-chart. A ***p*-chart** monitors the proportion of nonconforming items. Sometimes it is called a fraction nonconforming or fraction defective chart.

As with variables data, a *p*-chart is constructed by first gathering 25 to 30 samples of a fixed sample size of the attribute being measured. For attributes data, it is recommended that each sample size be at least 100; otherwise it is difficult to obtain good statistical results. For the type of control chart that we shall discuss, we assume that the size of each sample is the same.

The steps in constructing a *p*-chart are similar to those used for $\bar{x}$ and *R*-charts. Assume we have *k* samples, each of size *n*. For each sample, we compute the fraction nonconforming, *p*; that is, the number of nonconforming items divided by the number in the sample. The average fraction nonconforming, $\bar{p}$, is computed by summing the total number of nonconforming items in all samples and dividing by the total number of items (=*nk* if the sample size is constant) in all samples combined. Because the number of nonconforming items in each sample follows a binomial distribution, the standard deviation is

$$s = \sqrt{\frac{\bar{p}(1 - \bar{p})}{n}}$$

Using the principles we described earlier in this chapter, upper and lower control limits are given by

$$\text{UCL}_p = \bar{p} + 3s$$
$$\text{LCL}_p = \bar{p} - 3s$$

Whenever LCL_p turns out negative, we use zero as the lower control limit, because the fraction nonconforming can never be negative. We may now plot the fraction nonconforming on a control chart just as we did for the averages and ranges, and use the same procedures to analyze patterns in a *p*-chart as we did for $\bar{x}$- and *R*-charts. That is, we check that no points fall outside of the upper and lower control limits, and that no peculiar patterns (runs, trends, cycles, etc.) exist in the chart.

To illustrate a *p*-chart, the worksheet *Mower Test* in the Tracway database contains 30 samples of functional test results for 100 mowers at the completion of assembly. In row 104, the Excel function COUNTIF is used to compute the number in each sample that have passed the test. *PHStat* has a procedure for constructing *p*-charts (see *PHStat Note: p-charts*). Figure 5.14 shows the *p*-chart; the process appears to be in control.

FIGURE 5.14 *p*-chart Constructed with *PHStat* for Mower Test Data

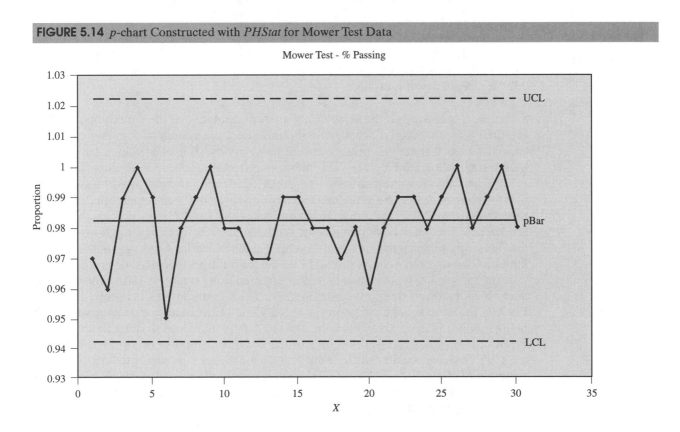

PHStat Note: p-charts

From the *PHStat* menu, select *Control Charts,* followed by *p Chart.* The dialog box, shown in Figure 5.15, prompts you for the cell range for the number of nonconformances and the sample size. This procedure also allows you to have nonconstant sample sizes; if so, enter the cell range of the sample size data. *PHStat* creates several new worksheets for the calculations and the actual chart.

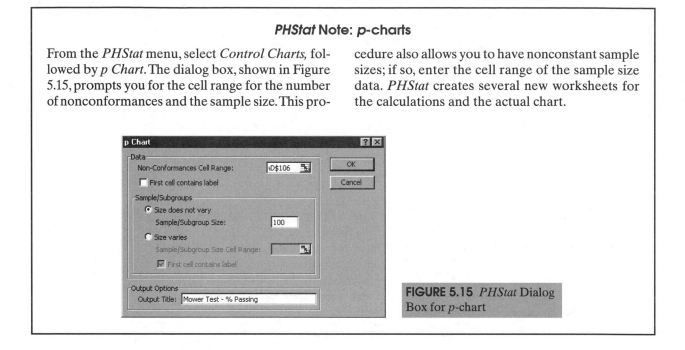

FIGURE 5.15 *PHStat* Dialog Box for *p*-chart

Statistical Issues in the Design of Control Charts

In designing control charts, we must consider three issues:

1. The selection of the sample data,
2. The sample size, and
3. The frequency of sampling.

Sampling is useful only if the sample data are representative of the entire population at the time they are taken. Each sample should reflect the system of common causes or special causes that may be present at that point in time. If special causes are present, then the sample should have a good chance of reflecting those special causes.

Consecutive measurement over a short period of time generally provides good samples for control charts; this is the method most often used. (Such samples are called **rational subgroups.**) It is also important to select samples from a single process. A process is a specific combination of equipment, people, materials, tools, and methods. We saw that selecting samples from each of several machines can lead to hugging the control limits. Separate control charts should be set up for multiple machines or processes.

The sample size is also important. We suggested using samples of size 5 for variables data; this is probably the most common in practice. Small samples, however, do not allow you to detect small changes in the mean value of the quality characteristic that is being monitored. For example, samples of size 5 only allow you to detect a shift in the mean of two standard deviations or more in the next sample with a probability of at least .95. To detect smaller shifts in the process mean, say only one standard deviation, a sample of about 20 must be used. Of course, you must also consider the cost of sampling. If it is expensive or very time-consuming to take a measurement, then smaller samples may be desirable.

The third issue is the frequency of sampling. It may not be economical to sample too often. There are no hard and fast rules for sampling frequency. Samples should be close enough so that special causes can be detected before a large amount of nonconforming product is made. This decision should take into account how often special causes are observed and the volume of production.

This discussion suggests that many statistical issues exist in implementing SPC; this is why users need to have a good understanding of statistical principles!

Process Capability Analysis

The purpose of SPC is to monitor a process over time in order to maintain a state of statistical control. However, just because a process is in control does not mean that it is capable of meeting specifications on the quality characteristic that is being measured. In golf, for example, you might consistently shoot between 85 and 90; however, this is far from meeting the "specification"—par! **Process capability analysis** involves comparing the distribution of process output to specifications when only common causes (natural variations in materials, machines and tools, methods, operators, and the environment) determine the variation. As such, process capability is meaningless if special causes occur in the process. Therefore, before conducting a process capability analysis, control charts should be used to ensure that all special causes have been eliminated and that the process is in control.

Process capability is measured by the proportion of output that can be produced within design specifications. By collecting data, constructing frequency distributions and histograms, and computing basic descriptive statistics such as the mean and variance, we can better understand the nature of process variation and its ability to meet quality standards.

There are three important elements of process capability: the design specifications, the centering of the process, and the range of variation. Let us examine three possible situations.

1. The natural variation in the output is smaller than the tolerance specified in the design (Figure 5.16). The probability of exceeding the specification limits is essentially zero; you would expect that the process will almost always produce output that conforms to the specifications, as long as the process remains centered. Even slight changes in the centering or spread of the process will not affect its ability to meet specifications.

FIGURE 5.16 Capable Process

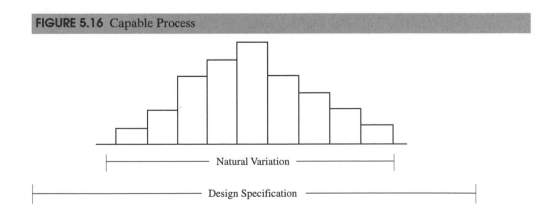

Natural Variation

Design Specification

2. The natural variation and the design specification are about the same (Figure 5.17). A very small percentage of output might fall outside the specifications. The process should be closely monitored to make sure that the centering of the process does not drift and that the spread of variation does not increase.

3. The range of process variation is larger than the design specifications (Figure 5.18). The probability of falling in the tails of the distribution outside the specification limits is significant. The only way to improve product quality is to change the process.

To illustrate process capability analysis, we will use the worksheet *Process Capability* in the Tracway database, which contains 200 samples of mower blade weights taken from the manufacturing process that has been shown to be in control. For optimum performance, the specifications of the blade are 5.00 ± 0.15, or between 4.85 and 5.15. Figure 5.19 shows the output of the *Descriptive Statistics* and *Histogram* tools in the *Analysis Toolpak* applied to these data. The process mean is 4.9828, slightly below the target specification. With a standard deviation of 0.098, we would expect nearly all process output to fall within ± three standard deviations of the mean, or $4.9828 \pm 3(0.098)$, or between 4.69 and 5.28. As you can see, all but one of the data points falls within this interval. This six–standard deviation spread represents the capability of the process. As long as the process remains in control, we would expect the blade weights to fall within this range.

The relationship between the process capability and the design specifications is often quantified by a measure called the **process capability index,** denoted by C_p. C_p is simply the ratio of the specification width to the process capability:

$$C_p = \frac{\text{USL} - \text{LSL}}{6s}$$

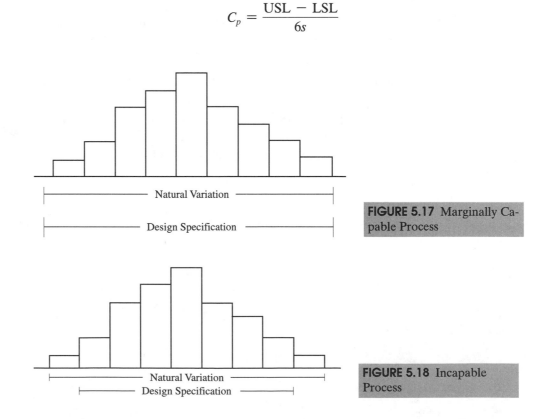

FIGURE 5.17 Marginally Capable Process

FIGURE 5.18 Incapable Process

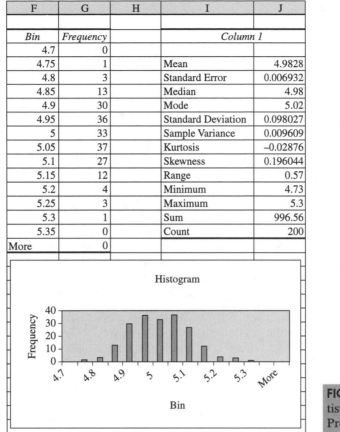

F	G	H	I	J
Bin	Frequency		Column 1	
4.7	0			
4.75	1		Mean	4.9828
4.8	3		Standard Error	0.006932
4.85	13		Median	4.98
4.9	30		Mode	5.02
4.95	36		Standard Deviation	0.098027
5	33		Sample Variance	0.009609
5.05	37		Kurtosis	–0.02876
5.1	27		Skewness	0.196044
5.15	12		Range	0.57
5.2	4		Minimum	4.73
5.25	3		Maximum	5.3
5.3	1		Sum	996.56
5.35	0		Count	200
More	0			

FIGURE 5.19 Summary Statistics and Histogram for Process Capability Analysis

For the Tracway example, $Cp = (5.15 - 4.85)/(.294) = 1.02$. Note that when the specification width is equal to the process capability, the index is 1.0. This means that the process is just barely capable of meeting specifications; any shift in the process mean will cause a significant proportion of the output to exceed one of the specification limits. You can see this visually on the histogram in Figure 5.19. Values of C_p greater than 1.0 signify that the process is quite capable of meeting specifications, whereas values lower than 1.0 mean that some nonconforming output will always be produced unless the process technology is improved.

Summary

Variation occurs in any process; the role of statistical quality control is to understand this variation and, in particular, identify and separate the special causes of variation that can usually be controlled from the common causes of variation that can be reduced only through changes in technology. Statistical process control is a methodology of plotting and analyzing data on control charts to determine if any special causes are present. For variables data, $\bar{x}$- and R-charts are used to monitor the process mean and process variability, respectively. For attributes data, p-charts are used to monitor the proportion of nonconformances in a sample. Any unusual patterns in the data on a control chart usually signal an out-of-control condition that requires corrective action. The natural variation in a controlled process is called the process capability, and is used to quantify the ability of a process to meet specifications.

Questions and Problems

1. Define the terms *process capability* and *statistical process control,* and explain their importance in manufacturing and service.
2. What are some reasons that production output varies?
3. Explain the difference between common causes of variation and special causes of variation.
4. What is the difference between variables data and attributes data?
5. Describe the meaning of the term *in control.*
6. Describe the steps involved in applying statistical process control.
7. Describe the difference between an $\bar{x}$- and an R-chart.
8. Given that the sample grand mean (based on 30 samples of 6 observations each) for the width of a chair seat is 27.104 inches, and the average range for each batch is 0.316 inches, identify the upper and lower control limits for $\bar{x}$ and R-charts.
9. Given that the sample grand mean (based on 25 samples of 10 observations each) for the weight of a satellite component is 0.806 grams, and the average range for each batch is 0.013 grams, identify the upper and lower control limits for $\bar{x}$- and R-charts.
10. Given that the sample grand mean (based on 30 samples of 8 observations each) for the weight of a pouch of stuffed crab is 0.503 pounds, and the average range for each batch is 0.068 pounds, identify the upper and lower control limits for $\bar{x}$ and R-charts.
11. Why would you not expect all observations to fall within control chart limits?
12. Interpret the following $\bar{x}$ and R-charts.

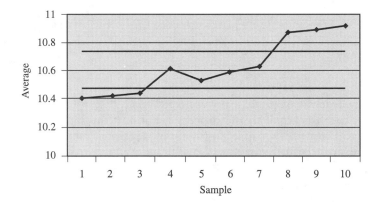

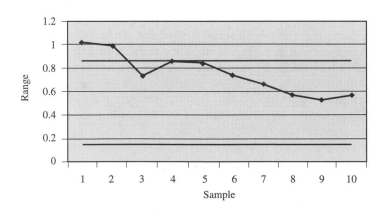

13. Interpret the following $\bar{x}$ and *R*-charts.

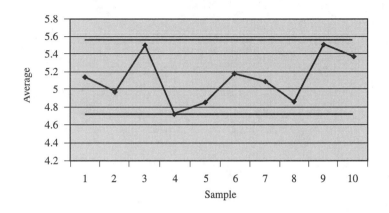

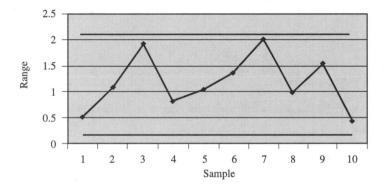

14. Interpret the following $\bar{x}$ and *R*-charts.

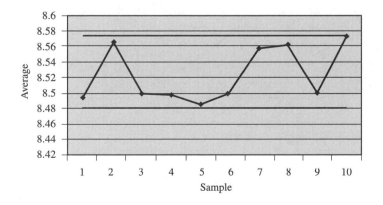

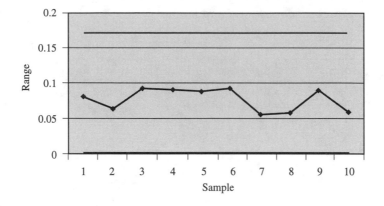

15. Interpret the following $\bar{x}$- and R-charts.

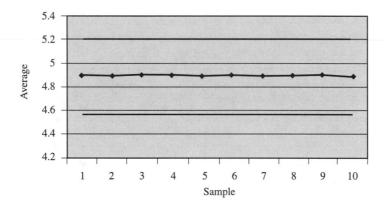

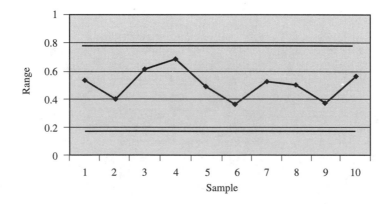

16. Interpret the following $\bar{x}$ and R-charts.

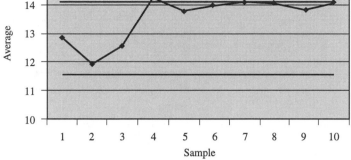

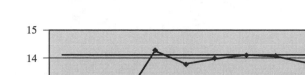

17. Interpret the following $\bar{x}$ and R-charts.

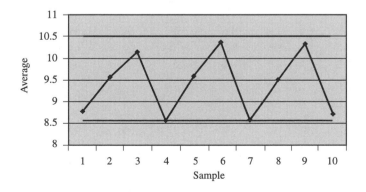

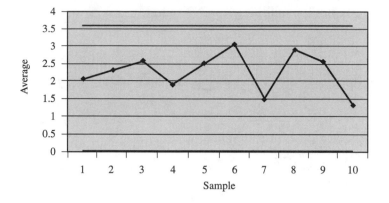

18. If 30 batches of 100 items are tested for nonconformity, and on average 96.0 of the samples contain no defects, identify the upper and lower control limits for a *p*-chart.
19. If 25 batches of 200 samples are run through a battery of tests, and on average 98.6 of the samples contain no defects, identify the upper and lower control limits for a *p*-chart.
20. If 50 batches of 100 items are tested for nonconformity, and on average 98.6 of the samples contain no defects, identify the upper and lower control limits for a *p*-chart.
21. If a plant has five machines processing food, with two shifts per day, how many process control chart sets should be developed?
22. If an operation produces output with a standard deviation of 0.35 pounds, and the upper control limit is 8 pounds and the lower control limit is 6 pounds, what is the process capability index?
23. If an operation produces output with a standard deviation of 0.12 inch, and the upper control limit is 3.60 inches and the lower control limit is 2.00 inches, what is the process capability index?
24. Compute control limits for the $\bar{x}$ and *R*-charts for the following 25 samples, each consisting of 5 observations. Draw the charts and interpret.

Sample					
1	105	100	99	96	103
2	102	100	99	100	100
3	98	104	98	106	97
4	99	101	99	99	99
5	95	97	104	102	97
6	102	107	100	101	100
7	97	98	105	96	101
8	102	101	102	100	105
9	101	98	103	99	100
10	96	97	100	96	104
11	97	97	100	99	96
12	105	103	102	100	96
13	96	103	102	99	105
14	97	99	99	100	99
15	102	103	99	95	102
16	100	104	96	100	99

17	92	104	105	97	96
18	97	98	96	99	99
19	100	101	104	95	103
20	104	98	96	104	97
21	103	97	97	98	100
22	101	97	96	104	98
23	102	100	98	104	99
24	96	97	105	102	97
25	98	99	97	98	100

25. Compute control limits for the $\bar{x}$ and R-charts for the following 50 samples, each consisting of 6 observations. Draw the charts and interpret.

Sample						
1	33	48	33	36	37	10
2	35	49	16	41	14	34
3	24	24	20	20	17	49
4	19	45	20	23	28	34
5	25	37	26	30	15	30
6	29	25	49	17	35	35
7	27	39	38	28	45	26
8	23	29	27	19	42	16
9	33	19	15	33	44	25
10	42	34	30	13	11	42
11	15	13	32	44	21	39
12	21	49	24	42	11	27
13	23	12	45	17	42	19
14	11	43	19	48	42	25
15	14	31	39	17	40	32
16	33	21	10	18	36	15
17	26	21	44	13	40	37
18	28	34	38	22	20	30
19	18	26	13	13	48	48
20	13	46	29	35	48	33
21	40	21	33	29	16	42
22	22	11	14	39	42	39
23	20	34	29	38	16	13
24	11	43	41	31	41	41
25	29	23	11	20	43	23
26	41	49	14	41	41	33
27	28	33	33	26	12	21
28	39	25	48	34	22	27
29	38	29	10	12	12	20
30	31	40	27	26	44	13
31	28	10	19	36	21	45
32	49	19	16	11	22	16
33	44	28	28	46	24	29
34	39	32	22	49	15	34

35	11	47	30	48	25	41
36	45	34	11	46	48	45
37	36	36	20	35	46	26
38	46	17	10	10	45	41
39	22	42	20	46	40	21
40	31	28	10	39	28	20
41	40	27	36	31	35	49
42	20	49	33	27	39	30
43	40	41	29	29	44	49
44	13	10	14	10	10	21
45	44	25	25	14	43	33
46	41	37	45	31	42	14
47	40	49	14	22	18	44
48	41	14	19	48	41	49
49	40	39	24	12	29	17
50	42	33	20	33	17	32

26. Hunter Nut Company produces cans of mixed nuts, advertised as containing no more than 20 percent peanuts. Hunter Nut Company wants to establish control limits for their process to ensure meeting this requirement. They have taken 30 samples of 144 cans of nuts from the production process at periodic intervals, inspected each can, and identified the proportion of cans that did not meet the peanut requirement. Compute the average proportion nonconforming and the upper and lower control limits for this process. Draw the *p*-chart and interpret the results.

Sample	Proportion Nonconforming
1	0.230
2	0.214
3	0.215
4	0.209
5	0.235
6	0.218
7	0.203
8	0.214
9	0.216
10	0.225
11	0.211
12	0.197
13	0.208
14	0.223
15	0.198
16	0.191
17	0.232
18	0.185
19	0.219

20	0.210
21	0.199
22	0.216
23	0.181
24	0.223
25	0.216
26	0.193
27	0.195
28	0.213
29	0.195
30	0.219

27. Doctor and Ramble produces high quality medicinal soap, advertised as 99 and 44/100 percent free of medically offensive pollutants. Twenty-five samples of 100 bars of soap were gathered at the beginning of each hour of production; the number of bars not meeting this requirement follows. Develop a *p*-chart for these data and interpret the results.

Sample	*Number Nonconforming*
1	0
2	1
3	1
4	0
5	2
6	5
7	1
8	2
9	1
10	0
11	0
12	1
13	0
14	2
15	0
16	1
17	3
18	2
19	3
20	5
21	4
22	7
23	3
24	5
25	8

References

Evans, James R., *Statistical Process Control for Quality Improvement,* Upper Saddle River, NJ: Prentice Hall, 1991.

Evans, James R. and Lindsay, William M., *The Management and Control of Quality,* 4th ed., Cincinnati, OH: South-Western, 1999.

General Motors Statistical Process Control Manual, Milwaukee, WI: American Society for Quality, 1986.

Statistical Quality Control Handbook, AT&T Technologies, Commercial Sales Clerk, Select Code 700-444, P.O. Box 19901, Indianapolis, IN 46219.

PART II

CHAPTER

6

Regression

Outline

Simple Linear Regression
    Least Squares Estimation
Measuring Variation about the Regression Line
    Coefficient of Determination and Correlation Coefficient
    Standard Error of the Estimate and Confidence Bands
Regression as Analysis of Variance
Assumptions of Regression Analysis
Application of Regression Analysis to Investment Risk
Multiple Linear Regression
    Interpreting Results from Multiple Linear Regression
Building Good Regression Models
    Using Adjusted R^2 to Evaluate Fit
    Correlation and Multicollinearity
    Best Subsets Regression
Regression with Ordinal and Nominal Independent Variables
Regression Models with Nonlinear Terms
Summary
Questions and Problems

In chapter 1 we discussed correlation—a measure of strength of the association between numerical variables. Decision makers are often interested in predicting the value of a dependent variable from the value of one or more independent, or explanatory, variables. For example, many colleges try to predict the success of their students as measured by their college GPA (the dependent variable) from various independent variables such as SAT scores, high school rank, high school GPA, type of school (public, private, college prep), and other variables. Such a model might be used for admission decisions. Another example is predicting the demand for a product (the dependent variable) as a function of price and advertising (the independent variables). This model might be used to help determine optimal values of price and advertising. **Regression analysis** is a tool for building statistical models that characterize relationships between a dependent variable and one or more independent variables, all of which are numerical.

    Two broad categories of regression models are used often in business settings: (1) regression models of time series data (in which the independent variable is time and the focus is on predicting the future), and (2) regression models of cross-sectional data (data collected for a single time period, or when time is not a factor, and which usually involve multiple independent variables). Time series regression is an important tool in *forecasting,* which is the subject of chapter 8. The distinction between the two types is not of great importance, however, and time is often an important variable that is included among a set of independent variables.

For example, in 1996, Tracway experienced some quality problems due to an increasing number of defects in materials received from suppliers. The company instituted an initiative in August 1997 to work with suppliers to reduce these defects, to more closely coordinate deliveries, and to improve materials quality through reengineering supplier production policies. To assess the impact of this program, Tracway measured the number of defects in supplier deliveries each month. Figure 6.1 shows a scatter diagram of the data, measured in defects per million items received.

This scatter diagram clearly indicates a change in the number of defects identified over time, with a significant decline after the supplier initiative was implemented. Tracway's operations manager, Henry Hudson, would like to predict what might have happened had the supplier initiative not been implemented, and how the number of defects might further be reduced in the near future. That is, he would like to characterize the pattern in the data through August 1997 and compare it to the pattern in the data after that time period.

In this scenario the dependent variable is the number of defects, and the independent variable is time. A regression model that involves a single independent variable is called *simple regression.* Other independent variables—for example, an indicator variable that denotes the actual supplier and the amount of resources devoted to improving supplier production policies—might also be included to explain the trend in the numbers of defects. A regression model that involves several independent variables is called *multiple regression.*

In this chapter we describe how to develop and analyze both single and multiple regression models. Our principal focus is to gain a basic understanding of the assumptions of regression models, statistical issues associated with interpreting regression results, and practical issues in using regression as a tool for making and evaluating decisions. We will investigate

FIGURE 6.1 Plot of Supplier Defects Detected at Delivery

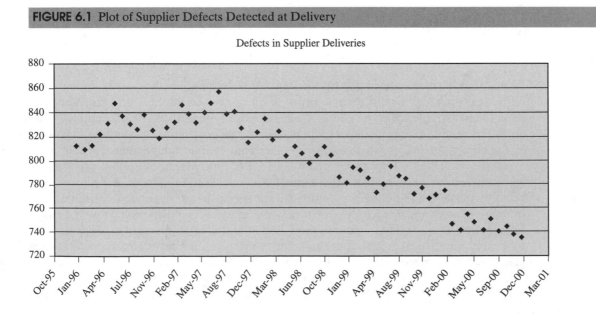

Defects in Supplier Deliveries

- Simple linear regression, focusing on developing the model, understanding the significance of regression and the use of hypothesis tests, and interpreting key statistics such as the coefficient of determination and standard error of the estimate;
- Multiple linear regression, including understanding how to select variables in models and evaluate goodness of fit, and incorporating ordinal and nominal variables in the models; and
- Developing regression models to capture nonlinearities in data.

We will use the worksheets *Defects after Delivery, Stock, Employee Success,* and *Engines* from the Tracway database in this chapter. Figure 6.2 shows portions of these for your reference.

	A	B	C	D	E	F
1	Defects after delivery					
2						
3		1996	1997	1998	1999	2000
4	January	812	828	824	782	771
5	February	810	832	836	795	775
6	March	813	847	818	792	747
7	April	823	839	825	786	742
8	May	832	832	804	773	756
9	June	848	840	812	781	749
10	July	837	849	806	796	743
11	August	831	857	798	788	751
12	September	827	839	804	784	741
13	October	838	842	813	772	745
14	November	826	828	805	777	738
15	December	819	816	786	769	736

	A	B	C	D	E
1		Stock			
2					
3	Date	S&P500	Tracway	S&P % change	Tracway % change
4	30-Jun-00	15300	$ 100.00		
5	3-Jul-00	15438	$ 101.50	0.90%	1.50%
6	5-Jul-00	15867	$ 102.50	2.78%	0.99%
7	6-Jul-00	14984	$ 97.10	-5.57%	-5.27%
8	7-Jul-00	15468	$ 97.70	3.23%	0.62%
9	10-Jul-00	15608	$ 99.50	0.91%	1.84%
10	11-Jul-00	16218	$ 103.10	3.91%	3.62%

	A	B	C	D	E	F	G
1		Employee Success					
2							
3	Duration	Yrseducation	College gpa	age	M/F	College Grad	Local
4	10	18	3.01	33	0	1	1
5	10	16	2.78	25	1	1	1
6	10	18	3.15	26	1	1	0
7	10	18	3.86	24	0	1	1
8	9.6	16	2.58	25	0	1	1
9	8.5	16	2.96	23	1	1	1
10	8.4	17	3.56	35	1	1	1

	A	B
1		Engines
2		
3	Sample	Time (min)
4	1	65.1
5	2	62.3
6	3	60.4
7	4	58.7
8	5	58.1
9	6	56.9
10	7	57.0

FIGURE 6.2 Portions of Worksheets in the Tracway Database Used in This Chapter

Simple Linear Regression

We first discuss the case of a single independent variable. The relationship between two variables can assume many forms, as illustrated in Figure 6.3. The relationship may be linear, one of many types of nonlinear forms, or there may be no relationship at all. To develop a regression model, you first must specify the type of function that best describes the data. This is important, because using a linear model for data that are clearly nonlinear, for example, would probably lead to poor business decisions and results. The type of relationship can usually be seen in a scatter diagram, and we recommend that you always create one first to gain some understanding of the nature of any potential relationship.

The simplest type of regression model is a linear relationship involving one independent variable, X, and one dependent variable, Y, as illustrated in Figure 6.4(a). We assume that for any value of X, we have a distribution of values of Y—a population—whose mean is $\beta_0 + \beta_1 X$. Therefore, $Y = \beta_0 + \beta_1 X$ represents the equation of a straight line (the **regression line**) through the means of these populations. Here, β_0 is the intercept of the line, that is, the value of Y when $X = 0$; and β_1 is the slope, which measures the change in Y as X is increased by one. However, individual data points will not lie on this line; therefore, we must include an error term to characterize the individual data points in the population. The mathematical form of this model is

$$Y = \beta_0 + \beta_1 X + \varepsilon$$

where ε is an error term. This is illustrated in Figure 6.4(b). For example, suppose that one observation of the ith dependent variable is Y_i when the value of the independent variable is X_i. Then the error associated with this data point is

$$\varepsilon_i = Y_i - \beta_0 - \beta_1 X_i$$

The error is positive if the data point lies above the line, and negative if it lies below. Another way of looking at this is that the error term ε_i represents the difference between the mean value of the dependent variable ($\beta_0 + \beta_1 X_i$) and the actual value, Y_i, for a given value of X.

LEAST SQUARES ESTIMATION

Because we will have only sample data available, we must estimate the values of β_0 and β_1. Let us call these estimates b_0 and b_1, respectively. Then $\hat{Y} = b_0 + b_1 X$ represents the

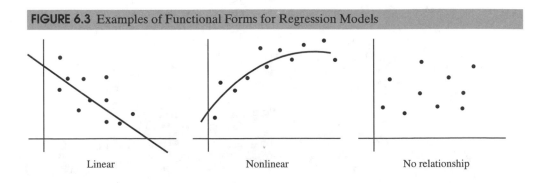

FIGURE 6.3 Examples of Functional Forms for Regression Models

Linear   Nonlinear   No relationship

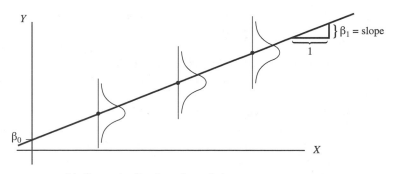

(a)   Regression line through population means

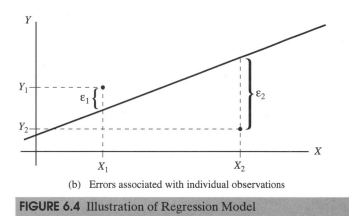

(b)   Errors associated with individual observations

FIGURE 6.4 Illustration of Regression Model

estimate of the population mean for any value of X within the range of the sample data. The best estimates of the population parameters are typically determined by choosing estimates b_0 and b_1 to minimize some function of the errors associated with all the data. The most common approach for doing this is called **least-squares regression,** which minimizes the sum of squares of the errors:

$$\sum_{i=1}^{n} (Y_i - [b_0 + b_1 X_i])^2$$

Note that X_i and Y_i are the known observations and that b_0 and b_1 are unknowns. Using calculus, we can show that the solution that minimizes this function is

$$b_1 = \frac{\sum_{i=1}^{n} X_i Y_i - n\overline{X}\,\overline{Y}}{\sum_{i=1}^{n} X_i^2 - n\overline{X}^2}$$

$$b_0 = \overline{Y} - b_1 \overline{X}$$

Although these calculations appear to be somewhat complicated, they can easily be performed in Excel, which has built-in capabilities to do this.

To illustrate simple linear regression, we will use the monthly data found on the worksheet *Defects After Delivery* in the Tracway database. Although the data appear to be nonlinear, as shown in Figure 6.1, we must remember that Tracway instituted a fundamental process change in its supplier management program in August 1997. Therefore, it makes little sense to view these data as one homogeneous series. We should view the data through and after August 1997 as independent groups. Thus we will illustrate a simple linear regression model for the data through August 1997 and leave estimating the model for the remainder of the data as an exercise.

Because the variables in a regression model must be numerical, some manipulation of the data is required to transform the dates in the first column into a numerical scale. First, we copied the data to a new worksheet and labeled the months consecutively, starting with January 1996 as month 1, as shown in Figure 6.5. This new column will represent the independent variable for the regression model. Next, we create a scatter diagram for the data using the Chart Wizard as described in chapter 2 (see Figure 6.6). After the chart has been created and is still selected (so that the *Chart* menu appears on the Excel menu bar), we apply the *Add Trendline* option from the *Chart* menu (see *Excel Note: Using the Add Trendline Option*). This results in the trendline shown in Figure 6.7. The regression model is $\hat{Y} = 1.5203X + 816.04$ (Excel expresses the model as $Y = b_1 X + b_0$). Thus the intercept, b_0, is 816.04 and the slope, b_1, is 1.5203. The slope

	A	B	C
1	Defects after delivery		
2			
3	Month	Time	Defects
4	Jan-96	1	812
5	Feb-96	2	810
6	Mar-96	3	813
7	Apr-96	4	823
8	May-96	5	832
9	Jun-96	6	848
10	Jul-96	7	837
11	Aug-96	8	831
12	Sep-96	9	827

FIGURE 6.5 Portion of Revised Worksheet with Numeric Date Variables

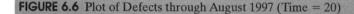

FIGURE 6.6 Plot of Defects through August 1997 (Time = 20)

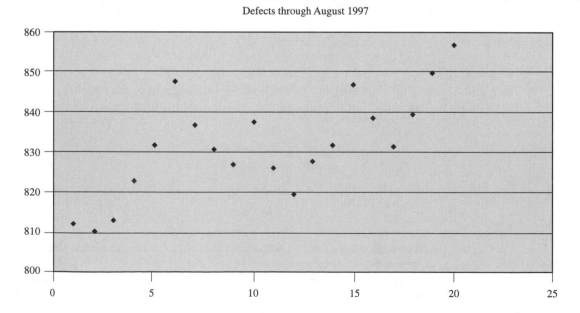

Defects through August 1997

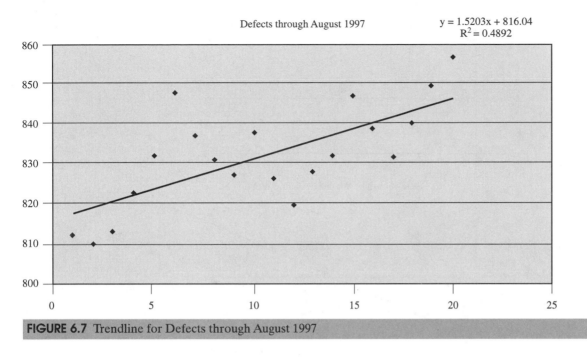

FIGURE 6.7 Trendline for Defects through August 1997

tells us that prior to the supplier defect reduction program, defects per million were increasing at a rate of about 1.5 per month. The prediction for September 1997 (month 21), if the new program had not been established, would be $\hat{Y}_{22} = 1.5203 \ (21) + 816.04 = 847.96$ or 848. This can also be found by using the Excel function TREND(*known_Y's, known_X's, new_X's*). Thus using the worksheet in Figure 6.5, we would estimate $\hat{Y}_{21} = \text{TREND}(\text{C4:C23,B4:B23,21}) = 848$.

Measuring Variation about the Regression Line

The objective of regression analysis is to explain the variation of the dependent variable around its mean value as the independent variable changes. Figure 6.8 helps to understand this. In Figure 6.8(a), the independent variable has no effect; thus β_1 would be zero and the model would reduce to $Y = \beta_0 + \epsilon$. In this case, the intercept β_0 would be the mean, $\overline{Y}$, and the variation between the observations and the mean $(Y - \overline{Y})$ is pure error. In Figure 6.8(b) we have the other extreme case in which all points lie on the regression line; that is, all of the variation in the data around the mean is explained by the independent variable. In this case, the error term is zero, and the value of each observation is equal to its predicted value: $Y = \hat{Y} = \beta_0 + \beta_1 X$. Thus the variation around the mean $(Y - \overline{Y})$ is simply the variation from the regression line to the mean, $(\hat{Y} - \overline{Y})$. Finally, Figure 6.8(c) shows the typical case in which some of the variation is explained by the independent variable, whereas some is also due to error. The total variation from the mean, $(Y - \overline{Y})$, can be expressed as $(\hat{Y} - \overline{Y}) + (Y - \hat{Y})$. The first term is the variation explained by regression, whereas the second is the variation due to error.

Because some points lie above the mean and others below it, we need to square the deviations from the mean to obtain a useful measure of the total variation in all the data; otherwise they will sum to zero. The sums of squares of the deviations of individual observations from the mean, $\Sigma(Y_i - \overline{Y})^2$, is called the total sum of squares,

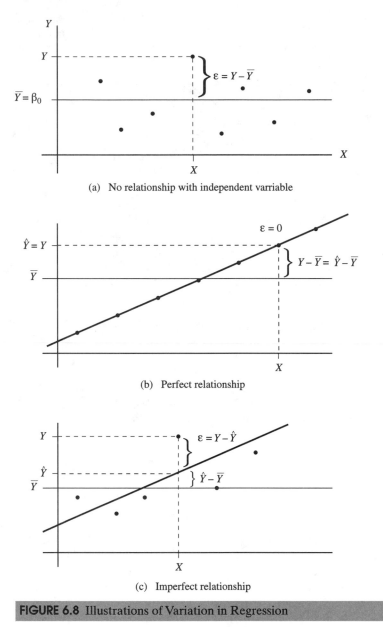

(a) No relationship with independent varriable

(b) Perfect relationship

(c) Imperfect relationship

FIGURE 6.8 Illustrations of Variation in Regression

or **SST.** Mathematically, this is equal to $\Sigma(\hat{Y} - \overline{Y})^2 + \Sigma(Y - \hat{Y})^2$, which is simply the sums of squares of the variation explained by regression, called **SSR,** and the sum of squares of the errors, or unexplained variation, **SSE.** (Another term often used for errors is *residuals.*) In other words,

$$SST = SSR + SSE$$

Figure 6.11 shows the calculations of these sums of squares on the worksheet. You can see that this relationship holds, because $3,142.00 = 1,537.02 + 1,604.98$. Sums of squares are useful in explaining the strength of regression relationships, obtaining variance estimates, and performing hypothesis tests.

Excel Note: Using the Add Trendline Option

The *Add Trendline* option is selected from the *Chart* menu. The dialog box in Figure 6.9 is displayed, and you may choose among a linear and a variety of nonlinear functional forms to fit the data. Selecting an appropriate nonlinear form requires some advanced knowledge of functions and mathematics, so we will restrict our discussion to the linear case. From the *Options* tab (see Figure 6.10) you may customize the name of the trendline, forecast forward or backward, set the intercept at a fixed value, and display the regression equation and *R*-squared value on the chart. The *R*-squared value will be described later in this chapter. Once Excel displays these results, you may move the equation and *R*-squared value for better readability by dragging them with a mouse. If you know you want a linear trendline, you may also click on the data series in the chart, and then add a trendline by clicking on the right mouse button (try it!).

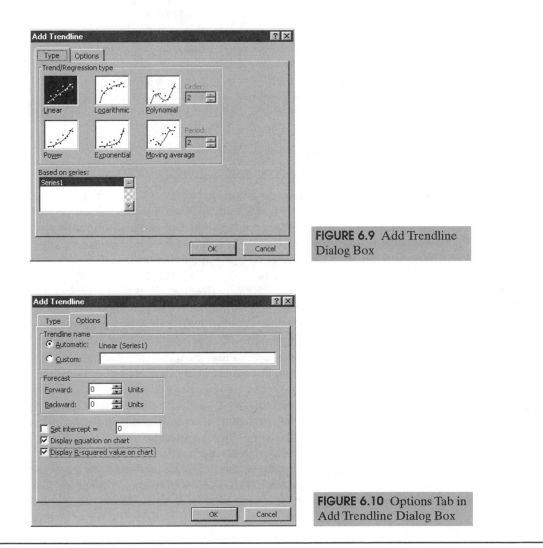

FIGURE 6.9 Add Trendline Dialog Box

FIGURE 6.10 Options Tab in Add Trendline Dialog Box

	A	B	C	D	E	F	G
1	Defects after delivery						
2					Sums of Squares Calculations for		
3	Month	Time	Defects	Estimate	SST	SSR	SSE
4	Jan-96	1	812	817.56	400.00	208.50	30.92
5	Feb-96	2	810	819.08	484.00	166.91	82.46
6	Mar-96	3	813	820.60	361.00	129.94	57.77
7	Apr-96	4	823	822.12	81.00	97.59	0.77
8	May-96	5	832	823.64	0.00	69.86	69.86
9	Jun-96	6	848	825.16	256.00	46.76	521.58
10	Jul-96	7	837	826.68	25.00	28.28	106.46
11	Aug-96	8	831	828.20	1.00	14.42	7.83
12	Sep-96	9	827	829.72	25.00	5.19	7.41
13	Oct-96	10	838	831.24	36.00	0.57	45.66
14	Nov-96	11	826	832.76	36.00	0.58	45.74
15	Dec-96	12	819	834.28	169.00	5.21	233.59
16	Jan-97	13	828	835.80	16.00	14.47	60.90
17	Feb-97	14	832	837.32	0.00	28.35	28.35
18	Mar-97	15	847	838.84	225.00	46.85	66.51
19	Apr-97	16	839	840.36	49.00	69.97	1.86
20	May-97	17	832	841.89	0.00	97.72	97.72
21	Jun-97	18	840	843.41	64.00	130.08	11.60
22	Jul-97	19	849	844.93	289.00	167.07	16.60
23	Aug-97	20	857	846.45	625.00	208.69	111.39
24		Average	832.00		3142.00	1537.02	1604.98
25					SST	SSR	SSE

FIGURE 6.11 Sums of Squares Calculations

COEFFICIENT OF DETERMINATION AND CORRELATION COEFFICIENT

The sums of squares provide information about the strength of the regression relationship. Specifically, the ratio SSR/SST gives the proportion of variation that is explained by the independent variable of the regression model, and is called the **coefficient of determination, R^2.** The value of R^2 will be between 0 and 1. A value of 1.0 indicates a perfect fit, whereas a value of 0 indicates that no relationship exists. For the supplier defect data, we see that $R^2 = 1,537.02/3,142.00 = 0.4892$. Note that this is the same value provided by the *Add Trendline* option in Excel. The value of R^2 means that approximately 48 percent of the variation in the dependent variable is explained by regression (i.e., the independent variable, time). The remaining variation is due to other factors that were not included in the model. Although we would like high values of R^2, it is difficult to specify a "good" value that signifies a strong relationship, because this depends on the application. For example, in marketing research studies, an R^2 of 0.6 or more is considered very good, whereas in many social science applications even smaller values are considered acceptable.

The square root of the coefficient of determination is the **sample correlation coefficient, R.** Values of R range from -1 to 1, where the sign is determined by the sign of the slope of the regression line. A correlation coefficient of $R = 1$ indicates perfect positive correlation; that is, as the independent variable increases, the dependent variable does also. $R = -1$ indicates perfect negative correlation—as X increases, Y decreases. As with R^2, a value of $R = 0$ indicates no correlation. Because R^2 measures the actual proportion of the variation explained by regression, it is generally easier to interpret than R.

STANDARD ERROR OF THE ESTIMATE AND CONFIDENCE BANDS

In chapter 4 we saw that sums of squares divided by their appropriate degrees of freedom provide estimates of variances, which we called mean squares. The sum of squares

(SSE) has two degrees of freedom because we estimated two parameters of the regression line, the slope and intercept. Thus $MSE = SSE/(n-2)$ is the variance of the errors about the regression line. The square root of MSE is called the **standard error of the estimate, S_{YX},** and is simply the standard deviation of the errors about the regression line. This is computed as

$$S_{YX} = \sqrt{\frac{SSE}{n-2}}$$

Intuitively, S_{YX} measures the spread of the data about the regression line. If the data are clustered close to the regression line, then the standard error will be small. For the Tracway data, $MSE = 1{,}604.98/18 = 89.17$, thus $S_{YX} = 9.44$.

The standard error can be used to develop **confidence bands** around the regression line that are analogous to confidence intervals for point estimates. You might think of a confidence band as a collection of confidence intervals, one for each estimate of the dependent variable. A $100(1-\alpha)\%$ confidence band around the regression line is

$$\hat{Y}_i \pm t_{\alpha/2,\,n-2}\, S_{YX}\, \sqrt{h_i}$$

where $\hat{Y}_i = b_0 + b_1 X_i$ is the predicted mean of Y for a given value X_i of the independent variable, and

$$h_i = \frac{1}{n} + \frac{(X_i - \overline{X})^2}{\displaystyle\sum_{i=1}^{n}(X_i - \overline{X})^2}$$

From this formula you can see that h_i varies with the value of X; in particular, h_i will be larger for values of X farther away from its mean, implying that the confidence intervals will be wider and that more uncertainty exists about the true population mean. Figure 6.12 shows an example of confidence bands.

FIGURE 6.12 Confidence Bands about the Regression Line

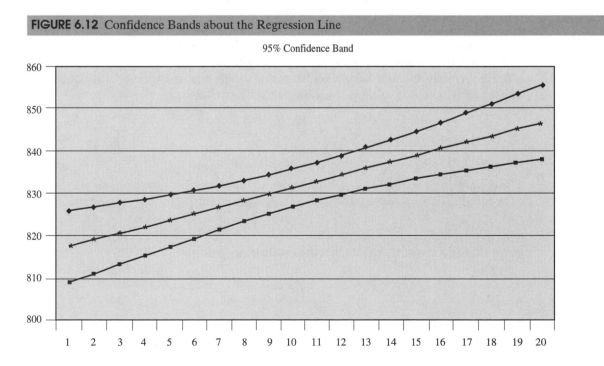

95% Confidence Band

Regression as Analysis of Variance

In chapter 4 we introduced the concept of analysis of variance (ANOVA), which determines whether the variation due to a particular factor is significantly larger than that due to error. You may recall that ANOVA is based on computing sums of squares and associated mean square values, and then conducting an *F*-test. ANOVA is commonly applied to regression to test for the significance of regression. **Significance of regression** is simply a hypothesis test of whether the regression coefficient β_1 is zero:

$$H_0: \beta_1 = 0$$
$$H_1: \beta_1 \neq 0$$

As we discussed earlier, if $\beta_1 = 0$, then any variation about the mean is due to other factors that are not explained by the independent variable chosen for the model (in our example, time).

In examining the sums of squares for a simple linear regression model with one explanatory variable, we see that because we estimate the mean, the total sum of squares, SST, has $n - 1$ degrees of freedom. Because SSE has $n - 2$ degrees of freedom, the regression sum of squares, SSR, has one degree of freedom. Thus MSR = SSR/1 represents the variance between observations explained by regression, while MSE = SSE/$(n - 2)$ represents the remaining variance. By dividing MSR by MSE, we obtain an *F* statistic. For the Tracway data, we have

$$F = \frac{\text{MSR}}{\text{MSE}} = \frac{1{,}537.02}{89.17} = 17.24$$

If this number is higher than the critical value from the *F*-distribution for a chosen level of significance, then we would reject the null hypothesis. Logically, if the null hypothesis is true (SST = SSE), then SSR (and MSR) would be zero. Therefore, the smaller the *F* ratio, the greater is the likelihood that H_0 is true. Likewise, the larger the *F* ratio, the greater is the likelihood that $\beta_1 \neq 0$ and that the independent variable explains more of the variation in the data about the mean.

An alternative to using the *F*-test for testing for significance of regression is to use a *t*-test. Actually, this test allows you to test a hypothesis that the population slope is equal to any specified value, β_1, including zero. The *t* statistic is

$$t = \frac{b_1 - \beta_1}{S_{YX}/\sqrt{\sum_{i=1}^{n}(X_i - \overline{X})^2}}$$

The denominator is simply the standard error of the slope. This statistic has $n - 2$ degrees of freedom. To test for significance of regression, set β_1 to zero. In our example, $b_1 = 1.5203$, $S_{YX} = 9.44$, and $\sum_{i=1}^{n}(X_i - \overline{X})^2 = 665$ (here, X_i is the numerical indicator corresponding to the month). Then the *t* statistic is

$$t = \frac{1.5203}{9.44/\sqrt{665}} = 4.15$$

Using a 5 percent significance level, the critical value for *t* with $n - 2 = 18$ degrees of freedom is 2.1009; therefore, we reject the null hypothesis that $\beta_1 = 0$.

Excel Note: Using the Regression Tool

From the *Tools* menu, select *Data Analysis* and the *Regression* tool. The dialog box shown in Figure 6.13 is displayed. In the box for the *Input Y Range,* specify the range of the dependent variable values. In the box for the *Input X Range,* specify the range for the independent variable values. This tool requires that independent variables be located in a continuous matrix, which sometimes calls for moving data around. Check *Labels* if your data range contains a descriptive label. You have the option of forcing the intercept to zero by checking *Constant is Zero;* however, you will usually not check this box, because adding an intercept term allows a better fit to the data. You also can set a Confidence Level (the default of 95 percent is commonly used) to provide confidence intervals for the intercept and slope parameters. In the Residuals section, you have the option of including a residuals output table by checking Residuals, Standardized Residuals (both of which are described later), and two plots. The Residual Plots generates a chart for each independent variable versus the residual, and the Line Fit Plots generates a chart for predicted versus observed values.

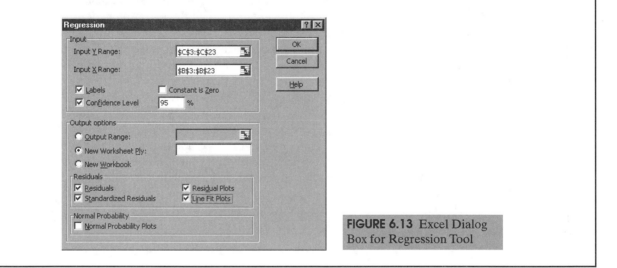

FIGURE 6.13 Excel Dialog Box for Regression Tool

The *Regression* tool in the *Analysis Toolpak* provides all the information to perform these tests (see *Excel Note: Using the Regression Tool*).

The summary output from the *Regression* tool is shown in Figure 6.14. In the *Regression Statistics* section are the correlation coefficient (called *Multiple R*), R^2, Adjusted R^2, standard error, and the sample size. The **Adjusted R^2** is a statistic that incorporates the sample size and the number of explanatory variables in the model, and is computed as

$$R^2_{adj} = 1 - \left[(1 - R^2) \frac{n-1}{n-2} \right]$$

In this example, $R_{adj}{}^2 = 1 - [(1 - .4892)(19/18)] = 0.461$. The Adjusted R^2 is useful when comparing this model with other models that include additional explanatory variables (such models will be discussed in the next section).

The ANOVA section presents the results of the analysis of variance. The *Significance F* measure represents the probability of wrongly concluding that the independent variable does significantly explain the variation in the dependent variable about

28	SUMMARY OUTPUT								
29									
30	*Regression Statistics*								
31	Multiple R	0.6994187							
32	R Square	0.48918652							
33	Adjusted R Square	0.460808							
34	Standard Error	9.44273954							
35	Observations	20							
36									
37	ANOVA								
38		*df*	*SS*	*MS*	*F*	*Significance F*			
39	Regression	1	1537.02406	1537.024	17.23791142	0.000598997			
40	Residual	18	1604.97594	89.16533					
41	Total	19	3142						
42									
43		*Coefficients*	*Standard Error*	*t Stat*	*P-value*	*Lower 95%*	*Upper 95%*	*Lower 95.0%*	*Upper 95.0%*
44	Intercept	816.036842	4.386449547	186.0358	5.14112E-31	806.8212464	825.252438	806.821246	825.2524378
45	Time	1.52030075	0.366173733	4.151856	0.000598997	0.75099769	2.28960381	0.75099769	2.289603814

FIGURE 6.14 Regression Output for Supplier Defects through August 1997

the mean when it does not. The extremely small value would lead us to conclude that time does indeed explain a significant amount of the variation in defects. Finally, the last section presents the estimated regression coefficients of the model, their standard errors, a *t* statistic, *p*-value, and confidence interval limits for the coefficients. The *t* statistics are associated with hypothesis tests of the individual regression coefficients. The results confirm the *t*-test we conducted earlier. Note that $9.44/\sqrt{665} = 0.366$ and is the standard error in the ANOVA results. The small *p*-values would lead us to reject the null hypotheses that either of these coefficients are zero. Note that the *p*-value associated with time is equal to the *Significance F* value. This will always be true for a regression model with one independent variable, because it is the only explanatory variable.

The regression tool also provides several charts. These include a *Line Fit Plot* (Figure 6.15), which is essentially a scatter diagram with the values predicted by the regression model included. (This is no different from the chart obtained using the *Add Trendline* option.) The *Residual Plot* (Figure 6.16) shows the deviations between the model's prediction and the actual value for each observation, or

$$\varepsilon_i = Y_i - \hat{Y}_i$$

FIGURE 6.15 Line Fit Plot from Regression Tool

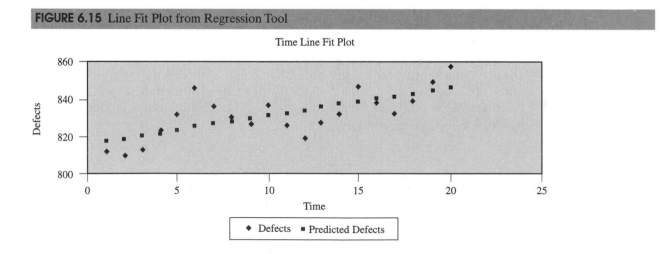

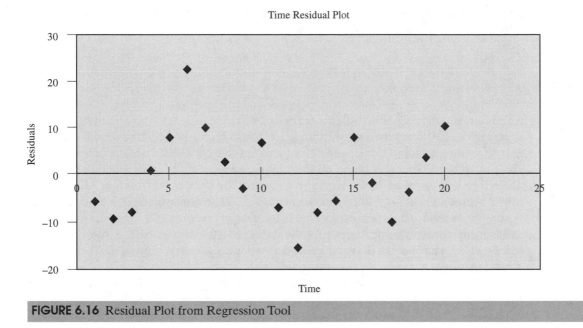

FIGURE 6.16 Residual Plot from Regression Tool

Assumptions of Regression Analysis

Regression analysis is predicated on some key assumptions about the data. Clearly the first assumption is linearity. This is usually checked by examining a scatter diagram of the data or examining the residual plot. If the model is appropriate, then the residuals should appear to be randomly scattered about zero, with no apparent pattern. If the residuals exhibit some well-defined pattern, such as a linear trend, a U-shape, and so on, then there is good evidence that some other functional form might better fit the data.

The second key assumption is that the errors for each individual value of X are normally distributed with a mean of zero and a constant variance. This can be verified by examining a histogram of the residuals associated with each value of the independent variable, and inspecting for a bell-shaped distribution, or using more formal goodness-of-fit tests as described in chapter 4.

The third assumption is **homoscedasticity,** which means that the variation about the regression line is constant for all values of the independent variable. This can also be evaluated by plotting the residuals and looking for large differences in the variances at different values of the independent variable.

Finally, residuals should be independent for each value of the independent variable. This is an important assumption when time is the independent variable. If successive observations appear to be correlated, for example, by becoming larger over time or exhibiting a cyclical type of pattern, then this assumption is violated. Correlation among successive observations over time is called **autocorrelation,** and can be identified by residual plots having clusters of residuals with the same sign. The pattern of residuals in Figure 6.16, a cyclical pattern above and below the regression line, might lead us to suspect autocorrelation, which can be evaluated more formally using a statistical test based on the **Durbin-Watson statistic.** The Durbin-Watson statistic is

$$D = \frac{\sum_{i=2}^{n} (\varepsilon_i - \varepsilon_{i-1})^2}{\sum_{i=1}^{n} \varepsilon_i^2}$$

This is a ratio of the squared differences in successive residuals to the sum of the squares of all residuals. When successive residuals are positively autocorrelated, D will approach zero. For our example, the value of D is computed to be 0.927. Critical values of the statistic have been tabulated based on the sample size and number of independent variables (see Levine, *et al.* in the references section for further information). For simple linear regression with $n = 20$, the critical value is 1.20, below which we would conclude that positive autocorrelation exists. That is the case in our example, suggesting that least squares regression is inappropriate for these data and that our statistical inferences may not be valid. Thus before drawing inferences about regression models and performing hypothesis tests, these assumptions should be checked!

PHStat provides a tool for simple linear regression that provides similar output as the Excel regression tool (see *PHStat Note: Simple Linear Regression*). *PHStat* also calculates the Durbin-Watson statistic (see Figure 6.17).

Application of Regression Analysis to Investment Risk

Investing in the stock market is highly attractive to everyone. However, stock investments do carry an element of risk. Risk associated with an individual stock can be measured in two ways. The first is **systematic risk,** which is the variation in stock price explained by the market—as the market moves up or down, the stock tends to move in the same direction. The Standard & Poor's (S&P) 500 index is the most commonly used measure of the market. For example, we generally see that stocks of consumer products companies are highly correlated with the S&P index whereas utility stocks generally show less correlation with the market. The second type of risk is called **specific risk,** and is the variation that is due to other factors such as the earnings potential of the firm, acquisition strategies, and so on. Specific risk is measured by the standard error of the estimate.

Systematic risk is characterized by a measure called *beta*. A beta value equal to 1.0 means that the specific stock will match market movements; a beta less than 1.0 indicates that the stock is less volatile than the market; a beta greater than 1.0 indicates that the stock has greater variance than the market. Thus stocks with large beta values are riskier than those with lower beta values. Beta values can be calculated by developing a regression model of a particular stock's returns (the dependent variable) against the average market returns (the independent variable). The slope of the regression line is the beta risk. This can be explained through the graph in Figure 6.19. If we plot the market returns against the returns of the individual stock and find the regression line, we would observe that if the slope equals one, the stock changes at the same rate as the market. However, if the stock price changes are less than the market changes, the slope

	A	B
1	Durbin-Watson Calculations	
2		
3	Sum of Squared Difference of Residuals	1488.087905
4	Sum of Squared Residuals	1604.97594
5	Durbin-Watson Statistic	0.927171473

FIGURE 6.17 Durbin-Watson Statistic from *PHStat* Regression Tool

PHStat Note: Simple Linear Regression

From the *PHStat* menu, select *Regression* and then *Simple Linear Regression*. Figure 6.18 shows the dialog box. In the *Data* section, you provide the ranges of the dependent and independent variables. Output options include regression sta-

tistics and ANOVA calculations (identical to Figure 6.14), residuals table, and residuals plot. You can also obtain a scatter diagram similar to Figure 6.15, the Durbin-Watson statistic, and exact confidence intervals.

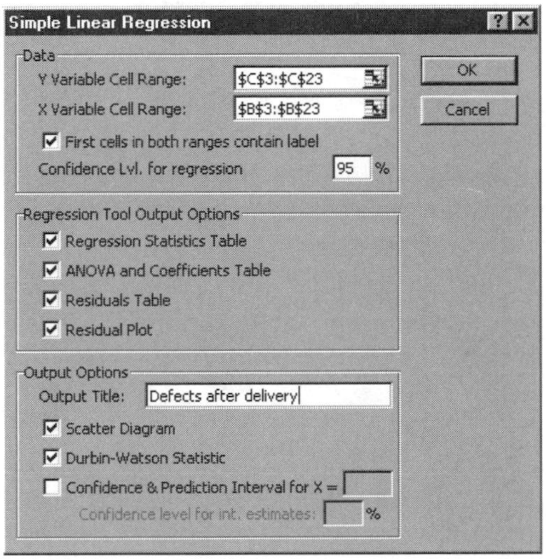

FIGURE 6.18 *PHStat* Dialog Box for Simple Linear Regression

of the regression line would be less than one, whereas the slope would be greater than one when the stock price changes exceed that of the market. A negative slope indicates a stock that moves in the opposite direction of the market (for example, if the market goes up, the stock price goes down).

The worksheet *Stock* in the Tracway database shows daily stock prices for Tracway for the period June 30 through December 31, 2000. Figure 6.20 shows a scatter diagram of the S&P 500 performance[1] and Tracway stock performance over this six-month period, respectively. You can see that a correlation appears to exist.

The percentage increase (negative values indicating a decrease) for both the S&P 500 (column D) and Tracway stock (column E) are given in the worksheet. These provide the data for the regression model

$$\text{Daily Change in Tracway Stock Price} = \beta_0 + \beta_1 \text{ S\&P Change}$$

Figure 6.21 shows the results of applying the *Regression* tool from Excel. The resulting model is

$$\text{Daily Change in Tracway Stock Price} = 0.00124 + 0.62124 \text{ S\&P Change}$$

The R^2 value of 0.90 shows that a large percentage of the variation is explained by the model. The slope of the regression line, β_1 (the beta risk of Tracway stock), is 0.62. This indicates Tracway is less risky than the average S&P 500 stock.

[1] These values are purely hypothetical for the purpose of this example.

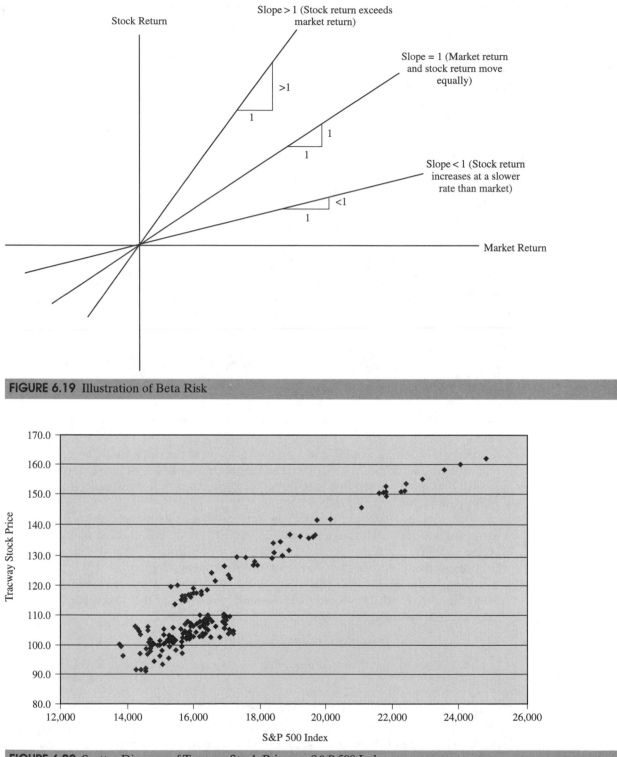

FIGURE 6.19 Illustration of Beta Risk

FIGURE 6.20 Scatter Diagram of Tracway Stock Prices vs S&P 500 Index

	A	B	C	D	E	F	G	H	I
1	SUMMARY OUTPUT								
2									
3	*Regression Statistics*								
4	Multiple R	0.950684862							
5	R Square	0.903801707							
6	Adjusted R Square	0.903019607							
7	Standard Error	0.010344035							
8	Observations	125							
9									
10	ANOVA								
11		*df*	*SS*	*MS*	*F*	*Significance F*			
12	Regression	1	0.123649065	0.123649065	1155.608972	2.20035E-64			
13	Residual	123	0.013160883	0.000106999					
14	Total	124	0.136809949						
15									
16		*Coefficients*	*Standard Error*	*t Stat*	*P-value*	*Lower 95%*	*Upper 95%*	*Lower 95.0%*	*Upper 95.0%*
17	Intercept	0.001239606	0.000926122	1.338490941	0.183205317	-0.000593595	0.003072807	-0.000593595	0.003072807
18	S&P%	0.621240017	0.018274856	33.9942491	2.20035E-64	0.585066074	0.65741396	0.585066074	0.65741396

FIGURE 6.21 Regression Results for Tracway Beta Risk

Multiple Linear Regression

Tracway's Human Resources department is concerned about the high rate of turnover it experiences in its sales staff. Senior managers have suggested that the department look closer at its recruiting policies, particularly trying to identify the characteristics of individuals that lead to greater retention. However, in a recent staff meeting, human resources managers could not agree on these characteristics. Some argued that years of education and grade point averages were good predictors. Others argued that hiring more mature applicants would lead to greater retention. To study these factors, the staff agreed to conduct a statistical study to determine the effect that years of education, college grade point average, and age when hired have on retention. A sample of 40 salespeople hired 10 years ago was selected to determine the influence of these variables on how long each individual stayed with the company.

In this example, we have one dependent variable (years with Tracway) and three independent variables (years of education, college grade point average, and age when hired). A regression model with more than one independent variable is called a **multiple regression** model. If all terms in the model are linear, we have a **multiple linear regression** model. Simple linear regression is just a special case of multiple linear regression.

A multiple linear regression model has the form

$$Y = \beta_0 + \beta_1 X_1 + \beta_2 X_2 + ... + \beta_k X_k + \varepsilon$$

where Y is the dependent variable

$X_1 ... X_k$ are the independent (explanatory) variables

β_0 is the intercept term

$\beta_1 ... \beta_k$ are the regression coefficients for the independent variables

ε is the error term

For the Tracway example, we have three independent variables, so the model is

$$\text{Retention (years)} = \beta_0 + \beta_1 \text{ Years education} + \beta_2 \text{ GPA} + \beta_3 \text{ Age} + \varepsilon$$

Similar to the simple linear regression case, we estimate the regression coefficients—called **partial regression coefficients**—as $b_0, b_1, b_2, \ldots, b_k$, and then can predict the value of the dependent variable using the model

$$\hat{Y} = b_0 + b_1 X_1 + b_2 X_2 + \ldots + b_k X_k$$

The partial regression coefficients represent the expected change in the dependent variable when the associated dependent variable is increased by one unit *while the values of all other independent variables are held constant.* Thus b_2 would represent the change in retention for a unit increase in GPA while holding Years education and Age constant.

As with simple linear regression, multiple linear regression uses least squares to estimate the intercept and slope coefficients that minimize the squared error terms over all observations. The principal assumptions discussed for simple linear regression also hold here. The data are found on the worksheet *Employee Success* in the Tracway database. The *Regression* tool from *Analysis Toolpak* provides the ability to perform multiple regression in addition to single-variable regression. The only difference is that the data for the independent variables are in three columns, so the *Input X Range* is specified as B3:D43. The output is shown in Figure 6.22; a check of residuals verifies the assumptions. (*PHStat* provides a similar tool; the options are identical to those discussed for simple linear regression.)

From Figure 6.22, we see that the model is

Retention $= -2.74 - 0.067$ Years education $+ 0.680$ GPA $+ 0.292$ Age

For example, if a person age 30 with 16 years of education and a college GPA of 2.50 applied, this regression model would predict that this applicant would stay with Tracway

Retention $= -2.74 - 0.067 \times \mathbf{16} + 0.680 \times \mathbf{2.50} + 0.292 \times \mathbf{30} = 6.648$ years

One point we should make is that it is dangerous to extrapolate a regression model outside the ranges covered by the observations. For example, if a person age 40 with 13 years of education and a GPA of 1.5 applied, this regression would predict 9.1 years with the firm. That may or may not be accurate, but the regression model considered no data with these characteristics.

FIGURE 6.22 Regression Results for Employee Duration with Education, GPA, and Age

SUMMARY OUTPUT								
Regression Statistics								
Multiple R	0.387559901							
R Square	0.150202677							
Adjusted R Square	0.079386234							
Standard Error	2.725526994							
Observations	40							
ANOVA								
	df	SS	MS	F	Significance F			
Regression	3	47.26784375	15.75594792	2.121014127	0.114635313			
Residual	36	267.4259062	7.428497396					
Total	39	314.69375						
	Coefficients	Standard Error	t Stat	P-value	Lower 95%	Upper 95%	Lower 95.0%	Upper 95.0%
Intercept	-2.73710846	4.504149393	-0.607685985	0.547210322	-11.87193479	6.397717875	-11.87193479	6.397717875
Yrseducation	-0.067054294	0.355164691	-0.188797748	0.851311676	-0.787360724	0.653252136	-0.787360724	0.653252136
College gpa	0.679981319	1.183551377	0.574526237	0.569184814	-1.720368968	3.080331607	-1.720368968	3.080331607
age	0.291535813	0.135043927	2.158822092	0.037605841	0.017654395	0.56541723	0.017654395	0.56541723

INTERPRETING RESULTS FROM MULTIPLE LINEAR REGRESSION

The results from the *Regression* tool are in the same format as we saw for simple linear regression. *Multiple R,* the **multiple correlation coefficient,** and *R Square,* the **coefficient of multiple determination,** indicate the strength of association between the dependent and independent variables. The low value of R^2 states that only 15 percent of the variation in the data is explained by these independent variables, a rather poor fit. We will discuss how to build better models in the next section.

The ANOVA section in Figure 6.22 tests for significance of the entire model. That is, it computes an F statistic for testing the hypotheses

$$H_0: \beta_1 = \beta_2 = \ldots = \beta_k = 0$$
$$H_1: \text{at least one } \beta_j \text{ is not } 0$$

The null hypothesis states that no linear relationship exists between the dependent and any of the independent variables, whereas the alternate hypothesis states that the dependent variable has a linear relationship with at least one independent variable. It cannot conclude that a relationship exists with every independent variable. The test is identical to the simple linear regression case. The F statistic is computed as MSR/MSE, except that it has k and $n - k - 1$ degrees of freedom. At a 5 percent significance level, we would fail to reject the null hypothesis because *Significance F* is greater than 0.05. Another interpretation is that the probability of getting these results in a random sample from a population with no relationship between retention and the independent variables is 0.114, well above a 5 percent significance level.

The last section in the results provide information to test hypotheses on individual regression coefficients. For example, to test the hypothesis that the population slope β_1 (associated with Years education) is zero, we compute a t statistic by dividing $b_1(-0.06705)$ by its standard error (0.355165), which equals -0.1888 as shown in the third column. This statistic has $n - k - 1$ degrees of freedom, or in this case, $40 - 3 - 1 = 36$. From Table A.3 in the appendix at the end of the book, we find $t_{36, 0.025} = 2.0281$. Therefore, we cannot reject the null hypothesis at the 0.05 significance level. This conclusion may also be drawn by examining the P-value in the next column of the results. On the other hand, a t test would conclude that the slope associated with Age is significant even though we could not reject the null hypothesis for significance of the overall regression model. Such anomalies can occur in multiple regression models for various reasons, including interdependencies among the variables. The F-test looks at the significance of the overall model; in our case, the low R^2 value suggested a poor fit, and even though Age alone appears significant, in combination with the other variables we could not conclude that all slopes were different from zero. This simply strengthens the importance of remembering that statistics is not an exact science (no pun intended), and results must always be viewed with caution.

We may also use the regression output information to compute confidence intervals for slope coefficients. A confidence interval for β_j would be

$$b_j \pm t_{n-k-1} \, s.e.$$

where *s.e.* is the standard error provided in the summary output.

As with any regression model, we need to look closer at the results in order to understand them. The results do not imply that more education is bad, or that college GPAs have nothing to do with success. It may be that those with more education are more mobile, and have moved on to other jobs. The same is true with grade point averages. But when specifically measuring how long this sample of 40 people hired 10 years ago stayed, those who were older tended to stay longer with Tracway. More years of education and/or higher grade point averages were not significant predictors of length of employment with Tracway. Other variables that we did not include in the model may improve the results. This leads to the question of how to build good regression models.

Building Good Regression Models

A good regression model should include only significant independent variables. Because years of education and GPA do not appear to significantly affect the dependent variable, we might drop them and evaluate a model involving only age. This is done in Figure 6.23. The new model is:

$$\text{Retention} = -2.01 + 0.300 \times \text{Age}$$

In this regression model, there is very little deterioration in model fit ($R^2 = 0.142$ versus 0.150 with the three-variable model). Age is again very significant, with *Significance F* of 0.017, indicating even greater significance than in the prior model. The prediction for a 30-year-old applicant with 16 years of education and a GPA of 2.50 would be 6.99 years, a little longer than the prior model's prediction, because the other variables, which adjusted the age prediction slightly, are not included.

USING ADJUSTED R^2 TO EVALUATE FIT

A useful way of examining the relative fit of different models is through the Adjusted R^2. Adding an independent variable to a regression model will always result in R^2 equal to or greater than the R^2 of the original model. This is true even when the new independent variable has little true relationship with the dependent variable. The Adjusted R^2, which we introduced earlier in the context of simple linear regression, reflects both the number of independent variables and the sample size. This helps to better understand the value of adding independent variables to the model. The Adjusted R^2 for a multiple linear regression model is computed as

$$\text{Adjusted } R^2 = 1 - \frac{\text{SSE}}{\text{SST}}\left(\frac{n-1}{n-k-1}\right)$$

FIGURE 6.23 Regression Results for Employee Duration with Age

	I	J	K	L	M	N	O	P	Q
	SUMMARY OUTPUT								
	Regression Statistics								
	Multiple R	0.376658199							
	R Square	0.141871399							
	Adjusted R Square	0.119289067							
	Standard Error	2.665805435							
	Observations	40							
	ANOVA								
		df	*SS*	*MS*	*F*	*Significance F*			
	Regression	1	44.64604247	44.64604247	6.282407021	0.01659192			
	Residual	38	270.0477075	7.106518619					
	Total	39	314.69375						
		Coefficients	*Standard Error*	*t Stat*	*P-value*	*Lower 95%*	*Upper 95%*	*Lower 95.0%*	*Upper 95.0%*
	Intercept	-2.014865684	3.042483099	-0.662243838	0.511811593	-8.174050928	4.144319561	-8.174050928	4.144319561
	age	0.30029287	0.119806943	2.506473024	0.01659192	0.057756386	0.542829354	0.057756386	0.542829354

where SSE = sum of squared errors (residuals)

SST = total sum of squares

n = number of observations

k = number of independent variables

Essentially, the adjustment term $(n - 1)/(n - k - 1)$ represents the ratio of the degrees of freedom of SSE and SST. For the Tracway example with all three independent variables, we have

$$\text{Adjusted } R^2 = 1 - \frac{267.4259}{314.6938}\left(\frac{39}{36}\right) = 0.0794$$

For the regression model with only Age as the independent variable (Figure 6.23), the Adjusted R^2 is 0.119. Note that while R^2 decreased by dropping the other two variables from the model, the Adjusted R^2 actually increased, indicating a better model. Thus the Adjusted R^2 provides a way to evaluate the effect of adding or removing variables to or from a model.

From a practical perspective, the independent variables selected should make some sense in attempting to explain the dependent variable (that is, you should have some reason to believe that changes in the independent variable will cause changes in the dependent variable even though causation cannot be proven statistically). From a statistical viewpoint, it is best to have as simple a model as possible. One approach to constructing a good model is to collect data on as many candidate independent variables as possible (plus of course the dependent variable), and then try to eliminate those that have little effect on the dependent variable. This can be viewed as an effort to obtain *model efficiency*. The modern use of statistics, however, makes model efficiency much less important. Modern computers provide the ability to deal with masses of data easily, and tools such as data mining can seek models and variable associations that analysts might never uncover. However, techniques such as data mining require a solid understanding of regression procedures to interpret computer output and to direct analysis. Analyzing the correlation matrix can help to identify appropriate independent variables.

CORRELATION AND MULTICOLLINEARITY

As discussed in chapter 2, correlation, a numerical value between −1 and +1, measures the linear relationship between pairs of variables. The higher the absolute value of the correlation, the greater the strength of the relationship. The sign simply indicates whether variables tend to increase together (positive) or not (negative). The *Correlation* tool in the Excel Analysis Toolpak computes the correlation between all pairs of variables (see *Excel Note: Using the Correlation Tool*). Table 6.1 shows the correlation matrix for the cross-sectional data gathered about the duration of employment with

TABLE 6.1   Correlation Matrix for Employee Duration with Tracway

	Duration	*Years Education*	*College GPA*	*Age When Hired*
Duration	1.0	0.1797	0.1774	0.3767
Years education		1.0	0.5867	0.4210
College GPA			1.0	0.2485
Age when hired				1.0

Excel Note: Using the Correlation Tool

From the *Tools* menu, select *Data Analysis* and the *Correlation* tool. The dialog box shown in Figure 6.24 is displayed. In the box for the *Input* *Range,* specify the range of the data for which you want correlations. As with other tools, check *Labels* if your data range contains a descriptive label.

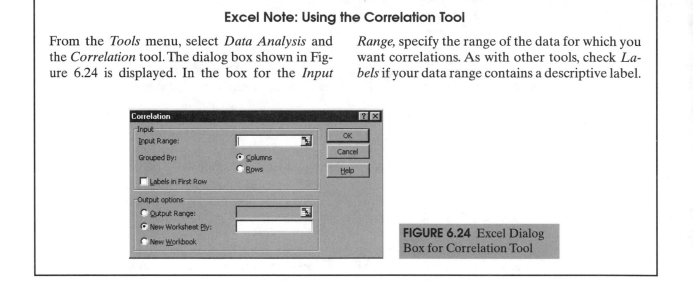

FIGURE 6.24 Excel Dialog Box for Correlation Tool

Tracway. You can see that Age has the strongest relationship with the dependent variable, followed by Years Education and College GPA. This information can be used to prioritize the independent variables for selection for inclusion in the model.

Including multiple variables in the regression model, however, may result in **multicollinearity,** a condition occurring when two or more independent variables in the same regression model contain high levels of the same information, explaining the variation in the dependent variable and the correlation with one another. Essentially, multicollinearity may be an issue when some set of independent variables predict each other better than they predict the dependent variable. Multicollinearity makes it difficult to distinguish the effects of these variables on the dependent variable. When multicollinearity is present, the β coefficients of the independent variables can be unstable, and even the signs of these β coefficients may change when different variables are included. Also, p-values can be inflated, resulting in the conclusion not to reject the null hypothesis for significance of regression when it should be rejected. Although a full discussion of multicollinearity is beyond the introductory scope of this book, it is important that you are aware of the problems that it may cause and seek expert advice when appropriate.

BEST SUBSETS REGRESSION

Best subsets regression evaluates either all possible regression models for a set of independent variables or the best subsets of models for a fixed number of independent variables. *PHStat* includes a useful tool for performing best subsets regression (see *PHStat Note: Best Subsets Regression*). Figure 6.25 shows the *PHStat* output for the *Employee Success* data. The Adjusted R^2 is typically used to compare models. We see that the maximum Adjusted R^2 value occurs for the model that includes only variable $X3$, Age. Another criterion is based on a statistic called Cp, which measures the difference of a fitted regression model from a *true* model, along with random error. When a regression model with p independent variables contains only random differences from a true model, the average value of Cp is $p + 1$. Thus good models are those for which

	A	B	C	D	E	F	G
1	Best Subsets Analysis						
2							
3	*R2T*	0.150203					
4	1 - *R2T*	0.849797					
5	n	40					
6	T	4					
7	n - T	36					
8							Consider
9		Cp	p+1	R Square	Adj. R Square	Std. Error	This Model?
10	X1	4.995759	2	0.032275	0.006808943	2.830924	No
11	X1X2	6.660513	3	0.040189	-0.011692645	2.85717	No
12	X1X2X3	4	4	0.150203	0.079386234	2.725527	Yes
13	X1X3	2.33008	3	0.142411	0.096054807	2.70074	Yes
14	X2	5.029296	2	0.031484	0.005996452	2.832081	No
15	X2X3	2.035645	3	0.149361	0.103380798	2.689774	Yes
16	X3	0.352938	2	0.141871	0.119289067	2.665805	Yes

FIGURE 6.25 *PHStat* Best Subsets Regression Results

PHStat Note: Best Subsets Regression

From the *PHStat* menu, select *Regression,* then *Best Subsets.* The dialog box that appears prompts you to enter the range for the dependent variable and the independent variables, as well as the confidence level for the regression. The tool creates a best subsets worksheet that contains a summary of the models analyzed. With a large number of variables, the analysis can take a significant amount of time and memory and may cause a fatal error in Excel, depending on the processor capability and amount of memory available.

Cp is close to or below $p + 1$. From Figure 6.25, *PHStat* suggests that we consider four models that meet this criterion. The tool also provides ANOVA output for each of the combinations for further analysis.

In considering alternative models, you should consider whether the regression assumptions can be validated, issues of interpreting the model in its application context, and the significance of regression. Best subsets regression does not point to an "optimal" model.

Regression with Ordinal and Nominal Independent Variables

Some data of interest in a regression study may be ordinal or nominal. For example, there clearly is a need for additional information in the Tracway employment prediction study. Some Tracway human resources staff have suggested that gender is a factor (some claiming that males have an advantage, others claiming that females are more stable employees and thus stay with the firm longer). Other factors might be whether or not a college degree was obtained, or whether the applicant is from the local area. These data, however, are nominal. Because regression analysis requires numerical data, we could include them by *coding* the variables.

Each of these variables is dichotomous; therefore, we can code them as either 0 or 1. For example, a male can be assigned a code of 0 and a female assigned a code of 1. Employees with a college degree can be assigned a code of 1 and those without assigned a code of 0. Finally, employees from the local area can be assigned a code of 1 and those from other geographic locations assigned a code of 0. These data are available on the worksheet *Employee Success* in the Tracway database.

We might begin by running a regression on the entire data set, yielding the output shown in Figure 6.26. The resulting model is

$$\hat{Y} = -1.33048 + 0.084 \text{ Years Education} - 0.745 \text{ GPA} + 0.182 \text{ Age}$$
$$+ 0.327 \text{ M/F} + 1.392 \text{ College Grad} + 3.492 \text{ Local}$$

Thus if an applicant has 16 years of education, a 2.50 GPA, is a 30-year-old male, a college graduate, and from outside the local area, this regression model would predict a length of employment of

$$-1.33 + 0.084 \times \mathbf{16} - 0.745 \times \mathbf{2.50} + 0.182 \times \mathbf{30}$$
$$+ 0.327 \times \mathbf{0} + 1.392 \times \mathbf{1} + 3.492 \times \mathbf{0} = 5.0 \text{ years}$$

This model has an R^2 of 0.47, indicating that all six available independent variables explain only 47 percent of the variance in the employment duration of the 40 employees in the database. Some of the variables have almost no power in explaining differences in employment duration. We have already seen that years of education and GPA are not significant. Although the estimated regression coefficient associated with gender indicates that females stay with Tracway about 0.3 years longer than males, it appears that gender has little significance because the p-value is 0.68. The variables that seem to have the most significant relationship with employment duration are age when hired, whether or not the applicant is from the local area, and possibly being a college graduate.

Figure 6.27 shows a regression for these three variables. Note that the Adjusted R^2 for this model has increased to 0.41. Next, we might consider dropping the variable College Grad. These results are shown in Figure 6.28. As you can see, the Adjusted R^2 declines to 0.39. Therefore, it appears that the three-variable model is the best. Even though the model explains only about 45 percent of the variation in the data, it may be

FIGURE 6.26 Regression Results with Additional Nominal Variables

	I	J	K	L	M	N	O	P	Q
SUMMARY OUTPUT									
Regression Statistics									
Multiple R	0.685822138								
R Square	0.470352005								
Adjusted R Square	0.37405237								
Standard Error	2.247401959								
Observations	40								
ANOVA									
	df	*SS*	*MS*	*F*	Significance F				
Regression	6	148.0168363	24.66947271	4.884255302	0.001136047				
Residual	33	166.6769137	5.050815567						
Total	39	314.69375							
	Coefficients	Standard Error	t Stat	P-value	Lower 95%	Upper 95%	Lower 95.0%	Upper 95.0%	
Intercept	-1.330477104	5.763506721	-0.230845069	0.818860412	-13.05642899	10.39547478	-13.05642899	10.39547478	
Yrseducation	0.083979089	0.48331756	0.17375551	0.863119116	-0.89933866	1.067296839	-0.89933866	1.067296839	
College gpa	-0.745109069	1.034889319	-0.719989138	0.476600602	-2.85060889	1.360390752	-2.85060889	1.360390752	
age	0.181607005	0.118173863	1.536778107	0.13388154	-0.058819717	0.422033728	-0.058819717	0.422033728	
M/F	0.327410634	0.778243368	0.420704689	0.676697966	-1.255938659	1.910759927	-1.255938659	1.910759927	
College Grad	1.391804392	1.426061927	0.975977526	0.336176258	-1.509542714	4.293151497	-1.509542714	4.293151497	
Local	3.492096285	0.792831286	4.404589408	0.000105319	1.879067626	5.105124944	1.879067626	5.105124944	

	J	K	L	M	N	O	P	Q
SUMMARY OUTPUT								
Regression Statistics								
Multiple R	0.676670252							
R Square	0.45788263							
Adjusted R Square	0.412706183							
Standard Error	2.176904964							
Observations	40							
ANOVA								
	df	*SS*	*MS*	*F*	*Significance F*			
Regression	3	144.092802	48.03093401	10.135428	5.57182E-05			
Residual	36	170.600948	4.738915222					
Total	39	314.69375						
	Coefficients	Standard Error	t Stat	P-value	Lower 95%	Upper 95%	Lower 95.0%	Upper 95.0%
Intercept	-1.815477807	2.48680335	-0.730044781	0.470087027	-6.858942122	3.227986508	-6.858942122	3.227986508
age	0.185323272	0.103248623	1.794922454	0.08106604	-0.024074365	0.39472091	-0.024074365	0.39472091
College Grad	1.189895496	0.775365171	1.53462593	0.133618475	-0.382615885	2.762406877	-0.382615885	2.762406877
Local	3.285074868	0.722833151	4.544720817	5.98404E-05	1.819103222	4.751046515	1.819103222	4.751046515

FIGURE 6.27 Three-Variable Regression Model Results

	J	K	L	M	N	O	P	Q
SUMMARY OUTPUT								
Regression Statistics								
Multiple R	0.649936892							
R Square	0.422417963							
Adjusted R Square	0.391197313							
Standard Error	2.216409667							
Observations	40							
ANOVA								
	df	*SS*	*MS*	*F*	*Significance F*			
Regression	2	132.932293	66.46614649	13.53008201	3.88914E-05			
Residual	37	181.761457	4.912471811					
Total	39	314.69375						
	Coefficients	Standard Error	t Stat	P-value	Lower 95%	Upper 95%	Lower 95.0%	Upper 95.0%
Intercept	-1.979163656	2.529601836	-0.782401257	0.438957635	-7.104618831	3.146291518	-7.104618831	3.146291518
age	0.229196592	0.10101206	2.269002248	0.02919116	0.024526916	0.433866267	0.024526916	0.433866267
Local	3.047598912	0.718888124	4.239322936	0.000143293	1.590994635	4.50420319	1.590994635	4.50420319

FIGURE 6.28 Two-Variable Regression Model Results

the best for the data available. The model predictions for the 30-year-old applicant we have been testing is

$$-1.815 + 0.185 \times \mathbf{30} + 1.190 \times \mathbf{1} + 3.285 \times \mathbf{0} = 4.93 \text{ years}$$

Multiple regression has been used effectively in many business applications. Kimes and Fitzsimmons[2] developed a model for La Quinta Motor Inns to evaluate proposed sites for new motels. This model included 35 variables, almost assuring high levels of multicollinearity. However, for the purpose used, this was not as important as having a comprehensive model to predict motel success. The cross-sectional study included 6 variables about competition, 18 variables about demand, 3 demographic variables, 4 market-related variables, and 4 physical variables. The characteristics of each proposed site could be entered into a spreadsheet containing the regression model and evaluated immediately.

---

[2] Kimes, S. E. and Fitzsimmons, J. A., "Selecting profitable hotel sites at La Quinta Motor Inns," *Interfaces*, Vol 19, No. 6, 1990, 83–94.

Regression Models with Nonlinear Terms

Linear regression models are not appropriate for every situation. If there is a reason to suspect a nonlinear relationship between the dependent variable and one or more independent variables, we might propose a nonlinear regression model to explain the relationships. One basis for selecting an appropriate model is to plot the dependent variable against the independent variable. If the relationship is clearly nonlinear, different forms of nonlinear models will probably fit the data better than a straight line. In the *Add Trendline* dialog box in Figure 6.8, you can see a variety of nonlinear forms of regression models involving a single variable. For example, a second order polynomial model would be

$$Y = \beta_0 + \beta_1 X + \beta_2 X^2 + \varepsilon$$

Multiple regression models might involve interaction terms:

$$Y = \beta_0 + \beta_1 X_1 + \beta_2 X_2 + \beta_{12} X_1 X_2 + \varepsilon$$

In this model, we are assuming that the relationship between X_1 and Y changes when the value of X_2 changes and vice-versa.

Although these models appear to be quite different from ordinary linear regression models, they both have the property that they are *linear in the parameters* (the betas). In other words, all terms are a product of a beta coefficient and some function of the data. In such cases, we can apply least squares to estimate the regression coefficients. We will illustrate this with another Tracway example.

As part of its efforts to remain competitive, Tracway tries to keep up with the latest in production technology. This is especially important in the highly competitive lawn mower line, where competitors can gain a real advantage if they develop more cost-effective means of production. The Tracway lawn mower division therefore spends a great deal of effort in testing new technology. When new production technology is introduced, firms often experience learning, resulting in a gradual decrease in the time required to produce successive units. (Think of your own experience in learning a task such as typing or playing a musical instrument.) Generally, the rate of improvement declines until the production time levels off.

One example is the production of a new design for lawn mower engines. To determine the time required to produce these engines, Tracway produced 50 units on its production line; test results are given on the worksheet *Engines* in the Tracway database. Figure 6.29 plots these data, which shows that a learning effect took place. The first unit took slightly over 61 minutes, with times decreasing until they reach just over 46 minutes, and a level of efficiency. Had Tracway based projections only on the first few units, the company could have made some poor business decisions. As Tracway is continually developing new technology, understanding the rate of learning can be useful in estimating future production costs without having to run extensive prototype trials.

As a basis for comparison, we will first fit a simple linear regression model to the data with time being the dependent variable and production unit number being the independent variable. The results are shown in Figure 6.30. The fit of this model is actually quite good, explaining about 85 percent of the change in production time. The model is

$$\text{Unit Production Time} = 58.18 - 0.29 \times \text{Unit number}$$

However, we can see that the model will mislead us for larger numbers of units produced. For example, this model says that the 200th engine will take $58.18 - 0.29 \times 200 = 0.18$ minutes, which is clearly not realistic. We also see from the residuals

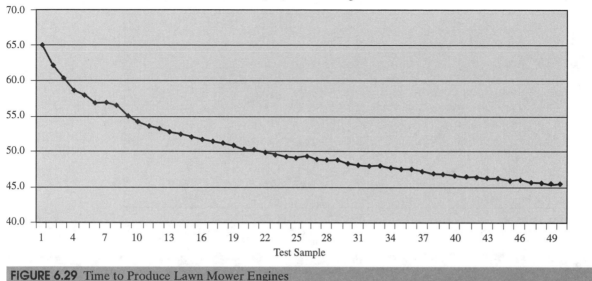

FIGURE 6.29 Time to Produce Lawn Mower Engines

D	E	F	G	H	I	J	K	L
SUMMARY OUTPUT								
Regression Statistics								
Multiple R	0.921357319							
R Square	0.848899309							
Adjusted R Square	0.845751378							
Standard Error	1.818268787							
Observations	50							
ANOVA								
	df	*SS*	*MS*	*F*	*Significance F*			
Regression	1	891.5529337	891.5529337	269.6689639	2.48594E-21			
Residual	48	158.6928663	3.306101381					
Total	49	1050.2458						
	Coefficients	*Standard Error*	*t Stat*	*P-value*	*Lower 95%*	*Upper 95%*	*Lower 95.0%*	*Upper 95.0%*
Intercept	58.18367347	0.522096433	111.4423884	1.29129E-59	57.13392885	59.23341809	57.13392885	59.23341809
Sample	-0.292614646	0.017818887	-16.42160053	2.48594E-21	-0.328441899	-0.256787393	-0.328441899	-0.256787393

FIGURE 6.30 Simple Linear Regression Model for Production Time

plot (Figure 6.31) that the errors are not evenly distributed around the regression line, an indication of an inappropriate model.

As an alternative, we might try a second order polynomial model:

$$Y = \beta_0 + \beta_1 X + \beta_2 X^2 + \varepsilon$$

This requires adding another column of data to the worksheet that represents the square of the unit number. The results of this model are given in Figure 6.32. The R^2 suggests a very strong fit, explaining over 96 percent of the variation. The residuals plots are somewhat better, but still do not appear random (Figure 6.33). The 200th engine would be predicted to take $61.8301 - 0.713356 \times 200 + 0.00825 \times 200^2 = 249.16$ minutes, which is clearly wrong. What is happening is that the curve, being a quadratic function, begins to extends upwards outside the range of the data. As you can see, selecting an appropriate model is not a trivial exercise but requires good knowledge of mathematical functions and their properties.

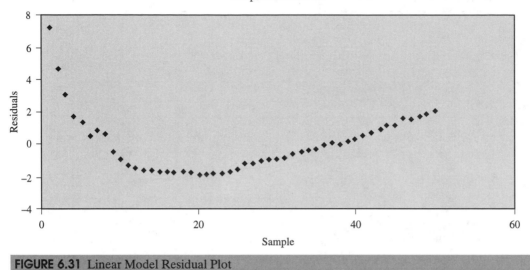

FIGURE 6.31 Linear Model Residual Plot

E	F	G	H	I	J	K	L	M
SUMMARY OUTPUT								
Regression Statistics								
Multiple R	0.980398299							
R Square	0.961180824							
Adjusted R Square	0.959528944							
Standard Error	0.931364547							
Observations	50							
ANOVA								
	df	*SS*	*MS*	*F*	*Significance F*			
Regression	2	1009.476124	504.7380619	581.8709175	6.95966E-34			
Residual	47	40.76967622	0.86743992					
Total	49	1050.2458						
	Coefficients	*Standard Error*	*t Stat*	*P-value*	*Lower 95%*	*Upper 95%*	*Lower 95.0%*	*Upper 95.0%*
Intercept	61.83010204	0.411494609	150.2573807	1.06122E-64	61.00228245	62.65792164	61.00228245	62.65792164
Sample	-0.713356404	0.037222154	-19.16483401	7.52013E-24	-0.788237649	-0.638475159	-0.788237649	-0.638475159
Sample sq	0.008249838	0.000707564	11.65949948	1.79834E-15	0.006826405	0.009673272	0.006826405	0.009673272

FIGURE 6.32 Second-Order Polynomial Linear Regression Model Results

A model that is often used to characterize learning situations is an exponential model:

$$Y = aX^b$$

This model is no longer linear in the regression coefficients (statisticians often call such a model *intrinsicly nonlinear*). This means that least squares regression cannot be applied because the assumptions will be violated. Fortunately, it is easy to transform this model to one that is linear in the coefficients by taking the natural logarithm of both sides of the equation. This yields the model

$$Ln\,Y = Ln\,a + b\,Ln\,X$$

In Excel, the natural logarithm of a number is obtained by the function =LN(*cell reference*). By performing this transformation on both the dependent and independent vari-

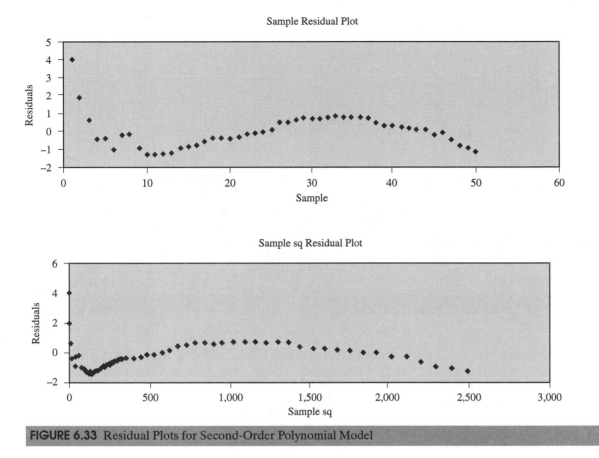

FIGURE 6.33 Residual Plots for Second-Order Polynomial Model

able data values, and applying the regression tool, we obtain the results in Figure 6.34. The new model is

$$Ln\ Y = 4.212171 - 0.097539\ Ln\ X$$

The fit of this model is good, with $R^2 = 0.9896$ (although when using logarithmic transformations, you need to keep in mind that the scale has been changed). Although the

FIGURE 6.34 Linear Regression Results for Logarithmic Transformation

E	F	G	H	I	J	K	L	M
SUMMARY OUTPUT								
Regression Statistics								
Multiple R	0.99479129							
R Square	0.98960971							
Adjusted R Square	0.989393245							
Standard Error	0.008978816							
Observations	50							
ANOVA								
	df	*SS*	*MS*	*F*	*Significance F*			
Regression	1	0.368566288	0.368566288	4571.6977	2.88602E-49			
Residual	48	0.003869718	8.06191E-05					
Total	49	0.372436006						
	Coefficients	*Standard Error*	*t Stat*	*P-value*	*Lower 95%*	*Upper 95%*	*Lower 95.0%*	*Upper 95.0%*
Intercept	4.212171076	0.004468069	942.7274156	4.3427E-104	4.203187426	4.221154725	4.203187426	4.221154725
log sample	-0.097539437	0.001442585	-67.61433058	2.88602E-49	-0.100439947	-0.094638926	-0.100439947	-0.094638926

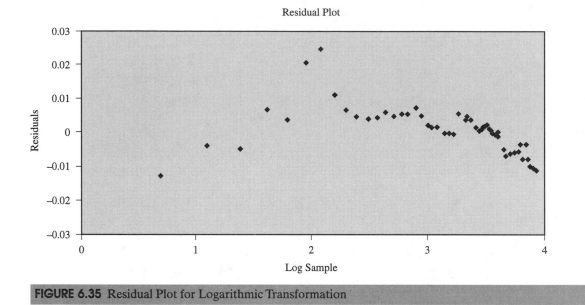

FIGURE 6.35 Residual Plot for Logarithmic Transformation

residual plot shows some apparent nonrandomness, note that the residuals are so tightly clustered around zero that this is a superior fit when compared with the other models (Figure 6.35).

To use this model to predict the time required for the 200th engine, we get

$$\text{Logarithm of engine number} = 4.212171 - 0.097539 \times \text{logarithm (200), or}$$
$$= 4.212171 - 0.097539 \times 5.298317 = 3.6954$$

To transform this back into the original data units, we find $e^{3.6954}$, where e is the base of natural logarithm, 2.71828 . . .), obtaining 40.26 minutes.

Summary

Regression is a powerful modeling tool to identify and understand relationships between independent and dependent variables. Regression is often applied to time series data as well as cross-sectional data. Simple linear regression involves a single independent variable; multiple regression models involve several independent variables. Ordinal and nominal data can be included in regression models through coding.

Regression models have important business applications in predicting the results of decisions. Good regression models should be based on fundamental knowledge that the set of independent variables can cause changes in the dependent variable. This enables managers to focus on variables they can control, with confidence that their decisions will lead to the results anticipated. New techniques such as data mining focus on the ability to predict rather than on statistical validity. However, a good fit says nothing about causation. Data may exhibit a statistical relationship, but in reality have little in common and may be due to a quirk of fate. As the celebrated quality management expert, W. Edwards Deming often said, there is no knowledge without theory.

Estimating parameters for a linear regression model is done using the method of least squares; Excel has various options for applying this theory, including the *Add Trendline* option in a scatter diagram and the *Regression* tool in the *Analysis Toolpak*.

The significance of regression is evaluated by viewing regression as analysis of variance. Key statistics used to evaluate the results are the coefficient of determination, correlation coefficient, and the ANOVA F-test. In using regression, it is important to pay attention to the underlying assumptions used in the least squares method: normally distributed errors and constant variance. If these are violated, the statistical significance of the results may be questionable.

In multiple regression models, we must be cautious of multicollinearity, which can be avoided by careful selection of independent variables that do not include overlapping information content. However, the need for this depends upon the intended use of the model. The existence of multicollinearity does not impede the ability of the regression model to predict. It may make more sense to include additional independent variables that have overlapping information if they make sense from a theoretical perspective (that is, the user expects the independent variable in question to have an impact on the dependent variable).

Questions and Problems

1. Describe the difference between dependent and independent variables in regression.
2. Explain the difference between time series data and cross-sectional data.
3. Develop a line chart and a simple linear regression model of Tracway total mower sales over time, using the data on the worksheet *Mower Unit Sales* in the Tracway database. You will need to add a column designating a numerical index for the month as the independent variable. Use the *Add Trendline* feature to show the fit for a linear model and for a polynomial model with five terms.
4. Develop a line chart and a simple linear regression model of Tracway total tractor sales over time, using the data on the worksheet *Tractor Unit Sales* in the Tracway database. You will need to add a column designating a numerical index for the month as the independent variable.
5. Develop a linear regression model for the sales of mowers in the North American region on the worksheet *Mower Unit Sales* in the Tracway database. You will need to add a column designating a numerical index for the month as the independent variable. Graph the data, adding a trendline.
6. Develop a linear regression model for the sales of tractors in the North American region on the worksheet *Tractor Unit Sales* in the Tracway database. You will need to add a column designating a numerical index for the month as the independent variable. Graph the data, adding a trendline.
7. Develop a 95 percent confidence band for the sales of mowers in the North American region on the worksheet *Mower Unit Sales* in the Tracway database.
8. Develop a 95 percent confidence band for the sales of tractors in the North American region on the worksheet *Tractor Unit Sales* in the Tracway database.
9. Compare the F statistic with the R^2 statistic in the regression of mower sales in the North American region versus time. You will need to add a column designating a numerical index for the month as the independent variable.
10. Autocorrelation involves relationships between errors and the errors of a given number of periods prior. Discuss how autocorrelation might be expected in cyclical data.
11. Describe the difference between systematic risk and specific risk in the context of financial investment.

Problems 12 through 23 use the database HATCO.xls, adopted from Hair, Anderson, Tatham, and Black in *Multivariate Analysis*, 5th edition, Prentice Hall, 1998. This database consists of data related to predicting the level of business obtained from HATCO's customers. The variables are

X1 Delivery speed
X2 Price level

X3 Price flexibility
X4 Manufacturer image
X5 Overall service
X6 Salesforce image
X7 Product quality
X8 Firm size   (0–small; 1–large)
X9 Usage level (dependent variable)

HATCO management considers the first seven of the independent variables (X1 through X7) to be possible factors in influencing usage level.

12. Develop a correlation matrix, and interpret the likely strength of X1 through X7 as variables to explain X9 (Usage level).
13. Construct a simple linear regression model of Usage level (X9) as a function of Overall service (X5) and interpret the result.
14. Construct a simple linear regression model of Usage level as a function of Delivery speed (X1) and interpret the result.
15. Construct a multiple regression model with Usage level as the dependent variable, and Delivery speed (X1) and Overall service (X5) as independent variables. Interpret the output.
16. If the regression of Usage level versus X5 explained 49 percent of the variation in Usage level, and the regression of Usage level versus X1 explained 46 percent of the variation in Usage level, why did the regression of Usage level versus X1 and X5 together explain only about 59 percent of the variation in Usage level?
17. Interpret the Adjusted R^2 measures between the three regression models in problems 13 through 15.
18. Construct the regression of Usage level as a function of all seven independent variables X1 through X7. Interpret the output.
19. How can the P-value from the t statistic for Delivery speed (0.983) be so much worse in this model than it was in the model obtained in problem 14 (which was 1.14E-14) or problem 15 (which was 5.65E-06)?
20. Construct a regression model using Price flexibility (X3), Overall service (X5), and Salesforce image (X6) as independent variables. Interpret the output compared with that in problem 18.
21. Compare the Adjusted R^2 of the models in problems 18 and 20.
22. Include the binary variable X8 (coded as 0 for small firms, and 1 for large firms) along with variables X3, X5, and X6 in a regression model, and compare with that in problem 20.
23. Segregate the HATCO data by firm size. (That is, rearrange data so that firm size is in the left of all X3, X5, X6, and X1. Select all five variables and sort.) Run separate regressions on the data for small firms and the data for large firms. Compare the difference in intercepts with the results of problem 22.
24. (From Horngren, Foster, and Datar, *Cost Accounting: A Managerial Emphasis,* 9th ed., 1997, Prentice Hall, 371.)
    The managing director of a consulting group has the following monthly data on total overhead costs and professional labor-hours to bill to clients.

Total Overhead Costs	Billable Hours
$340,000	3,000
$400,000	4,000
$435,000	5,000
$477,000	6,000
$529,000	7,000
$587,000	8,000

Generate a regression formula to identify the fixed overhead costs to the consulting group.
 a. What is the constant component of the consultant group's overhead?
 b. If a special job requiring 1,000 billable hours that would contribute a margin of $38,000 before overhead was available, would the job be attractive?

25. (From Horngren, Foster, and Datar, *Cost Accounting: A Managerial Emphasis,* 9th ed., 1997, Prentice Hall, 349.)
Cost functions are often nonlinear with volume, as production facilities are often able to produce larger quantities at lower rates than smaller quantities. Using the following data, plot the data and use the Chart, *Add Trendline* feature. Compare a linear trendline with a logarithmic trendline.

Units Produced	Costs
500	12,500
1,000	25,000
1,500	32,500
2,000	40,000
2,500	45,000
3,000	50,000

26. (From Horngren, Foster, and Datar, *Cost Accounting: A Managerial Emphasis,* 9th ed., 1997, Prentice Hall, 349.)
The Helicopter Division of Aerospatiale is studying assembly costs at its Marseilles plant. Past data indicates the following costs per helicopter:

Helicopter Number	Labor-Hours
1	2,000
2	1,400
3	1,238
4	1,142
5	1,075
6	1,029
7	985
8	957

Use linear regression, and compare the results with a second-order polynomial regression model. Using the model with the best fit, predict the hours required for a ninth helicopter.
27. For the data in problem 26, use an exponential regression model and estimate the hours required for the ninth helicopter.
28. (From Crask, Fox, and Stout, *Marketing Research: Principles & Applications,* Prentice Hall, 1995, 252.)
A real estate company hired a small market research firm to develop a model to calculate a ballpark price for a home based only on square footage. The real estate company felt that this model would be useful in helping customers set the list prices

of their homes. The market research firm wants a linear regression relating price as a function of square footage based on the following sample data.

List Price	Square Footage
75,900	1,750
61,000	1,590
110,000	2,100
83,500	1,800
94,600	1,890
54,500	1,360
96,000	2,050
70,700	1,760
50,800	1,500
69,400	1,650
87,500	1,700
105,000	1,920
76,500	1,800
103,200	2,150
59,000	1,600

29. Using the *Defects After Delivery* worksheet in the Tracway database, compare the following simple linear regression models against time. What do the results indicate?
   a. January 1996 through August 1997
   b. September 1997 through December 2000
   c. January 1996 through December 2000
30. Use the *PHStat* Best Subsets regression tool for the HATCO database to identify the best regression models with Usage level as the dependent variable.

References

Evans, J. R., *Operations Management: Quality Performance and Value,* 5th ed., St. Paul: West Publishing Company, 1996.

Harnett, D. L. and Horrell, J. F., *Data, Statistics, and Decision Models with Excel,* New York: John Wiley & Sons, 1998.

Kime, S. E. and Fitzsimmons, J. A., "Selecting profitable hotel sites at La Quinta Motor Inns," *Interfaces,* Vol. 20, No. 2, 1990, 12–20.

Lentner, M. and Bishop, T., *Experimental Design and Analysis,* 2nd ed., Blacksburg, VA: Valley Book Company, 1993.

Levine, D. M., Berenson, M. L. and Stephan, D., *Statistics for Managers Using Microsoft Excel,* Upper Saddle River, NJ: Prentice Hall, 1997.

Pindyck, R. S. and Rubinfeld, D. L., *Econometric Models and Economic Forecasts,* New York: McGraw-Hill, 1976.

Ragsdale, C. T., *Spreadsheet Modeling and Decision Analysis,* 2nd ed., Cincinnati: South-Western Publishing Co., 1998.

CHAPTER 7

Forecasting

Outline

Qualitative and Judgmental Methods
   Historical Analogy
   The Delphi Method
   Applying the Delphi Method
   Indicators and Indexes
Statistical Forecasting Models
   Moving Average Models
   Error Metrics and Forecast Accuracy
   Exponential Smoothing Models
   Incorporating Trend and Seasonality into Exponential Smoothing Models
Regression Models
   Incorporating Seasonality in Regression Models
The Practice of Forecasting
Summary
Questions and Problems
Appendix: *CB Predictor*

One of the major problems that managers face is forecasting future events in order to make good decisions. For example, forecasts of interest rates, energy prices, and other economic indicators are needed for financial planning; forecasts of sales are needed to plan production and workforce capacity; and forecasts of trends in demographics, consumer behavior, and technological innovation are needed for long-term strategic planning. The government invests significant resources on predicting short-run U.S. business performance using the Index of Leading Indicators. This index focuses on the performance of individual businesses, which often is highly correlated with the performance of the overall economy, and is used to forecast economic trends for the nation as a whole. In this chapter we introduce some common methods and approaches to forecasting, including both qualitative and quantitative techniques.

Managers may choose from a wide range of forecasting techniques. Selecting the appropriate method depends upon the characteristics of the forecasting problem such as the time horizon of the variable being forecast, as well as available information upon which the forecast will be based. The three major categories of forecasting approaches are *qualitative and judgmental techniques, statistical time series models,* and *explanatory/causal methods.* Qualitative and judgmental techniques rely on experience and intuition; they are necessary when historical data are not available or when the decision maker needs to forecast far into the future. For example, a forecast of when the next generation of a microprocessor will be available and what capabilities it might have will depend greatly on the opinions and expertise of individuals who understand the technology. Statistical time series models find greater applicability for short-range forecasting problems. A **time series** is a stream of historical data, such as weekly sales. Time series models assume that whatever forces have influenced sales in the recent past will continue into the near future; thus forecasts are developed by extrapolating these data into the future.

Explanatory/causal models seek to identify factors that explain statistically the patterns observed in the variable being forecast, usually with regression analysis. Although time series models use only time as the independent variable, explanatory/causal models generally include other factors. For example, forecasting the price of oil might incorporate independent variables such as the demand for oil measured in barrels, the proportion of oil stock generated by OPEC countries, and tax rates. Although we can never prove that changes in these variables actually cause changes in the price of oil, we often have evidence that a strong influence exists.

Surveys of forecasting practices [Sanders and Manrodt, 1994] have shown that both judgmental and quantitative methods are used for forecasting sales of product lines or product families, as well as for broad company and industry forecasts. Simple time series models are used for short- and medium-range forecasts, whereas regression analysis is the most popular method for long-range forecasting. However, many companies rely on judgmental methods far more than quantitative methods, and almost half judgmentally adjust quantitative forecasts.

In this chapter we focus on these three approaches to forecasting. Specifically, we will discuss

- Historical analogy and the Delphi method as approaches to judgmental forecasting;
- Moving average, exponential smoothing, and Holt-Winters models of time series forecasting, with a discussion of evaluating the quality of forecasts;
- The use of regression models for explanatory/causal forecasting; and
- Some insights into the practical issues associated with forecasting.

We will use three worksheets from the Tracway database—*Mower Unit Sales, Market Share Tractors,* and *World Tractor Unit Sales*—to illustrate these approaches in this chapter. Figure 7.1 shows portions of these for your reference.

Qualitative and Judgmental Methods

Qualitative, or judgmental, forecasting methods are valuable in situations for which no historical data are available, or in those that specifically require human expertise and knowledge. One example might be identifying future opportunities and threats as part of a SWOT (strengths, weaknesses, opportunities, and threats) analysis within a strategic planning exercise. Another use of judgmental methods is to incorporate nonquantitative information, such as the impact of government regulations or competitor behavior, in a quantitative forecast. Judgmental techniques range from simple methods such as manager's opinion or a group-based jury of executive opinion, to more structured approaches such as historical analogy and the Delphi method.

	A	B	C	D	E	F	G
1	Mower Unit Sales						
2							
3	Month	World	NA	SA	Europe	Pacific	China
4	Jan-96	7020	6000	200	720	100	0
5	Feb-96	9280	7950	220	990	120	0
6	Mar-96	9780	8100	250	1320	110	0
7	Apr-96	11100	9050	280	1650	120	0
8	May-96	11930	9900	310	1590	130	0
9	Jun-96	12240	10200	300	1620	120	0
10	Jul-96	10740	8730	280	1590	140	0

	A	B	C	D	E	F	G
1	Market Share Tractors						
2							
3	Month	World	NA	SA	Eur	Pac	China
4	Jan-96	0.102	0.070	0.250	0.110	0.210	
5	Feb-96	0.105	0.071	0.257	0.113	0.211	
6	Mar-96	0.106	0.073	0.256	0.112	0.213	
7	Apr-96	0.107	0.076	0.263	0.111	0.215	
8	May-96	0.109	0.077	0.265	0.110	0.213	
9	Jun-96	0.113	0.080	0.265	0.111	0.211	
10	Jul-96	0.114	0.083	0.266	0.106	0.219	

	A	B	C	D	E	F	G
1	World Tractor Unit Sales						
2							
3	Month	World	NA	SA	Eur	Pac	China
4	Jan-96	15518	8143	1000	5091	1000	284
5	Feb-96	16325	8592	1051	5310	1090	283
6	Mar-96	17129	8630	1016	6071	1127	285
7	Apr-96	17327	8947	1027	5856	1209	288
8	May-96	16278	8442	1057	5273	1221	286
9	Jun-96	15448	7500	1019	5315	1327	287
10	Jul-96	15905	6145	977	7170	1324	289

FIGURE 7.1 Portions of Tracway Database Used in This Chapter

HISTORICAL ANALOGY

One judgmental approach is **historical analogy,** in which a forecast is obtained through a comparative analysis with a previous situation. For example, if a new product is being introduced, the response of similar previous products to marketing campaigns can be used as a basis to predict how the new marketing campaign might fare. Of course, temporal changes or other unique factors might not be fully considered in such an approach. However, a great deal of insight can often be gained through an analysis of past experiences. For example, in early 1998 the price of oil was over $22 a barrel. However, in mid-1998, the price of a barrel of oil dropped to around $11. The reasons for this price drop included an oversupply of oil from new production in the Caspian Sea region, high production in non-OPEC regions, and lower than normal demand. In similar circumstances in the past, OPEC would meet and take action to raise the price of oil. Thus from historical analogy, we might forecast a rise in the price of oil. OPEC did in fact meet in mid-1998 and agreed to cut their production, but nobody believed that they would actually cooperate effectively, and the price continued to drop for a time. Analogies often provide good forecasts, but you need to be careful to recognize new or different circumstances. Another analogy is international conflict relative to the price of oil. Should war break out, the price of oil would be expected to rise, analogous to what it has done in the past.

THE DELPHI METHOD

A popular judgmental forecasting approach is called the **Delphi method.** The Delphi method uses a panel of experts, whose identities are typically kept confidential from one another, to respond to a sequence of questionnaires. After each round of responses, individual opinions, edited to ensure anonymity, are shared, allowing each to see what the other experts think. Seeing other experts' opinions helps to reinforce those in agreement, and possibly to consider other factors when they did not agree. In the next round, the experts revise their estimates, and the process is repeated, usually for no more than a total of two or three rounds. The Delphi method promotes unbiased exchanges of ideas and discussion, and usually results in some convergence of opinion. It is one of the better approaches to forecasting long-range trends and impacts. The following example shows how the Delphi method might be applied to a situation at Tracway, Inc.

APPLYING THE DELPHI METHOD

Sales data in Tracway's database shows that the mower business is relatively flat, whereas tractor sales have experienced significant growth, increasing from about 10 to nearly 17 percent in the past 5 years. This growth is not the same in all sales regions; for example, it appears that growth in North America, South America, and China is strong, but that sales in the European and Pacific regions are either steady or declining. With continued global expansion and increasing demand, Tracway faces a need to expand production capacity. However, before deciding upon new location of plants and their specific capacities, which involve substantial capital investment, management needs to better understand the growth that might be expected in the global market. Thus Mike Mortensen, Tracway's CEO, needs to address the question: Where will significant changes in regional markets occur in the future?

Mike hired three industry experts to provide their opinions of expected changes to Tracway's market share in each key region. In order to obtain forecasts with the least amount of bias, Mike decided to use the Delphi method. To keep the experts anonymous, they were identified only as A, B, and C. Each expert was asked to provide his or her estimates of the market for mowers and tractors by region over the next 10 years, which were then shared among the group. For the money budgeted, Mike was able to obtain the commitment of the three experts for two rounds of reports.

Delphi First Round

In the first round, Expert A forecast that worldwide mower sales would decline slightly, with decreases in the North American and European regions and some compensating increases in South America, the Pacific, and China. Because these last three regions had a much lower sales base, Expert A expected mower sales in total to be slightly lower. This expert saw much brighter prospects for the small tractor market, especially in North America. The South American region was forecasted to have stronger proportional increases, but lower absolute increases because they currently had a much lower sales level than did North America. In addition, the Chinese market for small tractors was forecasted to boom, and European demand for small tractors was expected to grow slightly. However, due to economic problems, demand in the Pacific region was highly uncertain.

Expert B had a strong reputation for his knowledge of the European region. He forecasted strong regional growth in demand for small tractors over the next 5 years, and steady demand for mowers. However, he also felt that the European Economic Community was expected to make it quite difficult for outside companies (such as Tracway) to compete.

Expert C was known for her expertise in the economies of the Pacific, Chinese, and South America regions. She forecast that demand for small tractors would increase substantially in South America and China. Pacific region demand for small tractors should increase, but a great deal of uncertainty would exist, especially in the first 5 years of the forecast period. Demand for mowers was expected to increase in South America to a small degree, and to be quite small in the Pacific region. After 5 years, she believed that the Pacific region would have a strong economic recovery.

Mike read the first round of reports and shared them with the team of experts. For the second round, Mike requested that each expert provide numerical forecasts for expected changes by region over a 5-year horizon, along with assessments of market risks.

Delphi Second Round

Table 7.1 shows the percent changes that each expert forecast. Expert A considered the North American and European markets to be very predictable and steady, with little risk and low growth. The South American region was expected to promise the greatest opportunities for growth, but there was a risk that rampant inflation could return and disrupt economies, leading to the real possibility of market declines. The Pacific region was viewed as the most turbulent, already suffering some economic hardship that could easily lead to political unrest, further deteriorating that market. Expert A considered the Chinese region to be safe, and a promising new market for small tractors. Expert B was very optimistic about the growth potential for the European region. However, regulatory conditions could make the market increase potential for Tracway quite low. Expert C was optimistic about the South American region. This expert did not expect inflation to get out of control, because the governments in that region had seen what damage inflation could do and were experienced in dealing with it. Expert C felt that the Pacific region would also be able to deal with its economic problems, given time. There was more concern about political factors in China, which could change the current strong growth in demand for small tractors.

Delphi Conclusions

The Delphi method ideally yields agreement among all of the participating experts, although this does not always occur. The value of Delphi is the learning that takes place because of the exchanges among the experts and, most important of all, the learning experienced by the decision maker. The process can stop when the decision maker is confident of the expected outcomes.

In this case, after the second round, Mike Mortensen felt confident that tractor sales growth would be strong, with the bulk of the increase being in the North American region (25 percent increase) and the South American region (50 percent increase). Sales were expected to be the same as last year in the European region (despite more optimistic impressions of Expert A and Expert B) and the Pacific region. Extremely high rates of growth were expected from the Chinese region, although the volumes involved

TABLE 7.1 Results of First Round of Delphi Method

	Expert A	*Expert B*	*Expert C*
Tractors—NA region	+20% to +25%		
Tractors—SA region	+50% to +70%		+30% to +60%
Tractors—European region	+10% to +20%	+20% to +30%	
Tractors—Pacific region	−20% to +30%		+20% to +100%
Tractors—Chinese region	+200% to +300%		+50% to +150%
Mowers—NA region	−10% to −5%		
Mowers—SA region	+30% to +50%		+10% to +20%
Mowers—European region	−10% to −5%	No change to +10%	
Mowers—Pacific region	No change to +10%		No change to +20%

were expected to be inconsequential for a few more years given the much higher volumes in North and South America.

The expectation for mower sales was much less optimistic. The vast majority of sales from mowers occurred in the North American region, and a slight decrease in sales (about 5 percent) was expected over the next year. The same was true for the European region, the only other region with significant mower sales volume. Sales in South America and the Pacific regions might provide pleasant surprises, but Mike was not counting on significant growth in mower demand, and was planning on holding mower production capacity at no more than its current level. In fact, slight decreases in capacity were planned.

INDICATORS AND INDEXES

Indicators and indexes generally play an important role in developing judgmental forecasts. **Indicators** are measures that are believed to influence the behavior of a variable we wish to forecast. By monitoring changes in indicators, we expect to gain insight about the future behavior of the variable to help forecast the future. For example, one variable that is important to the nation's economy is the gross domestic product (GDP), which is a measure of the value of all goods and services produced in the United States. Despite its shortcomings (for example, unpaid work such as housekeeping and child care is not measured; production of poor quality output inflates the measure, as does work expended on corrective action), it is a practical and useful measure of economic performance. Like most time series, the GDP rises and falls in a cyclical fashion. Predicting future trends in the GDP is often done by analyzing *leading indicators*—series that tend to rise and fall some predictable length of time prior to the peaks and valleys of the GDP. One example of a leading indicator is the formation of business enterprises; as the rate of new businesses grows, one would expect the GDP to increase in the future. Other examples of leading indicators are the percentage change in the money supply and net change in business loans. Other indicators, called *lagging indicators,* tend to have peaks and valleys that follow those of the GDP. Some lagging indicators are the consumer price index, prime rate, business investment expenditures, and inventories on hand. The GDP can be used to predict future trends in these indicators.

Indicators are often combined quantitatively into an **index.** The direction of movement of all the selected indicators are weighted and combined, providing an index of overall expectation. For example, financial analysts use the Dow Jones industrial average as an index of general stock market performance. Indexes do not provide a complete forecast, but rather a better picture of direction of change, and thus play an important role in judgmental forecasting.

The Department of Commerce began an Index of Leading Indicators to help predict future economic performance. Components of the index include

- Average weekly hours, manufacturing
- Average weekly initial claims, unemployment insurance
- New orders, consumer goods and materials
- New orders, nondefense capital goods
- Vendor performance—slower deliveries
- Building permits, private housing
- Stock prices, 500 common stocks (S&P)
- Money supply
- Interest rate spread
- Index of consumer expectations (Univ. of Michigan)

Business Conditions Digest included over 100 time series in seven economic areas. This publication was discontinued in March 1990, but information related to the Index of Leading Indicators was continued in *Survey of Current Business.* In December 1995, the U.S. Department of Commerce sold this data source to The Conference Board, which now markets the information under the title *Business Cycle Indicators;* information can be obtained at its Web site, http://www.conference-board.org/. The site includes excellent current information about the calculation of the index, as well as its current components.

Statistical Forecasting Models

Many forecasts are based on analysis of historical time series data, and are predicated on the assumption that the future is an extrapolation of the past. A naive approach is to eyeball a **trend**—a gradual shift in the value of the time series—by visually examining a plot of the data. For instance, Figure 7.2 shows a graph of mower sales for the Pacific region over the past 5 years (obtained from the worksheet *Mower Unit Sales* in the Tracway database). Looking at the trend, we might expect sales over the next year to increase by about 25 units.

Time series may also exhibit short-term *seasonal effects* (over a year, month, week, or even a day) as well as longer-term *cyclical effects* or nonlinear trends. For example, Figure 7.3 shows mower sales in Europe over the past 5 years. We can easily see that sales exhibit a seasonal pattern over the course of each year, with low sales in January and peaks in July, as well as a downward trend. The data suggests that sales might drop about 80 units over the next year while maintaining its seasonal pattern. At a neighborhood pharmacy, for example, seasonal patterns may occur over a day, with the heaviest volume of customers in the morning and around the dinner hour. The pattern might even vary by day of the week, being higher on Friday, Saturday, and Monday than on other days. Cycles relate to much longer term behavior, such as periods of inflation and recession, or bull-and-bear stock market behavior.

FIGURE 7.2 Graph of Mower Sales—Pacific Region Showing Upward Trend

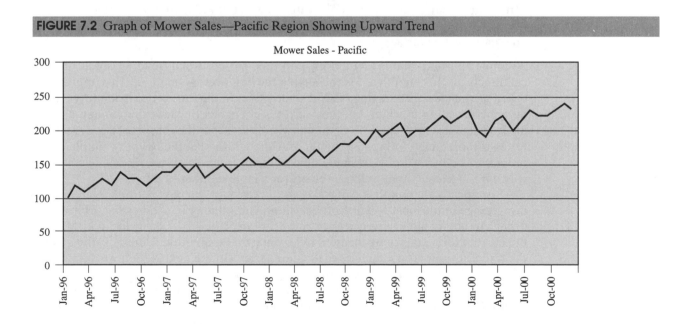

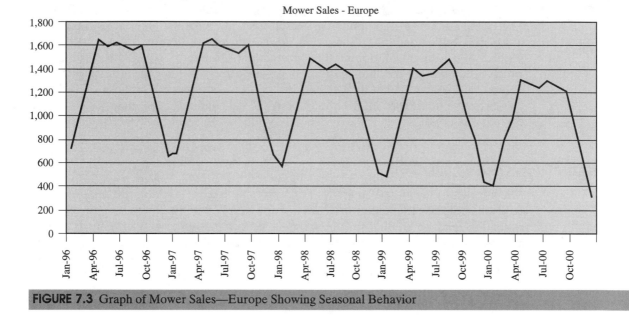

FIGURE 7.3 Graph of Mower Sales—Europe Showing Seasonal Behavior

Of course, such unscientific approaches may be a bit unsettling to a manager making important decisions. Subtle effects and interactions of seasonal and cyclical factors may not be evident from simple visual extrapolation of data. Statistical methods, which involve more formal analyses of time series, are invaluable in developing good forecasts. A variety of statistically based forecasting methods for time series are commonly used. Among the most popular are *moving average methods, exponential smoothing,* and *regression analysis.* These can be implemented very easily on a spreadsheet using basic functions available in Microsoft Excel and the tools contained in the *Analysis Toolpak;* these are summarized in Table 7.2. Finally, the CD-ROM accompanying this book contains an Excel add-in, *CB Predictor,* which contains a variety of forecasting methods with some intelligent technology. We will describe *CB Predictor* later in this chapter.

MOVING AVERAGE MODELS

A simple approach that is useful over short time periods when trend, seasonal, or cyclical effects are *not* significant is the **simple moving average** method. This approach is based on the idea of averaging random fluctuations in the time series to identify the underlying direction in which the time series is changing. Because the moving average method assumes that future observations will be similar to the recent past, it is most useful as a short-range forecasting method. Although this method is very simple, it has proven to be quite useful in stable environments, such as inventory management, in which it is necessary to develop forecasts for a large number of items.

Specifically, the simple moving average forecast for the next period is computed as the average of the most recent k observations. The value of k is somewhat arbitrary, although its choice affects the accuracy of the forecast. The larger the value of k, the more the current forecast is dependent on older data; the smaller the value of k, the quicker the forecast responds to changes in the time series. (In the next section we discuss how to select k by examining errors associated with different values.)

For example, suppose that we want to forecast Tracway's total market share for tractors for January 2001 using a three-period moving average ($k = 3$). From the work-

TABLE 7.2 Excel Support for Forecasting

Excel Functions	***Description***
TREND(*known_y's, known_x's, new_x's, constant*)	Returns values along a linear trend line.
GROWTH(*known_y's, known_x's, new_x's, constant*)	Calculates predicted exponential growth.
LINEST(*known_y's, known_x's, new_x's, constant, stats*)	Returns an array that describes a straight line that best fits the data.
FORECAST(*x, known_y's, known_x's*)	Calculates a future value along a linear trend.
Analysis Toolpak	
Moving average	Projects forecast values based on the average value of the variable over a specific number of preceding periods.
Exponential smoothing	Predicts a value based on the forecast for the prior period, adjusted for the error in that prior forecast.
Regression	Used to develop a model relating time series data to a set of variables assumed to influence the data.

sheet *Market Share Tractors* in the Tracway database, the fractional world market share is 0.1682 in October 2000, 0.1683 in November, and 0.1690 in December. The three-period moving average forecast for January 2001 is

$$\text{January 2001 forecast} = \frac{0.1682 + 0.1683 + 0.1690}{3} = 0.1685$$

Moving average forecasts can be generated easily on a spreadsheet. Figure 7.4 shows the computations for a three-period moving average forecast of Tracway's world market share for tractors for the 12 months of the year 2000, and the forecast for January 2001. Figure 7.5 shows a graph that contrasts the data with the forecasted values. Moving average forecasts can also be obtained from Excel's *Analysis Toolpak* (see *Excel Note: Forecasting with Moving Averages*).

Weighted Moving Averages

In the simple moving average approach, the data are weighted equally. This may not be desirable, because we might wish to put more weight on recent observations than on older observations, particularly if the time series is changing rapidly. For example, you

	A	B	C	D	E	F
1	**Moving Average Forecast - World Tractor Market Share**					
2						
3	**Month**	**Market Share**	**Moving Average**			
4	Oct-99	0.1525				
5	Nov-99	0.1521		=AVERAGE(B4:B6)		
6	Dec-99	0.1511				
7	Jan-00	0.1540	0.1519	Forecast for Jan-00		
8	Feb-00	0.1563	0.1524			
9	Mar-00	0.1579	0.1538			
10	Apr-00	0.1618	0.1560			
11	May-00	0.1624	0.1586			
12	Jun-00	0.1633	0.1607			
13	Jul-00	0.1655	0.1625			
14	Aug-00	0.1667	0.1637			
15	Sep-00	0.1692	0.1652			
16	Oct-00	0.1682	0.1672			
17	Nov-00	0.1683	0.1681			
18	Dec-00	0.1690	0.1686			
19			0.1685	Forecast for Jan-01		
20						

FIGURE 7.4 Moving Average Forecasts for World Tractor Market Share

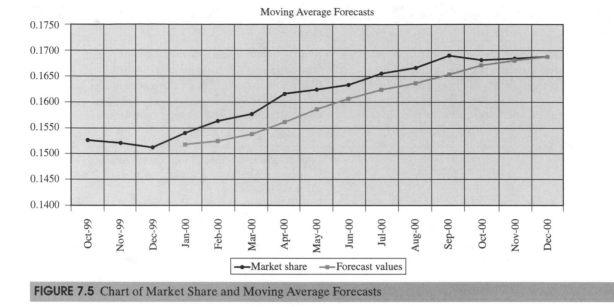

FIGURE 7.5 Chart of Market Share and Moving Average Forecasts

might assign a 60 percent weight to the most recent observation, 30 percent to the observation two periods prior, and the remaining 10 percent of the weight to the observation three periods prior. In this case the three-period weighted moving average forecast for January 2001 would be

$$\text{January 2001 Forecast} = \frac{0.1 \times 0.1682 + 0.3 \times 0.1683 + 0.6 \times 0.1690}{0.1 + 0.3 + 0.6}$$

$$= \frac{0.1687}{1} = 0.1687$$

Note that this value is higher than the equally weighted case, and we would expect a better forecast because the market share is increasing. Different weights can easily be incorporated into Excel formulas. This leads us to the questions of how to measure forecast accuracy, and also how to select the best parameters for a forecasting model.

ERROR METRICS AND FORECAST ACCURACY

The quality of a forecast depends on how accurate it is in predicting future values of a time series. The error in a forecast is the difference between the forecast and the actual value of the time series (once it is known!). In Figure 7.5, this is simply the vertical distance between the forecast and the data for the same time period. Note that the moving average forecast tends to consistently underestimate the actual market share; this is due to the increasing trend in the time series. We might be able to reduce this bias by selecting different parameters. In the simple moving average model, different values for k will produce different forecasts. How do we know, for example, if a 2-, 3-, or 4-period; 3-period weighted; or maybe even a 12-period moving average model would be the best predictor of Tracway's market share? We might first generate different forecasts using each of these models as shown in Figure 7.6 for the last two years' of market share data and compare them against the actual data as shown in Figure 7.7.

Because of the trend, all models lag the time series; in particular, the 12-month moving average model can be seen to be lagging the data significantly, because the larger number of observations in each calculation makes the forecast slow to respond

Excel Note: Forecasting with Moving Averages

From the *Tools* menu, select *Data Analysis,* and then *Moving Average.* Excel displays the dialog box shown in Figure 7.8. Enter the *Input Range* of the data, the *Interval* (the value of k), and the first cell of the *Output Range.* You may also obtain a chart of the data and the moving averages, as well as a column of standard errors, by checking the appropriate boxes. However, we do not recommend using the chart or error options because the forecasts are not aligned correctly with the data (the forecast value aligned with a particular data point represents the forecast for the *next* month), and thus can be misleading. Rather, we recommend that you generate your own chart as we did in Figure 7.5. Figure 7.9 shows the results produced by the *Moving Average* tool. Note that the forecast for Jan-00 is aligned with the actual value for Dec-99 on the chart. Compare this to Figure 7.5 and you can see the difference.

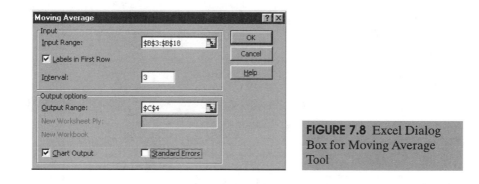

FIGURE 7.8 Excel Dialog Box for Moving Average Tool

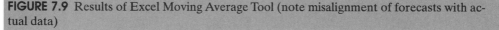

FIGURE 7.9 Results of Excel Moving Average Tool (note misalignment of forecasts with actual data)

	A	B	C	D	E	F	G
1		Tractor					3-period
2		Market					weighted
3	Date	Share	MA2	MA3	MA4	MA12	(0.1, 0.3, 0.6)
4	Jan-99	0.1521					
5	Feb-99	0.1467					
6	Mar-99	0.1468	0.1494				
7	Apr-99	0.1458	0.1468	0.1485			0.1473
8	May-99	0.1464	0.1463	0.1464	0.1479		0.1462
9	Jun-99	0.1492	0.1461	0.1464	0.1464		0.1463
10	Jul-99	0.1512	0.1478	0.1472	0.1471		0.1480
11	Aug-99	0.1519	0.1502	0.1489	0.1482		0.1501
12	Sep-99	0.1520	0.1516	0.1508	0.1497		0.1514
13	Oct-99	0.1525	0.1519	0.1517	0.1511		0.1519
14	Nov-99	0.1521	0.1522	0.1521	0.1519		0.1523
15	Dec-99	0.1511	0.1523	0.1522	0.1521		0.1522
16	Jan-00	0.1540	0.1516	0.1519	0.1519	0.1498	0.1516
17	Feb-00	0.1563	0.1526	0.1524	0.1524	0.1500	0.1530
18	Mar-00	0.1579	0.1551	0.1538	0.1534	0.1508	0.1551
19	Apr-00	0.1618	0.1571	0.1560	0.1548	0.1517	0.1570
20	May-00	0.1624	0.1598	0.1586	0.1575	0.1530	0.1601
21	Jun-00	0.1633	0.1621	0.1607	0.1596	0.1544	0.1617
22	Jul-00	0.1655	0.1628	0.1625	0.1613	0.1555	0.1629
23	Aug-00	0.1667	0.1644	0.1637	0.1632	0.1567	0.1645
24	Sep-00	0.1692	0.1661	0.1652	0.1645	0.1580	0.1660
25	Oct-00	0.1682	0.1680	0.1672	0.1662	0.1594	0.1681
26	Nov-00	0.1683	0.1687	0.1681	0.1674	0.1607	0.1684
27	Dec-00	0.1690	0.1683	0.1686	0.1681	0.1621	0.1684

FIGURE 7.6 Alternative Moving Average Forecasting Models

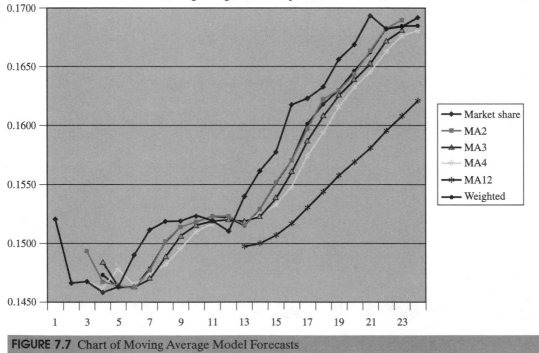

FIGURE 7.7 Chart of Moving Average Model Forecasts

to the current changes. The 2-period moving average and the 3-period weighted models are nearly identical in results, and are the best among these models because they do not smooth out the trend in the data as much.

To analyze the accuracy of these models more precisely, we can define *error metrics* that compare quantitatively the forecast with the actual observations. Three metrics that are commonly used are the *mean absolute deviation, mean square error,* and *mean absolute percentage error.* The **mean absolute deviation (MAD)** is the average difference between the actual value and the forecast, averaged over the range of forecasted values.

$$\text{MAD} = \frac{\sum_{i=1}^{n} |A_t - F_t|}{n}$$

where A_t is the actual value of the time series at time t, F_t is the forecast value for time t, and n is the number of forecast values (*not* the number of data points because we do not have a forecast value associated with the first k data points). MAD provides a robust measure of error, and is less affected by extreme observations.

Mean square error (MSE) is probably the most commonly used error metric. It penalizes larger errors because squaring larger numbers has a greater impact than squaring smaller numbers. The formula for MSE is

$$\text{MSE} = \frac{\sum_{i=1}^{n} (A_t - F_t)^2}{n}$$

Again, n represents the number of forecast values used in computing the average.

A third commonly used metric is **mean absolute percentage error (MAPE).** MAPE is the average of absolute errors divided by actual observation values, expressed as a percentage.

$$\text{MAPE} = \frac{\sum_{i=1}^{n} \frac{|A_t - F_t|}{A_t}}{n} \times 100$$

The values of MAD and MSE depend upon the measurement scale of the time series data. For example, forecasting profit in the range of millions of dollars would result in very large MAD and MSE values, even for very accurate forecasting models. On the other hand, market share is measured in proportions, and therefore even bad forecasting models will have small values of MAD and MSE. Thus these measures have no meaning except in comparison with other models used to forecast the same data. Generally, MAD is less affected by extreme observations, and is preferable to MSE if such extreme observations are considered rare events with no special meaning. MAPE is different in that the measurement scale is eliminated by dividing the absolute error by the time series data value. This allows a better relative comparison. Although these comments provide some guidelines, there is no universal agreement on which measure is best.

These measures can be used to compare the moving average forecasts in Figure 7.8. The results, shown in Table 7.3, verify that both the weighted moving average model and the 2-period moving average model provide the best forecasts, although the weighted model has slightly lower error metric values. In view of the previous discussion, we would conclude that the weighted model is best among these five moving average models.

TABLE 7.3	Error Metrics for Moving Average Models of Tracway Tractor Market Share				
	MA2	*MA3*	*MA4*	*MA12*	*3-Period Weighted*
MAD	0.0019	0.0024	0.003	0.0084	0.0018
MSE	0.000005	0.000008	0.000012	0.000074	0.000005
MAPE	1.18%	1.49%	1.86%	5.10%	1.14%

EXPONENTIAL SMOOTHING MODELS

A versatile, yet highly effective approach for short-range forecasting is **simple exponential smoothing.** The basic simple exponential smoothing model is

$$F_{t+1} = (1 - \alpha)F_t + \alpha A_t$$
$$= F_t + \alpha(A_t - F_t)$$

where F_{t+1} is the forecast for time period $t + 1$, F_t is the forecast for period t, A_t is the observed value in period t, and α is a constant between 0 and 1, called the **smoothing constant.**

Using the two forms of the forecast equation, we can interpret the simple exponential smoothing model in two ways. In the first model, the forecast for the next period, F_{t+1}, is a weighted average of the forecast made for period t, F_t, and the actual observation in period t, A_t. The second form of the model, obtained by simply rearranging terms, states that the forecast for the next period, F_{t+1}, equals the forecast for the last period, F_t, plus a fraction α of the forecast error made in period t, $A_t - F_t$. Thus to make a forecast once we have selected the smoothing constant, we need only know the previous forecast and the actual value. By repeated substitution for F_t in the equation, it is easy to demonstrate that F_{t+1} is a decreasingly weighted average of all past time series data. Thus the forecast actually reflects *all* the data, provided that α is strictly between 0 and 1.

For the Tracway market share data, if the forecast for January 2000 is 0.151, the actual market share for January 2000 is 0.154, and $\alpha = 0.7$, then the forecast for February would be

$$\text{Market Share}_{\text{Feb-00}} = 0.151 + (0.7)(0.154 - 0.151) = 0.1531$$

If February's actual market share was found to be 0.156, the forecast for March would be

$$\text{Market Share}_{\text{Mar-00}} = 0.1531 + (0.7)(0.156 - 0.1531) = 0.15513$$

Because the simple exponential smoothing model requires only the previous forecast and the current time series value, it is very easy to calculate; thus it is highly suitable for environments such as inventory systems where many forecasts must be made. The smoothing constant α is usually chosen by experimentation in the same manner as choosing the number of periods to use in the moving average model. Different values of α affect how quickly the model responds to changes in the time series. For instance, a value of $\alpha = 0$ would simply repeat last period's forecast, whereas $\alpha = 1$ would forecast last period's actual demand. The closer α is to 1, the quicker the model responds to changes in the time series because it puts more weight on the actual current observation than on the forecast.

An Excel spreadsheet for evaluating exponential smoothing models for Tracway's tractor market share data using values of α between 0.1 and 0.9 is shown in Figure 7.10. A smoothing constant of $\alpha = 0.9$ provides the least error. This result is compatible with

	A	B	C	D	E	F	G	H	I	J	K
1	Exponential Smoothing Model										
2											
3		Tractor									
4		Market	Smoothing Constant								
5	Date	Share	0.1	0.2	0.3	0.4	0.5	0.6	0.7	0.8	0.9
6	Jan-99	0.1521	0.1521	0.1521	0.1521	0.1521	0.1521	0.1521	0.1521	0.1521	0.1521
7	Feb-99	0.1467	0.1521	0.1521	0.1521	0.1521	0.1521	0.1521	0.1521	0.1521	0.1521
8	Mar-99	0.1468	0.1516	0.1510	0.1505	0.1499	0.1494	0.1489	0.1483	0.1478	0.1472
9	Apr-99	0.1458	0.1511	0.1502	0.1494	0.1487	0.1481	0.1476	0.1473	0.1470	0.1469
10	May-99	0.1464	0.1506	0.1493	0.1483	0.1476	0.1470	0.1466	0.1463	0.1461	0.1459
11	Jun-99	0.1492	0.1502	0.1487	0.1478	0.1471	0.1467	0.1465	0.1464	0.1464	0.1464
12	Jul-99	0.1512	0.1501	0.1488	0.1482	0.1479	0.1479	0.1481	0.1483	0.1486	0.1489
13	Aug-99	0.1519	0.1502	0.1493	0.1491	0.1493	0.1496	0.1500	0.1504	0.1507	0.1510
14	Sep-99	0.1520	0.1503	0.1498	0.1499	0.1503	0.1507	0.1511	0.1514	0.1516	0.1518
15	Oct-99	0.1525	0.1505	0.1503	0.1505	0.1510	0.1514	0.1516	0.1518	0.1519	0.1520
16	Nov-99	0.1521	0.1507	0.1507	0.1511	0.1516	0.1519	0.1522	0.1523	0.1524	0.1525
17	Dec-99	0.1511	0.1508	0.1510	0.1514	0.1518	0.1520	0.1521	0.1522	0.1522	0.1521
18	Jan-00	0.1540	0.1509	0.1510	0.1513	0.1515	0.1516	0.1515	0.1514	0.1513	0.1512
19	Feb-00	0.1563	0.1512	0.1516	0.1521	0.1525	0.1528	0.1530	0.1532	0.1535	0.1537
20	Mar-00	0.1579	0.1517	0.1525	0.1534	0.1540	0.1545	0.1550	0.1554	0.1557	0.1560
21	Apr-00	0.1618	0.1523	0.1536	0.1547	0.1556	0.1562	0.1567	0.1571	0.1574	0.1577
22	May-00	0.1624	0.1533	0.1552	0.1568	0.1581	0.1590	0.1598	0.1604	0.1609	0.1614
23	Jun-00	0.1633	0.1542	0.1567	0.1585	0.1598	0.1607	0.1613	0.1618	0.1621	0.1623
24	Jul-00	0.1655	0.1551	0.1580	0.1599	0.1612	0.1620	0.1625	0.1628	0.1631	0.1632
25	Aug-00	0.1667	0.1561	0.1595	0.1616	0.1629	0.1638	0.1643	0.1647	0.1650	0.1653
26	Sep-00	0.1692	0.1572	0.1609	0.1632	0.1645	0.1653	0.1658	0.1661	0.1664	0.1666
27	Oct-00	0.1682	0.1584	0.1626	0.1650	0.1664	0.1672	0.1678	0.1683	0.1686	0.1689
28	Nov-00	0.1683	0.1594	0.1637	0.1659	0.1671	0.1677	0.1681	0.1682	0.1683	0.1683
29	Dec-00	0.1690	0.1603	0.1646	0.1667	0.1676	0.1680	0.1682	0.1683	0.1683	0.1683
30											

FIGURE 7.10 Exponential Smoothing Forecasts for Tractor Market Share

the results of the moving average model; putting high weights on the most recent data causes the forecasts to react more quickly to the upward trend in the data.

Excel's *Analysis Toolpak* also has an exponential smoothing tool (see *Excel Note: Forecasting with Exponential Smoothing*).

INCORPORATING TREND AND SEASONALITY INTO EXPONENTIAL SMOOTHING MODELS

Many time series exhibit trends and/or seasonality. Like simple moving average models, simple exponential smoothing models also tend to lag systematic changes in the data. Thus it is beneficial to include trend and seasonality explicitly into the approach, making exponential smoothing more useful for many business forecasting situations. The technique we describe is based on the work of two researchers, C. C. Holt, who developed the basic approach, and P. R. Winters, who extended Holt's work. Hence, this approach is commonly referred to as the Holt-Winters model.

The Holt-Winters model decomposes a time series value A_t into three components for each time period t: a base component B_t, for which seasonality influences have been removed; a trend component T_t, and a seasonal component S_t. We assume that the "season" lasts c time periods before repeating. For example, mower sales typically show seasonal effects over the course of a year; thus if the data are given by month, $c = 12$. In other instances, a season might be only a portion of a year. For example, grocery purchasing patterns might show a seasonal effect within a month as more goods are purchased at the beginning of a month when payroll checks are cashed. In this case, the season for weekly data would correspond to $c = 4$.

The first step in building the model is to calculate the seasonal factors. These calculations are shown in column D, rows 2 through 13, of Figure 7.11 for the first year of

	A	B	C	D	E	F	G
1	Month	Forecast	Tractors	Seasonal	Base	Trend	MAPE
2	Jan-96		15518	0.999415	15526.85		
3	Feb-96		16325	1.051399	15526.85	0	
4	Mar-96		17129	1.103182	15526.85	0	
5	Apr-96		17327	1.115947	15526.85	0	
6	May-96		16278	1.048348	15526.85	0	
7	Jun-96		15448	0.994934	15526.85	0	
8	Jul-96		15905	1.024357	15526.85	0	
9	Aug-96		14422	0.928874	15526.85	0	
10	Sep-96		14258	0.918309	15526.85	0	
11	Oct-96		14061	0.905612	15526.85	0	
12	Nov-96		15378	0.990424	15526.85	0	
13	Dec-96		14272	0.9192	15526.85	0	
14	Jan-97	15517.77	14289	0.999415	14296.94	-1229.92	8.603%
15	Feb-97	13738.65	16530	1.051399	15722.04	1425.102	16.887%
16	Mar-97	18916.42	17320	1.103182	15699.98	-22.0622	9.218%
17	Apr-97	17495.72	18842	1.115947	16884.14	1184.161	7.144%
18	May-97	18941.86	17826	1.048348	17004.01	119.8706	6.259%
19	Jun-97	17037.13	17669	0.994934	17759.15	755.1422	3.577%

FIGURE 7.11 Forecasting with Trend and Seasonality

Excel Note: Forecasting with Exponential Smoothing

From the *Tools* menu, select *Data Analysis,* and then *Exponential Smoothing.* Similar to the Moving Average dialog box, you enter the *Input Range* of the time series data, the *Damping Factor* $(1 - \alpha)$ (*not* the smoothing constant as we have defined it!), and the first cell of the *Output Range.* You also have options for labels, to chart output, and to obtain standard errors. As opposed to the Moving Average tool, the chart generated by this tool does correctly align the forecasts with the actual data, as shown in Figure 7.12. You can see that the exponential smoothing model follows the pattern of the data quite closely, although it tends to lag with an increasing trend in the data.

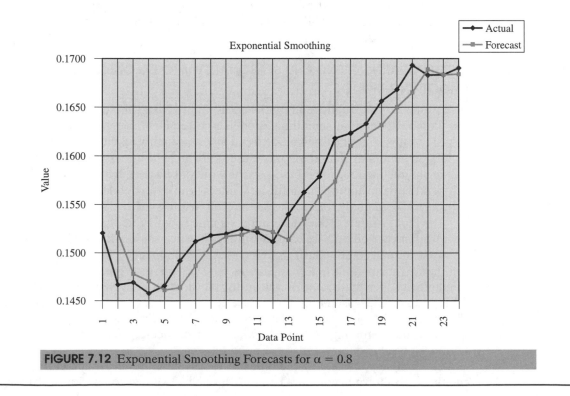

FIGURE 7.12 Exponential Smoothing Forecasts for $\alpha = 0.8$

the Tracway data. For the monthly data for world tractor unit sales, $c = 12$. If $\overline{A}$ is the average value of the time series over a season, then

$$S_t = A_t / \overline{A}$$

represents the seasonal factor for period t. Thus the formula in cell D2 is =C2/AVERAGE(C2:C13). From the formula for S_t it is easy to show that the average value of $S_t = 1.0$ for any one season. We also see that the actual time series values, A_t, are equal to $S_t \overline{A}$. Therefore, S_t simply represents the proportion of the average value over the course of a season attributed to the seasonal factor.

We can use these seasonal factors to *deseasonalize* the time series in future time periods using the formula

$$B_t = A_t / S_{t-c}$$

Note that the base components for the first year are simply the average value by virtue of the calculations as shown in column E of Figure 7.11. Once the data are deseasonalized, we can isolate the trend factor (column F) by taking the difference of two successive base values:

$$T_t = B_t - B_{t-1}$$

For the first year, all trend components are zero. However, for January 1997, the trend component is $14{,}296.94 - 15{,}526.85 = -1{,}229.92$.

We are now in a position to calculate forecasts. The forecast for period $t + 1$ is

$$F_{t+1} = (B_t + T_t) S_{t+1-c}$$

Essentially, we are taking the base value plus the trend component, which represents the (deseasonalized) forecast that includes a trend, and adjusting it for seasonality. For January 1997, the forecast is

$$
\begin{aligned}
F_{\text{Jan97}} &= (B_{\text{Dec96}} + T_{\text{Dec96}}) S_{\text{Jan96}} \\
&= (15{,}226.85 + 0)0.999415 \\
&= 15{,}517.77
\end{aligned}
$$

(Note: These values are drawn from the spreadsheet in Figure 7.11; manual calculations will produce slightly different results due to rounding errors.) When the actual value for January 1997 is obtained, we can compute the mean absolute percentage error (MAPE):

$$100 \, |15{,}517.77 - 14{,}289.1| / 14{,}289.1 = 8.6027\%$$

Next, we can compute the forecast for February 1997 as

$$F_{\text{Feb97}} = (14{,}296.94 - 1{,}229.92)1.051399 = 13{,}738.65$$

If we continue in this fashion, we can obtain forecasts for successive years as shown in Figure 7.11. However, notice that as we project further into the future we would continue to use the seasonal factors computed for the first year. This may not be wise, because the seasonal factors may change over time. The Holt-Winters model incorporates the spirit of exponential smoothing in updating the seasonal components, trend, and base components using smoothing constants.

Seasonality factors are updated by the formula

$$S_t = \gamma(A_t / B_t) + (1 - \gamma)S_{t-c}$$

where γ is a smoothing constant with $0 \leq \gamma \leq 1$. Thus the seasonal components are a weighted average of the current and past values. The higher the value of γ, the greater the emphasis given to more recent seasonal variation.

Base forecasts are smoothed using the formula

$$B_t = \alpha(A_t/S_{t-c}) + (1 - \alpha)(B_{t-1} + T_{t-1})$$

with a smoothing constant α $(0 \leq \alpha \leq 1)$. To understand this, note that prior to observing A_t, the projected deseasonalized value is $B_{t-1} + T_{t-1}$. At time t, the current deseasonalized value is A_t/S_{t-c}; thus B_t is simply a weighted average of these two terms.

The current trend value formula is

$$T_t = \beta(B_t - B_{t-1}) + (1 - \beta)T_{t-1}$$

where a third smoothing constant, β $(0 \leq \beta \leq 1)$, is used to reflect the change in the base forecast from the prior to the current time period, and $1 - \beta$ is multiplied times the previous trend value.

The final step is to generate the trend and seasonally adjusted forecast, F_{t+1}.

$$F_{t+1} = (B_t + T_t)S_{t+1-c}$$

The worksheet in Figure 7.11 can be modified easily to include these smoothing formulas, and the results are shown in Figures 7.13 and 7.14. Extending this through December 2000 yields an average MAPE of 7.47 percent. Like ordinary exponential smoothing, selecting different smoothing constants results in different MAPE values. However, because this model requires three separate smoothing constants, finding the best combination is more difficult.

Regression Models

We introduced regression in the previous chapter as a means of developing relationships between dependent and independent variables. In fact, the first example of simple linear regression was a forecasting application. Thus simple linear regression using time as the independent variable is one approach to forecasting. One disadvantage of simple linear regression as a forecasting tool is clearly the assumption of linearity. As we saw in chapter 5, the mower defect data are not linear across the entire range of the data; therefore, we could develop a regression line for only a portion of the data. Thus

FIGURE 7.13 Holt-Winters Exponential Smoothing Model Results

	A	B	C	D	E	F	G	H	I
1	Month	Forecast	Tractors	Seasonal	Base	Trend	MAPE	Smoothing constants	
2	Jan-96		15518	0.999415	15526.85			Base	0.7
3	Feb-96		16325	1.051399	15526.85	0		Trend	0.3
4	Mar-96		17129	1.103182	15526.85	0		Seasonal	0.9
5	Apr-96		17327	1.115947	15526.85	0			
6	May-96		16278	1.048348	15526.85	0			
7	Jun-96		15448	0.994934	15526.85	0			
8	Jul-96		15905	1.024357	15526.85	0			
9	Aug-96		14422	0.928874	15526.85	0			
10	Sep-96		14258	0.918309	15526.85	0			
11	Oct-96		14061	0.905612	15526.85	0			
12	Nov-96		15378	0.990424	15526.85	0			
13	Dec-96		14272	0.9192	15526.85	0			
14	Jan-97	15517.77	14289	0.976785	14665.91	-258.283	8.603%		
15	Feb-97	15148.16	16530	1.075742	15327.72	17.74332	8.360%		
16	Mar-97	16928.84	17320	1.109954	15593.62	92.19196	2.258%		
17	Apr-97	17504.53	18842	1.137797	16524.64	343.84	7.097%		
18	May-97	17684.04	17826	1.050609	16963.35	372.3009	0.797%		
19	Jun-97	17247.83	17669	1.001386	17632.1	461.2358	2.385%		

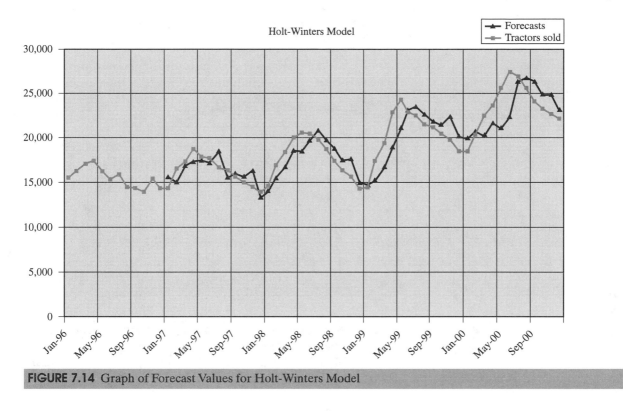

FIGURE 7.14 Graph of Forecast Values for Holt-Winters Model

it does not reflect changes as accurately as short-range forecasting models. One advantage that regression models do have is that they can forecast as far into the future as you wish. However, the forecast errors are expected to increase the further into the future forecasts are made.

If the time series is not linear, one alternative is to use a nonlinear function for a trendline. Excel provides a variety of forms in the *Add Trendline* option (see Figure 7.15). Figure 7.16 shows a fourth-degree polynomial trendline for European market share of mowers. You can see that this function captures the general trend in the data.

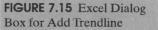

FIGURE 7.15 Excel Dialog Box for Add Trendline

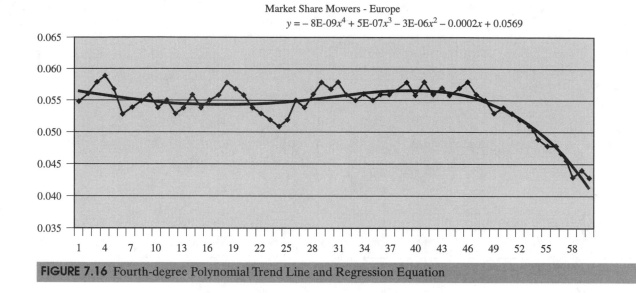

Market Share Mowers - Europe
$$y = -8E\text{-}09x^4 + 5E\text{-}07x^3 - 3E\text{-}06x^2 - 0.0002x + 0.0569$$

FIGURE 7.16 Fourth-degree Polynomial Trend Line and Regression Equation

Selecting the appropriate function requires some knowledge of the mathematical properties of functions and some experimentation.

The Excel functions TREND, GROWTH, LINEST, and FORECAST, summarized in Table 7.2, also provide limited forecasting ability for linear or exponential time series.

INCORPORATING SEASONALITY IN REGRESSION MODELS

Quite often, time series data exhibit seasonality, especially on an annual basis. World tractor sales in the North American region are one example. As we have seen, moving average and exponential smoothing models will always lag, and linear regressions against time will try to fit the seasonal pattern with a straight line. One approach to incorporating seasonality into a regression model is to use ordinal variables for the seasonal components, creating a multiple regression model as described in chapter 6. With monthly data, as we have for tractor sales, we have 12 seasonal components. Thus we define 12 ordinal variables. Each month's variable will have an observed value of 0, except for the month corresponding to the actual observation, which is assigned a value of 1. This model picks up both trend from the regression coefficient for time, and seasonality from the ordinal variables for each month.

If we included all 12 seasonality variables in the regression model, we would encounter a problem of dependence among the independent variables, because the time column could be expressed as a weighted sum of the remaining columns of independent variables, violating an important theoretical assumption for using regression. Therefore, we will use only the first 11 ordinal variables, and the model is

$$\text{Tractors}_{\text{world}} = \beta_0 + \beta_1 \text{Time} + \beta_2 \text{January} + \beta_3 \text{February} + \beta_4 \text{March} + \beta_5 \text{April} + \beta_6 \text{May} + \beta_7 \text{June} + \beta_8 \text{July} + \beta_9 \text{August} + \beta_{10} \text{September} + \beta_{11} \text{October} + \beta_{12} \text{November}$$

The first 12 observations of the data set for the regression analysis would be as follows:

Actual	Time	Jan.	Feb.	Mar.	Apr.	May	Jun.	Jul.	Aug.	Sep.	Oct.	Nov.
15,518	1	1	0	0	0	0	0	0	0	0	0	0
16,325	2	0	1	0	0	0	0	0	0	0	0	0
17,129	3	0	0	1	0	0	0	0	0	0	0	0
17,327	4	0	0	0	1	0	0	0	0	0	0	0
16,278	5	0	0	0	0	1	0	0	0	0	0	0
15,448	6	0	0	0	0	0	1	0	0	0	0	0
15,905	7	0	0	0	0	0	0	1	0	0	0	0
14,422	8	0	0	0	0	0	0	0	1	0	0	0
14,258	9	0	0	0	0	0	0	0	0	1	0	0
14,061	10	0	0	0	0	0	0	0	0	0	1	0
15,378	11	0	0	0	0	0	0	0	0	0	0	1
14,272	12	0	0	0	0	0	0	0	0	0	0	0

The forecast for December of the first year will be $\beta_0 + \beta_1(12)$. The variable coefficients (betas) for each of the other 11 months will show the adjustment relative to December. For example, the January forecast (Time = 1) would be $\beta_0 + \beta_1(1) + \beta_2(1)$. The forecast for the *following* January (Time = 13) would be $\beta_0 + \beta_1(13) + \beta_2(1)$.

Using the *Regression* tool in Excel, the regression model obtained from all 60 observations of data is

$$\text{Tractors}_{\text{world}} = 10{,}457.5 + 167.7\,\text{Time} + 770.6\,\text{January} + 2{,}678.4\,\text{February}$$
$$+3{,}965.4\,\text{March} + 5{,}351.5\,\text{April} + 5{,}537.7\,\text{May} + 5{,}277.7\,\text{June}$$
$$+4{,}612.3\,\text{July} + 3{,}402.7\,\text{August} + 2{,}499.6\,\text{September}$$
$$+1{,}595.1\,\text{October} + 1{,}218.4\,\text{November}$$

Figure 7.17 gives the regression output for this model. The R^2 for this model is 0.851, not ideal, but fairly good. The MAPE (calculated by spreadsheet) was 6.3 percent, slightly better than the Holt-Winters model's forecast. Figure 7.18 shows a graph of the seasonal regression fit.

The Practice of Forecasting

In practice, managers use a variety of judgmental and quantitative forecasting techniques. Statistical methods alone cannot account for such factors as sales promotions, unusual environmental disturbances, new product introductions, large one-time orders, and so on. Many managers begin with a statistical forecast and adjust it to account for intangible factors. Others may develop independent judgmental and statistical forecasts, and then combine them, either objectively by averaging or in a subjective manner. It is impossible to provide universal guidance as to which approaches are best, for they depend on a variety of factors, including the presence or absence of trends and seasonality, the number of data points available, length of the forecast time horizon, and the experience and knowledge of the forecaster. Often, quantitative approaches will miss significant changes in the data, such as reversal of trends, whereas qualitative forecasts may catch them, particularly when using indicators as discussed earlier in this chapter.

Let us see how the different forecasts developed for Tracway might be assessed by Mike Mortensen to forecast demand for Tracway mowers and tractors. The Delphi forecast gave him confidence that the strong North American region would provide a solid base for future demand for Tracway profits. If growth for the tractor business increased in the South American and Pacific regions, this should assure Tracway prosperity. Even

	A	B	C	D	E	F	G	H	I
1	SUMMARY OUTPUT								
2									
3	*Regression Statistics*								
4	Multiple R	0.922313							
5	R Square	0.850662							
6	Adjusted R Square	0.812533							
7	Standard Error	1567.342							
8	Observations	60							
9									
10	ANOVA								
11		*df*	*SS*	*MS*	*F*	*Significance F*			
12	Regression	12	657675052.2	54806254	22.31016	1.9564E-15			
13	Residual	47	115458339.4	2456560					
14	Total	59	773133391.5						
15									
16		*Coefficients*	*Standard Error*	*t Stat*	*P-value*	*Lower 95%*	*Upper 95%*	*Lower 95.0%*	*Upper 95.0%*
17	Intercept	10457.52	821.9209897	12.72326	7.82E-17	8804.026551	12111.0069	8804.026551	12111.00694
18	time	167.7431	11.92317327	14.06867	1.82E-18	143.756828	191.729444	143.756828	191.7294442
19	Jan	770.5883	999.9128833	0.770655	0.444768	-1240.975031	2782.15169	-1240.97503	2782.151688
20	Feb	2678.366	998.4189355	2.682607	0.010051	669.8079165	4686.92377	669.8079165	4686.923771
21	Mar	3965.439	997.0653397	3.97711	0.000239	1959.60399	5971.27368	1959.60399	5971.273683
22	Apr	5351.504	995.8526681	5.373791	2.35E-06	3348.108492	7354.89903	3348.108492	7354.899028
23	May	5537.697	994.7814362	5.566748	1.21E-06	3536.45699	7538.93745	3536.45699	7538.937448
24	Jun	5277.741	993.8521011	5.310389	2.92E-06	3278.370378	7277.11168	3278.370378	7277.111679
25	Jul	4612.339	993.0650614	4.644549	2.77E-05	2614.551576	6610.12624	2614.551576	6610.12624
26	Aug	3402.69	992.4206556	3.428677	0.001271	1406.199229	5399.18114	1406.199229	5399.181141
27	Sep	2499.584	991.9191617	2.519947	0.015193	504.1016024	4495.06576	504.1016024	4495.065765
28	Oct	1595.141	991.5607964	1.608717	0.114376	-399.6200913	3589.9022	-399.620091	3589.902197
29	Nov	1218.417	991.3457151	1.229054	0.22517	-775.9114079	3212.74551	-775.911408	3212.745505

FIGURE 7.17 Output for Seasonal Regression Model of World Tractor Sales

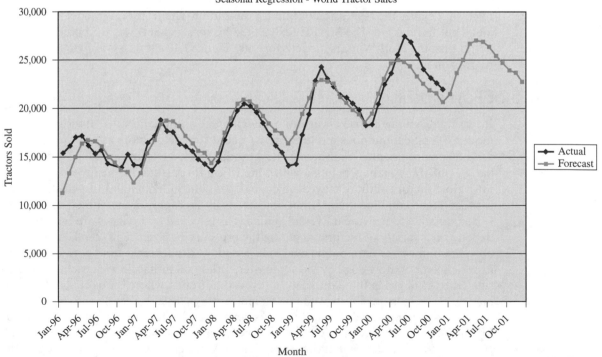

FIGURE 7.18 Regression-Based Forecasts

if one of those regions should prove to have gains less than expected, the Chinese market promised to help as well.

In the immediate future, Mike was concerned about forecasting 12 months ahead for each product by region. The first model considered was the seasonal regression model for each product in each region. This is the same model that we used for world tractor sales, only with Tracway's sales by product per region used as the dependent variable. For the North American region's tractor sales, the resulting regression is

$$\begin{aligned}
\text{Tracway North American tractor sales} = &-155.5 + 30.042\ \text{Time} + 152.458\ \text{January} \\
&+ 280.417\ \text{February} + 392.375\ \text{March} \\
&+ 514.333\ \text{April} + 564.292\ \text{May} \\
&+ 528.250\ \text{June} + 442.208\ \text{July} \\
&+ 352.167\ \text{August} + 256.125\ \text{September} \\
&+ 178.083\ \text{October} + 94.042\ \text{November}
\end{aligned}$$

This yields the following forecasts for each month:

Jan.	Feb.	Mar.	Apr.	May	Jun.	Jul.	Aug.	Sep.	Oct.	Nov.	Dec.	Total 2001
1,830	1,988	2,129	2,281	2,361	2,355	2,300	2,240	2,173	2,125	2,071	2,007	**25,860**

The same model was used for each product in each region, yielding the results in Table 7.4. Looking at the R^2 values, we see that some models are very good, whereas others, such as the models for European and Pacific tractor sales, are not as good. However, they are better than a simple regression of sales against time, because these models also include seasonality. The β_{time} coefficient shows the trend in the models. There are negative trends for both products in Europe, and for tractors in the Pacific region. The FC_{2001} value provides the total annual forecast for each region by product. The sales for each region in the last year (year 2000) are shown next, and the last line gives the calculated percentage increase implied. European sales for both products are projected to decline.

The Delphi forecasts were for a longer period of 5 years. Mike considered the forecast change in the world market, divided each by five to get a rough approximation of expected change per year, and adjusted each forecast considering Tracway's market share. This yielded Mike's expected increases by region as follows:

	NA Tractor	SA Tractor	Europe Tractor	Pacific Tractor	China Tractor	NA Mower	SA Mower	Europe Mower	Pacific Mower
%	5%	10%	20%	0%	25%	−1%	25%	−1%	0%
$Sales_{2000}$	24,430	10,890	6,550	2,740	1,510	91,850	3,870	11,610	2,600
FC_{2001}	25,650	11,980	7,860	2,740	1,890	90,930	4,840	11,500	2,600

TABLE 7.4   Regression Model Forecasting Results for Tracway Products

	NA Tractor	SA Tractor	Europe Tractor	Pacific Tractor	China Tractor	NA Mower	SA Mower	Europe Mower	Pacific Mower
R^2	0.840	0.983	0.464	0.370	0.961	0.990	0.979	0.988	0.947
β_{time}	30.04	13.38	−2.83	−0.06	4.37	4.21	1.63	−7.27	2.05
FC_{2001}	25,860	12,948	6,542	3,229	2,159	92,326	4,093	10,647	2,955
$Sales_{2000}$	24,430	10,890	6,550	2,740	1,510	91,850	3,870	11,610	2,600
%	+5.9%	+18.9%	−0.002%	+17.8%	+43.0	+0.05	+5.8%	−8.3%	+13.7%

Thus Mike has developed two numeric estimates by product by region.

	NA Tractor	SA Tractor	Europe Tractor	Pacific Tractor	China Tractor	NA Mower	SA Mower	Europe Mower	Pacific Mower
Regression	25,860	12,948	6,542	3,229	2,159	92,326	4,093	10,647	2,955
Mike	25,650	11,980	7,860	2,740	1,890	90,930	4,840	11,500	2,600

These forecasts are not radically different, but some differences exist. Research has indicated that more accurate forecasts can sometimes be obtained by combining forecasts. This can be done in a number of ways. First, weights could be assigned to each forecast, and the forecasts can be combined as a weighted average. Different weights could be used to reflect the level of confidence of the forecaster. Mike is more confident in his subjective forecast, and will assign it a weight of 0.7. This leaves a weight of 0.3 for the regression-based forecast. The combined forecast is calculated as follows:

	NA Tractor	SA Tractor	Europe Tractor	Pacific Tractor	China Tractor	NA Mower	SA Mower	Europe Mower	Pacific Mower
Regression	25,860	12,948	6,542	3,229	2,159	92,326	4,093	10,647	2,955
×0.3	**7,758**	**3,884**	**1,963**	**969**	**648**	**27,698**	**1,228**	**3,194**	**887**
Mike's	25,650	11,980	7,860	2,740	1,890	90,930	4,840	11,500	2,600
×0.7	**17,955**	**8,386**	**5,502**	**1,918**	**1,323**	**63,651**	**3,388**	**8,050**	**1,820**
Total	25,713	12,270	7,465	2,887	1,971	91,349	4,616	11,244	2,707

This forecast, predicting 50,306 tractors and 109,916 mowers to be sold by Tracway in 2001, would involve an annual increase of 9 percent for tractor sales and no change in sales of mowers. This gives Mike a prediction that is detailed enough to allow for planning production over the next 12 months, because each product's demand is predicted by region.

Summary

The late quality guru, W. Edwards Deming, often stated that "Management is prediction." Thus forecasting is a crucial element in all business decisions because the future is uncertain. A variety of forecasting techniques are available to support decision making. Qualitative methods, such as Delphi, provide some structure to enhance judgment, but provide no statistical objectivity. Time series methods, such as the moving average method and exponential smoothing models, provide a means to extrapolate past trends into the future. A significant amount of analysis is needed to determine the best parameters for these models to minimize forecast errors. These models simply react to movements in data with little understanding of the causes of change. Regression models, on the other hand, are explanatory/causal models, based upon theories of what makes the forecast variable change, and provide an additional means of predicting future variable values.

Although forecasting has long been recognized as being important (the Delphi method gets its name from the oracle in ancient Greece), nobody has developed the ideal means of forecasting. No quantitative model can capture all the factors that govern the future. Therefore, good managers need to understand that no forecasting method is completely reliable. However, the use of forecasting models combined with good judgement will generally outperform seat-of-the-pants decisions.

Questions and Problems

1. Obtain last year's daily Dow Jones industrial averages (from the Internet, from the business pages of a newspaper, or from a business magazine). The business pages of newspapers just after the close of business December 31 generally publish a graph of these data. These graphs typically show a lot of variance over short periods, as well as interesting shapes over the year. What factors do you expect to be the reason for these changes? What implications do these factors have on the ability to forecast the future?

2. Obtain data on the price of a barrel of oil (from the Internet, from the business pages of a newspaper, or from a business magazine). Most of these sources will provide you with a graph, typically showing a lot of variance over short periods. What factors do you expect to be the reason for these changes? What implications do these factors have on the ability to forecast the future?

3. Contrast quantitative and judgmental forecasting techniques.

4. Describe the difference between statistical time series models and explanatory/causal methods.

5. Discuss the types of forecasts for which simple time series models and regression models are applicable.

6. Are judgmental or quantitative forecasts more commonly used for forecasting product sales? Why?

7. Apply the concept of historical analogy to forecast the success of a specific candidate in the next presidential election.

8. Tracway began sales of tractors in the Chinese region in 1998. How could the concept of historical analogy be applied to predict the future sales of tractors in the Chinese region?

9. What type of forecasting situation is the Delphi method suitable for?

10. What makes a good leading indicator?

11. Find the last report of the Index of Leading Indicators. These occur at the beginning of every month, and are reported in the news (print and broadcast). What did the indicators predict this month?

12. Discuss the difference between trends, cycles, and seasonal effects.

13. Calculate 3-, 4-, and 12-period simple moving averages to predict Tracway's market share for mowers and tractors in the North American region for January 2001.

14. Generate a 3-period moving average forecast for Tracway market share in the North American region for January 2000 using weights of 0.2 three periods prior, 0.3 two periods prior, and 0.5 one period prior.

15. Compare the MAD, MSE, and MAPE for the 3-period unweighted, 3-period weighted (using weights of 0.2, 0.3, and 0.5), 4-period unweighted, and 12-period unweighted moving average forecasts of Tracway's mower market share in the North American region.

16. Compare the MAD, MSE, and MAPE for the 3-period unweighted, 3-period weighted (using weights of 0.2, 0.3, and 0.5), 4-period unweighted, and 12-period unweighted moving average forecasts of Tracway's tractor market share in the North American region.

17. Based on the relative performances of the four models in problems 16 and 17, what can you conclude about the best fitting moving average model?

18. Calculate exponential smoothing models to predict Tracway's market share for mowers and tractors in the North American region for January 2001, given a forecast for December 2000 of 0.1 for mowers and 0.2 for tractors. Use alpha = 0.3, alpha = 0.6, and alpha = 1.0.

19. Compare the MAD, MSE, and MAPE for three exponential smoothing forecasting models (one using an alpha of 0.3, the second using an alpha of 0.6, and the last an alpha of 1.0) of Tracway's mower market share in the North American region. Use a starting forecast for January 1996 of 0.1. Which smoothing constant gives the better forecasts?

20. Compare the MAD, MSE, and MAPE for three exponential smoothing forecasting models (one using an alpha of 0.3, the second using an alpha of 0.6, and the last an alpha of 1.0) of Tracway's tractor market share in the North American region. Use a starting forecast for January 1996 of 0.07. Which smoothing constant gives the better forecasts?

21. Based on the relative performances in problems 19 and 20, what can you conclude about generalizing the value of alpha?

22. Use a Holt-Winters model to forecast Tracway mower market share in the North American region. Identify the forecast for January 2001. Identify the MAPE of this model over the period January 1997 through December 2000.

23. Use a Holt-Winters model to forecast Tracway tractor market share in the North American region. Identify the forecast for January 2001. Identify the MAPE of this model over the period January 1997 through December 2000.

24. Compare forecasts using the Excel functions TREND and GROWTH on the North American region mower market share with forecasts for January 2001 obtained from the FORECAST function and from developing a regression model. The FORECAST function and the regression model require generating a time variable ranging from 1 (January 1996) through 61 (January 2001).

25. Compare forecasts using the Excel functions TREND and GROWTH on the North American region tractor market share with forecasts for January 2001 obtained from the FORECAST function and from developing a regression model. The FORECAST function and the regression model require generating a time variable ranging from 1 (January 1996) through 61 (January 2001).

26. Generate a seasonal regression for the North American region market share for mowers, using 11 dummy variables for seasonality. Identify the R^2 statistic for this regression.

27. Generate a seasonal regression for the North American region market share for tractors, using 11 dummy variables for seasonality. Identify the R^2 statistic for this regression.

28. Compare the MAPEs of the mower and tractor market share models for the North American region.

29. What advantage do regression models have over moving average, exponential smoothing, and Holt-Winters models with respect to forecasting?

30. Spreadsheet models provide good forecasting tools for cash flow situations. Bodie and Merton's *Finance* (Prentice Hall, 1998, page 422) includes a spreadsheet involving a 3-year model of cash flow based upon percent of sales. The key forecast variable is sales, which in this case is $200 million growing at the rate of 40 percent per year. Other relationships and data needed to build the model are

    Cost of goods sold = 55% of sales

    Gross margin = Sales − cost of goods sold

    Selling, general, and administration expenses = 15% of sales

    EBIT (earnings before interest and tax) = Gross margin − selling, general, and administration

    Net income = EBIT − interest and taxes

    Change to shareholder equity = Net income − dividends

Projected dividends for each of the next 3 years are $5.4 million, $4.82 million, and $4.02 million

Projected interest expense for each of the next 3 years are $30 million, $45.21 million, and $64.04 million

Projected taxes values for each of the next 3 years are $12 million, $10.72 million, and $8.94 million

Develop a spreadsheet model to forecast change to shareholder equity for the current year and two more years.

Appendix: *CB Predictor*

CB Predictor is an Excel add-in that was developed by Decisioneering, Inc., the makers of *Crystal Ball.* The student version of *CB Predictor,* included with this text, includes the time series forecasting approaches we discussed in this chapter and several others; however, the student version does not have the regression option, although the commercial version does.

Excel Note: Using *CB Predictor*

After *CB Predictor* has been installed, it may be accessed in Excel from the *Tools* menu; if it does not appear, make sure the appropriate box is checked in the *Tools/Add-Ins* window. When *CB Predictor* is started, the dialog box shown in Figure 7A.1 appears. The dialog box contains four tabs that query you for information one step at a time. *Input Data* allows you to enter the data on which to base your forecast; *Data Attributes* allows you to specify the type of data and whether or not seasonality is present; *Method Gallery* allows you to select one of eight time series methods—single moving average, double moving average, single exponential smoothing, double exponential smoothing, seasonal additive, seasonal multiplicative, Holt-Winters Additive, or Holt-Winters multiplicative (see Figure 7.A.2). The graphs shown in the *Method Gallery* suggest the method that is best suited for the data. For example, single moving average and exponential smoothing best apply to nonseasonal data with no trend; double moving average and double exponential smoothing (which we have not described in this chapter) are best for nonseasonal data with a trend. However, *CB Predictor* will run each method you select and will recommend the one that best forecasts your data. The final tab, *Results,* allows you to specify a variety of reporting options.

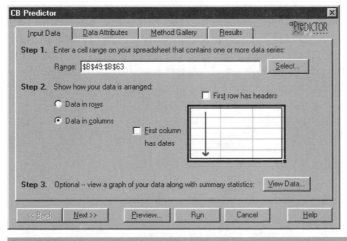

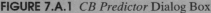

FIGURE 7.A.1 *CB Predictor* Dialog Box

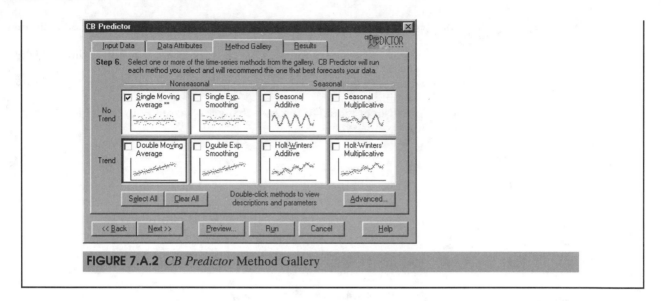

FIGURE 7.A.2 *CB Predictor* Method Gallery

We will illustrate the use of *CB Predictor* for the data we have used in this chapter (see the *Excel Note: Using CB Predictor* for basic information on using the add-in). First, consider the World Tractor Market Share data from January 99 through December 00. Using Single Moving Average with a user-defined number of periods as 2 (*CB Predictor* also has an option to select the best number of periods automatically), we obtain the results shown in Figure 7.A.3. You can see that these compare with Figure 7.8, which we calculated manually using Excel. If we use Double Exponential Smoothing (because the data appear to exhibit a trend) and allow *CB Predictor* to select the best number of periods, we obtain the results shown in Figure 7.A.4. Comparing the MAD for both cases in the *CB Predictor* Report output, we find that for the single moving average, MAD = .001854 while MAD = .001597 for the double moving average case, an improvement that we suspected would occur.

As another example, Figure 7.A.5 shows the results for the World Tractor Unit Sales. All methods were selected in the *Method Gallery,* and *CB Predictor* found the best fit to be for *Double Exponential Smoothing.* Figures 7.A.6(a) and (b) show portions of the Report output that summarizes the best fitting model and second through fourth best as well. Theil's U statistic is a relative error measure that compares the results with a naïve forecast. A value less than 1 means that the forecasting technique is better than guessing; a value equal to 1 means that the technique is about a good as guessing; and a value greater than 1 means that the forecasting technique is worse than guessing.

We encourage you to experiment with *CB Predictor* for other time series in the Tracway database.

	A	B	C
1	**Results Table for II9 Mktshare Tractors**		
2	Created: 8/5/99 at 10:47:27 AM		
3			
30	Series	Column B ▼	
31			
32		Data	
33	Date	Historical Data	Fit & Forecast
34	Period 1	0.152	
35	Period 2	0.147	
36	Period 3	0.147	0.149
37	Period 4	0.146	0.147
38	Period 5	0.146	0.146
39	Period 6	0.149	0.146
40	Period 7	0.151	0.148
41	Period 8	0.152	0.150
42	Period 9	0.152	0.152
43	Period 10	0.153	0.152
44	Period 11	0.152	0.152
45	Period 12	0.151	0.152
46	Period 13	0.154	0.152
47	Period 14	0.156	0.153
48	Period 15	0.158	0.155
49	Period 16	0.162	0.157
50	Period 17	0.162	0.160
51	Period 18	0.163	0.162
52	Period 19	0.166	0.163
53	Period 20	0.167	0.164
54	Period 21	0.169	0.166
55	Period 22	0.168	0.168
56	Period 23	0.168	0.169
57	Period 24	0.169	0.168
58	Period 25		0.169

FIGURE 7.A.3 *CB Predictor* Results for Single Moving Average

	A	B	C
1	**Results Table for II9 Mktshare Tractors**		
2	Created: 8/5/99 at 10:56:07 AM		
3			
30	Series	Column B ▼	
31			
32		Data	
33	Date	Historical Data	Fit & Forecast
34	Period 1	0.152	
35	Period 2	0.147	
36	Period 3	0.147	
37	Period 4	0.146	0.143
38	Period 5	0.146	0.146
39	Period 6	0.149	0.146
40	Period 7	0.151	0.150
41	Period 8	0.152	0.154
42	Period 9	0.152	0.154
43	Period 10	0.153	0.152
44	Period 11	0.152	0.153
45	Period 12	0.151	0.152
46	Period 13	0.154	0.151
47	Period 14	0.156	0.154
48	Period 15	0.158	0.159
49	Period 16	0.162	0.160
50	Period 17	0.162	0.164
51	Period 18	0.163	0.165
52	Period 19	0.166	0.164
53	Period 20	0.167	0.167
54	Period 21	0.169	0.169
55	Period 22	0.168	0.171
56	Period 23	0.168	0.170
57	Period 24	0.169	0.168
58	Period 25		0.169

FIGURE 7.A.4 *CB Predictor* Results for Double Moving Average

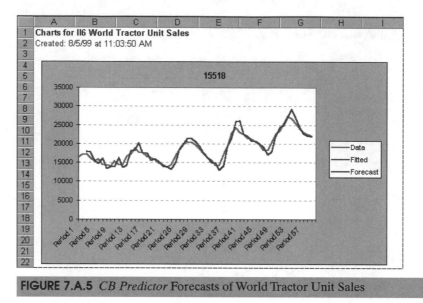

FIGURE 7.A.5 *CB Predictor* Forecasts of World Tractor Unit Sales

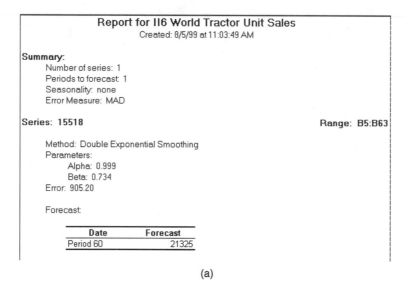

(a)

FIGURE 7.A.6 *CB Predictor* Report for Best-Fitting Forecasting Model

Method Errors:

	Method	RMSE	MAD	MAPE
Best:	Double Exponential Smoothing	1202.3	905.2	4.98%
2nd:	Double Moving Average	1403.1	1034.8	5.55%
3rd:	Single Exponential Smoothing	1269.5	1049.8	5.60%
4th:	Single Moving Average	1709.5	1432.5	7.54%

Method Statistics:

	Method	Durbin-Watson	Theil's U
Best:	Double Exponential Smoothing	1.824	0.959
2nd:	Double Moving Average	1.249	1.083
3rd:	Single Exponential Smoothing	0.911	1
4th:	Single Moving Average	0.546	1.293

Method Parameters:

	Method	Parameter	Value
Best:	Double Exponential Smoothing	Alpha	0.999
		Beta	0.734
2nd:	Double Moving Average	Periods	2
3rd:	Single Exponential Smoothing	Alpha	0.999
4th:	Single Moving Average	Periods*	2
		* = user defined	

(b)

FIGURE 7.A.6 (*continued*)

References

Bodie, Z. and R. C. Merton, *Finance,* Upper Saddle River, NJ: Prentice Hall, 1998.

Cryer, J. D., *Time Series Analysis,* Boston: PWS Publishers, 1986.

Goodwin, P. and Wright, G., "Improving judgmental time series forecasting: A review of the guidance provided by research," *International Journal of Forecasting,* 9, 1993, 147–161.

Newbold, P. and Bos, T., *Introductory Business Forecasting,* Cincinnati: South-Western Publishing Co., 1990.

Sanders, Nada R. and Manrodt, Karl B., "Forecasting Practices in U.S. Corporations: Survey Results," *Interfaces,* 24, March–April 1994, 2.

CHAPTER 8

Selection Models and Risk Analysis

Outline

Decision Criteria and Selection
  Decisions Involving a Single Alternative
  Sensitivity Analysis
  Decisions Involving Mutually Exclusive Alternatives
  Decisions Involving Nonmutually Exclusive Alternatives
  Decisions Involving Uncertainty
Monte Carlo Simulation for Risk Analysis
Applications of Monte Carlo Simulation
  Project Management
  Budget-Constrained Product Selection
Case Study: Simulation and Risk Analysis in New Product Screening at Cinergy
  Corporation
Summary
Questions and Problems
Appendix: Additional *Crystal Ball* Options
  Correlated Assumptions
  Freezing Assumptions
  Overlay Charts
  Trend Charts
  Sensitivity Charts

Up to this point, we have discussed many different statistical approaches for gathering data and converting it into useful information. This chapter focuses on *using* data and information to make decisions, particularly those that involve an element of risk. Managers make many kinds of decisions. Some of these decisions are repetitive, perhaps on an annual or quarterly basis. These might include selecting new employees from a pool of applicants or selecting specific business improvement projects from a pool of proposals. These types of decisions have little financial impact and are not considered very risky. Other decisions, such as deciding where to locate a plant or warehouse or determining whether to pursue a major investment opportunity commit the firm to spending large sums of money. These usually are one-time decisions and generally involve a higher level of risk because of uncertain data and imperfect information.

For example, suppose that Tracway is considering a proposal to develop an Internet-based sales system. This system will involve substantial money for development and for daily operations. Although projections suggest that the revenue impact can be substantial, this venture entails a considerable amount of risk because the future revenues are highly uncertain. Some issues Tracway must consider include what criteria should be used to evaluate this project, how risk can be quantified and assessed, and how a decision should be chosen.

In this chapter we present various approaches for evaluating and making decisions using simple "what if?" analysis through more complex simulation models and decision analysis techniques. Specifically, we will discuss

- Common types of decisions: acceptance/rejection of a single proposal, selecting from a set of mutually exclusive alternatives, selecting nonmutually exclusive alternatives, and decisions involving probabilistic events;
- Decision criteria used to evaluate these decisions, including net present value, internal rate of return, expected value, return-to-risk ratio, and opportunity loss;
- The use of data tables for sensitivity analysis;
- Single and multistage decision trees for modeling decision problems; and
- Concepts of risk analysis, the use of statistical measures such as the standard deviation and coefficient of variation to measure risk, and Monte Carlo simulation with *Crystal Ball* for evaluating models involving risk.

These approaches draw upon many of the statistical concepts presented in previous chapters, and thus illustrate the importance of good data collection and analysis. Most of these approaches can be implemented easily on spreadsheets, providing better communication and improved understanding.

Decision Criteria and Selection

Business decisions usually fall into one of four categories:

1. Decisions involving the acceptance or rejection of a proposal or project, for example, a new marketing campaign, acquisition of another company, or the purchase of a new machine. Such decisions are usually based on whether or not acceptance meets some acceptance criteria such as return on investment or some measure of added value.
2. Decisions involving the selection of the best decision among a set of mutually exclusive alternatives, for example, the choice of one marketing campaign among four competing proposals, selecting a new hire from a pool of candidates, or selecting a location to build a new plant. These decisions are often made by ranking the alternatives according to some criteria and selecting the best.
3. Decisions among a set of nonmutually exclusive alternatives (i.e., for which more than one may be chosen), for example, selecting research and development projects or choosing stocks or other investment instruments to create a portfolio. These decisions are usually made by ranking the alternatives and selecting those that meet threshold criteria or budgetary limitations.
4. Decisions involving uncertainty—those involving a sequence of choices and chance events in which the objective is to choose the best strategy (i.e., a set of choices that are contingent upon the occurrence of chance events). These decisions are usually made by computing the expected value associated with each choice.

DECISIONS INVOLVING A SINGLE ALTERNATIVE

Most business ventures are evaluated on the basis of financial criteria. Two common criteria for evaluating decisions for which financial impacts are the most important are *net present value* and *internal rate of return*. We will review the basic concepts of net present value to provide a foundation for our discussion of decision analysis approaches; more complete discussions can be found in basic finance texts, for example, Gallagher and Andrew (1997).

Net present value (NPV) measures the worth of a stream of cash flows, taking into account the time value of money. That is, a cash flow of F dollars t time periods in the future is worth $F/(1 + i)^t$ dollars today, where i is the **discount rate,** or required rate of return from an investment. The discount rate reflects the opportunity costs of spending funds now versus achieving a return through another investment, as well as the risks associated with not receiving returns until a later time. The sum of the present values of all cash flows over a stated time horizon is the net present value.

$$NPV = \sum_{t=0}^{n} \frac{F_t}{(1 + i)^t}$$

where F_t = cash flow in period t.

A positive NPV means that the investment will provide added value because the projected return exceeds the discount rate. Projects with a negative NPV should be rejected.

The **internal rate of return (IRR)** is the estimated rate of return for a project. It is the discount rate that makes the total present value of all cash flows sum to zero.

$$\sum_{t=0}^{n} \frac{F_t}{(1 + \text{IRR})^t} = 0$$

IRR is often used to compare a project against a predetermined *hurdle rate,* a rate of return required by management to accept a project. If IRR is greater than the hurdle rate, the project is accepted; otherwise, it is rejected. Net present value and internal rate of return can be computed in Excel using standard functions (see *Excel Note: Using the NPV and IRR Functions*).

Excel Note: Using the NPV and IRR Functions

The Excel function NPV(*rate,value1,value2, . . .*) calculates the net present value of an investment by using a discount rate and a series of future payments (negative values) and income (positive values). *Rate* is the rate of discount over the length of one period (i), and *value1, value2, . . .* are 1 to 29 arguments representing the payments and income. The values must be equally spaced in time and are assumed to occur at the end of each period. The NPV investment begins one period before the date of the *value1* cash flow and ends with the last cash flow in the list. The NPV calculation is based on *future* cash flows. If the first cash flow (such as an initial investment) occurs at the beginning of the first period, then it must be added to the NPV result and *not* included in the function arguments.

The Excel function for internal rate of return is IRR(*values, guess*). *Values* represents the series of cash flows (at least one of which must be positive and one of which must be negative). *Guess* is a number believed close to the value of IRR that is used to facilitate the mathematical algorithm used to find the solution. Occasionally, the function might not converge to a solution; in those cases you should try a different value for *guess*. In most cases the value of *guess* can be omitted from the function.

For Tracway's proposed Internet sales system, cash flows can be estimated only 12 months into the future because of the rapid degree of change in technology. We assume that expenditures and operating expenses will be incurred at the end of every month and that revenues are collected at the end of every month. The company's discount rate is 12 percent per year. Figure 8.1 shows a spreadsheet model for cash flows expected from the project. The formula in cell E20, the net present value of the net profit, is =NPV($B$3/12,E7:E18)+E6. Note that the initial investment is not included in the NPV calculation because it is not a future cash flow value. Because the NPV of the net profit is $276.38, it indicates that the proposal is just barely breaking even when the time value of money is factored in. This is supported by the low IRR of only 1.03 percent.

SENSITIVITY ANALYSIS

One of the limitations of any one spreadsheet is that it is based on a fixed set of assumptions. In fact, these assumptions are what a decision model consists of—relationships between inputs that describe the modeler's opinion. For example, the discount rate is most likely only an estimate, because the company's true cost of capital may change in the future. Tracway CEO Mike Mortensen might like to know what would happen if this assumption were changed. **Sensitivity analysis** involves changing key input values and examining critical outputs, with the purpose of identifying how much change from assumed inputs would matter with respect to the outputs of interest. Of course, one approach would be to change the rate in cell B3 and recalculate the spreadsheet. However, this would have to be done for each value. A better approach is to use a *data table* in Excel (see *Excel Note: Constructing Data Tables*).

Figure 8.2 shows a one-way data table for examining the sensitivity of the discount rate to NPV. The formula in cell H2 is simply =E20, a copy of the NPV calculation. The cell reference for the column input is cell B3. We see that discount rates lower than about 12 percent (actually about 12.3 percent) result in a positive net present value, whereas those greater than this value yield a negative NPV. This suggests that any uncertainty in the discount rate should be carefully analyzed. Should it increase (for example, because of an increase in the discount rate by the Federal Reserve), Tracway's decision to adopt the proposal would not be a good business decision. Tracway would be better off to invest its money on some alternative than to undertake the project.

	A	B	C	D	E
1	**Internet Project Proposal**				
2					
3	Discount rate	12.0%			
4		Development	Operating		
5	Month	Expense	Expense	Revenue	Net Profit
6	Initial investment	$ 30,000.00	$ -	$ -	$ (30,000.00)
7	January	$ 20,000.00	$ 5,000.00	$ -	$ (25,000.00)
8	February	$ 10,000.00	$ 7,000.00	$ -	$ (17,000.00)
9	March	$ 10,000.00	$ 8,000.00	$ 1,000.00	$ (17,000.00)
10	April	$ 10,000.00	$ 9,000.00	$ 3,000.00	$ (16,000.00)
11	May	$ 5,000.00	$ 10,000.00	$ 6,000.00	$ (9,000.00)
12	June	$ 5,000.00	$ 10,000.00	$ 10,000.00	$ (5,000.00)
13	July	$ 5,000.00	$ 10,000.00	$ 15,000.00	$ -
14	August	$ 5,000.00	$ 10,000.00	$ 21,000.00	$ 6,000.00
15	September	$ -	$ 10,000.00	$ 28,000.00	$ 18,000.00
16	October	$ -	$ 10,000.00	$ 36,000.00	$ 26,000.00
17	November	$ -	$ 10,000.00	$ 45,000.00	$ 35,000.00
18	December	$ -	$ 10,000.00	$ 55,000.00	$ 45,000.00
19					
20	Net Present Values	$97,669.21	$101,757.23	$199,702.82	$276.38
21					
22	IRR	1.03%			

FIGURE 8.1 Spreadsheet for Evaluating Tracway Internet Project Proposal

---

Excel Note: Constructing Data Tables

A data table computes the value of a formula based on a range of values of one or two variables that influence the formula (called *input cells*). Input values are listed either down a column (column-oriented) or across a row (row-oriented). Formulas used in a one-variable data table must refer to an input cell.

To create a one-way data table, type the list of values you want to substitute in the input cell either down one column or across one row. If the input values are listed down a column, type the formula in the row above the first value and one cell to the right of the column of values. Type any additional formulas to the right of the first formula. If the input values are listed across a row, type the formula in the column to the left of the first value and one cell below the row of values. Type any additional formulas below the first formula. Select the range of cells that contains the formulas and values you want to substitute. From the *Data* menu, click *Table*. If the data table is column-oriented, type the cell reference for the input cell of the formula in the *Column input cell* box. If the data table is row-oriented, type the cell reference for the input cell in the *Row input cell* box.

To create a two-variable data table, the formula must refer to two different input cells. In a cell on the worksheet, enter the formula that refers to the two input cells. Type one list of input values in the same column, below the formula. Type the second list in the same row, to the right of the formula. Select the range of cells that contains the formula and both the row and column of values. From the *Data* menu, click *Table*. In the *Row input cell* box, enter the reference for the input cell for the input values in the row. In the *Column input cell* box, enter the reference for the input cell for the input values in the column.

Two-way data tables allow you to investigate the impact of two key input data values in decision models. Figure 8.3 shows a two-way data table for simultaneously changing the initial investment and discount rate assumptions. This analysis shows that Tracway can tolerate higher values of the discount rate if it can reduce the initial investment in the project. Such analyses provide useful information to consider in making alternative decisions. In reality, however, not only are the initial investment and the discount rate uncertain, but so are all the cash flows in the model. Incorporating assumptions about uncertainty in a model is the science of risk analysis, which we shall introduce later in this chapter.

G	H
Data Table	NPV
	$276.38
10.0%	$ 1,965.13
10.5%	$ 1,539.39
11.0%	$ 1,116.03
11.5%	$ 695.03
12.0%	$ 276.38
12.5%	$ (139.93)
13.0%	$ (553.92)
13.5%	$ (965.60)
14.0%	$ (1,374.98)
14.5%	$ (1,782.08)
15.0%	$ (2,186.90)
15.5%	$ (2,589.46)
16.0%	$ (2,989.78)
16.5%	$ (3,387.86)
17.0%	$ (3,783.71)
17.5%	$ (4,177.36)
18.0%	$ (4,568.81)

FIGURE 8.2 One-Way Data Table for Evaluating Discount Rate Scenarios

	J	K	L	M	N
	Initial Investment		Discount Rate		
	$276.38	10%	12%	14%	16%
$	20,000.00	$11,965.13	$10,276.38	$ 8,625.02	$ 7,010.22
$	25,000.00	$ 6,965.13	$ 5,276.38	$ 3,625.02	$ 2,010.22
$	30,000.00	$ 1,965.13	$ 276.38	$ (1,374.98)	$ (2,989.78)
$	35,000.00	$ (3,034.87)	$ (4,723.62)	$ (6,374.98)	$ (7,989.78)
$	40,000.00	$ (8,034.87)	$ (9,723.62)	$(11,374.98)	$(12,989.78)

FIGURE 8.3 Two-Way Data Table for Initial Investment and Discount Rate

DECISIONS INVOLVING MUTUALLY EXCLUSIVE ALTERNATIVES

When only one alternative can be selected from among many, the best choice can usually be identified by evaluating each alternative according to some criterion. However, when key data are uncertain, sensitivity analysis can provide invaluable insight, as the following example illustrates.

Tracway engineers have proposed a change in metal processing that should result in reduced costs for Tracway mower and tractor production. There are three options to fuel this system: natural gas (NG), bunker oil (BO), and wood (W). Each of the three fuels involves different investment costs, operating expense rates, and material cost rates.

Operating expenses are functions of the quantity processed, which is expected to be 1 million tons during the first year, growing at the rate of 10 percent per year. Material cost is also calculated on the basis of a ton of metal processed. Material costs for BO and NG depends on the price of a barrel of oil, P. Specific cost parameters (all in millions of dollars) are

		NG	*BO*	*W*
Investment	Year 1	$6.00	$6.00	$4.00
	Year 2	0	0	$2.00
Operating expense rate/ton		$0.50	$0.60	$1.00
Material expense/ton		$(0.30 + 0.01P)	$0.02P	$0.10

There are two major sources of uncertainty. The first is demand growth. The expected rate of growth in metal processed is 10 percent, but it could easily range from 5 to 15 percent. Second, the future price of a barrel of oil (P) is highly uncertain. In 1972, it was about $3 per barrel. In the early 1980s, the price rose to about $35 per barrel. Currently, it varies between $15–$20.

This is a typical cash flow decision problem, usually analyzed with ordinary spreadsheet models. An Excel model for this problem is given in Figure 8.4. The spreadsheet is relatively straightforward. Yearly demands are given in row 8, increasing by the growth rate in cell B3. For each alternative, we compute the total cost for each year. The net present value of the annual cash flows is computed using the NPV function after adding the initial investment in year 0. In column I, we use logical IF and AND functions to determine the lowest-cost option, designated by a 1, by checking if the discounted cost is less than the other two alternatives. For example, the formula for cell I14 is =IF(AND(H14 < H20,H14 < H26),1,0). At a growth rate of 10 percent per year and an expected price of $18 per barrel, the bunker oil option has a slight advantage over the natural gas system. The wood system is a bit more expensive.

To examine the impact of changes in the two key parameters on the model, we can construct two-way data tables for each alternative. In this model, the key variables are expected to be the growth rate (cell B3) and the price of a barrel of oil (cell B4). The

	A	B	C	D	E	F	G	H	I
1	**Metal Processing Fuel Decision Model**								
2									
3	*Demand growth rate*	10%							
4	*Oil price ($/barrel)*	$18.00							
5	*Cost of capital*	12%							
6									
7	**Year**	**0**	**1**	**2**	**3**	**4**	**5**		
8	Demand (millions of tons)		1.000	1.100	1.210	1.331	1.464		
9									
10	*NATURAL GAS*								
11	Investment ($millions)	6							
12	Operating cost ($millions)		0.500	0.550	0.605	0.666	0.732	**Net Present**	**Best**
13	Material cost ($millions)		0.480	0.528	0.581	0.639	0.703	**Value**	**Option**
14	Total cost ($millions)	6.000	0.980	1.078	1.186	1.304	1.435	$10.222	0
15									
16	*BUNKER OIL*								
17	Investment ($millions)	6							
18	Operating cost ($millions)		0.600	0.660	0.726	0.799	0.878	**Net Present**	**Best**
19	Material cost ($millions)		0.360	0.396	0.436	0.479	0.527	**Value**	**Option**
20	Total cost ($millions)	6.000	0.960	1.056	1.162	1.278	1.406	$10.135	1
21									
22	*WOOD*								
23	Investment ($millions)	4	2						
24	Operating cost ($millions)		1.000	1.100	1.210	1.331	1.464	**Net Present**	**Best**
25	Material cost ($millions)		0.100	0.110	0.121	0.133	0.146	**Value**	**Option**
26	Total cost ($millions)	4.000	3.100	1.210	1.331	1.464	1.611	$10.524	0

FIGURE 8.4 Spreadsheet for Fuel Decision Model

results of such an analysis using two-way data tables are shown in Figure 8.5, with the best costs (in millions of dollars of net present cost) highlighted. From Figure 8.5, it is clear that the bunker oil option is best at low prices of oil; the natural gas option is best at a price of $20 per barrel; and for prices of $25 per barrel or more, the wood option is best. We also observe that wood is relatively better at lower demand growth rates. Natural gas has a greater advantage at higher growth rates, but the price per barrel of oil

L	M	N	O
Natural Gas	**Net Present Values**		
Oil Price		Growth Rate	
$10.222	5%	10%	15%
$ 5.00	$ 9.349	$ 9.662	$ 10.003
$ 10.00	$ 9.546	$ 9.877	$ 10.239
$ 15.00	$ 9.743	$ 10.092	$ 10.474
$ 20.00	$ 9.940	$ 10.308	$ 10.710
$ 25.00	$ 10.137	$ 10.523	$ 10.945
$ 30.00	$ 10.334	$ 10.738	$ 11.181
Bunker oil			
Oil Price		Growth Rate	
$10.135	5%	10%	15%
$ 5.00	$ 8.758	$ 9.015	$ 9.297
$ 10.00	$ 9.152	$ 9.446	$ 9.768
$ 15.00	$ 9.546	$ 9.877	$ 10.239
$ 20.00	$ 9.940	$ 10.308	$ 10.710
$ 25.00	$ 10.334	$ 10.738	$ 11.181
$ 30.00	$ 10.728	$ 11.169	$ 11.652
Wood			
Oil Price		Growth Rate	
$10.524	5%	10%	15%
$ 5.00	$ 10.120	$ 10.524	$ 10.967
$ 10.00	$ 10.120	$ 10.524	$ 10.967
$ 15.00	$ 10.120	$ 10.524	$ 10.967
$ 20.00	$ 10.120	$ 10.524	$ 10.967
$ 25.00	$ 10.120	$ 10.524	$ 10.967
$ 30.00	$ 10.120	$ 10.524	$ 10.967

FIGURE 8.5 Data Table Analysis of Oil Price and Growth Rate Scenarios (Best options are highlighted)

clearly seems more important than the growth rate. Based on this analysis, Tracway managers might wish to seek better information about the future prices of oil and growth rate of demand before reaching a final decision.

DECISIONS INVOLVING NONMUTUALLY EXCLUSIVE ALTERNATIVES

If several nonmutually exclusive alternatives are being considered, various ranking criteria such as return on investment (ROI) or more general benefit/cost ratios provide a basis for evaluation and selection. ROI is computed as

$$\text{ROI} = \frac{\text{annual revenue} - \text{annual costs}}{\text{initial investment}}$$

Proposals are typically ranked in order of highest ROI first, and are selected until total initial investment exceeds a budget. Benefit/cost analysis is based on examining the ratios of expected benefits by expected costs. In business applications, benefits can usually be quantified as revenues or cost savings. Both benefits and costs should be converted to present values in order to account for the time value of money. Ratios greater than 1.0 indicate that a proposal should be adopted if sufficient resources exist to support it.

To illustrate the application of benefit/cost analysis, we will consider the evaluation of potential Tracway projects. Every quarter, Tracway departments propose projects to apply technology to improve operations to the Information Systems department. Departmental accountants estimate expected benefits, following guidelines issued by Tracway's Accounting department. For consistency, Tracway has found it best to have the Information Systems department develop cost estimates for proposed projects. In the current period, 13 projects have come before the Finance Committee, which allocates the project development budget. The proposals are shown in Figure 8.6, with estimated benefits consisting of added revenue and cost reduction as well as estimated costs, all computed as net present values.

Projects are coded by the Submitting department. A-series projects involve application of technology in marketing Tracway products. B-series projects are in the production area, with no expected impact on increased revenues, but substantial reductions in operating expenses. C-series projects combine revenue increases with cost reductions, but involve heavy expenses in project implementation. D-series projects are expected to have a strong impact on increased revenue, but also increased operating expenses.

Benefit/cost ratios provide a way to evaluate these diverse projects. First, those projects with negative net present values (projects A3, C8, and D12) do not pay for their

	A	B	C	D	E
1	Project	Cost	Revenue Impact	Cost Reduction	ROI
2	A1	$175,600.00	$ -	$ 200,358.00	1.14
3	A2	$126,512.00	$ 422,580.00	$ (103,420.00)	2.52
4	A3	$198,326.00	$ 415,625.00	$ (226,413.00)	0.95
5	B4	$421,618.00	$ -	$ 486,312.00	1.15
6	B5	$322,863.00	$ -	$ 456,116.00	1.41
7	B6	$398,810.00	$ -	$ 508,213.00	1.27
8	B7	$212,506.00	$ -	$ 356,067.00	1.68
9	C8	$813,620.00	$ 416,283.00	$ 386,229.00	0.99
10	C9	$850,418.00	$ 583,260.00	$ 398,014.00	1.15
11	D10	$522,615.00	$ 916,426.00	$ (155,106.00)	1.46
12	D11	$486,283.00	$ 816,420.00	$ (103,210.00)	1.47
13	D12	$683,407.00	$ 758,420.00	$ (75,896.00)	1.00
14	D13	$722,813.00	$ 950,128.00	$ (120,063.00)	1.15

FIGURE 8.6 Tracway Information System Project Proposals

implementation costs, and therefore can be eliminated. Thus benefit/cost ratios of less than 1 correspond to negative NPVs. Suppose that the company sets a benefit/cost threshold of 1.2, meaning that project benefits must be at least 20 percent higher than costs. The following projects meet this criterion.

Rank	Project	Benefit/Cost Ratio	Implementation Cost
1	A2	2.52	$126,512
2	B7	1.68	$212,506
3	D11	1.47	$486,283
4	D10	1.46	$522,615
5	B5	1.41	$322,863
6	B6	1.27	$398,810

This ranking can be used a number of ways. If sufficient budget is available to cover the implementation costs, all projects could be adopted because they all satisfy management's threshold criteria. If the budget is limited, the projects could be funded in order of benefit/cost ratio until the budget runs out. Using this approach, any residual budget might be used to fund another project that ranks lower.

Benefit/cost analysis is often used in evaluating social projects where benefits generally cannot be quantified (such as improved police protection). Even in business, such intangible benefits as customer goodwill, obtaining market share, or having added flexibility in production may be important factors in a decision. Nevertheless, as a quantitative technique, benefits need to be converted into some numerical measure. When this is viable, this approach can be useful when comparing multiple alternatives.

DECISIONS INVOLVING UNCERTAINTY

Many decisions involve selection from a small set of mutually exclusive alternatives with uncertain consequences. Once a decision is made, one of a set of possible outcomes, or chance events, occurs. Considerable uncertainty usually exists about the outcomes, and this uncertainty can be expressed as a probability of occurrence. For example, an investor might wish to choose one of three types of investments:

1. Aggressive stock fund,
2. Balanced stock and bond fund, or
3. Pure bond fund.

The outcomes, or events, that might result are

- Market rises,
- Market falls, or
- Market remains stable.

To provide the basis for making a decision, the investor would have to estimate the return or loss—generally called a **payoff**—from making a particular decision and having a particular outcome occur, as well as an assessment of the probability that each outcome will occur. For example, our investor might determine that, over a specified period of time, the payoffs associated with each decision and event are

| | Event | | |
Decision	Market Rises	Market Falls	Market Stable
Aggressive	1,000	−1,500	0
Balanced	600	−500	200
Bond	200	300	100

The investor might also estimate that based on current economic conditions, the probability that the market will rise is 0.5, the probability that it will fall is 0.2, and the probability that it will remain stable is 0.3.

Expected Monetary Value and Risk

A decision criterion used in these types of problems is **expected monetary value (EMV),** that is, we compute the expected payoff for each decision based on the probabilities that the chance events will occur, and select the alternative with the best expected value. *PHStat* provides tools for computing EMV and other decision information (see *PHStat Note: Using the Expected Monetary Value Tool*). From the results in Figure 8.7, we see that action 2 (balanced stock and bond fund) has the best expected monetary value, $260, given the assumptions made about the probabilities of the events.

The expected value, however, does not account for any risk associated with a decision. **Risk** is the chance of an unexpected consequence, usually undesirable. Risk analysis focuses on understanding the degree of uncertainty in a situation; the higher the uncertainty, the greater the risk. As a simple example, suppose we know the possible returns of two projects as given in Table 8.1(a). Can you tell which is riskier? You might think that because Project A has a wider range of possible returns, particularly on the low side, it must be riskier than Project B. Project A has an expected value of only $7,750 as compared to Project B's expected value of $8,000.

However, suppose you know the probability distribution of the returns for each project as shown in Table 8.1(b). There is much less likelihood of achieving a return below $8,000 for Project A than for Project B. On this basis, we might conclude that Project B is riskier than Project A because we would be more uncertain of the outcome—in fact, there is an 80 percent chance of realizing a return of $8,000 or more from Project A but only a 60 percent chance for Project B. Using the formula for the variance of a random variable we presented in chapter 3, we can compute the standard deviation of returns to be $993.70 for Project A and $1,414.20 for Project B. When the expected values are roughly comparable, standard deviation is an important measure of risk. The higher the standard deviation, the greater are the chances that the actual outcome will differ from the expected value, leading to outcomes that might not be acceptable. In Figure 8.7, we see that the aggressive stock fund has the highest standard deviation, and therefore is the riskiest from this perspective.

Another key measure of risk is the *coefficient of variation,* defined in chapter 4 as the ratio of the standard deviation to the mean. This is particularly useful when

PHStat Note: Using the Expected Monetary Value Tool

From the *PHStat* menu, select *Decision Making* and then *Expected Monetary Value.* The dialog box is shown in Figure 8.8; you need only specify the number of actions (alternatives) and events. *PHStat* creates a worksheet in which to enter your data. You may customize the worksheet to change the row and column labels in the Probabilities & Payoff Table for your specific problem (this is similar to the chi-square application discussed in chapter 4). After you enter the data, the expected values and other statistical information are automatically computed (see Figure 8.7). The *Expected Opportunity Loss* option in the dialog box will be discussed shortly.

	A	B	C	D	E
1	Investment Options				
2					
3	Probabilities & Payoff Table:				
4		P	Aggressive	Balanced	Bond
5	Market rises	0.5	1000	600	200
6	Market falls	0.2	-1500	-500	300
7	Market stable	0.3	0	200	100
8					
9	Statistics	Aggressive	Balanced	Bond	
10	Expected Monetary Value	200	260	190	
11	Variance	910000	174400	4900	
12	Standard Deviation	953.9392	417.61226	70	
13	Coefficient of Variation	4.769696	1.606201	0.3684211	
14	Return to risk ratio	0.209657	0.6225871	2.7142857	
15					
16	Expected Opportunity Loss	420	360	430	
17			EVPI		

FIGURE 8.7 Completed *PHStat* Worksheet for Expected Monetary Value

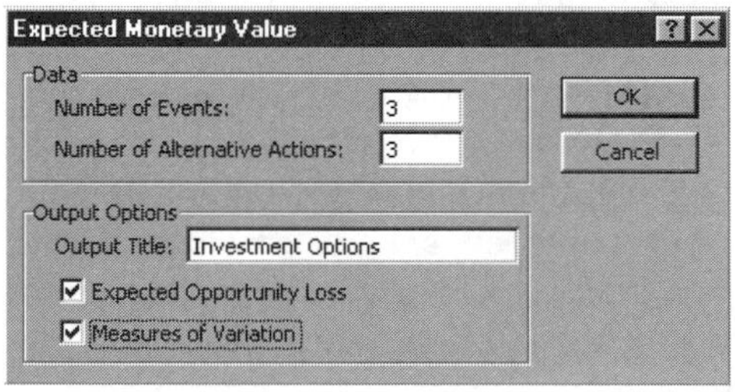

FIGURE 8.8 *PHStat* Dialog Box for Expected Monetary Value Decision Making

comparing alternatives that have different expected values. For the two projects we are considering, the respective coefficients of variation are

$$\text{Project A: CV} = 993.7/7{,}750 = 0.1282$$
$$\text{Project B: CV} = 1{,}414.2/8{,}000 = 0.1768$$

Although Project B has a higher expected return, it is also relatively more risky because the coefficient of variation is larger.

The **return-to-risk ratio** is simply the reciprocal of the coefficient of variation, that is, the expected value divided by the standard deviation. Although it provides the same information as the coefficient of variation, it is easier to understand because its measure is similar to the decision maker's objective. That is, if the objective is to maximize return, a higher return-to-risk ratio is often considered better. In the previous example,

TABLE 8.1	Illustration of Risk Differences	

Potential Returns

Project A	Project B
$4,000	
$5,000	
$6,000	$6,000
$7,000	$7,000
$8,000	$8,000
$9,000	$9,000
$10,000	$10,000

(a)

Potential Returns and Probabilities

Project A	Probability	Project B	Probability
$4,000	0.02		
$5,000	0.03		
$6,000	0.05	$6,000	0.20
$7,000	0.10	$7,000	0.20
$8,000	0.70	$8,000	0.20
$9,000	0.08	$9,000	0.20
$10,000	0.02	$10,000	0.20

(b)

the return-to-risk ratio for Project A is 7.80 and the ratio for Project B is 5.656. On a risk-adjusted basis, Project A provides a higher return.

Applying these ideas to the example in Figure 8.7, the return-to-risk ratio of the balanced fund is 0.623. Although the pure bond fund has a smaller expected value, its return-to-risk ratio is much higher, 2.71, indicating that this decision is relatively less risky. We can understand this by examining the payoffs. For the pure bond fund, the investor cannot lose any money. However, with the balanced fund, if the market falls, the investor stands to lose $500. Even more risk exists with the aggressive stock fund—a chance of losing $1,500—and is verified by the low return-to-risk ratio. An investor who has a low tolerance for risk might wish to forego a higher expected return for the comfort of a lower risk.

Opportunity Loss and Expected Value of Perfect Information

The **expected opportunity loss** in row 16 of Figure 8.7 represents the average additional amount the investor would have achieved by making the right decision instead of a wrong one. To find the expected opportunity loss, we first create an **opportunity loss table** as shown in Figure 8.9. We ask the question: What is the best decision if a particular event would occur? For example, if the event "market rises" occurs, then the best decision would have been to select the aggressive stock fund and realize a return of $1,000. Thus no opportunity is lost. However, if the investor selects the balanced fund, then he or she achieves a return of only $600, losing the opportunity of an extra $400. Likewise, the opportunity loss associated with choosing the bond fund is $1,000 − $200 = $800. In general, the opportunity loss is the difference between the payoff for a particular decision and the best decision, given the occurrence of each event. Once the

	A	B	C	D	E	F
1	Investment Options					
2						
3	Payoff Table:					
4		Aggressive	Balanced	Bond		
5	Market rises	1000	600	200		
6	Market falls	-1500	-500	300		
7	Market stable	0	200	100		
8						
9						
10	Opportunity Loss Table:					
11		Optimum	Optimum		Alternatives	
12		Action	Profit	Aggressive	Balanced	Bond
13	Market rises	Aggressive	1000	0	400	800
14	Market falls	Bond	300	1800	800	0
15	Market stable	Balanced	200	200	0	100

FIGURE 8.9 *PHStat* Output for Opportunity Loss Table

opportunity loss table is constructed, the expected opportunity loss for each action is found by weighting the values by the event probabilities. This is given in row 16 in Figure 8.7. We see that the balanced fund has the smallest expected opportunity loss. *It will always be true that the decision having the best expected value will also have the minimum expected opportunity loss.*

The minimum expected opportunity loss is called the **expected value of perfect information (EVPI).** EVPI represents the maximum improvement in the expected return that can be achieved if the decision maker is able to acquire—before making a decision—perfect information about the future event that will take place. For example, if we know with certainty that the market will rise, then the optimal decision is to choose the aggressive stock fund and receive a return of $1,000. Likewise, if we know that the market will fall, we should chose the bond fund with a return of $300. Finally, if the market is stable, we should choose the balanced fund with a return of $200. By weighting these outcomes by the probabilities of occurrence, we find that the expected return will now be

$$\text{Expected return with perfect information} = 0.5(\$1,000) + 0.2(\$300) + 0.3(\$200) = \$620$$

Because the expected value without having the perfect information is only $260, we would have increased our average return by $620 − $260 = $360. This is the expected value of perfect information. EVPI is often used to assess the value of acquiring less than perfect information; one would never want to pay more than the EVPI for any information about the future event, no matter how good.

Decision Trees

Another approach to structuring a decision problem involving uncertainty is to use a graphical model called a **decision tree.** Decision trees consist of a set of **nodes** and **branches.** Nodes are points in time at which events take place. The event can be a selection of a decision from among several alternatives, represented by a **choice node,** or an outcome over which the decision maker has no control, an **event node.** Event nodes are conventionally depicted by circles, whereas choice events are expressed by boxes (see Figure 8.10). Many decision makers find decision trees are more useful than the tabular form because *sequences* of decisions and outcomes over time can be modeled easily. The CD-ROM accompanying this book contains an Excel add-in called *TreePlan,* which allows you to construct decision trees and perform calculations within an Excel worksheet. The disk contains all documentation and explanations of how to use *TreePlan,* and we encourage you to take advantage of it for many of the problems in this chapter.

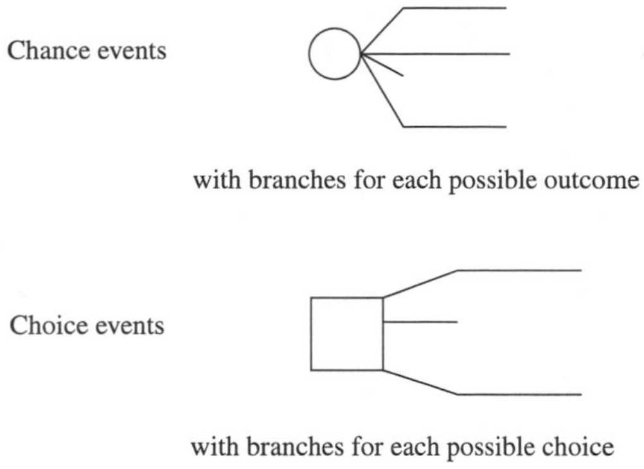

Chance events

with branches for each possible outcome

Choice events

with branches for each possible choice

FIGURE 8.10 Decision Tree Symbols

To illustrate the application of decision analysis techniques using decision trees, we will consider one of the Tracway projects from Figure 8.6. Project A1 involves developing a group support system to enable Tracway employees to conduct meetings electronically. The proposed system involves development expenses of $50,000 to purchase software, $10,000 to hire a consultant to help with installing the system, and four Tracway Information Systems personnel for a 6-week development period with a labor cost of $30,000. Tracway fringe benefits are 20 percent of labor, adding another $6,000. Eight personal computers are required for the system, at an estimated cost of $2,000 each, for a hardware cost of $16,000. These estimated costs total $112,000 for the project. To operate the project, two people are needed on a full-time basis at an estimated cost of $68,000. With fringes, this amounts to $81,600, growing in years two and three at the rate of 5 percent inflation per year. However, uncertainty exists as to whether the system can be installed successfully using internal expertise. The review team has estimated a 70 percent chance of successful installation with an 84 percent availability (accounting for expected downtime).

The main benefit to Tracway is expected to be reduction of travel expenses, which are estimated at $500 per person per meeting. An average of five people travel to each meeting, and it is expected that the system will serve 50 meetings per year (low-usage scenario), resulting in a savings of $125,000, to as high as 100 meetings per year (high-usage scenario), resulting in a savings of $250,000. However, with the system availability of 0.84, these savings can only be estimated as $105,000 and $210,000, respectively. The project is to be evaluated on a 3-year basis, using a discount rate of 12 percent per year.

The proposal could be made more reliable by hiring consultants to do most of the installation (thereby increasing the probability of a successful implementation to 0.9). This second decision alternative, called the buy-up proposal, is expected to increase the availability of the system to 95 percent. The costs would be the same except for an increase to $100,000 for the consultants and a reduction in labor development costs for Tracway Information Systems personnel. The benefits increase because of the higher system reliability increase to $118,750 for the low-usage scenario, and $237,500 for the high-usage case.

Finally, a less expensive version of the system can be obtained by buying a turnkey software package that requires no consulting expertise to install. This is a riskier proposition, and the Information Systems group is willing to estimate only a 0.5 probability of full successful system installation. This alternative reduces the total project development expenses to $77,414. However, this system is expected to be more unreliable, and available only 60 percent of the time. Figure 8.11 shows a spreadsheet model for computing the net present value of these proposals under both usage scenarios.

	A	B	C	D	E	F	G
		Original proposal		Buy-up proposal		Buy-down proposal	
1							
2							
3	Development expenses						
4	Software	$ 50,000		$ 50,000		$ 20,000	
5	Consultant	$ 10,000		$ 100,000			
6	Labor	$ 30,000		$ 8,000		$ 40,000	
7	Fringes (20%)	$ 6,000		$ 1,600		$ 8,000	
8	Hardware	$ 16,000		$ 16,000		$ 9,414	
9							
10	Total	$ (112,000)		$ (175,600)		$ (77,414)	
11							
12	Operating expenses						
13	Year 1	$ 81,600		$ 81,600		$ 81,600	
14	Year 2	$ 85,680		$ 85,680		$ 85,680	
15	Year 3	$ 89,964		$ 89,964		$ 89,964	
16							
17	System availability	0.84		0.95		0.6	
18		Low usage	High usage	Low usage	High usage	Low usage	High usage
19	Savings benefits	$ 125,000	$ 250,000	$ 125,000	$ 250,000	$ 125,000	$ 250,000
20	Year 1	$ 105,000	$ 210,000	$ 118,750	$ 237,500	$ 75,000	$ 150,000
21	Year 2	$ 105,000	$ 210,000	$ 118,750	$ 237,500	$ 75,000	$ 150,000
22	Year 3	$ 105,000	$ 210,000	$ 118,750	$ 237,500	$ 75,000	$ 150,000
23							
24	Net benefits						
25	Year 1	$ 23,400	$ 128,400	$ 37,150	$ 155,900	$ (6,600)	$ 68,400
26	Year 2	$ 19,320	$ 124,320	$ 33,070	$ 151,820	$ (10,680)	$ 64,320
27	Year 3	$ 15,036	$ 120,036	$ 28,786	$ 147,536	$ (14,964)	$ 60,036
28							
29	Net present values	($65,003.03)	$187,189.25	($95,577.85)	$189,639.61	($102,471.97)	$77,665.38

FIGURE 8.11 Financial Analysis of Information Systems Proposals

A decision tree for this problem constructed in *TreePlan* is shown in Figure 8.12. This is an example of a **single-stage decision tree,** one having a single set of decisions followed by a set of chance events. A decision tree is evaluated by "folding back" the tree from right to left. When we encounter an event node, we compute the expected value of all events that emanate from the node, because each branch will have an associated probability. For example, the value of the top right chance node in Figure 8.12 is found by taking the expected value of the payoffs associated with high and low usage.

$$\$187,189 \times 0.50 + (\$65,003) \times 0.50 = \$61,093$$

Likewise, the expected value corresponding to the branch "Original proposal" is

$$\$61,093 \times 0.7 + (\$112,000) \times 0.3 = \$9,165.10$$

When we encounter a choice node (in this case, the only choice node is the first node in the tree), we take the best of the expected values of all nodes that follow. Because we are dealing with net present values of benefits less costs, the best decision is to pursue the buy-up proposal having an expected value of $24,768.

Multistage decision trees involve a sequence of interrelated decisions and chance events. Suppose, for example, that if either the original or buy-down proposals failed, Tracway would consider hiring a consultant to salvage the project. Because some of the work would already have been performed, the consultant fees would be $60,000, but there is still a 10 percent chance of failure. The other alternative is to scrap the project entirely. Figure 8.13 shows a decision tree for this situation. Note that the payoffs now include the additional cost of the consultant along those paths that have been added to the original decision tree. From an expected value basis, the best decision strategy is first to pursue the original proposal. If the original proposal succeeds, no further decisions

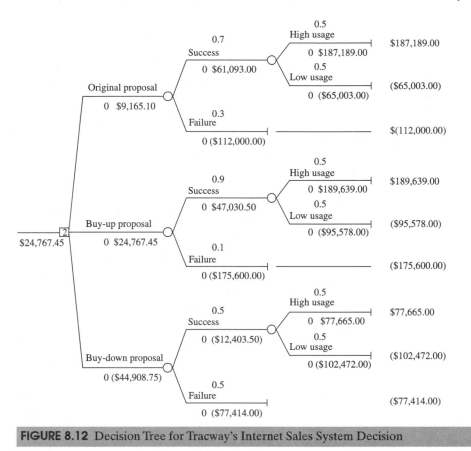

FIGURE 8.12 Decision Tree for Tracway's Internet Sales System Decision

need to be made. However, if the original proposal fails, Tracway should hire the consultant (having the best expected value, despite its being negative).

You can see that in both decision trees, considerable risk exists. The only case for which Tracway will realize a positive return is if the implementation is successful *and* usage turns out to be high. In the multistage case, assuming the chance events are independent, the probability of a positive return for the optimal decision strategy is

$$P(success) \times P(high\ usage) + P(failure) \times P(success\ after\ hiring\ consultant) \times P(high\ usage) = (0.7)(0.5) + (0.3)(0.9)(0.5) = 0.485$$

Despite the positive expected value, such a risk might not be acceptable.

Monte Carlo Simulation for Risk Analysis

To evaluate risk we need to characterize the probability distributions and compute essential statistics such as the standard deviation and coefficient of variation for the outputs of key variables in a decision model. An easy way of doing this in a spreadsheet model is to use Monte Carlo simulation. *Monte Carlo simulation*—sampling from input distributions to estimate the distribution of an output variable—provides probability distributions of the potential outcomes of decisions, and thus a means of evaluating risk. For example, we could answer such questions as What is the probability that we will

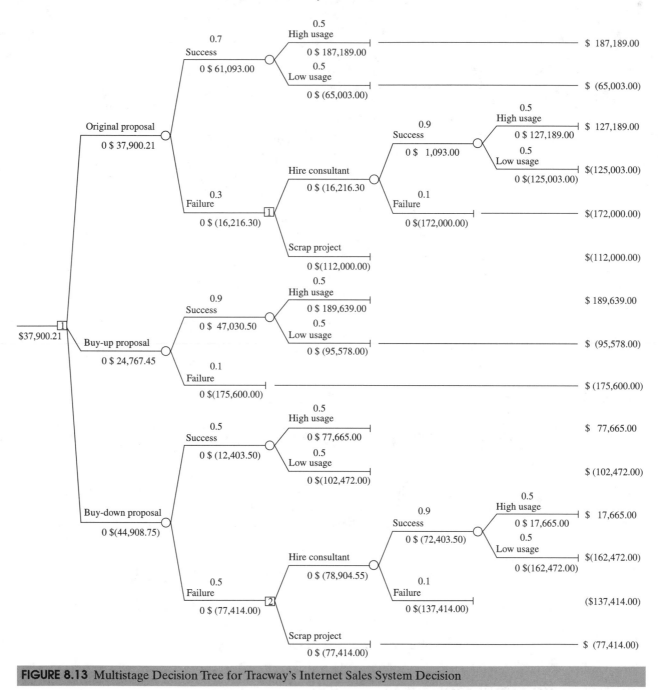

FIGURE 8.13 Multistage Decision Tree for Tracway's Internet Sales System Decision

incur a financial loss? What is the probability that we will run out of inventory? What are the chances the project will be completed on time?

Crystal Ball automates the process of performing Monte Carlo simulation on spreadsheets. The appendix to chapter 3 provided an introduction to *Crystal Ball,* and the appendix to this chapter describes some advanced capabilities. *If you have not read the appendix to chapter 3, we suggest that you to do so now.* We will illustrate the application of *Crystal Ball*–based risk analysis to Tracway's proposed Internet sales system.

Because the proposal is new, no historical data are available to characterize the assumptions of uncertainty in the spreadsheet model in Figure 8.1. Therefore, Tracway analysts must use subjective, judgmental assumptions. Conservative estimates are that development expenses each month will have a mean equal to the estimates in Figure 8.1, with a standard deviation of 10 percent of the mean, normally distributed. We use the *Crystal Ball* function (see chapter 3) CB.Normal(*mean, standard deviation*) to model these assumptions.[1] Operating expenses are more certain; they are also assumed to be normally distributed with a mean equal to the estimates in Figure 8.1, but with a standard deviation equal to 5 percent of the mean. Revenues are expected to grow as estimated in Figure 8.1; however, the value of the first year's revenue (March) is assumed to be anywhere between $800 and $1,200, uniformly distributed. This is modeled as CB.Uniform(800, 1,200). Revenues in succeeding months are assumed to be multiples of the March value (using the same ratios as in Figure 8.1). Thus April's revenue is assumed to be three times that of March, and so on. The discount rate is assumed to have a triangular distribution, with a low estimate of 10.5 percent, most likely value of 12 percent, and high value of 13 percent. Cells E20 (NPV) and B22 (IRR) are defined as forecast cells. Figure 8.14 shows an example of the spreadsheet under these assumptions.

Figures 8.15 through 8.18 show the results of a simulation of 1,000 trials. The net present value ranges from −$52,130.15 to +$46,124.46 with an expected value of −$791.33, standard deviation of $22,831.82, and coefficient of variation equal to −28.85. The return-to-risk ratio is therefore −0.046. The mean standard error is $722.01. This means that for any other 1,000-trial simulation, we can expect the mean to fall roughly within three standard errors of the estimated mean, or −$791.33 ± 3(722.01) or from −$2,957.36 to $1,374.70, with a high level of confidence.

	A	B	C	D	E
1	**Internet Project Proposal**				
2					
3	Discount rate	12.0%			
4		Development	Operating		
5	Month	Expense	Expense	Revenue	Net Profit
6	Initial investment	$ 36,137.58	$ -	$ -	$ (36,137.58)
7	January	$ 20,012.45	$ 5,350.81	$ -	$ (25,363.26)
8	February	$ 10,700.93	$ 7,424.14	$ -	$ (18,125.07)
9	March	$ 12,430.72	$ 7,743.91	$ 1,020.24	$ (19,154.39)
10	April	$ 10,671.81	$ 9,436.82	$ 3,060.72	$ (17,047.91)
11	May	$ 5,535.50	$ 9,873.90	$ 6,121.44	$ (9,287.95)
12	June	$ 5,231.79	$ 10,368.35	$ 10,202.40	$ (5,397.73)
13	July	$ 5,151.80	$ 9,705.66	$ 15,303.61	$ 446.14
14	August	$ 5,918.39	$ 10,481.91	$ 20,404.81	$ 4,004.51
15	September	$ -	$ 9,329.72	$ 28,566.73	$ 19,237.02
16	October	$ -	$ 10,051.02	$ 36,728.66	$ 26,677.64
17	November	$ -	$ 9,198.21	$ 45,910.82	$ 36,712.61
18	December	$ -	$ 10,128.97	$ 56,113.22	$ 45,984.26
19					
20	Net Present Values	$109,228.63	$101,918.18	$202,802.71	($8,344.10)
21					
22	IRR	0.22%			

FIGURE 8.14 *Crystal Ball* Model for Internet Project Proposal Simulation (assumption and forecast cells are highlighted)

---

[1] We could use the Assumption feature of *Crystal Ball;* however, the student version is limited to six assumption cells. The *Crystal Ball* functions serve the same purpose; however, not defining these as assumption cells limits some of the advanced analysis capabilities of the software as described in the appendix to this chapter.

Forecast: Net present value

Cell E20 **Statistics**

Statistic	Value
Trials	1,000
Mean	($791.33)
Median	($235.74)
Mode	---
Standard Deviation	$22,831.82
Variance	$521,291,997.73
Skewness	-0.03
Kurtosis	1.91
Coeff. of Variability	-28.85
Range Minimum	($52,130.15)
Range Maximum	$46,124.46
Range Width	$98,254.61
Mean Std. Error	$722.01

FIGURE 8.15 *Crystal Ball* Summary Statistics for NPV Forecast

Figure 8.16 shows that there is only a 49.6 percent probability that the NPV will be positive. Likewise, Figure 8.17 shows that the IRR ranges from −4.68 percent to 5.58 percent, with an average of 0.76 percent. Clearly, although this project has significant upside potential, it has significant downside risk. Figure 8.18 shows the probability that IRR will exceed Tracway's threshold of 4 percent IRR for new ventures. Because the probability is only 6.9 percent, Tracway will probably reject this proposal.

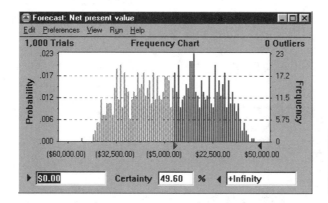

Forecast: Net present value

1,000 Trials **Frequency Chart** **0 Outliers**

$0.00 Certainty **49.60** % +Infinity

FIGURE 8.16 *Crystal Ball* Forecast Chart Showing Certainty Level for a Positive NPV

Forecast: IRR

Cell B22 **Statistics**

Statistic	Value
Trials	1,000
Mean	0.76%
Median	0.94%
Mode	---
Standard Deviation	2.32%
Variance	0.05%
Skewness	-0.18
Kurtosis	1.96
Coeff. of Variability	3.04
Range Minimum	-4.68%
Range Maximum	5.58%
Range Width	10.27%
Mean Std. Error	0.07%

FIGURE 8.17 *Crystal Ball* Summary Statistics for IRR Forecast

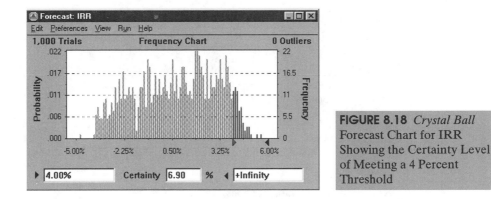

FIGURE 8.18 *Crystal Ball* Forecast Chart for IRR Showing the Certainty Level of Meeting a 4 Percent Threshold

Applications of Monte Carlo Simulation

In this section we present two additional examples of Monte Carlo simulation using *Crystal Ball*. The case study later in the chapter describes a more comprehensive application of *Crystal Ball* to an actual problem faced by Cinergy Corporation.

PROJECT MANAGEMENT

Project management is concerned with scheduling the activities of a project involving interrelated activities. An important aspect of project management is identifying the expected completion time of the project. Activity times can be fixed or uncertain. We often assume that uncertain activity times have a beta or triangular distribution, especially when times are estimated judgmentally. Analytical methods such as PERT (Project Evaluation and Review Technique), discussed in most operations management texts, allow us to determine probabilities of project completion times under a normality assumption. This assumption may not always be valid. Furthermore, the PERT approach assumes that the expected activity times define the critical path. Simulation can provide a more realistic characterization of the project completion time and the associated risks. We will illustrate risk analysis in project management through the following example.

A consulting firm has been hired to assist in the evaluation of new software. The manager of the Information Systems department is responsible for coordinating all of the activities involving consultants and the company's resources. The following activities have been defined, along with minimum (a), most likely (b), and maximum (c) times for each in working days. The target project completion date is 140 working days. Because this is a new application, activity times are assumed to be triangular, with certain activity times constant. Table 8.2 shows the list of activities and time estimates.

Figure 8.19 shows a spreadsheet designed to compute the activity schedule and slack, from which we may compute the project completion time and identify the critical path. The expected activity times (column E) are computed using the formula

$$\text{Expected activity time} = \frac{a + 4b + c}{6}$$

TABLE 8.2 Activity and Time Estimate List

Activity		Predecessors	Min	Likely	Max
A	Select steering committee	—	15	15	15
B	Develop requirements list	—	40	45	60
C	Develop system size estimates	—	10	14	30
D	Determine prospective vendors	—	2	2	5
E	Form evaluation team	A	5	7	9
F	Issue request for proposal	B,C,D,E	4	5	8
G	Bidders conference	F	1	1	1
H	Review submissions	G	25	30	50
I	Select vendor short list	H	3	5	10
J	Check vendor references	I	3	3	10
K	Vendor demonstrations	I	20	30	45
L	User site visit	I	3	3	5
M	Select vendor	J,K,L	3	3	3
N	Volume sensitive test	M	10	13	20
O	Negotiate contracts	M	10	14	28
P	Cost benefit analysis	N,O	2	2	2
Q	Obtain board of directors approval	P	5	5	5

and the variance of the time for each activity (column F) is computed as

$$\text{Variance} = \frac{(c - a)^2}{36}$$

These formulas are based on the assumption that activity times have a beta probability distribution, the standard assumption in the analytical modeling approach.

Activities A, B, C, and D have no immediate predecessors, and therefore have early start times of 0. The early start time for each other activity is the maximum of the early finish times for the activity's immediate predecessor. For example, cell G9 has the formula =H5; cell G10 has the formula =MAX(H6,H7,H8,H9). Early finish times are com-

FIGURE 8.19 Spreadsheet for Project Management Calculations

	A	B	C	D	E	F	G	H	I	J	K
1	Project Management Model										
2											
3			Most		Activity		Early	Early	Latest	Latest	
4	Activity	Min	Likely	Max	Time	Variance	Start	Finish	Start	Finish	Slack
5	A	15	15	15	15.00	0.00	0.00	15.00	24.67	39.67	24.67
6	B	40	45	60	46.67	11.11	0.00	46.67	0.00	46.67	0.00
7	C	10	14	30	16.00	11.11	0.00	16.00	30.67	46.67	30.67
8	D	2	2	5	2.50	0.25	0.00	2.50	44.17	46.67	44.17
9	E	5	7	9	7.00	0.44	15.00	22.00	39.67	46.67	24.67
10	F	4	5	8	5.33	0.44	46.67	52.00	46.67	52.00	0.00
11	G	1	1	1	1.00	0.00	52.00	53.00	52.00	53.00	0.00
12	H	25	30	50	32.50	17.36	53.00	85.50	53.00	85.50	0.00
13	I	3	5	10	5.50	1.36	85.50	91.00	85.50	91.00	0.00
14	J	3	3	10	4.17	1.36	91.00	95.17	117.67	121.83	26.67
15	K	20	30	45	30.83	17.36	91.00	121.83	91.00	121.83	0.00
16	L	3	3	5	3.33	0.11	91.00	94.33	118.50	121.83	27.50
17	M	3	3	3	3.00	0.00	121.83	124.83	121.83	124.83	0.00
18	N	10	13	20	13.67	2.78	124.83	138.50	126.83	140.50	2.00
19	O	10	14	28	15.67	9.00	124.83	140.50	124.83	140.50	0.00
20	P	2	2	2	2.00	0.00	140.50	142.50	140.50	142.50	0.00
21	Q	5	5	5	5.00	0.00	142.50	147.50	142.50	147.50	0.00
22											
23		Project completion time				147.50					

puted as the early start time plus the activity time (e.g., H5 = G5 + E5). The early finish time for the last activity, Q, represents the earliest time the project can be completed; that is, the minimum project completion time. Thus the project completion time in cell F23 is set equal to the value of cell H21.

To compute late start and late finish times, we set the late finish time of the terminal activity equal to the project completion time. The late start time is computed by subtracting the activity time from the late finish time (e.g., I21 = J21 − E21). The late finish time for any other activity, say *X*, is defined as the minimum late start of all activities to which activity *X* is an immediate predecessor. For example, the formula for cell J21 is =H21; for J20, the formula is =I21; and for J17, the formula is =MIN(I18, I19). Finally, slack is computed as the difference between the late finish and early finish (e.g., K5 = J5 − H5). The activity times in Figure 8.19 are the expected values. Based on these, the critical path consists of those activities with zero slack, namely B-F-G-H-I-K-M-O-P-Q, and has an expected duration of 147.5 days.

In the analytical approach found in most textbooks, probabilities of completing the project within a certain time are computed assuming that

1. The distribution of project completion times is normal (as a result of the central limit theorem);
2. The expected project completion time is the sum of the expected activity times along the critical path, which is found using the expected activity times; and
3. The variance of the distribution is the sum of the variances of those activities along the critical path, which is found using the expected activity times.

Thus for this example, the variance of the critical path is 56.63 (found by adding the variances of those activities with zero slack). The probability that the project will be completed within 140 days is found by computing the *z*-value.

$$z = \frac{140 - 147.5}{7.53} = -.996$$

Using Table A.2 in the appendix at the end of the book, this corresponds to an area between $-\infty$ and 140 of .1587.

The problem with these assumptions is that variations in activity times may yield different critical paths than the one resulting from expected times. In addition, actual activity times might not have a beta distribution, and further, the distribution of project completion times might not be normal. Simulation can easily address these issues and provide a more accurate representation of risk.

To apply *Crystal Ball* to this situation, we assumed that each activity time had a triangular distribution with the specified parameters (minimum, most likely, and maximum). Because the student version of *Crystal Ball* is limited to six assumption cells, we must use the *Crystal Ball* functions as an alternative to defining each activity time as an assumption. Thus we replace the formulas in each activity time cell by CB.Triangular(*Minimum, Likeliest, Maximum*). For example, the formula in cell E10 would be CB.Triangular(B10, C10, E10). Doing this has no detrimental impact on the ultimate distribution of forecast cell values; however, it does not allow us to use certain options in *Crystal Ball,* for example, the sensitivity chart. Finally, the forecast cell is F23, project completion time.

Figure 8.20 shows a portion of the *Crystal Ball* report for 1,000 replications of the spreadsheet in Figure 8.19. We see that the expected project completion time is higher than that predicted in the original spreadsheet, and that the distribution range is rather

Crystal Ball **Report**
Simulation started on 9/27/96 at 15:01:34
Simulation stopped on 9/27/96 at 15:03:33

Forecast: Project completion time

Summary:
Display Range is from 130.00 to 180.00
Entire Range is from 127.03 to 188.00
After 1,000 Trials, the Std. Error of the Mean is 0.30

Statistics:	Value
Trials	1,000
Mean	155.22
Median	154.65
Mode	–
Standard Deviation	9.47
Variance	89.76
Skewness	0.17
Kurtosis	2.96
Coeff. of Variability	0.06
Range Minimum	127.03
Range Maximum	188.00
Range Width	60.97
Mean Std. Error	0.30

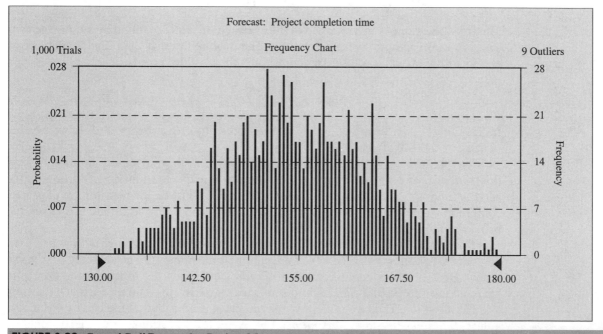

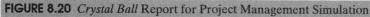
FIGURE 8.20 *Crystal Ball* Report for Project Management Simulation

wide. In fact, the simulation results determine that the probability that the project will be completed before 147.5 days is only about 0.20. The probability that the project will be completed by 140 days is only about .05, significantly different from that predicted using the standard assumptions. Thus it is highly unlikely that the project will be completed within 140 days, and it probably will take longer than 147 days.

BUDGET-CONSTRAINED PRODUCT SELECTION

This example shows how Monte Carlo simulation and statistical reasoning can be combined with more traditional selection models to provide insights that traditional models cannot. A company's research and development efforts have resulted in eight potential new products. The proposed selling price, estimated annual sales, annual cost, and initial investment required have been determined by a team from accounting, marketing, and other areas of the company. However, all products cannot be selected because the budget allocated for initial investment is limited. One criterion for selecting products is to maximize the weighted average return, where the rate of return (ROR) for product k is defined as

$$\text{ROR}_k = (\text{price}_k \times \text{annual sales}_k - \text{annual cost}_k)/\text{initial investment}_k$$

and the weighted average return is

$$\frac{\sum_k I_k \, \text{ROR}_k}{\sum_k I_k}$$

The best solution to this selection problem can be found by a simple "greedy" algorithm: Rank the products in descending order by ROR, and select the products in rank order until the total investment exceeds the budget. The spreadsheet in Figure 8.21 shows an example. Based on the ROR, the products would be ranked in order 4, 8, 3, 5, 2, 6, 1, 7. Once we select products 4 and 8, we cannot select product 3 because it would cause the budget to be exceeded.

An analytic solution such as this does not take into account any risk factors. For example, the annual sales as well as the annual costs might be uncertain. To illustrate, suppose that the values in column C represent the mean annual sales, but that actual sales

FIGURE 8.21 Product Selection Analysis Spreadsheet

	A	B	C	D	E	F	G
1	Constrained Product Selection Model						
2							
3	Product	Price	Annual sales	Annual cost	Initial investment	Average rate of return	Decisions
4	1	$ 9	10000	$ 75,000	$ 160,000	0.094	0
5	2	$ 2	500000	$ 950,000	$ 400,000	0.125	0
6	3	$850	200	$ 125,000	$ 250,000	0.180	0
7	4	$ 45	100000	$ 4,250,000	$ 800,000	0.313	1
8	5	$ 4	1000	$ 3,000	$ 6,000	0.167	0
9	6	$ 17	80000	$ 1,300,000	$ 500,000	0.120	0
10	7	$475	50	$ 22,000	$ 30,000	0.058	0
11	8	$ 23	200000	$ 4,500,000	$ 500,000	0.200	1
12				Total invested	$ 1,300,000		
13				Budget	$ 1,500,000		

are normally distributed with a standard deviation equal to 10 percent of the mean. In addition, suppose that the annual costs are uniformly distributed with limits equal to plus or minus 10 percent of the mean value. Because annual costs should be correlated with sales, we will use the correlation feature of *Crystal Ball* to correlate the annual sales with the annual costs of each product, using a correlation coefficient of 0.85.

Figure 8.22 shows the frequency charts for the rates of return for each product. The left grabbers have been positioned at zero to show the probability that the rates of return will be positive. Thus for product 4 we see that even though the mean rate of re-

FIGURE 8.22 *Crystal Ball* Results Showing Certainty Levels for a Positive ROR for Each Product

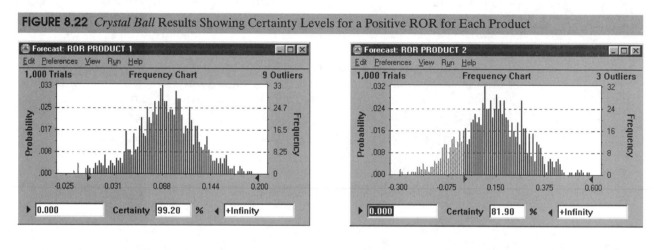

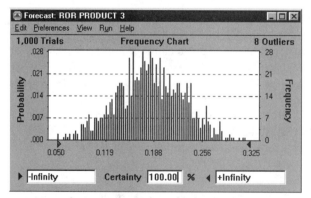

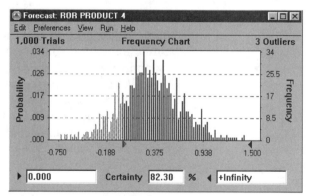

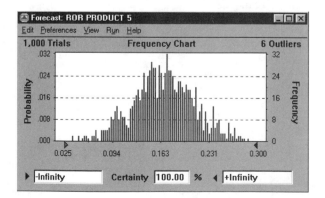

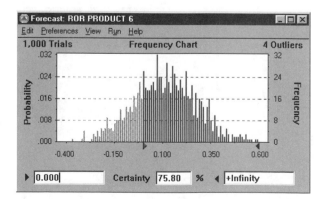

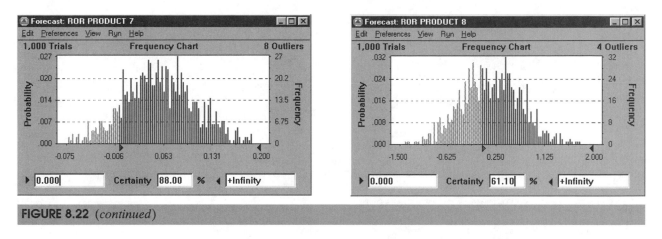

FIGURE 8.22 (*continued*)

turn is 0.313, there is an 18 percent chance that it will actually be negative. For product 8 the probability that the ROR will be positive is only 0.611. The risks uncovered by the simulation might sway the company to select a different mix of products instead of the optimal solution based upon expected values.

Case Study: Simulation and Risk Analysis in New Product Screening at Cinergy Corporation[2]

Cinergy Corporation was created in October 1994 by a merger of The Cincinnati Gas & Electric Company and PSI Energy. Cinergy is the nation's 13th-largest electric utility company, with approximately 11,000 megawatts of generating capacity, annual revenues of approximately $3 billion, and 8,000 employees. The company spans 25,000 square miles in north central, central, and southern Indiana, southwestern Ohio, and northern Kentucky, and serves the energy needs of 1.4 million electric customers and 435,000 gas customers.

A common situation faced by Cinergy and many other companies is the screening of new product ideas, which clearly involves much uncertainty. At Cinergy, the new product screening process starts with a product idea assessment including market potential, annual sales, and profit estimates. *Crystal Ball* is used to help identify the risks involved with new product development.

In one case, a new energy service product called the Uninterruptible Personal Computer (PC) Power Service was considered for introduction. This product and service would provide several benefits for a home computer, including an uninterruptible power supply, protection against power line surges and sags, and electric sinusoidal wave enhancement (i.e., improved power quality). The first step in the assessment process is to estimate the market potential for the product. This was accomplished through primary and secondary market research, leading to the spreadsheet in Figure 8.23.

Growth rates; customer forecasts; the saturation of computers, home offices, and home businesses; and the purchase intentions among the different subgroupings of the target market are all uncertain. For many of these, no historical information was

---

[2] We are indebted to Bruce Sailers and Cinergy Corporation for providing this case study.

	A	B	C	D	E	F	G
1	**Uninterrupted PC Power Supply Service**						
2	**Estimated Customer Potential**						
3	Market Research Information:						
4							
5	Percent of Households with a PC:						34%
6		Compound 5-year Growth Rate:					7.7%
7	Percent of PC Owners Who Have a Home Office:						55%
8		Compound 5-year Growth Rate:					13%
9	Percent of Home Office PC Owners Who Have a Home Business:						29%
10		Compound 5-year Growth Rate:					10%
11							
12	**Target Market Size**						
13	Year	Estimated Cinergy Households	Household Random Error	Cinergy Households	Households with a PC	PC Owners with a Home Office	PC Owners & Home Business
14	1997	1,228,000	0	1,228,000	417,520	229,636	66,594
15	1998	1,244,000	0	1,244,000	449,669	259,489	73,253
16	1999	1,261,000	0	1,261,000	484,294	293,223	80,578
17	2000	1,278,000	0	1,278,000	521,585	331,342	88,636
18	2001	1,293,000	0	1,293,000	561,747	374,416	97,500
20	**Purchase Intent for UPS System & Service**						
21			Very Serious	Somewhat Serious	Purchase Intent		
22	PC only		4.5%	24.0%	8.4%		
23	PC & Home Office		8.0%	23.5%	11.1%		
24	PC & Home Business		6.5%	23.5%	9.9%		
25							
26	Assume 80% of very serious purchase:				80%		
27	Assume 20% of somewhat serious purchase:				20%		
28							
29	**Estimated Customer Potential for UPS System & Service**						
30							
31	Year	PC Only Customers	Home Office Customers	Home Business Customers	Market Potential		
32	1997	15,782	18,098	6,593	40,473		
33	1998	15,975	20,672	7,252	43,899		
34	1999	16,050	23,604	7,977	47,631		
35	2000	15,980	26,940	8,775	51,695		
36	2001	15,736	30,738	9,653	56,127		

FIGURE 8.23 Spreadsheet for Cinergy New Product Analysis

available to assign probability distributions. The saturation values and growth rates for computers, home offices, and home businesses were obtained from secondary sources, and subjective estimates of the uncertainty related to these values were obtained by reading additional material and industry reviews, and talking with experts in the field. The percent of households with a PC, PC owners who have a home office, and home office PC owners with a home business were modeled by uniform distributions; growth rate assumptions were triangular.

For the household random error term, historical data was available that suggested errors are random and within .5 percent of the actual values. Therefore, a normally distributed assumption was made for these cells. The standard deviation of this random error term increases throughout the forecast horizon because there is more uncertainty related to the household forecast for 2002 than for 1997. Purchase intent values were obtained from a primary research study that was designed to estimate these values within ±3 percent. Normal distributions were used.

Finally, the market potential cells are *Crystal Ball* forecast cells. Cinergy was interested in making inferences regarding the market potential for this product and therefore information needs to be gathered on them. However, these same cells are also used as input into another spreadsheet that projects the number of customers purchasing the product each year (i.e., adoptions) using a mathematical model called the Bass diffusion model. This is shown in Figure 8.24.

We will not discuss the intricacies of the Bass diffusion model here. However, the parameters that are included in the model are uncertain. These values can be estimated from secondary sources such as other utility programs that involve this same type of technology and were modeled using triangular distributions.

	A	B	C	D	E	F	G	H	I
1	**Sales Forecast**								
2				**Bass Diffusion Model**					
3-5			$Adopt_t = \left(p + q\left(\dfrac{CumAdopt_{t-1}}{Population_t}\right) + bX\right)*(Population_t - CumAdopt_{t-1})$						
6									
7									
8		p	0.1	(Coefficient of Innovation)					**Legend:**
9		q	0.6	(Coefficient of Imitation)					Pop - Market Potential
10		b	0.0000						Adopt - Current Year Adoptions
11									CA - Cummulative Adoptions
12	t	X	Pop	Adopt	CA	CA/Pop	Pop-CA		t - Time Period (Year)
13	0		40,473	-		0.0%	40,473		
14	1	0%	40,473	4,047	4,047	10.0%	36,426		
15	2	0%	43,899	6,190	10,237	23.3%	33,662		
16	3	0%	47,631	8,561	18,798	39.5%	28,833		
17	4	0%	51,695	10,467	29,266	56.6%	22,429		
18	5	0%	56,127	11,090	40,355	71.9%	15,772		

FIGURE 8.24 Sales Forecast Model

Once sales projections are made, financial estimates can be developed. At the early stages of a product's assessment, many uncertainties exist. Warranty costs, advertising expenditures, administrative costs, billing, and initial investments are all uncertain until just before the decision is made to introduce a new product. Often they are uncertain even after this decision. The financial spreadsheet is shown in Figure 8.25.

Most of the assumptions were modeled using triangular or normal distributions. A truncated normal was used for the inflation factor, having a mean of 3 percent, a standard deviation of 1 percent, and a minimum value of 2 percent. The main variable of interest is the project's net present value, which was a *Crystal Ball* forecast cell.

The last piece of information needed was the number of iterations to use. Cinergy management wished to estimate the NPV to within $10,000 with 95 percent confidence. An estimate of the standard deviation was obtained from running a preliminary analysis with 1,000 iterations. Calculations showed that 5,000 replications were necessary to achieve this precision.

The *Crystal Ball* output is shown in Figure 8.26. The mean of the NPV is $399,065 with a relatively small standard error due to the large sample size. This provided a high degree of confidence that the mean NPV value is positive. However, this does not say that no risk exists for this project. For any single trial, there is a 21.4 percent chance of the NPV being negative. Every manager has a different degree of aversion to risk. However, at this stage in the product's development, an almost 80 percent chance of returning a positive NPV is encouraging. It was recommended that this product move forward to the next phase in the product development process.

The sensitivity analysis also showed that the coefficients of the Bass model are important. This makes sense, because these values directly determine the number of customers each year. As with most products, the financial projections are sensitive to the units sold. This suggests that if there is time to perform further research, any effort expended to estimate the Bass model coefficients as accurately as possible will be time well spent.

	A	B	C	D	E	F	G
1	**Financial Analysis**						
2							
3	**Assumptions:**						
4	Price of UPS system:					$	300.00
5	Price of Installation:					$	100.00
6	Price of Service Contract:					$	150.00
7	Percentage of Customers Electing Service Contract:						15.0%
8	Percentage of Customers Electing Installation Service:						5%
9							
10	Cost of UPS System to Cinergy:					$	200.00
11	Installation and Fulfillment Costs per Unit:						
12	Order Processing					$	1.25
13	Billing					$	1.00
14	Product Installation						
15		Hours of technician time					2
16		Cost per hour (fully loaded or contract)				$	40.00
17							
18	Service Contract Costs:						
19	Hours of technician time						2
20	Materials (batteries, etc.)					$	25.00
21	Systems serviced each year						30%
22							
23	*Administrative Costs - 3 FTE fully loaded (Manager, Asst, Clerk)*					$	200,000
24	Inflation Factor:						3%
25	Taxes:						
26	Federal						35%
27	State						8.9%
28	Acquisition Costs Per Customer:						
29	Year 3 - 5					$	50.00
30							
31	*Initial Investment*					$	300,000

	A	B	C	D	E	F	G
33	**Summary of Analysis:**						
34	Year	Customers	Average Revenue per Cust	Average Cost per Cust	Average Profits per Cust	Total Profit	
35	1	4,047	$ 327.50	$ 383.94	$ (56.44)	$ (135,260)	
36	2	6,190	$ 327.50	$ 327.45	$ 0.05	$ 171	
37	3	8,561	$ 327.50	$ 285.76	$ 41.74	$ 211,600	
38	4	10,467	$ 327.50	$ 281.85	$ 45.65	$ 282,912	
39	5	11,090	$ 327.50	$ 281.27	$ 46.23	$ 303,572	
40							
41	**Initial Investment:**			$ 300,000			
42	**NPV @ 14%:**			49,479			
43	**Internal Rate of Return:**			17%			
44							
45							
46	**Financial Analysis:**						
47							
48	Year	Customers	Product Revenue	Service Contract Revenue	Total Revenue		
49	1997	4,047	$ 1,234,335	$ 91,058	$ 1,325,393		
50	1998	6,190	$ 1,887,950	139,275	2,027,225		
51	1999	8,561	$ 2,611,105	192,623	2,803,728		
52	2000	10,467	$ 3,192,435	235,508	3,427,943		
53	2001	11,090	$ 3,382,450	249,525	3,631,975		
54							
55	Year	UPS System Cost	Installation and Fulfillment Costs	Acquisition Costs	Maintenance Service Costs	Administrative Costs	Total Costs
56	1997	$ 809,400	$ 25,294	$ 500,000	$ 19,122	$ 200,000	$ 1,553,816
57	1998	$ 1,238,000	$ 38,688	515,000	$ 29,248	206,000	2,026,936
58	1999	$ 1,712,200	$ 53,506	428,050	$ 40,451	212,180	2,446,387
59	2000	$ 2,093,400	$ 65,419	523,350	$ 49,457	218,545	2,950,171
60	2001	$ 2,218,000	$ 69,313	554,500	$ 52,400	225,101	3,119,314
61							
62	Year	Profits Before Taxes	State Tax	Federal Tax	Total Annual Profit		
63	1997	$ (228,423)	$ (20,330)	$ (72,833)	$ (135,260)		
64	1998	289	26	92	171		
65	1999	357,341	31,803	113,938	211,600		
66	2000	477,772	42,522	152,338	282,912		
67	2001	512,661	45,627	163,462	303,572		

FIGURE 8.25 Financial Analysis Spreadsheet

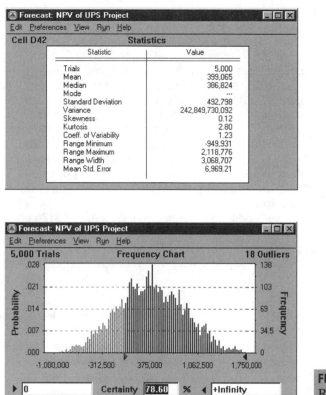

FIGURE 8.26 *Crystal Ball*
Results of NPV Evaluation

Summary

Making good decisions is essential to business success. This chapter presented a variety of examples and approaches for evaluating and selecting decisions. Decision criteria include net present value, internal rate of return, and expected value. Benefit/cost analysis provides a way of looking at the financial impacts of decisions, considering both direct costs and expected benefits, be they revenue increases or cost savings. "What if?" analysis and spreadsheet data tables provide a useful means to study the impact of changes in the assumptions of models.

Decision trees capture the structure of decision strategies when it is important to understand the impact of chance events that result from decisions. One disadvantage of decision trees is that decision strategies are based on expected values and do not explicitly include an assessment of risk. Another limitation of decision trees is that they are practical for only a small number of actions and events.

Monte Carlo simulation is a valuable tool for risk assessment because it allows you to characterize the distribution of outputs in decision models for any probabilistic assumptions that you wish to make for the model inputs. Software such as *Crystal Ball* automates the process on spreadsheets and provides complete statistical information and the ability to quantify risk.

Questions and Problems

1. Explain the concepts of net present value and internal rate of return. Why are they important for business decision making? Why might you use one criterion over the other?

2. Discuss how a reasonable value for the discount rate can be established in a personal context as well as in a business context.

3. Suppose that an investment costs $5,000 on January 1 of this year, and returns $1,000 at the end of this year and each of the following 5 years.
   a. Calculate the net present value (as of January 1 this year) of these cash flows using a discount rate of 10 percent per year.
   b. Calculate the internal rate of return, ignoring the discount rate assumption.

4. An investment requires an initial cash outlay of $100,000, and additional outlays of $50,000 at the end of each of the first 3 years. This investment is expected to result in incomes of $40,000 at the end of the first year, $70,000 at the end of the second year, $90,000 at the end of the third year, and $120,000 at the end of the fourth year.
   a. Calculate the net present value using a discount rate of 15 percent per year.
   b. Calculate the internal rate of return for these cash flows, ignoring the discount rate assumption.

5. A prospective product is expected to have sales of $100,000 in its first year. The rate of sales growth is debatable, but is expected to be somewhere between 5 and 15 percent per year. Cost of sales are expected to be $45,000 in the first year, growing by $5,000 each year thereafter. Indirect costs assigned to this product include the following:

Salaries:	$40,000 first year, increasing $1,000 per year
Benefits:	10 percent of salaries
Administrative expense:	$5,000 first year, increasing 4 percent per year
Depreciation	$8,000 every year
Interest	$2,000 for years 1 through 3, $3,000 for year 4

   a. Develop a spreadsheet and analyze earnings before tax for each year, assuming sales growth rates of 5, 7, 9, 10, 11, 13, and 15 percent.
   b. Compare the net present values for the rates of growth, using a discount rate of 12 percent per year.

6. An MBA student nearing graduation has been offered a job package that includes a retirement package that will involve first year investment (coming from her paycheck as well as company matching funds) of 15 percent of her annual pay, which initially would be $70,000. She can select a retirement option that has averaged 15 percent growth on the year's beginning balance each year. This growth rate could, however, be as low as 5 percent or as high as 25 percent. The MBA's average annual raise could range from 3 to 20 percent per year, with the most likely value 7 percent per year. The MBA plans on working 20 years before retiring to study her first love of philosophy.
   a. Calculate the expected value of her retirement plan after 20 years, as well as the value using the minimum and maximum rates for all assumptions.
   b. How realistic is such an analysis? What is the principal problem of using such an approach? What might be a better approach?

7. Oil field exploration involves high levels of risk. Geological exploration often provides prospective investors with estimates of the thickness of the hydrocarbon deposit (the oil), estimates of the oil field area, saltwater saturation, and porosity of the oil-bearing material. A model for estimating the original oil in place (OOIP) in barrels is

$$\text{OOIP} = 7758hA(1 - Sw)\phi$$

where h is hydrocarbon thickness in feet, A is the productive area in acres, Sw is saltwater saturation, and ϕ is the porosity. The worst, most likely, and best estimated values for each parameter are as follows:

	Worst	Most Likely	Best
h	15	30	100
A	100	200	700
Sw	0.9	0.6	0.1
ϕ	0.08	0.2	0.47

Given a development cost of $20 million, a value per barrel of $12, and a cost of production of $6 per barrel, calculate profit based on the worst, most likely, and best scenarios.

8. Compare the money spent on buying a house for $100,000 versus renting an apartment over a 15-year period. Assume that a loan for $95,000 can be obtained at the rate of 7 percent per year (payable monthly). The value of the house increases at the rate of 5 percent per year. House taxes cost the owner 12 percent of the value of the house each year. House insurance is $150 the first year, growing at the rate of 5 percent per year. Utilities cost $2,400 per year, growing at the rate of 3 percent per year. Calculate the amortized payment with the Excel function =PMT(.07/12, 180, 95000), reflecting a 7 percent annual rate of interest with 15 years of monthly payments for a loan of $95,000. Compare the net present value of these expenses with that of renting a house for $9,600 per year the first year, growing at a rate of 5 percent per year. Utilities for rent are $1,200 per year the first year, growing at the rate of 3 percent per year.

9. In the housing situation in problem 8, assume that $10,000 was required for down payment and closing costs. In the rental option, this $10,000 would be placed in savings (with a rate of interest of 3 percent per year on a positive beginning balance, paying 7 percent interest if the beginning balance is negative). The difference between the housing payment + house taxes + house insurance − rent is added savings (this value might go negative later in the analysis). Calculate the value of the house versus the value of the savings account after 15 years.

10. Use a data table to calculate the net present value of the money expended for buying or renting, as well as the value of the asset in each case, assuming real estate growth rates of 3, 4, 5, 6, and 7 percent per year.

11. The cost accountant of a large truck fleet is evaluating options for dealing with the large volume of flat tires experienced. Currently, the company repairs tires on the open market by having the driver take the flat tire to the nearest tire dealer. Last year this cost an average of $30 per flat tire. The volume of flat tires experienced per year was 10,000 last year, and the expected rate of growth in flat tires is 10 percent per year. However, some feel that flat growth will be as low as 5 percent, others as high as 15 percent. A complicating factor is that the cost to repair a tire grows an average of 3 percent per year.

   The company has two alternatives. A tire dealer has offered to fix all the company's flat tires for a fixed rate of $36 per tire over a 3-year period. The other alternative is for the company to go into the tire repair business for themselves. This option is expected to require an investment in equipment of $200,000, with a salvage value of $50,000 after 3 years. It would require an overhead expense of $40,000 per year in the first year, $45,000 the second year, and $50,000 the third year. The variable cost for fixing a flat tire is $12 per tire for the 3-year period of analysis.

   Compare the net present costs over 3 years for each of these three options, under conditions of tire growth ranging from 5 to 15 percent per year in increments of 1 percent.

12. A company has surplus cash available to invest at the end of each quarter. The chief financial officer (CFO) has requested a report that will display the options available, ranked by internal rate of return. These are to be short-term investments, no longer than 9 months before payment is due. The CFO's policy is that a maximum

of $100,000 can be invested in any one option. Expected cash flows for six alternatives follow. Develop the list showing IRR.

Investment	Present	End of 1st Quarter	End of 2nd Quarter	End of 3rd Quarter
ABC Corp	−$40,000	0	20,000	25,000
1st Bank	−100,000	101,000		
5th Bank	−100,000		102,500	
FBN Air	−50,000			53,500
OM Farms	−100,000		30,000	75,000
OTB	−80,000	82,500		

13. A firm's information systems department receives many requests for proposed projects to improve the system. Each project proposal is processed, using the submitting department's estimated benefits and the information systems department's estimated project costs. The costs are incurred within 3 months of project adoption (and are treated as occurring at the present). Estimated benefits are calculated as of the end of 12 months, 24 months, and 36 months after project completion. Company policy is to disregard any benefits beyond 36 months, as technology will probably outdate systems by that time. The company discount rate is 18 percent per year. Calculate net present values for these eight proposed projects.

Department	Cost	Benefits@12 Mo	Benefits@24 Mo	Benefits@36 Mo
Production	300,000	100,000	120,000	150,000
Production	260,000	150,000	200,000	0
Marketing	220,000	150,000	200,000	300,000
Marketing	520,000	250,000	240,000	220,000
Marketing	360,000	200,000	180,000	150,000
Transport	360,000	200,000	200,000	200,000
Admin	580,000	0	500,000	400,000

14. The information systems group has received nine proposed projects shown in the table below. These projects also have resource requirements in the form of systems analysis and programming. Assume that during this period 200 hours of systems analysis time and 300 hours of programmer time is available. Recommend projects to adopt, seeking to maximize net present value to the firm.

Project	Net Present Value	Systems Analysis Hours	Programmer Hours
Mkt4	$512,862	100	120
Mkt7	$103,841	50	60
Prod8	$90,439	20	30
Admin	$86,521	40	80
Mkt6	$42,106	50	70
Prod9	$12,655	30	100
Trans3	−$8,312	40	50
Mkt8	−$36,783	20	80
Mkt5	−$89,112	50	80

15. A company is considering two investments. The expected outcomes have been estimated in net present value terms with the following probabilities. Calculate the expected outcome for each investment. Identify the decision by a very pessimistic decision maker, a risk-neutral decision maker, and a very optimistic decision maker.

Investment A		Investment B	
+1 million	0.3 probability	−100,000	0.1 probability
+2 million	0.6 probability	0	0.1 probability
+3 million	0.1 probability	+1 million	0.2 probability
		+2 million	0.3 probability
		+3 million	0.2 probability
		+4 million	0.1 probability

16. The manager of a toy store is faced with the opportunity to buy this year's fad toy. He can buy cartons of 100 at various quantity discounts. If he buys 100, they cost him $50 each. If he buys 200, 300, or 400, they cost him $45 each. If he buys 500 or more, they cost him $40 each. Demand is expected to be at least 100. The manager estimates that there is a 10 percent chance that demand will be no more than 100, a 20 percent chance it will be 200, a 40 percent chance it will be 300, a 20 percent chance it will be 400, and a 10 percent chance it will reach 500. The store retails these toys at $60 each. If any are left over, they are worthless. Calculate the expected monetary value and expected opportunity loss for the options of buying 100, 200, 300, 400, or 500 of these toys.

17. An investor can invest in three highly speculative opportunities. The returns and standard deviations are as follows:

	Expected Return	Standard Deviation
Investment A	50,000	25,000
Investment B	40,000	24,000
Investment C	30,000	10,000

Based on the coefficient of variation, which of these is the least risky investment?

18. An information systems consultant is bidding on a project that involves some uncertainty. Based on past experience, if all went well (probability 0.1) the project would cost $1.2 million to complete. If moderate debugging were required (probability 0.7) the project would probably cost $1.4 million. If major debugging problems were encountered (probability 0.2) the project could cost $1.8 million. Assume that the firm is bidding competitively, and the expectation of successfully gaining the job at a bid of $2.2 million is 0, at $2.1 million is 0.1, at $2.0 million is 0.2, at $1.9 million is 0.3, at $1.8 million is 0.5, at $1.7 million is 0.8, and at $1.6 million is practically certain.
    a. Calculate the expected monetary value for the given bids.
    b. Calculate the expected value of perfect information.

19. Jim Bridger developed a new ski slope in the wilds of Montana. This operation holds great promise for success, but business depends on the snowfall. Too little snowfall would drive business way down, whereas too much snow would make it hard for customers to get to the resort. Jim is faced with the decision of how much to advertise. A massive advertising campaign has been drawn together by a local ad agency with a nominal price tag of $10 million. Jim asked for a more economical alternative, which the ad agency grudgingly put together with a price tag of $1 million. The

following table shows the expected profit including the cost of the ad campaigns for various levels of snow.

	Too Little Snow	Great Snow	Too Much Snow
Probabilities	0.2	0.5	0.3
Major ad campaign	−$7 million	+$40 million	+$15 million
Minor ad campaign	0	+$24 million	+$6 million

Identify the expected monetary value of each option, as well as the expected value of perfect information.

20. Gulf Exploration is considering making a bid for oil drilling rights off the Mexican coast. The company has decided to bid $520 million for these rights. At this bid, experts have told Gulf Exploration that it has about a 60 percent probability of winning the job. If the firm should win the contract, it can drill on its own, it can join a joint venture, or it can sell its rights. Should the firm drill, costs of drilling are expected to be $80 million. These expenses in the joint venture would be only $45 million. The negotiation process involved in selling the rights is expected to cost $2 million.

The outcomes for the two drilling options are as follows:

	Big Find	Average Find	Dry (Wet) Hole
Drill on own:	$900 million	$600 million	$250 million
Probabilities	0.6	0.2	0.2
Joint venture	$750 million	$500 million	$200 million
Probabilities	0.6	0.3	0.1
Sale of rights	$600 million		

Note that the costs have not been deducted from these values. Develop a decision tree to analyze this problem.

21. Farben Chemical is faced with a serious lawsuit over contentions of damage from pollution generation. The CEO has gathered much of the corporate legal staff as well as other top decision makers to discuss their options. The outcome of this discussion is as follows:

Initial options: Settle completely loss of $6 billion
      Negotiate   50 percent chance of settling for $2 billion
              50 percent chance of the choice:
                settle for $5 billion
                fight in court with:
                   40 percent chance win, legal cost $200 million
                   60 percent chance lose $8 billion
     Fight in court   40 percent chance win, legal cost $100 million
             60 percent chance lose $10 billion

 a. Draw a decision tree and identify the expected value of each of the initial options.
 b. What rationale might lead to a different decision than that of minimizing expected monetary loss?
 c. What would be the value of perfect knowledge of a trial's outcome?

22. A hotel wants to analyze its room pricing structure prior to a major remodeling effort. Currently, rates and average number of rooms sold are as follows. Each market segment has its own normally distributed elasticity of demand to price.

Room Type	Rate	Average Sold/Day	Price Elasticity of Demand
Standard	$85	250	mean −1.5, std deviation 0.3
Gold	98	100	mean −2, std deviation 0.4
Platinum	139	50	mean −1, std deviation 0.3

The elasticities show the response to price increase. For example, if the price of a standard room is reduced by 1 percent, the number of rooms sold each day is expected to increase by 1.5 percent. The projected number of rooms sold can be determined by the following formula:

$$\text{Projected rooms sold} = \text{elasticity} \times (\$ \text{ price change}) \times (\text{average daily sales/room rate})$$

Develop a *Crystal Ball* model to compute a 90 percent confidence interval of projected revenue for the hotel.

23. The manager of an apartment complex has observed that the number of units rented during any given month varies between 30 and 40. Rent is $500 per month. Operating costs average $15,000 per month, but vary somewhat. Operating costs are assumed to be normal with a standard deviation of $300. Develop a spreadsheet model and *Crystal Ball* analysis of the profitability of this business. Identify
    a. the probability that monthly profit is positive
    b. the probability that monthly profit will exceed $4,000
    c. the 90 percent confidence range of monthly profit
    d. the probability that profit will be between $1,000 and $3,000
    e. the distribution best fitting the forecast

24. Consider the project network in the following figure. All activity times are triangular with lower limit *a*, likely value *m*, and upper limit *b*.

Activity	Lower	Likely	Upper
A	1	3	4
B	3	5	7
C	1	4	5
D	1	2	4

Develop a spreadsheet to simulate this project using *Crystal Ball*, and discuss the results.

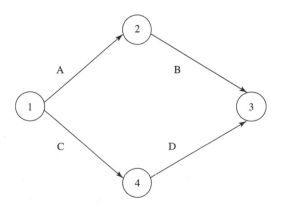

25. Consider the problem of installing a new software system. The activities and time parameters are as follows:

	Activity	Immediate Predecessors	Min	Most Likely	Max	Expected
A	Requirements analysis	–	2	3	4	3
B	Programming	A	6	7	9	7.17
C	Hardware acquisition	A	3	3	3	3
D	Train users	B	12	12	12	12
E	Implementation	B,C	3	5	7	5
F	Testing	E	1	1	2	1.17

    a. Compute the expected project completion time and find the critical path.

    b. Develop a spreadsheet model for this situation and simulate it using *Crystal Ball*. Write a memo to management explaining the results and assessing the risks associated with completing the project by specified target dates of 23 and 24 weeks.

26. A power plant construction project consists of 10 activities, with the following activity time parameters and precedence relationships.

	Activity	Min	Most Likely	Max	Immediate Predecessors
A	Design plant	9	12 months	18	none
B	Select site	2	8 months	12	A
C	Select vendor	3	4 months	6	A
D	Select personnel	1	3 months	5	A
E	Prepare site	9	12 months	16	B
F	Manufacture generator	12	18 months	21	C
G	Prepare operating procedures	3	5 months	8	C
H	Install generator	4	4 months	5	E,F
I	Train operators	9	9 months	9	D,G
J	Get license	6	6 months	36	H,I

    a. Determine the mean and variance for each activity.

    b. Calculate the critical path based on the mean activity times. What is the expected project completion time and its variance?

    c. Compute the probability that the project will be completed within 44 months.

    d. Develop an Excel model for this problem using the activity durations given. Simulate 500 replications using *Crystal Ball*. Contrast your results with the analytical solution.

    e. Repeat the *Crystal Ball* simulation in part (d) assuming that activity times are as follows:

Activity	Duration
A	lognormal(12,2)
B	normal(8,2)
C	lognormal(4,1)
D	normal(3,1)
E	lognormal(12,1)
F	21- lognormal(3,1)
G	lognormal(5,1)
H	lognormal(4,5)
I	9
J	6 + exponential(5)

How do the results compare with part (d)?

Appendix: Additional *Crystal Ball* Options

Crystal Ball includes several options that provide additional modeling and analysis capabilities. In this appendix we will describe these and provide some additional examples, extending the discussion of the financial model in the appendix to chapter 3.

CORRELATED ASSUMPTIONS

Normally, each assumption is independent of the others. In many situations, we might wish to explicitly model dependencies between variables. *Crystal Ball* allows you to use correlation coefficients to define dependencies between assumptions.[3] This can be done only after assumptions have been defined. For example, suppose that we wish to correlate the inflation factors between the fixed cost of goods sold and the unit cost of good sold in Figure 3A.1. We select one of these cells, for example, the fixed cost of goods sold (B4), then select *Define Assumption* from the *Cell* menu. When the distribution dialog box appears, click the *Correlate . . .* button. The Correlation dialog box, shown in Figure 8A.1, appears. The *Select Assumption* button provides a list of the assumptions that you have defined. We select the other assumption to correlate, unit cost of goods sold, and then enter a correlation coefficient.

You may enter a correlation coefficient in one of three ways. First, you can enter a value between -1 and 1 in the Coefficient Value box. Second, you may drag the slider control along the Correlation Coefficient scale; the specific value you select is displayed in the box to the left of the scale. Third, you may click *Calc . . .* and enter ranges of cells in the spreadsheet that contain empirical values that should be used to calculate a correlation coefficient. After the correlation coefficient is specified, *Crystal Ball* displays a sample correlation chart as shown in Figure 8A.2. The solid line indicates where values of a perfect correlation would fall; the points represent the actual pairing of assumption values that would occur during the simulation.

You must be cautious when using this option because it is possible that some correlations might conflict with others, preventing *Crystal Ball* from running. The User Manual describes how to handle these situations.

FREEZING ASSUMPTIONS

The *Freeze Assumptions . . .* command on the *Cell* menu allows you to temporarily exclude certain assumptions from a simulation. This allows you to see the effect that

FIGURE 8A.1 *Crystal Ball* Dialog Box for Correlation

---

[3] In the student version of *Crystal Ball,* only one pairwise correlation can be defined for each model.

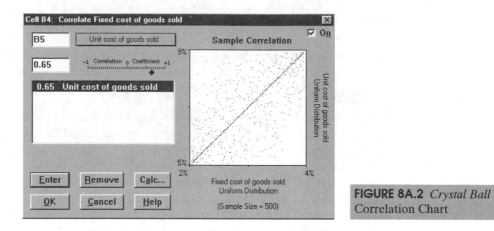

FIGURE 8A.2 *Crystal Ball* Correlation Chart

certain assumptions might have on the forecast cells while holding others constant to their spreadsheet values.

OVERLAY CHARTS[4]

If a simulation has multiple, related forecasts, the overlay chart feature allows you to superimpose the frequency data from selected forecasts on one chart in order to compare differences and similarities that might not be apparent. This option is invoked from the *Run* menu by selecting *Open Overlay Chart.*

TREND CHARTS

If a simulation has multiple related forecasts, you can view the certainty ranges of all forecasts on a single chart, called a trend chart. Trend charts are particularly useful for time-related forecasts. The trend chart displays certainty ranges in a series of patterned bands. For example, the band representing the 90 percent certainty range shows the range of values into which a forecast has a 90 percent chance of falling. Figure 8A.3 shows a trend chart for the 3-year cumulative profits in our example.

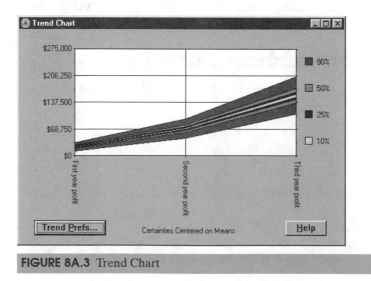

FIGURE 8A.3 Trend Chart

---

[4] The overlay chart is not available in the student version.

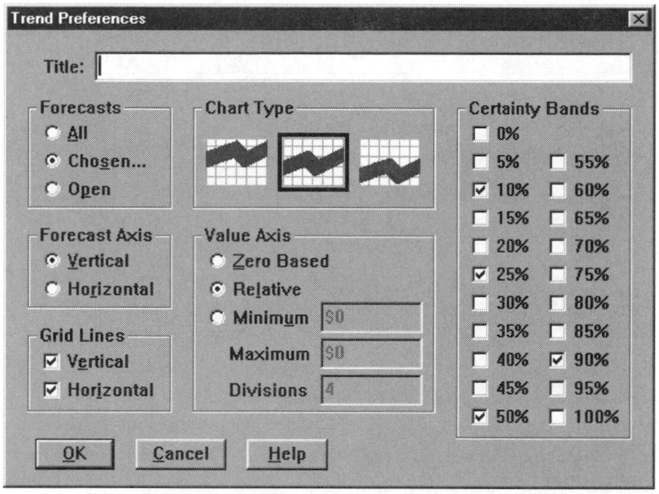

FIGURE 8A.4 *Crystal Ball* Dialog Box for Trend Preferences

Clicking the *Trend Preferences . . .* button displays the dialog box shown in Figure 8A.4. This allows you to customize the trend chart and select the number and type of certainty bands as well as to change the chart type.

SENSITIVITY CHARTS

The uncertainty in a forecast is the result of the combined effect of the uncertainties of all assumptions as well as the formulas used in the model. An assumption might have a high degree of uncertainty yet have little effect on the forecast because it is not weighted heavily in the model formulas. On the other hand, an assumption with a relatively low degree of uncertainty might influence a forecast greatly. **Sensitivity** refers to the amount of uncertainty in a forecast that is caused by both the uncertainty of an assumption as well as the model itself. The sensitivity chart feature of *Crystal Ball* allows you to determine the influence that each assumption cell has on a forecast cell.

To create a sensitivity chart, you must ensure that the *Sensitivity Analysis* box is checked in the *Run Preferences* dialog box before running the simulation. After the simulation is completed, select *Open Sensitivity Chart* from the *Run* menu. The assumptions (and possible other forecasts) are listed on the left, beginning with the assumption having the highest sensitivity. The sensitivity chart for the profitability example is shown in Figure 8A.5. We see that cell C9, the first year sales in the spreadsheet model of Figure 3A.1, influences the total profit forecast the most. The inflation factor for unit sales ranks second, followed by the other inflation factor assumptions. Note that the other inflation factors have a negative influence on total profit because they contribute to cost, not revenue.

The sensitivities in Figure 8A.5 are measured by rank correlation coefficients. Positive coefficients indicate that an increase in the assumption is associated with an increase in the forecast; negative coefficients imply the reverse. The larger the value of the correlation coefficient, the stronger is the relationship. You may also express sensitivities as a percentage of the contribution to the variance of the forecast by opening the *Sensitivity Prefs . . .* dialog box, shown in Figure 8A.6. This dialog box also allows you to select different forecasts for the sensitivity chart. Figure 8A.7 shows the sensitivity chart for total profit, ranked by contribution to variance.

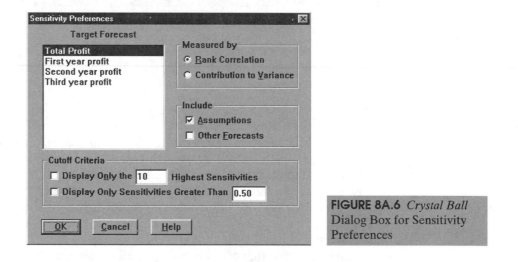

FIGURE 8A.5 Sensitivity Chart Example for Rank Correlation

FIGURE 8A.6 *Crystal Ball* Dialog Box for Sensitivity Preferences

FIGURE 8A.7 Sensitivity Chart Ranked by Contribution to Variance

References

Gallagher, T. J. and J. D. Andrew, Jr., *Financial Management: Principles and Practice,* Upper Saddle River, NJ: Prentice Hall, 1997.

Keeney, R. L., *Value-Focused Thinking: A Path to Creative Decisionmaking,* Cambridge, MA: Harvard University Press, 1992.

Nas, T. F., *Cost-Benefit Analysis: Theory and Application,* Newbury Park, CA: Sage, 1996.

Sharpe, P. and Keelin, T., "How SmithKline Beecham makes better resource-allocation decisions," *Harvard Business Review,* March–April 1998, 45–57.

CHAPTER
9

Introduction to Optimization

Outline

Constrained Optimization
Types of Optimization Problems
    Linear Optimization Example: Transportation Problem
    Integer Optimization Example: Project Selection
    Nonlinear Optimization Example: Hotel Pricing
Spreadsheet Optimization
    Solving the Optimal Pricing Problem
Solving Linear Optimization Models
    Interpreting Solver Reports
    Difficulties with Solver
Solving Integer Optimization Models
Solving Nonlinear Optimization Models
Risk Analysis of Optimization Results
Combining Optimization and Simulation
    A Portfolio Allocation Model
    Using *OptQuest*
    Interpreting Results
    Adding a Requirement
Summary
Questions and Problems

Throughout this book we have explored the role of data in managerial decisions. Although many decisions involve only a limited number of alternatives and can be addressed using statistical analysis, selection models, or simulation, others have a very large or even an infinite number of possibilities. To identify the best decision in these situations, we often use techniques of **optimization**—the process of selecting values of decision variables that *minimize* or *maximize* some quantity of interest—usually with constraints that limit the choices. This quantity we seek to minimize or maximize is called the **objective function,** and the set of decision variable values that maximize or minimize the objective function is called the **optimal solution.**

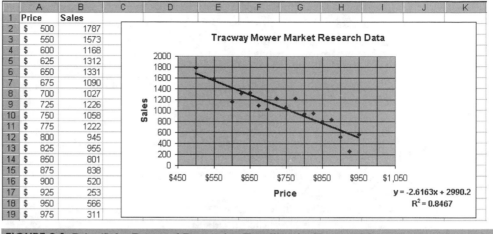

	Price	Sales
1	Price	Sales
2	$ 500	1787
3	$ 550	1573
4	$ 600	1168
5	$ 625	1312
6	$ 650	1331
7	$ 675	1090
8	$ 700	1027
9	$ 725	1226
10	$ 750	1058
11	$ 775	1222
12	$ 800	945
13	$ 825	955
14	$ 850	801
15	$ 875	838
16	$ 900	520
17	$ 925	253
18	$ 950	566
19	$ 975	311

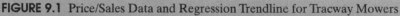

FIGURE 9.1 Price/Sales Data and Regression Trendline for Tracway Mowers

To illustrate an optimization model, suppose that Tracway wishes to determine the best pricing for one of its garden tractors to maximize revenue over the next fiscal year. A market research study has collected data that estimate the expected annual sales for different levels of pricing as shown in Figure 9.1. Plotting these data on an x-y scatter chart suggests that sales and price have a linear relationship; adding a trendline and regression equation confirms a high correlation between price and sales as shown in the accompanying chart. Thus the regression equation *Sales* $= -2.6163 \times$ Price $+ 2{,}990.2$ is a good predictor of expected sales for any pricing decision within the relevant range of the data.

Because revenue equals price multiplied by sales, an equation for revenue is

$$\text{Revenue} = \text{Price}(-2.6163 \times \text{Price} + 2{,}990.2)$$
$$= -2.6163 \times (\text{Price})^2 + 2{,}990.2 \times \text{Price}$$

The problem is to determine the best value of price to maximize the revenue. Figure 9.2 shows a tabulation of revenue for various levels of price. We see that as the price

FIGURE 9.2 Tabulation and Plot of Revenue as a Function of Price

	Price	Revenue
22	Price	Revenue
23	$ 500	$841,025
24	$ 550	$853,179
25	$ 600	$852,252
26	$ 625	$846,883
27	$ 650	$838,243
28	$ 675	$826,333
29	$ 700	$811,153
30	$ 725	$792,702
31	$ 750	$770,981
32	$ 775	$745,990
33	$ 800	$717,728
34	$ 825	$686,196
35	$ 850	$651,393
36	$ 875	$613,320
37	$ 900	$571,977
38	$ 925	$527,363
39	$ 950	$479,479
40	$ 975	$428,325
41	$ 1,000	$373,900

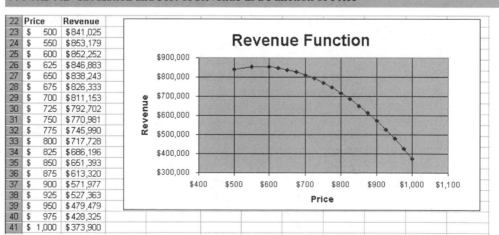

increases from $500, the revenue increases and then falls off. The maximum revenue appears to be at a price somewhere between $500 and $600. Later in this chapter we will learn how to find the optimal price exactly.

Optimization is a very broad and complex topic; we can hardly scratch the surface of this important topic in a short chapter. Our principal focus in this chapter is to introduce you to basic concepts of optimization to provide some idea of its applications in business and important issues involved in modeling, solving, and interpreting solutions to practical business problems. The key concepts we will discuss are

- Formulating linear, integer, and nonlinear optimization models in a spreadsheet environment;
- Using the Solver option included with Excel to find solutions to optimization models;
- Interpreting solution reports, with an emphasis on the managerial information contained in the output; and
- Exploring the use of simulation and risk analysis to better understand the implications of solutions to optimization models.

Constrained Optimization

In the Tracway example we posed in the introduction to this chapter, we could estimate the optimal price rather easily by developing a simple data table in a spreadsheet that evaluates the objective function for various values of the decision variables. Most practical optimization problems have **constraints**—limitations or requirements that decision variables must satisfy. The presence of constraints usually makes identifying an optimal solution considerably more difficult. Some examples of constraints are as follows:

- The amount of material used to produce a set of products cannot exceed the available amount of 850 square feet.
- The amount of money spent on research and development projects cannot exceed the assigned budget of $300,000.
- Contractual requirements specify that at least 500 units of product must be produced.
- A mixture of fertilizer must contain exactly 30 percent nitrogen.
- We cannot produce a negative amount of product (*nonnegativity*).

Constraints are generally expressed mathematically as equations or inequalities. For the constraint examples, we might write the following:

- Amount of material used ≤850 square feet
- Amount spent on research and development ≤$300,000
- Number of units of product produced ≥500
- Amount of nitrogen in mixture/total amount in mixture = .30
- Amount of product produced ≥0

The left-hand side of each of these expressions is called a **constraint function.** When represented mathematically, a constraint function is a function of the decision variables. For example, suppose that in the first case the material requirements of three products are 3.0, 3.5, and 2.3 square feet per unit. If A, B, and C represent the number of units of each product to produce, then 3.0A represents the amount of material used to produce A units of product A, 3.5B represents the amount of material used to produce B units of product B, and so on. Note that dimensions of these terms are (square feet/unit)(units) = square feet. Therefore, the constraint that limits the amount of material that can be used can be expressed as

$$3.0A + 3.5B + 2.3C \leq 850$$

As another example, if two ingredients contain 20 and 33 percent nitrogen, respectively, then the fraction of nitrogen in a mixture of X lbs. of the first ingredient and Y lbs. of the second ingredient is expressed by the constraint function

$$(.20X + .33Y)/(X + Y)$$

If the fraction of nitrogen in the mixture must be 0.30, then we would have

$$(.20X + .33Y)/(X + Y) = 0.3$$

This can be rewritten as a linear equation

$$(.20X + .33Y) = 0.3(X + Y)$$

or

$$-0.1X + 0.03Y = 0$$

Any solution that satisfies all constraints of a problem is called a **feasible solution.** An optimization problem that has no feasible solutions is called **infeasible.** The presence of constraints makes finding optimal solutions more difficult than for unconstrained problems. In fact, it may be very difficult to even identify a feasible solution, much less an optimal one. Thus to solve constrained optimization problems, we generally rely on special solution procedures.

Types of Optimization Problems

In addition to classifying optimization problems by whether or not they have constraints, we may also classify them by their mathematical structure. The most common types of optimization problems are *linear, integer,* and *nonlinear.* A **linear optimization problem** (often called a **linear program**) has two basic properties. First, the objective function and all constraints are *linear functions* of the decision variables. This means that each function is simply a sum of terms, each of which is some constant multiplied by a decision variable, for example

$$2A + 3B - 12C$$

Second, all variables are *continuous*, meaning that they may assume any real value (typically nonnegative).

In an **integer linear optimization problem,** some or all of the variables are restricted to be whole numbers. If only a subset of variables are restricted to be integer while others are continuous, we call this a **mixed integer linear optimization problem.** A special type of integer problem is one in which variables can be only zero or one. These *binary variables* help us to model logical "yes or no" decisions. Integer linear optimization models are generally more difficult to solve than pure linear models. Finally, in a **nonlinear optimization problem,** the objective function and/or constraint functions are *nonlinear functions* of the decision variables; that is, the terms cannot be written as a constant times a variable. An example is

$$3A^2 + 4/B - 6AB$$

Note that the example involving the mixture of ingredients to meet a nitrogen requirement that we discussed earlier was formulated originally as a nonlinear constraint. However, through simple algebra we were able to convert it to a linear form. Nonlinear optimization models are considerably more difficult to solve than either linear or integer models. We will illustrate an example of each type of problem next.

LINEAR OPTIMIZATION EXAMPLE: TRANSPORTATION PROBLEM

Tracway produces its most popular model of lawn tractor in its St. Louis, Greenwood, and Camarillo plants and ships these units to major distribution centers in Atlanta, Chicago, San Diego, and Singapore. In planning production for the next year, unit cost of shipping between any plant and distribution center, plant capacities, and distribution center demands are estimated to be as given in the spreadsheet in Figure 9.3. The problem Tracway faces is to determine how much to ship between each plant and distribution center to minimize the total transportation cost, not exceed available capacity, and meet customer demands.

To develop a linear optimization model, we first define the decision variables as the amount to ship between each plant and distribution center; these are specified in cells B14:E16 in the spreadsheet.[1] The sum of the rows and columns represent the total shipped from each plant and the total shipped to each distribution center, respectively. Note that the cost of shipping between any two locations is computed as the product of the unit cost and amount shipped. For example, the cost of shipping between St. Louis and Atlanta is \$35 × St. Louis–Atlanta shipments; this is the product of cells B5 and B14. If we sum these for every plant–distribution center pair, we have an expression for the total shipping cost as an Excel formula:

$$\text{Total cost} = \text{B5*B14} + \text{C5*C14} + \text{D5*D14} + \text{E5*E14}$$
$$+ \text{B6*B15} + \text{C6*C15} + \text{D6*D15} + \text{E6*E15}$$
$$+ \text{B7*B16} + \text{C7*C16} + \text{D7*D16} + \text{E7*E16}$$

This value is stored in cell A20. To simplify this expression, you could also use the SUMPRODUCT function in Excel, and write this as

$$\text{Total cost} = \text{SUMPRODUCT(B5:E5;B14:E14)} + \text{SUMPRODUCT(B6:E6;B15:E15)}$$
$$+ \text{SUMPRODUCT(B7:E7;B16:E16)}$$

	A	B	C	D	E	F
1	Tracway Transportation Linear Optimization Problem					
2						
3			Distribution Center			
4	Plant	Atlanta	Chicago	San Diego	Singapore	Capacity
5	St. Louis	\$ 35	\$ 40	\$ 60	\$ 120	12000
6	Greenwood	\$ 30	\$ 30	\$ 45	\$ 130	8000
7	Camarillo	\$ 60	\$ 65	\$ 50	\$ 100	5000
8	Demand	9000	3000	9500	1500	
9						
10						
11	Transportation plan					
12			Distribution Center			Total
13	Plant	Atlanta	Chicago	San Diego	Singapore	shipped
14	St. Louis	0	0	0	0	0
15	Greenwood	0	0	0	0	0
16	Camarillo	0	0	0	0	0
17	Demand met	0	0	0	0	
18						
19	Total cost					
20	\$ -					

FIGURE 9.3 Spreadsheet Model for Tracway Transportation Problem

---

[1] We will develop optimization models in the context of spreadsheets; the traditional way is to do it mathematically. Actually, we are doing both: If you replace the cell references by a name such as X, Y, or STLOUIS_ATLANTA, you will have constructed a mathematical model for the problem!

To ensure that we do not exceed the capacity of any plant, the total shipped from each plant (cells F14:F16) cannot be greater than the plant capacities (cells F5:F7). For example,

$$\text{Total shipped from St. Louis (cell F14)} = B14 + C14 + D14 + E14$$
$$= SUM(B14:E14) \leq 12{,}000 \text{ (cell F5)}$$

The constraints for the other two plants are similar. Can you write them?

To ensure that demands are met, the total shipped to each distribution center (cells B17:E17) must equal or exceed the demands (cells B8:E8). Thus for Atlanta,

$$\text{Total shipped to Atlanta (cell B17)} \geq B14 + B15 + B16 = SUM(B14:B16)$$
$$= 9{,}000 \text{ (cell B8)}$$

Can you write the constraints for the other distribution centers?

Finally, we need to ensure that all decision variables are nonnegative, or

$$B14{:}E16 \geq 0$$

Later in this chapter we will see how to solve this model.

Many types of problems can be modeled as linear programs. Table 9.1 provides a summary of just a few of them.

TABLE 9.1   Generic Examples of Linear Optimization Models

Type of Model	Decision Variables	Objective Function	Typical Constraints
Product mix	Quantities of products to produce and sell	Maximize contribution to profit	Resource limitations (e.g., production time, labor, material); maximum sales potential; contractual requirements
Process selection	Quantities of product to make using alternative processes	Minimize cost	Demand requirements; resource limitations
Blending	Quantity of materials to mix to produce one unit of product	Minimize cost	Specifications on acceptable mixture
Production planning	Quantities of product to produce in each of several periods; amount of inventory to hold between successive periods	Minimize production and inventory costs	Limited production rates; material balance equations (production + available inventory − inventory held to next period = demand)
Portfolio selection	Amounts to invest in different financial instruments	Maximize future expected return	Limit on available funds; sector requirements and restrictions (minimum and maximum amounts in different types of instruments)
Multiperiod investment planning	Amounts to invest in various instruments each year	Maximize return	Limit on available funds; cash balance equations between periods
Media selection	Number of advertisements in different media	Minimize cost	Budget limitation; requirements on number of customers reached; media requirements and restrictions

INTEGER OPTIMIZATION EXAMPLE: PROJECT SELECTION

Tracway's research and development (R&D) group has identified five potential new engineering and development projects; however, the firm is constrained by its available budget and human resources. The data are given in the spreadsheet in Figure 9.4. Each project is expected to generate a return (given by the net present value), but requires a fixed amount of cash and personnel. Because the resources are limited, all projects cannot be selected. Projects cannot be partially completed; therefore either the project must be undertaken completely or not at all.

To model this situation, we define the decision variables to be binary (that is, either zero or one), corresponding to either not selecting or selecting each project, respectively. These are defined in cells B9:F9. The objective function, computed in cell B13, is the total return, which can be expressed as the sum of the product of the return from each project and the binary decision variable.

$$\text{Total return} = B5*B9 + C5*C9 + D5*D9 + E5*E9 + F5*F9$$

To develop the constraints, note that if a project is selected, we must use both the cash and personnel requirements from the amounts available. These constraints can be written as

$$\text{Cash used} = B6*B9 + C6*C9 + D6*D9 + E6*E9 + F6*F9 \le G6$$
$$\text{Personnel used} = B7*B9 + C7*C9 + D7*D9 + E7*E9 + F7*F9 \le G7$$

The left-hand sides of these functions can be found in cells B10 and B11.

Constraint functions of binary variables can be used to model many different logical conditions. For instance, suppose that the R&D group has determined that at most one of projects 1 and 2 should be pursued. This can be modeled as

$$B9 + C9 \le 1$$

Similarly, the constraint "If project 4 is chosen, then project 2 must also be chosen" can be modeled as

$$B9 \ge E9$$

or equivalently,

$$B9 - E9 \ge 0$$

Note that if project 4 is chosen, then the value of cell E9 must be 1. From the constraint, the value of B9 must therefore be greater than or equal to 1 (i.e., project 2 must be chosen). On the other hand, if project 4 is not chosen (E9 = 0), then the constraint reduces

FIGURE 9.4 Spreadsheet Model for Project Selection Problem

	A	B	C	D	E	F	G
1	Project Selection Model						
2							
3							Available
4		Project 1	Project 2	Project 3	Project 4	Project 5	Resources
5	Expected Return (NPV)	$180,000	$220,000	$150,000	$140,000	$200,000	
6	Cash requirements	$ 55,000	$ 83,000	$ 24,000	$ 49,000	$ 61,000	$ 150,000
7	Personnel requirements	5	3	2	5	3	12
8							
9	Project selection decisions	0	0	0	0	0	
10	Cash expended	$ -					
11	Personnel used	0					
12							
13	Total Return	$ -					

to B9 $\geq$ 0, and project 2 can either be selected or not. Binary variables are also used to model fixed costs of production or other start-up activities. We will solve this problem later in this chapter.

NONLINEAR OPTIMIZATION EXAMPLE: HOTEL PRICING

The Marquis Hotel is considering a major remodeling effort and needs to determine the best combination of rates and room sizes to maximize revenues. Currently the hotel has 450 rooms with the following history:

Room Type	Rate	Daily Avg. No. Sold	Revenue
Standard	$85	250	$21,250
Gold	$98	100	9,800
Platinum	$139	50	6,950
Total revenue			$38,000

Each market segment has its own price/demand elasticity. Estimates are

Room Type	Price Elasticity of Demand
Standard	−1.5
Gold	−2.0
Platinum	−1.0

This means, for example, that a *1 percent decrease* in the price of a standard room will *increase* the number of rooms sold by *1.5 percent*. Similarly, a 1 percent increase in the price will decrease the number of rooms sold by 1.5 percent. For any pricing structure (in $), the projected number of rooms of a given type sold can be found using the formula

Historical average number of rooms sold + Elasticity × (New price − Current price)
× Historical average number of rooms sold/Current price

The hotel owners want to keep the price of a standard room between $70 and $90; a gold room between $90 and $110; and a platinum room between $120 and $149. Although the rooms may be renovated, there are no plans to expand beyond the current 450-room capacity.

Figure 9.5 shows a spreadsheet model for this situation. The decision variables, the new prices to charge, are given in cells B12:B14. The projected numbers of rooms rented

	A	B	C	D	E	F
1	Marquis Hotel Problem					
2						
3		Current	Average		Total Room	
4	Room type	Rate	Daily Sold	Elasticity	Capacity	
5	Standard	$ 85.00	250	-1.5	450	
6	Gold	$ 98.00	100	-2		
7	Platinum	$ 139.00	50	-1		
8						
9					Projected	
10					Rooms	Projected
11	Room type	New Price	Price Range		Sold	Revenue
12	Standard	$ 85.00	$ 70.00	$ 90.00	250	$21,250.00
13	Gold	$ 98.00	$ 90.00	$ 110.00	100	$ 9,800.00
14	Platinum	$ 139.00	$ 120.00	$ 149.00	50	$ 6,950.00
15				Totals	400	$38,000.00

FIGURE 9.5 Spreadsheet Model for Marquis Hotel Pricing Problem

are computed in cells E12:E14 using the given formula. By multiplying the number of rooms rented by the new price for each room type, the projected revenue is calculated, as given in cells F12:F14. Note that because the projected number of rooms sold is a function of price, the revenue functions are nonlinear. The total revenue in cell F15 represents the objective function.

In addition, we have the following constraints: (1) the new price must fall within the allowable price range, and (2) the total projected number of rooms sold must not exceed 450. These can be expressed as

$$\text{B12:B14} \geq \text{C12:C14}$$
$$\text{B12:B14} \leq \text{D12:D14}$$

and

$$\text{E15} \leq \text{E5}$$

Spreadsheet Optimization

Microsoft Excel contains an add-in called *Solver,* which allows you to find optimal solutions to constrained optimization problems formulated as spreadsheet models. (Check the list of available add-ins under *Tools/Add-Ins.* If Solver is not listed, you will have to reinstall Excel, using a custom installation.) Solver was developed and is maintained by Frontline Systems, Inc. (www.frontsys.com). Frontline Systems also sells a more powerful, industrial-strength version of Solver. Although we will describe how to use Solver, we encourage you to visit this Web site for additional examples, tutorials, updates, and other information about the software. Also, Excel provides a set of examples of optimization models that are useful to study. These can be found in the Excel file *Solvsamp.xls,* which should be included if Solver is installed. The easiest way to find this file is to search for it in your computer. We encourage you to study these examples for additional insight into formulating optimization models.

To use Solver, you should design your spreadsheet to include the following:

1. A cell for the value of each decision variable,
2. A cell that calculates the objective function value, and
3. Cells for the constraint functions.

If you examine the examples we developed in this chapter, you will see that all of them include these cells. It is usually convenient to lay out your variables in rows or columns and provide descriptive labels either to the left of the columns or above the rows; this improves the readability and manageability of your models. You should also consider using different fonts, borders, or shading to enhance the readability of your spreadsheets.

In Solver, decision variables are called *adjustable cells,* or *changing cells,* and the objective function cell is called the *target cell.* Solver identifies values of the changing cells that minimize or maximize the target cell value. Solver is easier to use if you define a cell for each of the constraint functions in your model (that is, the left-hand sides of the constraints). For example, in the transportation problem example, the capacity constraints are expressed as

$$\text{Amount shipped from a plant} \leq \text{plant capacity}$$

Thus, for the St. Louis plant, this constraint is F14 ≤ F5, where F14 = SUM(B14:E14). Notice that the left-hand side of this inequality is a function of the decision variables and is referenced in one cell of the spreadsheet. The right-hand side of this constraint is a constant value specified in a cell in the data section of the spreadsheet. You should try to write your constraints so that the left-hand side is contained in a single cell, and the right-hand side is a constant (although Solver does allow you to enter any numeric expression on the right-hand side). Constraints are entered through a special dialog box in Solver that we will describe later.

As you become more proficient in using spreadsheets and Solver, you should consider creating range names for the decision variables and constraint functions. This allows you to locate and manipulate elements of the model more easily. For example, in the project selection model, you might define the range B9:F9 as *Decisions,* and the range B5:F5 as *Return.* The total return can then be computed easily as *SUMPRODUCT(Decisions, Return).* In this chapter, however, we will stick with using cell references in all formulas.

SOLVING THE OPTIMAL PRICING PROBLEM

Figure 9.6 shows a simple spreadsheet model of the optimal pricing problem presented earlier in this chapter. The price is entered in cell B3, sales is computed using the regression equation in cell B4, and the revenue is found by multiplying cells B3 and B4. Solver is started by selecting *Tools*/Solver . . . in Excel. The *Solver Parameters* dialog box shown in Figure 9.7 will then be displayed. First, set the target cell by either typing B5 in the *Set Target Cell* box or clicking on cell B5 in the spreadsheet. Next, select the type of optimization option (Max or Min); Max is the default. Finally, define the changing cell by either entering B3 in the appropriate box or clicking in the *By Changing Cells* box and then clicking on cell B3 in the spreadsheet. Because this model is nonlinear, you need not select any additional options. When you click *Solve* in the upper right of the dialog box, Solver will find the optimal solution and display the dialog box shown in Figure 9.8. Ignore the reports (these will apply to linear programming models) and click *OK* to keep the Solver solution found in the spreadsheet. The final result is shown in Figure 9.9. As we observed earlier by examining Figure 9.2, the optimal price is between $500 and $600.

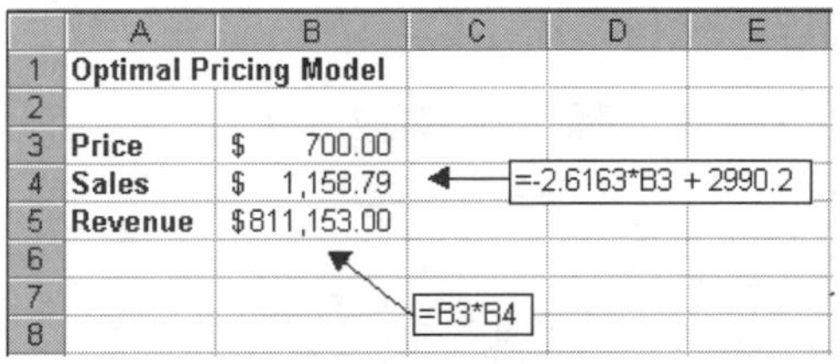

FIGURE 9.6 Spreadsheet Model for Garden Tractor Pricing

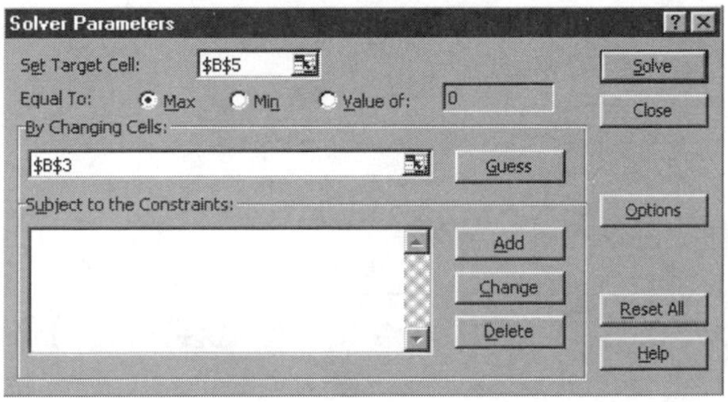

FIGURE 9.7 Solver Parameters Dialog Box

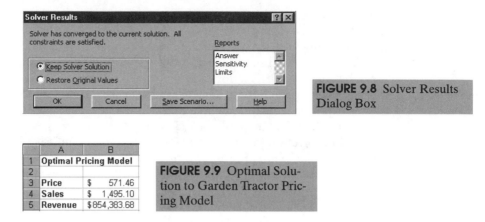

FIGURE 9.8 Solver Results Dialog Box

FIGURE 9.9 Optimal Solution to Garden Tractor Pricing Model

	A	B
1	Optimal Pricing Model	
2		
3	Price	$ 571.46
4	Sales	$ 1,495.10
5	Revenue	$854,383.68

Solving Linear Optimization Models

To illustrate how to use Solver for linear programming models, we will solve the Tracway transportation model. As before, you first enter the target cell, optimization objective, and changing cells in the *Solver Parameters* dialog box. For the Tracway example, this is shown in Figure 9.10. Note that the changing cells are defined by the range B14:E16.

To add constraints, click the *Add* button. The *Add Constraint* dialog box (Figure 9.11) will appear. *Cell Reference* refers to the left-hand side of a constraint; *Constraint* refers to the right-hand side. In either case, you may enter a single cell reference or a range of cells. The drop-down menu in the center of the dialog box allows you to choose the type of constraint (<=, =, >=, int, or binary). "Int" restricts the cell reference range to integers, and "binary" restricts it to 0 or 1. For example, the plant capacity constraints are expressed as

Total shipped from each plant (cells F14:F16) ≤ plant capacities (cells F5:F7)

In the cell reference box, you may either enter the range F14:F16 directly or highlight the range in the spreadsheet using your mouse (which is generally easier). Then click on

FIGURE 9.10 Setting Target Cell and Changing Cell Parameters in Solver

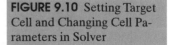

FIGURE 9.11 Add Constraint Dialog Box

the Constraint box and enter the right-hand side range, F5:F7, or highlight this range using the mouse. If you then click the *Enter* button, the Constraint dialog box will remain, allowing you to enter other constraints. For the Tracway problem, you will need to enter the demand constraints

Total shipped to each distribution center (cells B17:E17) $\geq$ demand (cells B8:E8)

When all constraints are entered, click the *OK* button to return to the *Solver Parameters* dialog box. The constraints will be displayed as shown in Figure 9.12. You may add, change, or delete these as necessary by clicking the appropriate buttons.

For linear models, you must select the *Options* button. This displays the *Solver Options* dialog box shown in Figure 9.13. Always check the boxes for *Assume Linear Model* and *Assume Non-Negative* when these are conditions of the problem. (You do not have to enter nonnegativity constraints explicitly in the model.) If you do not check *Assume Linear Model,* Solver will treat your model as nonlinear, and the output reports will not be in the proper form to interpret. Generally, you may leave the other options at their default values for linear models. Return to the *Solver Parameters* dialog box by clicking *OK*.

To find the optimal solution, click the *Solve* button. The *Solver Results* dialog box will appear as shown in Figure 9.14, with the message "Solver found a solution." If a solution could not be found, Solver will notify you with a message to this effect. This generally means that you have an error in your model, or you have included conflicting constraints that no single solution can satisfy. In such cases, you need to re-examine your model.

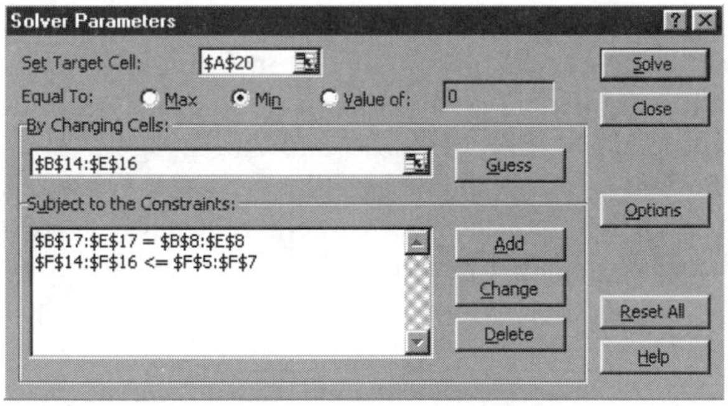

FIGURE 9.12 Constraint Function Definitions for Tracway Transportation Problem

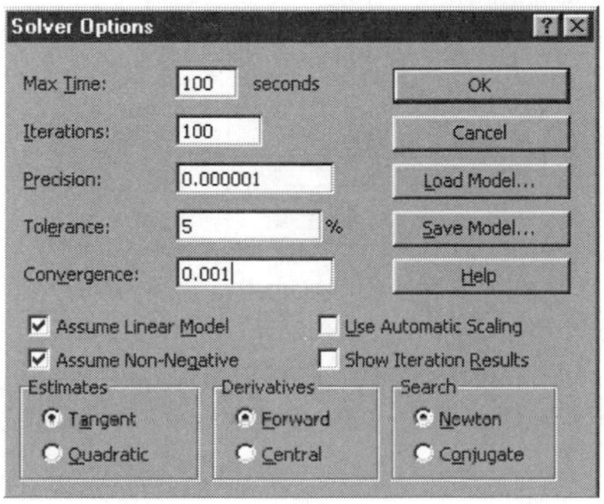

FIGURE 9.13 Solver Options Dialog Box

FIGURE 9.14 Solver Results
Dialog Box

Solver generates three reports: answer, sensitivity, and limits. To add them to your
Excel workbook, hold the *Ctrl* key, click on each of them, and then click *OK*. The optimal solution is shown in Figure 9.15. The minimum total cost is $1,010,000, obtained by
the plan in cells A13:E16.

Interpreting Solver Reports

The answer report (Figure 9.16) provides basic information about the solution, including the values of the optimal objective function and decision variables. The Status column in the Constraints section tells whether each constraint is binding or not binding.
A **binding constraint** is one that is satisfied as an equality. For example, we see that the
amounts shipped out of both the Greenwood and Camarillo plant are equal to the plant
capacities, and the amounts shipped to every destination are equal to the demands.
However, the amount shipped out of St. Louis (10,000) is less than the capacity (12,000).
This difference is called *slack* and is listed in the last column of that section of the answer report. The slack on a binding constraint will always be zero.

The sensitivity report (Figure 9.17) provides a variety of useful information for
managers. In the Adjustable Cells section, the final value for each decision variable is
given, along with its reduced cost, objective coefficient, and allowable increase and decrease. The **reduced cost** tells how much the objective coefficient needs to change in order for a variable to become positive in an optimal solution. For example, we see that
no units are shipped between St. Louis and San Diego at the current unit cost of 60.
However, if the unit cost is reduced by at least 5—the value of the reduced cost—then
it will be profitable to ship along that route. If a variable is currently positive in the solution, its reduced cost is always zero.

	A	B	C	D	E	F
1	**Tracway Transportation Linear Optimization Problem**					
2						
3			**Distribution Center**			
4	**Plant**	*Atlanta*	*Chicago*	*San Diego*	*Singapore*	**Capacity**
5	*St. Louis*	$ 35	$ 40	$ 60	$ 120	**12000**
6	*Greenwood*	$ 30	$ 30	$ 45	$ 130	**8000**
7	*Camarillo*	$ 60	$ 65	$ 50	$ 100	**5000**
8	**Demand**	**9000**	**3000**	**9500**	**1500**	
9						
10						
11	**Transportation plan**					
12			**Distribution Center**			**Total**
13	**Plant**	*Atlanta*	*Chicago*	*San Diego*	*Singapore*	**shipped**
14	*St. Louis*	9000	1000	0	0	**10000**
15	*Greenwood*	0	2000	6000	0	**8000**
16	*Camarillo*	0	0	3500	1500	**5000**
17	**Demand met**	**9000**	**3000**	**9500**	**1500**	
18						
19	**Total cost**					
20	$ 1,010,000					

FIGURE 9.15 Optimal Solution to Tracway Transportation Problem

Microsoft Excel 8.0a Answer Report
Worksheet: [Transportation LP model.xls]Sheet1
Report Created: 5/23/99 1:54:06 PM

Target Cell (Min)

Cell	Name	Original Value	Final Value
$A$20	Total cost	$ -	$ 1,010,000

Adjustable Cells

Cell	Name	Original Value	Final Value
$B$14	St. Louis Atlanta	0	9000
$C$14	St. Louis Chicago	0	1000
$D$14	St. Louis San Diego	0	0
$E$14	St. Louis Singapore	0	0
$B$15	Greenwood Atlanta	0	0
$C$15	Greenwood Chicago	0	2000
$D$15	Greenwood San Diego	0	6000
$E$15	Greenwood Singapore	0	0
$B$16	Camarillo Atlanta	0	0
$C$16	Camarillo Chicago	0	0
$D$16	Camarillo San Diego	0	3500
$E$16	Camarillo Singapore	0	1500

Constraints

Cell	Name	Cell Value	Formula	Status	Slack
$F$14	St. Louis shipped	10000	$F$14<=$F$5	Not Binding	2000
$F$15	Greenwood shipped	8000	$F$15<=$F$6	Binding	0
$F$16	Camarillo shipped	5000	$F$16<=$F$7	Binding	0
$B$17	Demand met Atlanta	9000	$B$17=$B$8	Not Binding	0
$C$17	Demand met Chicago	3000	$C$17=$C$8	Not Binding	0
$D$17	Demand met San Diego	9500	$D$17=$D$8	Not Binding	0
$E$17	Demand met Singapore	1500	$E$17=$E$8	Not Binding	0

FIGURE 9.16 Solver Answer Report

Microsoft Excel 8.0a Sensitivity Report
Worksheet: [Transportation LP model.xls]Sheet1
Report Created: 5/23/99 1:54:07 PM

Adjustable Cells

Cell	Name	Final Value	Reduced Cost	Objective Coefficient	Allowable Increase	Allowable Decrease
$B$14	St. Louis Atlanta	9000	0	35	5	1E+30
$C$14	St. Louis Chicago	1000	0	40	5	5
$D$14	St. Louis San Diego	0	5	60	1E+30	5
$E$14	St. Louis Singapore	0	15	120	1E+30	15
$B$15	Greenwood Atlanta	0	5	30	1E+30	5
$C$15	Greenwood Chicago	2000	0	30	5	5
$D$15	Greenwood San Diego	6000	0	45	5	5
$E$15	Greenwood Singapore	0	35	130	1E+30	35
$B$16	Camarillo Atlanta	0	30	60	1E+30	30
$C$16	Camarillo Chicago	0	30	65	1E+30	30
$D$16	Camarillo San Diego	3500	0	50	5	15
$E$16	Camarillo Singapore	1500	0	100	15	1E+30

Constraints

Cell	Name	Final Value	Shadow Price	Constraint R.H. Side	Allowable Increase	Allowable Decrease
$F$14	St. Louis shipped	10000	0	12000	1E+30	2000
$F$15	Greenwood shipped	8000	-10	8000	1000	2000
$F$16	Camarillo shipped	5000	-5	5000	1000	2000
$B$17	Demand met Atlanta	9000	35	9000	2000	9000
$C$17	Demand met Chicago	3000	40	3000	2000	1000
$D$17	Demand met San Diego	9500	55	9500	2000	1000
$E$17	Demand met Singapore	1500	105	1500	2000	1000

FIGURE 9.17 Solver Sensitivity Report

The *allowable increase* and *allowable decrease* values tell how much an individual objective coefficient can change before the optimal values of the decision variables will change, *with all other model parameters held constant.* (The value "1E + 30" is interpreted as infinity.) For example, if the unit cost of shipping between St. Louis and Chicago either increases or decreases by more than 5, then the optimal values of the decision variables will change. Note that if the objective coefficient of any one variable that has positive value in the current solution changes but stays within the range specified by the allowable increase and allowable decrease, the optimal decision variables will stay the same, but the objective function value will change. To illustrate this, suppose that the unit cost between St. Louis and Chicago were changed to 42 (an increase of 2, within the allowable range). Then each of the 1,000 units shipped between these locations would cost $2 more—a total increase of $2,000. However, if the objective coefficient of St. Louis–Singapore were decreased by 10, the total cost will not change because the current value of this variable is 0. If an objective coefficient changes beyond the allowable increase or allowable decrease, we must solve the problem again with the new value.

The Constraints section of the sensitivity report lists the Final Value of the constraint function (the left-hand side), the Shadow Price, the Constraint R.H. (right-hand) Side, and an Allowable Increase and Allowable Decrease. The **shadow price** tells how much the value of the objective function will change as the right-hand side of a constraint is increased by one, *with all other model parameters held constant*. Whenever a constraint has positive slack, the shadow price is zero. For example, the amount shipped out of St. Louis is less than the plant capacity. Increasing the capacity by one unit will not change the solution because the current capacity is not fully used. However, consider the Greenwood plant. All 8,000 units of capacity are used. If the plant could produce one additional unit, the total transportation cost will decrease by $10 (because the shadow price is −10). Similarly, if the demand at Singapore is increased by one unit, the total cost will increase by $105.

The shadow price is a valid predictor of the change in the objective function value for each unit of increase in the constraint right-hand side up to the value of the allowable increase. Similarly, the negative of the shadow price predicts the change in the objective function value for each unit the constraint right-hand side is decreased, up to the value of the allowable decrease. Beyond these ranges, the problem must be solved with the new value.

The limits report (Figure 9.18) shows the lower limit and upper limit that each variable can assume while satisfying all constraints and holding all of the other variables constant. Generally, this report provides little useful information for decision making and can effectively be ignored.

DIFFICULTIES WITH SOLVER

Several common functions in Excel can cause difficulties when using Solver because they are discontinuous at some point and introduce nonlinearities into what might appear to be a linear model. For example, in the formula IF(A12 < 45, 0, 1), the cell value jumps from 0 to 1 when the value of cell A12 crosses 45. In such situations, Solver cannot guarantee that any solution it finds is truly optimal. Common Excel functions to avoid are

- ABS
- MIN
- MAX
- INT
- ROUND
- IF
- COUNT

These functions are useful in general modeling tasks with spreadsheets, but should be avoided in optimization models.

	Target		
Cell	Name	Value	
$A$20	Total cost	$1,010,000	

Microsoft Excel 8.0a Limits Report
Worksheet: [Transportation LP model.xls]Sheet1
Report Created: 5/23/99 1:54:08 PM

	Adjustable		Lower	Target	Upper	Target
Cell	Name	Value	Limit	Result	Limit	Result
$B$14	St. Louis Atlanta	9000	9000	1010000	9000	1010000
$C$14	St. Louis Chicago	1000	1000	1010000	1000	1010000
$D$14	St. Louis San Diego	0	0	1010000	0	1010000
$E$14	St. Louis Singapore	0	0	1010000	0	1010000
$B$15	Greenwood Atlanta	0	0	1010000	0	1010000
$C$15	Greenwood Chicago	2000	2000	1010000	2000	1010000
$D$15	Greenwood San Diego	6000	6000	1010000	6000	1010000
$E$15	Greenwood Singapore	0	0	1010000	0	1010000
$B$16	Camarillo Atlanta	0	0	1010000	0	1010000
$C$16	Camarillo Chicago	0	0	1010000	0	1010000
$D$16	Camarillo San Diego	3500	3500	1010000	3500	1010000
$E$16	Camarillo Singapore	1500	1500	1010000	1500	1010000

FIGURE 9.18 Solver Limits Report

A poorly scaled model—one in which the parameters of the objective function and constraint functions differ by several orders of magnitude (as in the transportation example where costs are in tens and supplies/demands in thousands)—may cause round-off errors in internal computations or error messages such as "The conditions for Assume Linear Model are not satisfied." This does not happen often (but may in older versions of Solver); if it does, you should consult the Frontline Systems Web site for additional information. Usually, all you need to do is to keep the solution that Solver found, and run Solver again starting from that solution.

Solving Integer Optimization Models

Integer optimization models are set up in the same manner as linear models in Solver, except that any integer variables must be defined as such in the *Add Constraint* dialog box by using the "int" or "bin" options. For example, to define all the variables for the Project Selection model as binary, we would select *bin* for the range of these variables in the drop-down menu in the *Add Constraint* dialog box as shown in Figure 9.19. Figure 9.20 shows the constraints after they are entered in the *Solver Parameters* dialog box. You should still choose *Assume Linear Model* in the *Solver Options* dialog box. *For integer models you also need to ensure that the value of* Tolerance *in the* Solver Options *dialog box is set to zero to guarantee finding an optimal solution.* The solution for this example is shown in Figure 9.21. However, because integer models are discontinuous by

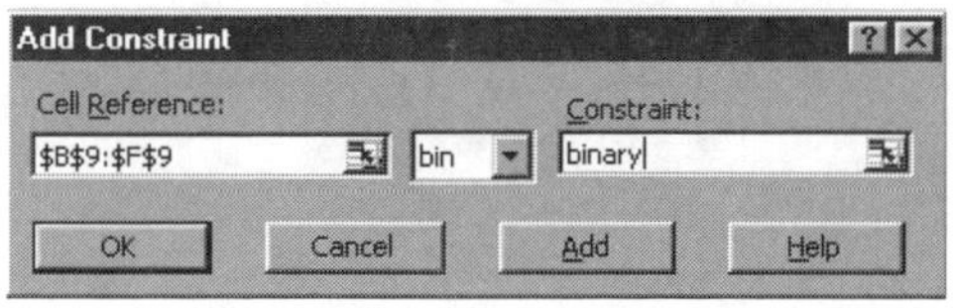

FIGURE 9.19 Defining Binary Variables in Solver

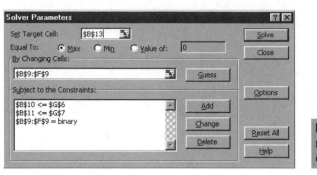

FIGURE 9.20 Solver Parameters Dialog Box for Project Selection Model

	A	B	C	D	E	F	G
1	**Project Selection Model**						
2							
3							**Available**
4		Project 1	Project 2	Project 3	Project 4	Project 5	**Resources**
5	**Expected Return (NPV)**	$180,000	$220,000	$150,000	$140,000	$200,000	
6	**Cash requirements**	$ 55,000	$ 83,000	$ 24,000	$ 49,000	$ 61,000	**$ 150,000**
7	**Personnel requirements**	5	3	2	5	3	**12**
8							
9	**Project selection decisions**	1	0	1	0	1	
10	**Cash expended**	$ 140,000					
11	**Personnel used**	10					
12							
13	**Total Return**	$530,000					

FIGURE 9.21 Optimal Solution to Project Selection Model

their very nature, the sensitivity analysis report cannot be interpreted in the same manner as for linear programs and thus should be ignored.

Solving Nonlinear Optimization Models

Nonlinear optimization models are formulated with Solver in the same fashion as linear or integer models, except that you should *not* choose *Assume Linear Model* in the *Options* box. Figure 9.22 shows the *Solver Parameters* dialog box for the Marquis Hotel model. The optimal solution is shown in Figure 9.23. The optimal prices predict a demand for all 450 rooms with a total revenue of $39,380.65.

The information contained in the answer report (Figure 9.24) is the same as for linear models. However, for nonlinear models, the sensitivity report (Figure 9.25) is quite

FIGURE 9.22 Solver Parameters Dialog Box for Marquis Hotel Pricing Problem

	A	B	C	D	E	F
1	**Marquis Hotel Problem**					
2						
3		Current	Average		Total Room	
4	Room type	Rate	Daily Sold	Elasticity	Capacity	
5	Standard	$ 85.00	250	-1.5	450	
6	Gold	$ 98.00	100	-2		
7	Platinum	$ 139.00	50	-1		
8						
9					Projected	
10					Rooms	Projected
11	Room type	New Price	Price Range		Sold	Revenue
12	Standard	$ 76.87	$ 70.00	$ 90.00	286	$21,974.39
13	Gold	$ 90.00	$ 90.00	$ 110.00	116	$10,469.39
14	Platinum	$ 145.04	$ 120.00	$ 149.00	48	$ 6,936.87
15				Totals	450	$39,380.65

FIGURE 9.23 Optimal Solution to Marquis Hotel Pricing Problem

	A	B	C	D	E	F	G
1	Microsoft Excel 8.0a Answer Report						
2	Worksheet: [Marquis Hotel example.xls]Sheet1						
3	Report Created: 5/27/99 8:15:12 AM						
4							
5							
6	Target Cell (Max)						
7		Cell	Name	Original Value	Final Value		
8		$F$15	Totals Revenue	$ 38,000.00	$ 39,380.65		
9							
10							
11	Adjustable Cells						
12		Cell	Name	Original Value	Final Value		
13		$B$12	Standard New Price	$ 85.00	$ 76.87		
14		$B$13	Gold New Price	$ 98.00	$ 90.00		
15		$B$14	Platinum New Price	$ 139.00	$ 145.04		
16							
17							
18	Constraints						
19		Cell	Name	Cell Value	Formula	Status	Slack
20		$E$15	Totals Sold	450.0000001	$E$15<=$E$5	Binding	0
21		$B$12	Standard New Price	$ 76.87	$B$12<=$D$12	Not Binding	13.12523944
22		$B$13	Gold New Price	$ 90.00	$B$13<=$D$13	Not Binding	20
23		$B$14	Platinum New Price	$ 145.04	$B$14<=$D$14	Not Binding	3.958573139
24		$B$12	Standard New Price	$ 76.87	$B$12>=$C$12	Not Binding	$ 6.87
25		$B$13	Gold New Price	$ 90.00	$B$13>=$C$13	Binding	$ -
26		$B$14	Platinum New Price	$ 145.04	$B$14>=$C$14	Not Binding	$ 25.04

FIGURE 9.24 Solver Answer Report for Marquis Hotel Pricing Problem

	A	B	C	D	E
1	Microsoft Excel 8.0a Sensitivity Report				
2	Worksheet: [Marquis Hotel example.xls]Sheet1				
3	Report Created: 5/27/99 8:15:12 AM				
4					
5					
6	Adjustable Cells				
7				Final	Reduced
8		Cell	Name	Value	Gradient
9		$B$12	Standard New Price	$ 76.87	$ -
10		$B$13	Gold New Price	$ 90.00	$ (42.69)
11		$B$14	Platinum New Price	$ 145.04	$ -
12					
13	Constraints				
14				Final	Lagrange
15		Cell	Name	Value	Multiplier
16		$E$15	Totals Sold	450.0000001	12.08293129

FIGURE 9.25 Solver Sensitivity Report for Marquis Hotel Pricing Problem

different. In the Adjustable Cells section, the "Reduced Gradient" is analogous to the Reduced Cost in linear models. For this problem, however, the objective function coefficient of each price depends on many parameters, and therefore the reduced gradient is more difficult to interpret in relation to the problem data. The "Lagrange Multiplier" in the Constraints section is similar to shadow prices for linear models. For nonlinear models, the Lagrange multipliers give the *approximate* rate of change in the objective function as the right-hand side of a binding constraint is increased by one unit. Thus for the Marquis Hotel pricing problem, if the number of available rooms is increased by 1 to 451, the total revenue would increase by approximately $12.08. For linear models, shadow prices give the *exact* rate of change within the allowable increase and decrease limits. Thus you should be somewhat cautious when interpreting these values, and will need to solve the models with these values to find the true effect of changes to constraints.

Risk Analysis of Optimization Results

It is rare that any optimization model is completely deterministic; in most cases, some of the data will be uncertain. This implies that inherent risk exists in using the optimal solution obtained from a model. Using the capabilities of risk analysis software such as *Crystal Ball,* these risks can be better understood and mitigated. To illustrate this, we will use the Marquis Hotel pricing problem.

In the Marquis problem, the price-demand elasticities of demand are only estimates, and most likely are quite uncertain. Because we probably will not know anything about their distributions, let us conservatively assume that the true values might vary from the estimates by plus or minus 25 percent. Thus we model the elasticities by uniform distributions. Using the optimal prices identified by Solver earlier in this chapter, let us see what happens to the forecast of the number of rooms sold under this assumption using *Crystal Ball*.

In the spreadsheet in Figure 9.23, we select cells D5:D7 as assumption cells with uniform distributions having minimum and maximum values equal to 75 percent and 125 percent of the estimated values, respectively. The total rooms sold (E15) is defined as a forecast cell. The model was replicated 1,000 times, creating the report in Figure 9.26. We see that the mean number of rooms sold under these prices is 450, which should be expected because the mean values of the elasticities were used to derive the optimal prices. However, because of the uncertainty associated with the elasticities, the probability that *more* than 450 rooms will be sold (demanded) is about 50 percent! This sug-

Statistic	Value
Trials	1,000
Mean	450.06
Median	450.21
Mode	---
Standard Deviation	5.60
Variance	31.35
Skewness	-0.02
Kurtosis	2.17
Coeff. of Variability	0.01
Range Minimum	437.29
Range Maximum	462.27
Range Width	24.98
Mean Std. Error	0.18

FIGURE 9.26 *Crystal Ball* Statistics Report for Total Rooms Sold

gests that if the assumptions of the uncertain elasticities are true, the hotel might anticipate that demand will exceed its room capacity about half the time, resulting in many unhappy customers.

We could use these results, however, to identify the appropriate hotel capacity to ensure, for example, that only a 10 percent chance exists that demand will exceed capacity. Figure 9.27 shows the forecast chart when the certainty level is set at 90 percent and the left grabber is anchored. We could interpret this as stating that if the hotel capacity were about 458 rooms, then demand will exceed capacity at most 10 percent of the time. So if we shift the capacity constraint down by 8 rooms to 442 and find the optimal prices associated with this constraint, we would expect demand to exceed 450 only about 10 percent of the time. Figure 9.28 shows the Solver results for this case, and Figure 9.29 shows the results of a *Crystal Ball* run confirming that at these prices, demand will exceed 450 less than 10 percent of the time.

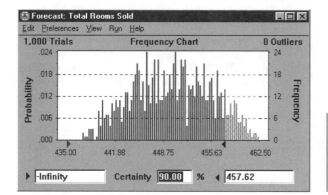

FIGURE 9.27 Forecast Chart to Identify Capacity Needed for a 10 Percent Probability of Demand Exceeding Capacity

	A	B	C	D	E	F
4	Room type	Rate	Daily Sold	Elasticity	Capacity	
5	Standard	$ 85.00	250	-1.500	442	
6	Gold	$ 98.00	100	-2.000		
7	Platinum	$ 139.00	50	-1.000		
8						
9					Projected	
10					Rooms	Projected
11	Room type	New Price	Price Range		Sold	Revenue
12	Standard	$ 78.55	$ 70.00	$ 90.00	278	$21,872.59
13	Gold	$ 90.00	$ 90.00	$ 110.00	116	$10,469.38
14	Platinum	$ 146.72	$ 120.00	$ 149.00	47	$ 6,928.58
15				Totals	442	$39,270.55

FIGURE 9.28 Solver Solution for a Hotel Capacity of 442 Rooms

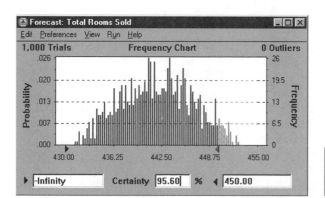

FIGURE 9.29 Forecast Chart Showing Certainty Level of Not Exceeding 450 Rooms

Combining Optimization and Simulation

OptQuest, also a product of Decisioneering, Inc., enhances the analysis capabilities of *Crystal Ball* by allowing you to search for optimal solutions within spreadsheet simulation models. To find an optimal set of decision variables for any simulation-based model, you generally need to search in a heuristic or ad hoc fashion. This usually involves running a simulation for an initial set of variables, analyzing the results, changing one or more variables, rerunning the simulation, and repeating this process until a satisfactory solution is obtained. This process can be very tedious and time consuming, and often how to adjust the variables from one iteration to the next is not clear.

OptQuest overcomes this limitation by automatically searching for optimal solutions within *Crystal Ball* simulation model spreadsheets. Within *OptQuest,* you describe your optimization problem and search for values of decision variables that maximize or minimize a predefined objective. Additionally, *OptQuest* is designed to find solutions that satisfy a wide variety of constraints or a set of goals that you may define.

A PORTFOLIO ALLOCATION MODEL

We will use a portfolio allocation model to illustrate the steps of setting up and running an optimization problem using *Crystal Ball* and *OptQuest.* An investor has $100,000 to invest in four assets. The expected annual returns, and minimum and maximum amounts with which the investor will be comfortable allocating to each investment follow:

Investment	Annual Return	Minimum	Maximum
1. Life insurance	6%	$ 2,500	$5,000
2. Bond mutual funds	7%	$30,000	none
3. Stock mutual funds	11%	$15,000	none
4. Savings account	4%	none	none

The major source of uncertainty in this problem is the annual return of each asset. In addition, the decision maker faces other risks; for example, unanticipated changes in inflation or industrial production, the spread between high and low grade bonds, and the spread between long and short term interest rates. One approach to incorporating such risk factors in a decision model is arbitrate pricing theory (APT).[2] APT provides estimates of the sensitivity of a particular asset to these types of risk factors. Let us assume that the risk factors per dollar allocated to each asset have been determined as follows:

Asset	Risk Factor/Dollar Invested
1. Life insurance	−0.5
2. Bond mutual funds	1.8
3. Stock mutual funds	2.1
4. Savings account	−0.3

The investor may specify a target level for the weighted risk factor, leading to a constraint that limits the risk to the desired level. For example, suppose that our investor will tolerate a weighted risk per dollar invested of at most 1.0. Thus, the weighted risk

---

[2] See Schniederjans, M., T. Zorn, and R. Johnson, "Allocating Total Wealth: A Goal Programming Approach," *Computers and Operations Research,* 20, 7, 1993, 679–685.

for a $100,000 total investment will be limited to 100,000. If our investor allocates $5,000 in life insurance, $50,000 in bond mutual funds, $15,000 in stock mutual funds, and $30,000 in a savings account (which fall within the minimum and maximum amounts specified), the total expected annual return would be

$$.06(\$5,000) + .07(\$50,000) + .11(\$15,000) + .04(\$30,000) = \$6,650.$$

However, the total weighted risk associated with this solution is

$$-0.5(5,000) + 1.8(50,000) + 2.1(15,000) - 0.3(30,000) = 110,000$$

Because this is greater than the limit of 100,000, this solution could not be chosen.

The decision problem, then, is to determine how much to invest in each asset to maximize the total expected annual return, remain within the minimum and maximum limits for each investment, and meet the limitation on the weighted risk.

USING *OPTQUEST*

The basic process for using *OptQuest* is described as follows:

1. Create a *Crystal Ball* model of the decision problem.
2. Define the decision variables within *Crystal Ball*.
3. Invoke *OptQuest* from the *Crystal Ball* toolbar or the corresponding menu.
4. Create a new optimization file.
5. Select decision variables.
6. Specify constraints.
7. Select the forecast.
8. Modify *OptQuest* options.
9. Solve the optimization problem.
10. Save the optimization files.
11. Exit *OptQuest*.

Creating the *Crystal Ball* Spreadsheet Model

An important task in using *OptQuest* is to create a useful spreadsheet model. A spreadsheet for this problem is shown in Figure 9.30. Problem data are specified in rows 4 through 8. On the bottom half of the spreadsheet, we specify the model outputs, namely the values of the decision variables, objective function, and constraints (the total weighted risk and total amount invested). You can see that this particular solution is not feasible because the total weighted risk exceeds the limit of 100,000.

Now that the basic model is developed, we define the assumptions and forecast cells in *Crystal Ball*. We will assume that the annual returns for life insurance and mutual funds are uncertain, but that the rate for the savings account is constant. We will make the following assumptions in the *Crystal Ball* model:

- Cell B4: uniform distribution with minimum 4% and maximum 6%
- Cell B5: normal distribution with mean 7% and standard deviation 1%
- Cell B6: lognormal distribution with mean 11% and standard deviation 4%

We define the forecast cell to be the total expected return, cell B16. As would be the case with any *Crystal Ball* application, you would select *Run Preferences* from the *Run* menu and choose appropriate settings. Set the number of trials per simulation to 500.

	A	B	C	D	E
1	Portfolio Allocation Model				
2		Annual			Risk factor
3	Investment	Return	Minimum	Maximum	per dollar
4	Life insurance	5.0%	$ 2,500	$ 5,000	-0.5
5	Bond mutual funds	7.0%	$ 30,000	none	1.8
6	Stock mutual funds	11.0%	$ 15,000	none	2.1
7	Savings account	4.0%	none	none	-0.3
8	Total amount available	$ 100,000		Limit	100,000
9					
10		Amount			Total weighted
11	Decision variables	invested			risk
12	Life insurance	$ 5,000.00			146,000.00
13	Bond mutual funds	$ 50,000.00			
14	Stock mutual funds	$ 30,000.00			Total amount
15	Savings account	$ 15,000.00			invested
16	Total expected return	$ 7,650.00			$ 100,000.00
17					

Constraints · Decision variables · Objective

FIGURE 9.30 Portfolio Allocation Spreadsheet Model

Define Decision Variables

The next step is to identify the decision variables in the model. This is something that is not done in a regular *Crystal Ball* application; however, it is required in order to use *OptQuest*. This is accomplished using the *Define Decision Variables* option in the *Cell* menu. Position the cursor on cell B12. From the *Cell* menu, choose *Define Decision Variables*. Set the minimum and maximum values according to the problem data (i.e., columns C and D in the spreadsheet), as shown in Figure 9.31.

Next, we repeat the process of defining decision variables for cells B13, B14, and B15. When the maximum limit is "none," you may use a value of $100,000 because this is the total amount available. You are now in a position to call *OptQuest* by clicking on the *OptQuest* bottom on the *Crystal Ball* toolbar or selecting it from the corresponding menu.

Creating a New Optimization File

From the opening screen in *OptQuest,* select *New* from the *File* menu. This option allows you to create different optimization files for the same simulation. This brings up the wizard tool that will step you through the process of setting up your optimization model. You will then see the screen shown in Figure 9.32. You will need to select the subset of decision variables from your *Crystal Ball* model that will be used for opti-

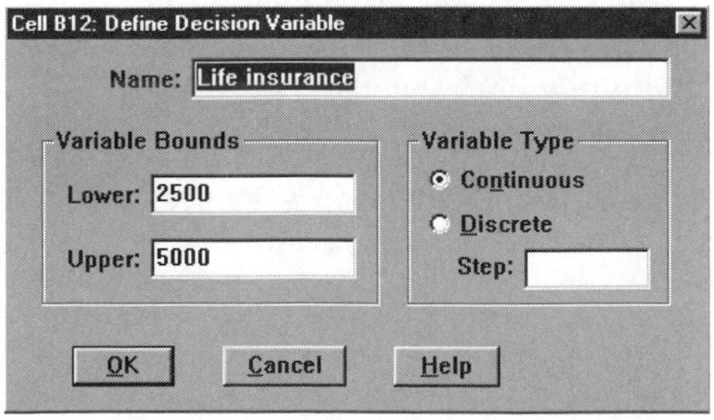

Cell B12: Define Decision Variable

Name: Life insurance

Variable Bounds

Lower: 2500

Upper: 5000

Variable Type

⦿ Continuous

○ Discrete

Step:

OK   Cancel   Help

FIGURE 9.31 Define Decision Variable Dialog Box

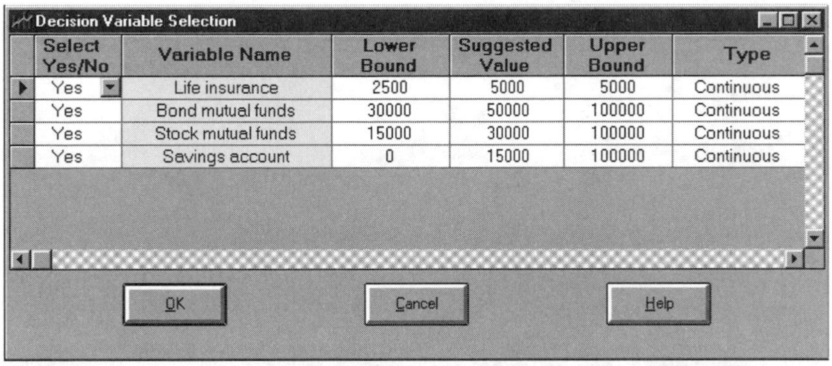

Select Yes/No	Variable Name	Lower Bound	Suggested Value	Upper Bound	Type
Yes	Life insurance	2500	5000	5000	Continuous
Yes	Bond mutual funds	30000	50000	100000	Continuous
Yes	Stock mutual funds	15000	30000	100000	Continuous
Yes	Savings account	0	15000	100000	Continuous

FIGURE 9.32 *OptQuest Decision Variable Selection* Screen

mization, the forecast cell and corresponding statistic that will be used as the objective to minimize or maximize, any forecast cells and corresponding statistics that will be used as goals, and any additional restrictions or constraints that you may wish to specify.

Select Decision Variables

Every decision variable in the *Crystal Ball* model appears in the *Decision Variable Selection* screen. The first column indicates whether the variable has been selected for optimization. To select one variable you may either type *Yes,* double-click to toggle between *Yes* and *No,* or make your selection from the drop-down menu. Initially, all decision variables are selected as optimization variables. For each selected variable, a lower and an upper bound must be given in the appropriate columns. If you would like to include a starting solution that *OptQuest* will improve upon, you can suggest the values of the selected variables in the *Suggested Value* column. The suggested value by default is the value that appears in the corresponding cell in your *Crystal Ball* model. If the suggested values are out of range or do not meet the problems constraints, these values are ignored. The *Type* column indicates whether a variable is discrete or continuous. The variable type can be changed in this window or in the Define Decision Variable window of *Crystal Ball.* A step size is associated with discrete variables. A variable of the type Discrete__2, for example, has a step size of 2. Therefore, if the lower and upper bounds for this variable are 0 and 7, respectively, the only feasible values are 0, 2, 4, and 6. To change the step size, you must click on the Discrete item of the drop-down menu and enter the new step size in the dialog box. In Figure 9.32, we see that all decision variables are selected for the optimization model.

Specify Constraints

The next screen displayed allows you to specify any constraints (see Figure 9.33). A *constraint* is any limitation or requirement that restricts the possible solutions to the problem. In our example, we have two constraints. The first constraint limits the total weighted risk to 100,000, and the second ensures that we do not allocate more than $100,000 in total to all assets. In the *OptQuest* screen, a listing of all previously selected decision variables is displayed. Constraints may only use these variables. You then type the constraints one by one, placing a single constraint on each line. (To facilitate the process, you may click on the decision variable names in the right-hand column to move the name to where the cursor is.) Constraints should be one in each line. An asterisk must be used to indicate the product of a constant and a variable (e.g., 3*X).

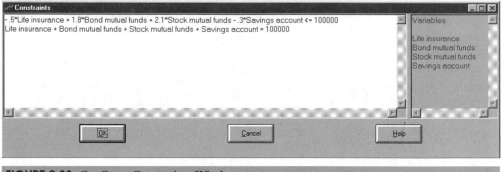

FIGURE 9.33 *OptQuest* Constraints Window

Thus, in our example, the risk constraint is:

$$-0.5*\text{Life insurance} + 1.8*\text{Bond mutual funds} + 2.1*\text{Stock mutual funds}$$
$$- 0.3*\text{Savings account} <= 100000$$

and the total investment constraint is:

$$\text{Life insurance} + \text{Bond mutual funds} + \text{Stock mutual funds}$$
$$+ \text{Savings account} <= 100000$$

The newly entered constraints are saved by clicking the OK button.

Select the Forecast

Every *OptQuest* run requires the selection a statistic of at least one forecast cell to act as the objective function to be minimized or maximized. You can select a forecast to be a *Maximize Objective* or a *Minimize Objective* from the drop-down menu in the *Select Objective/Requirements* column.

In addition to an objective, you may choose to set optimization *requirements*. Requirements are used to constrain forecast statistics to fall within specified lower and upper target values. This is done by choosing the *Requirement* option from the drop-down menu in the *Select Objective/Requirements* column and will be illustrated in other examples. In the *Crystal Ball* model, we have only defined one forecast, whose mean value we wish to maximize as shown in Figure 9.34.

FIGURE 9.34 *OptQuest* Forecast Selection Window

Select Objective / Requirements	Name	Forecast Statistic	Lower Bound	Upper Bound	Units
Maximize Objective	Total expected return	Mean			Dollars

Modify *OptQuest* Options

Next, a window with the following three tabs appears:

- Time
- Settings
- Preferences

The *Time* tab allows you to specify the total time that the system is allowed to search for the best values for the optimization variables. You may either enter the total number of minutes or a date and time when the process must stop. Performance will depend on the speed of your microprocessor. The default optimization time is 10 minutes; however, you are able to choose any time limit you desire. Selecting a very long time limit does not present a problem, because you are always able to terminate the search by selecting *Stop* in the *Run* menu or pressing the Esc key. Additionally, you will be given the option to extend the search and carry the optimization process farther once the selected time has expired.

The *Settings* tab window allows you to change the number of simulation trials to be performed during every call to *Crystal Ball*. For this example, select 500 trials. This value, of course, can also be changed in the *Run Preferences . . .* option in *Crystal Ball*. A short description of the optimization file can also be entered in this screen. Finally, the name of the log file can be changed. The log file records data related to the search, which can also be displayed by choosing the *Log* option of the *View* menu. The log file is particularly useful when the search abnormally terminates (e.g., due to a system crash), because a text editor can be used to read the information contained in this file and the search does not result in a wasted effort.

In the *Preferences* tab screen you can select which *Crystal Ball* runs to save (default is *Only Best*). Finally, in the *Advanced* tab screen, you are able to turn on and off the Neural Network Accelerator; we recommend leaving this on.

Solve the Optimization Problem

The optimization process is initiated from the next dialog box or from the *Run* menu. As the simulation is running, you may also select three additional options from the *View* menu: *Performance Graph, Bar Graph,* or *Log.* The Performance Graph shows a plot of the value of the objective as a function of the number of simulations evaluated. The Bar Graph shows how the value of each decision variable changes during the optimization search procedure. Finally, the Optimization Log provides details of the sequence of best solutions generated during the search.

As the optimization progresses, the sequence of best solutions identified during the search is displayed on the *Status and Solutions* screen. Each time a better solution is identified, a new line is added to the screen, showing the new objective value and values of the decision variables. In the upper left corner of the *Status and Solutions* screen, you can monitor the time remaining and the simulation trial number currently under evaluation. (This information disappears when the time limit is reached.)

Figure 9.35 shows the *Status and Solutions* screen upon completion of the optimization using a 266 MHz laptop. Note that the first solution does *not* correspond to the solution in the spreadsheet in Figure 9.30, because that solution is not feasible. *OptQuest* identifies an initial feasible solution to begin the search process.

Saving an Optimization File

The *Save* and *Save As . . .* options in the *File* menu allow you to save the current optimization model for future use. Note that the file that you save refers to the optimization

Status and Solutions

OptQuest for Crystal Ball

Optimization File
d:\statistics and data analysis\chapter 9 optimization\portfolio.opt
Portfolio allocation model

Optimization is Complete

Simulation	Maximize Objective Total expected return Mean	Life insurance	Bond mutual funds	Stock mutual funds	Savings account
54	6919.91	2956.13	30736.9	27518.2	38788.7
59	6924.45	3300.27	30727.8	27538.0	38433.9
64	6930.77	3016.43	30431.3	27790.6	38761.6
79	6935.87	2940.54	30018.2	28046.4	38994.9
88	6942.12	2849.42	30000.0	28154.1	38996.5
100	6943.51	2937.15	30000.0	28161.4	38901.4
Best: 145	6943.81	2963.46	30000.0	28161.9	38874.6

FIGURE 9.35 *OptQuest* Status and Solutions Window

problem and the *OptQuest* options only, and not to the *Crystal Ball* simulation model (which is saved in the Excel file). The optimization files are automatically given the extension name .OPT. The saved optimization file may be recalled by choosing *Open . . .* from the *File* menu.

Exit OptQuest

To exit, choose *Exit* from the *File* menu. *OptQuest* will now save the best simulations for you and will restore the one you select when you exit. After choosing *Exit* you will be given the opportunity to paste the best values found for the optimization variables in your *Crystal Ball* model. The results are shown in Figure 9.36. You can see that both constraints are satisfied (to within a small decimal fraction). Alternatively, other values can be pasted by highlighting the corresponding row on the *Status and Solutions* window accessible from the *View* menu.

FIGURE 9.36 *OptQuest* Results for Portfolio Allocation Model

	A	B	C	D	E
1	**Portfolio Allocation Model**				
2		*Annual*			*Risk factor*
3	*Investment*	*Return*	*Minimum*	*Maximum*	*per dollar*
4	Life insurance	5.0%	$ 2,500	$ 5,000	-0.5
5	Bond mutual funds	7.0%	$ 30,000	none	1.8
6	Stock mutual funds	11.0%	$ 15,000	none	2.1
7	Savings account	4.0%	none	none	-0.3
8	Total amount available	$ 100,000		*Limit*	100,000
9			Constraints		
10		*Amount*			*Total weighted*
11	*Decision variables*	*invested*			*risk*
12	Life insurance	$ 2,963.46			99,995.88
13	Bond mutual funds	$ 30,000.00		Decision	
14	Stock mutual funds	$ 28,161.90		variables	*Total amount*
15	Savings account	$ 38,874.60			*invested*
16	*Total expected return*	$ 6,900.97		Objective	$ 99,999.96
17					

INTERPRETING RESULTS

You should note that the "best" *OptQuest* solution identified may not be the true optimal solution to the problem, but will hopefully be close to the actual optimal solution. The accuracy of the results depends on the time limit you select for searching, the number of decision variables, and the complexity of the problem. With more decision variables, you need a larger number of simulations.

After solving an optimization problem with *OptQuest,* you probably would want to examine the *Crystal Ball* simulation using the optimal values of the decision variables in order to assess the risks associated with the recommended solution. Figure 9.37 shows the *Crystal Ball* forecast chart associated with the best solution. Although the mean value was optimized, we see that a high amount of variability exists in the actual return because of the uncertainty in the returns of the individual investments. In fact, the total returns varied from about $4,500 to over $12,000.

ADDING A REQUIREMENT

A *requirement* is a forecast statistic that is restricted to fall within a specified lower and upper bound. The forecast statistic may be one of the following:

Mean
Median
Mode
Standard Deviation
Variance
Percentile (as specified by the user)
Skewness
Kurtosis
Coefficient of Variation
Range (Minimum, maximum, and width)
Standard error

For example, to reduce the uncertainty of returns in the portfolio while also attempting to maximize the expected return, we might want to restrict the standard deviation to be no greater than 1,000. To add such a requirement in *OptQuest,* select *Forecast* from the *Tools* menu. This will bring up the *Forecast Selection Screen.* Because we have only

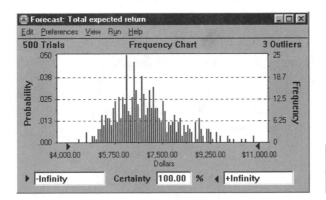

FIGURE 9.37 *Crystal Ball* Forecast Chart for *OptQuest* Solution

Simulation	Maximize Objective Total expected return:1 Mean	Requirement Total expected return:2 Std_Dev	Life insurance	Bond mutual funds	Stock mutual funds	Savings account
1	6943.81	1179.61 - Infeasible	2963.46	30000.0	28161.9	38874.6
2	6480.69	767.349	4913.51	45229.9	15000.0	34856.6
9	6708.03	958.209	3585.40	37574.6	21587.7	37252.3
15	6726.09	960.032	4925.39	37671.8	21614.3	35788.5
60	6731.68	980.145	3833.62	36616.5	22287.6	37262.2
61	6732.99	979.012	3883.71	36753.3	22241.5	37121.5
66	6733.25	978.725	3883.93	36790.0	22229.6	37096.4
71	6742.88	985.035	3917.32	36662.5	22413.5	37006.8
91	6758.16	996.177	4134.30	36297.4	22751.0	36817.3
96	6760.73	997.745	4208.33	36247.3	22797.8	36746.6
116	6761.06	997.778	4238.71	36246.6	22798.5	36716.2
Best: 126	6763.47	999.194	4292.27	36210.8	22839.9	36657.0

FIGURE 9.38 *OptQuest* Results with Standard Deviation Requirement

one forecast in the model, this row will be highlighted. The same cell may be simultaneously selected as an objective and as a goal. This can be achieved by highlighting the *Forecasts Name* in the *Forecast Selection* window and choosing *Duplicate* from the *Edit* menu. This creates a new row, with the forecast named Total Expected Return:2. From the drop-down menu in the first column, select *Requirement.* Click on the *Forecast Statistic* cell and using the drop-down menu, choose *Standard Deviation;* then set the upper bound to 1,000. Finally, click OK.

You may now run the new model. The results are shown in Figure 9.38. The best solution among those with standard deviations less than or equal to 1,000 is identified.

Summary

Optimization involves selecting values for decision variables that minimize or maximize some quantity, usually with constraints that limit the choices that can be made. There are three basic types of optimization problems: linear, in which the objective and constraint functions all have linear terms; integer linear, in which some or all decision variables are restricted to be whole numbers; and nonlinear, in which the objective and/or one or more constraint functions have nonlinear terms. Many practical problems in business ranging from production to marketing to finance can be formulated as optimization models.

The Solver tool in Excel provides the capability of solving optimization models that are formulated on a spreadsheet. Solver reports provide useful managerial information for sensitivity analysis—the process of examining the effect of small changes in model parameters on the optimal solution. You must realize that any model, and optimization models in particular, are only approximations of the real problem that decision makers face. This is why techniques such as sensitivity analysis and examining the effects of uncertainty on optimal solutions are important.

Questions and Problems

1. The International Chef, Inc., markets three blends of oriental tea: premium, Duke Grey, and breakfast. The firm uses tea leaves from India, China, and new domestic California sources.

Quality	Tea Leaves		
	Indian	*Chinese*	*Californian*
Premium	40%	20%	40%
Duke Grey	20%	30%	40%
Breakfast	20%	40%	40%

Net profit per pound for each blend is $0.50 for premium, $0.30 for Duke Grey, and $0.20 for breakfast. The firm's regular weekly supplies are 20,000 pounds of Indian tea leaves and 22,000 pounds of Chinese tea leaves. Because it is new, and until it proves itself, no more than 16,000 pounds of Californian tea is to be used in a week. The marketing research department reports that there is an almost unlimited market for premium and fine blends. However, the maximum expected sale for breakfast blend is 2,000 pounds. Develop a linear optimization model to determine the optimal mix to maximize profit.

2. Metropolitan Airport Services, Inc., is considering purchasing cars for transportation service between the municipal airport and hotels in the downtown area. They are considering station wagons, minibuses, and large buses. Purchase prices are $45,000 for each station wagon, $90,000 for each minibus, and $200,000 for each large bus. The board of directors has authorized a maximum budget of $5,000,000 for purchases. Because of the heavy air travel in the area, these vehicles would be utilized at maximum capacity regardless of the type of vehicle purchased.

   Expected net annual profit would be $1,500 per station wagon, $3,500 per minibus, and $5,000 per large bus. The company has hired 30 drivers for these vehicles, each qualified to drive any one of the three vehicle types. The maintenance department has the capacity to handle an additional 80 station wagons. A minibus is equivalent to 1 ⅔ station wagons for maintenance purposes, and a large bus is equivalent to 2 station wagons for maintenance purposes. Develop a linear optimization model to determine the optimal number of each type of vehicle to purchase in order to maximize profit.

3. A company in Victoria, Texas, produces bottles of aspirin products as follows:

Product	Sales Price
Super seltzer	$3.00
Capsules	$3.50
Cheap seltzer	$2.00
Tablets	$2.50

The company ships these products to two distributors, located in Hearne and Cuero, Texas. There is unlimited demand at each distributor. Shipping costs per bottle and contracted minimum quantities for each distributor are as follows:

		Hearne	*Cuero*
Shipping cost/bottle		$0.21	$0.22
Minimum demand	Super seltzer	700	1,000
	Capsules	800	1,500
	Cheap seltzer	1,000	800
	Tablets	1,800	5,000

Raw material costs and maximum available quantities are as follows:

	Cost/Ounce	*Maximum Ounces*
Acetylsalicylic acid	$0.60	50,000
Sodium	$0.30	25,000

The production costs per bottle and raw materials required per bottle are as follows:

	Production Cost/Bottle	*Ounces Acet. Acid*	*Ounces Sodium*
Super seltzer	$0.25	2	3
Capsules	0.35	4	0
Cheap seltzer	0.15	2	2
Tablets	0.10	3	0

Because capsules have become an insurance problem, the total number of bottles of capsules produced is to be no more than 20 percent of the total number of bottles produced. Develop a linear optimization model, and solve it using Solver.

4. You have inherited $1 million from a relative. You plan to invest this money (in varying amounts) in up to four long-term investment instruments (stocks, bonds, savings, and real estate). You evaluate investments in stocks and bonds at the beginning of each of the next six years. Each dollar invested in stocks at the beginning of the year is expected to return an average of $1.15 in time for immediate reinvestment one year later. Each dollar invested in bonds at the beginning of each year is expected to return $1.30 three years later (a profit of 30 percent in three years). Credit union savings returns $1.05 one year later, and each dollar invested in real estate is expected to return $1.30 four years later. A maximum of $200,000 can be invested in real estate in any one year.

   You want to diversify your investments to minimize risk. The total invested in stocks in a given year should not exceed 30 percent of the total investment in the other alternatives for that year. At least 25 percent of the total investment should be in credit union savings certificates. You also want to have $150,000 available in cash (which can be immediately reinvested) at the end of the third year as leverage in negotiating with your relatives. Develop a model to maximize the cash on hand at the end of the sixth year.

5. A city council is reviewing housing proposals for a new development area. There is some dispute among various interest groups as to what the goals are. The zoning committee has recommended three types of housing: single-family houses, deluxe condominiums, and apartments, and have also provided the following data:

	Family	*Condos*	*Apartment*
Land usage, acres/unit	0.25	0.40	0.125
Families housed/unit	1	4	6
Tax base generated/unit	$50,000	$100,000	$25,000
Utility installation expense/unit	$ 4,000	$ 8,000	$ 6,000

Twenty acres are available for zoning. Utility installation expense is to be held to no more than $1 million.

A public opinion survey has been conducted, and the city council has reviewed this survey. Important issues are to provide housing to families, generate a tax base, and minimize installation costs. Use a linear optimization model to identify the solutions associated with maximizing families housed, and also for maximizing the tax base added.

6. Larry Doyle was recently named by Governor McGraw as campaign director for his upcoming reelection campaign. Governor McGraw thinks that if he can get his message to two million people in the state, he has a good chance of winning a large chunk of votes at the state Libertarian Party Convention. Larry has obtained the following information about advertising media availability and cost.

Medium	Voter Exposure per $1,000 Spent	Cost per Insertion	Maximum Units
Prime-time TV	10,000	$5,000	60
Nonprime-time TV	4,000	$4,000	60
Radio	3,500	$3,000	100
Newspaper	1,500	$2,000	120
Billboards	750	$1,000	150

Governor McGraw has a campaign fund of $6 million available, which according to state election law cannot be exceeded. As a traditionalist, Governor McGraw has specified that he wants to place at least one ad in each of the 50 largest newspapers in the state (just before it is time for them to make their editorial recommendations to voters). Formulate and solve a linear model to maximize voter exposure.

7. Solve the following linear programming model using Solver and interpret the results.

$$\text{Max} \quad 6X + 7Y$$
$$\text{Subject to} \quad 12X + 14Y \le 168$$
$$X \le 10$$
$$Y \ge 5$$
$$X, Y \ge 0$$

8. Solve the following linear programming model using Solver and interpret the results.

$$\text{Max} \quad 3X + 7Y$$
$$\text{Subject to} \quad X + Y \le 10$$
$$3X + Y \ge 50$$
$$X, Y \ge 0$$

9. Solve the following linear programming model using Solver and interpret the results.

$$\text{Max} \quad 3X + 7Y$$
$$\text{Subject to} \quad X - Y \le 10$$
$$3X + 7Y \ge 50$$
$$X, Y \ge 0$$

10. A small canning company specializes in gourmet canned foods. They can five combinations of ham, lima beans, and jalapeno peppers.

Product (16-oz. cans)	Maximum Demand (Includes signed contracts)	Signed Contracts/Day (Minimum demands)
Ham & beans	10,000 cans/day	5,000 cans/day
Jalapeno ham & beans	4,000	1,000
Lima beans	6,000	1,000
Jalapeno lima beans	4,000	2,000
Jalapeno peppers	1,000	0 (new product)

The production department obtains input materials and fills 16-oz. cans. All quantities are in ounces; all costs and sales prices/can are in dollars. There is a maximum production limit of 24,000 cans/day. Canning costs are constant.

Product	Ham	Lima Beans	Jalapenos	Water	Can Cost	Price
Ham & beans	4	9	0	3	.05	2.31
Jalapeno ham & beans	3	9	1	3	.05	2.00
Lima beans	0	14	0	2	.05	.85
Jalapeno lima beans	0	12	1	3	.05	.90
Jalapeno peppers	0	0	12	4	.05	1.35
Cost of materials	$.40/oz.	$.05/oz.	$.10/oz.	free		

The company has a contract with a ham supplier for daily delivery of up to 30,000 ounces of ham at $.30/ounce. They also have a contract with a lima bean supplier for up to 100,000 ounces of lima beans per day at $.05/ounce. They do not have to pay for materials they do not use. They grow their own jalapenos, which cost $.10/ounce to pick, with no limitations on the supply.

Recommend a daily production schedule to maximize profit. Answer the following questions, treating each independently from the others. (You do not have to make additional Solver runs; all questions may be answered from the sensitivity analysis information.)

a. There is a rumor that the market for Jalapeno Ham & Beans is changing. Would there be any change in recommendations if the price for this product changed from $2.00 to $2.05? How about a price drop to $1.95/can?

b. If the price of Jalapeno Peppers increased to $1.40/can, would your recommendation change? Why or why not? What would the new daily profit be?

c. Your ham supplier is willing to provide additional ham up to another 20,000 ounces per day at the price of $.41/ounce. How many of these additional ounces do you recommend buying in addition to the normal daily purchase (which would still be $.40/ounce)? Why or why not?

d. The lima bean supplier is willing to provide up to 20,000 *additional* ounces per day at the price of $.06/ounce. How many ounces do you recommend buying in addition to the normal purchase at the old price? Why or why not?

e. There is a monthly sales meeting coming up. Do you have any recommendations concerning which products to advertise (increase demand), and which not to? Why?

11. You are in the business of producing and selling 100-pound bags of health food for pet pigs. You plan to advertise that each bag will provide a pig its minimum weekly requirements of protein (200 grams), calcium (300 grams), and fiber (100 grams), and will contain no more than 500 calories. You have found supplies at a reasonable cost for three possible ingredients.

	Cost	Protein	Calcium	Fiber	Calories
Corn	$.03/lb	100 g/lb	2 g/lb	1 g/lb	50/lb
Fishbones	$.005/lb	1 g/lb	50 g/lb	none	2/lb
Sawdust	$.001/lb	none	none	200 g/lb	1/lb

You plan to sell each bag for $1. Develop an optimization model and solve. Answer the following questions, treating each independently from the others. (You do not have to make additional Solver runs; all questions may be answered from the sensitivity analysis information.)

a. How much would the cost of corn have to drop to make it worth adding more?

b. If the cost of fishbones increased to $.006 per pound, what would the impact be?

c. If the cost of sawdust increased to $.005 per pound, what would the impact be?

d. If you reduced the advertised amount of protein from 200 grams/bag to 100 grams/bag, how much would that enable you to save? Why?

e. If you increased the advertised proportion of fiber from 100 grams/bag to 200 grams/bag, how much would your cost increase? Why?

12. Boing Corp. produces airplanes for large smugglers, medium-sized revolutions, and small governments. They produce three models, the Raven, the Hawk, and the Falcon.

	Contracts (minimums)	Maximum Demand	Fuselages	Missile Launchers	Cannons	Profit/ Plane
Ravens	0	40	1	4	0	$ 5 million
Hawks	15	30	1	2	2	$20 million
Falcons	0	50	1	4	4	$30 million

Develop a linear optimization model and solve it. Answer the following questions independently of each other.

a. If 40 extra cannons could be obtained for a marginal cost of $2 million per cannon, would it pay? What is the marginal benefit of cannons? For how many additional cannons would Boing be confident of this benefit?

b. If Boing could obtain up to 8 extra fuselages for a marginal cost of $6 million each, would it pay to acquire any? What is the marginal benefit? How many extra fuselages would Boing be confident of this benefit?

c. If huge bribes would have the effect of increasing demand, which plane's demands should be increased?

d. If a wealthy unofficial goods transporter wanted to know how much he/she would have to pay to get a Falcon, what price would be required?

e. If the government wanted to obtain missile launchers from Boing, how many could Boing let go for $1 million per launcher?

13. A department store chain is planning to open a new store. They need to decide how to allocate the 100,000 square feet of available floor space among seven departments. Data on expected performance of each department per month, in terms of square feet (sf) is as follows:

Department	Investment per sf	Risk as a Percent of $ Invested	Minimum sf	Maximum sf	Expected Profit per sf
Electronics	$ 100	24	6,000	30,000	$12.00
Furniture	50	12	10,000	30,000	6.00
Men's clothing	30	5	2,000	5,000	2.00
Clothing	600	10	3,000	40,000	30.00
Jewelry	900	14	1,000	10,000	20.00
Books	50	2	1,000	5,000	1.00
Appliances	400	3	12,000	40,000	13.00

The company has gathered $20,000,000 to invest in floor stock. The risk element is a measure of risk associated with investment in floor stock. The idea is that Electronics loses $10 for every $100 invested per month, based upon past records at other places for outdated inventory, pilferage, breakage, etc. Electronics is the highest risk item. Expected profit is after covering risk. Develop a linear optimization model to maximize profit that includes a constraint to measure total investment, as well as a constraint to measure dollars at risk. Report investment, square footage, and the average risk ratio for each solution.

Additional questions:

a. You may find a solution that doesn't use all available floor space. If you are trying to maximize profit, how can that be?

b. What rate of interest should the chain consider for the opportunity to obtain additional investment capital? Note that the model deals with monthly operations. How much additional money (per month) would that rate apply for?

c. If the chain obtains another $1,000,000 of investment capital for stock, what would the solution be? (A new solution is required.) What would the marginal value of capital be in that case?

d. (Return to the original model, with $20 million investment) Some planning committee members are concerned about risk. Identify the solutions (to include investment, square footage, and risk ratio) if risk were to be limited to 10 percent of investment.

14. Gulf Coast Oil Company is a petroleum refining company headquartered in Cut-and-Shoot, Texas. The company does not operate its own oil well. Instead, it purchases crude oil from a number of drilling companies on a long-term contract basis. The company has three refineries located in Houston, Corpus Christi, and Fort Worth, and has three distribution depots located in San Antonio, Texarkana, and El Paso.

The transportation problem faced by Gulf Coast Oil is to supply the required quantity of gasoline to each of the distribution depots. Each depot has specific demands, and each refinery has specific capacities. These parameters and the costs of moving one load of fuel from each refinery to each depot are as follows:

Source	Capacity	Depot	Demand
Houston	150	San Antonio	200
Corpus Christi	100	Texarkana	120
Fort Worth	250	El Paso	180

From	To	Unit Cost
Houston	San Antonio	20
	Texarkana	9
	El Paso	5
Corpus Christi	San Antonio	6
	Texarkana	10
	El Paso	18
Fort Worth	San Antonio	2
	Texarkana	15
	El Paso	12

Develop and solve a linear optimization model to minimize the cost of transportation.

15. Liquid Gold, Inc., transports radioactive waste from nuclear power plants to disposal sites around the country. Each plant has an amount of material that must be moved each period. Each site has a limited capacity per period. The cost of transporting between sites follows (some combinations of plants and storage sites are not to be used, and no figure is given).

Plant	Material	Cost to Site: S51	S62	S73	S87	Site	Capacity
P1	20,876	105	86	x	23	S51	285,922
P2	50,870	86	58	41	x	S62	308,578
P3	38,652	93	46	65	38	S73	111,955
P4	28,951	116	27	94	x	S87	208,555
P5	87,423	88	56	82	89		
P6	76,190	111	36	72	x		
P7	58,237	169	65	48	x		

Find the least-cost solution for these data.

16. The personnel director of a company that recently absorbed another firm, and is now downsizing, must relocate five information systems analysts from recently closed locations. Unfortunately, there are only three positions available. Salaries are fairly uniform among this group (those with higher pay were already given the opportunity to begin anew). Moving expenses will be used as the means of determining who will be sent where. Estimated moving expenses are as follows:

Analyst	Moving Cost to: Gary	Salt Lake City	Fresno
Arlene	$8,000	$ 7,000	$ 5,000
Bobby	$5,000	$ 8,000	$12,000
Charlene	$9,000	$15,000	$16,000
Douglas	$4,000	$ 8,000	$13,000
Emory	$7,000	$ 3,000	$ 4,000

Model this as an integer optimization model to minimize cost and identify which analysts to relocate to the three locations. Solve the model both as a pure linear model and as an integer model. What do you find? This will not be true in general!

17. You have the responsibility of providing analytic support to a company committee in charge of administering new computer projects. This committee has a budget of $2,500,000 to fund projects. There are four company departments (A, B, C, and D) that have submitted project proposals. Each proposal includes estimates of total cost, number of systems analysts required, number of special programmers required, and estimated cash flow for the next year, estimated after tax profit for the next year, and net present value. There are 12 systems analysts available, and 6 special programmers that could be devoted to these projects. The board of directors has given minimum required limits for next year's cash flow and after-tax profits. Cash flow from these projects is to be at least $300,000. After-tax profits from these projects is to be at least $200,000. The board would like to maximize the net present value of the selected projects, subject to the above limits, and the restriction that

projects must be either adopted or not adopted. (You cannot recommend partial project funding.)

	Project Cost ($1,000)	Estimated Analysts (people)	Systems Programmers (people)	Cash Flow	Net Present After-Tax Profit ($1,000)	Value ($1,000)
A01	230	3	0	50	20	100
A02	370	4	1	75	30	190
A03	180	2	0	40	20	80
A04	90	1	2	10	10	30
A05	570	4	1	160	70	220
B06	750	3	0	240	110	390
B07	370	3	1	100	40	180
B08	250	3	0	55	20	140
B09	190	2	0	30	10	90
B10	200	1	2	0	10	90
C11	310	2	0	50	20	70
C12	430	3	1	125	10	10
C13	680	3	0	205	100	170
C14	550	1	3	0	50	100
D15	290	1	1	100	40	140
D16	200	1	1	50	20	90
D17	150	1	2	0	10	110

The letter in the project name indicates the department that submitted the project. An additional limit, for political purposes, is that each of these four departments receive funding for at least one project. Model this problem and find a solution yielding the maximum net present value, identifying the measures for all other features the committee considered important. Then identify the solution if the budget were cut to $2,400,000, $2,300,000, $2,200,000, $2,100,000, and $2,000,000. Report the measures of attainment on all scales (estimated cost, analysts, programmers, cash flow, after-tax profit, and net present value) for each solution.

18. Many high-technology products such as crystals and alloys can be manufactured more efficiently in the weightless environment of earth orbit. You are planning production operations for a space flight. Five products are being considered. Unit profits, volumes, weights, labor hours per unit, and maximum demands follow. Model and solve this problem as an integer optimization problem. Also solve this as a pure linear model. How much does it "cost" to enforce the integer restrictions?

Products	Alloy1	Alloy2	Crystal1	Crystal2	Interferon
Profit ($/unit)	10	1.7	3.5	1.6	2.6
Volume (CF/unit)	9	3	10	7	13
Weight (lb/unit)	59	18	26	26	10
Manhours (/unit)	2.2	0.5	0.7	0.2	1.1
Demand ($\leq$)	22	69	90	40	85

Volume available: 600 CF

Weight allowable: 2,100 lb.

Manhours available: 40 hr.

19. Larsen E. Whipsnade is a young entrepreneur. His latest invention is the air-adjustable basketball shoe with pump, similar to those advertised by more expensive brand names. Larsen contacted a supplier of Victor basketball shoes, a little-known brand with low advertising. This supplier would provide shoes at the nominal price of $6 per pair of shoes. Larsen needed to know the best price at which to sell these shoes.

    As a business student with strong economics training, Larsen remembered that the volume sold is affected by the product's price—the higher the price, the lower the volume. He asked his friends and acquaintances what they would pay for a premium pair of basketball shoes that were a "little off-brand." Based on this data, he developed the formula

$$\text{Volume} = 1{,}000 - 20 \text{ Price}$$

    There are some minor expenses involved, including a $50 fee for selling shoes in the neighborhood (a fixed cost), as well as his purchase price of $6 per shoe. Develop an appropriate objective function and identify the optimal price level for this nonlinear model using Solver.

20. Larsen (problem 19) did very well selling Victor shoes. His shoe supplier told him of a new product, Abibas, that was entering the market. This shoe would be a product substitute for Victors, so that the higher the price of either shoe, the greater the demand for the other. Larsen interviewed more potential clients to determine price response and cross-elasticities. This yielded the following relationships:

$$\text{Volume of Victors} = 1{,}000 - 20 \, P_v + 1 \, P_a$$
$$\text{Volume of Abibas} = 800 + 2 \, P_v - 18 \, P_a$$

    where P_v = price of Victors, and P_a = price of Abibas. Develop a new profit function and use Solver to identify the optimal prices for the two shoes.

21. Kern's Meats has developed a sausage that consists of a blend of the finest meats available locally, along with hot peppers for flavor, okra for fiber, and club soda for additional sodium. Sausages are to each weigh exactly one pound. The meat purchased is not uniform; the variance in the content of meat is shown in the following table along with other important data.

	Pork	Beef	Goat	Peppers	Okra	Soda
Cost	$1.50/lb	$2.00/lb	$0.60/lb	$0.25/lb	$0.20/lb	$0.01/lb
Fiber	0.05 cc/lb	0.1 cc/lb	0.2 cc/lb	0.03 cc/lb	0.8 cc/lb	0
Sodium	0.05 cc/lb	0.02 cc/lb	0.03 cc/lb	0	0	0.01 cc/lb
Variance in meat content	0.1	0.1	0.3			

The mixture is to contain at least 50 percent meat (pork, beef, and goat) by weight, at least 0.35 cc of fiber, and no more than 0.02 cc of salt. Soda should be no more than 10 percent of the sausage by weight. Define decision variables as the number of pounds of each material per sausage. The meat requirement constraint that incorporates the variance is

$$\text{Pork} + \text{Beef} + \text{Goat} - z(\text{SQRT}[.1 \text{ Pork} + .1 \text{ Beef} + .3 \text{ Goat}])$$
$$\geq 0.5(\text{Pork} + \text{Beef} + \text{Goat} + \text{Peppers} + \text{Okra} + \text{Soda})$$

where z is the value of the standard normal distribution corresponding to a probability of actually achieving the meat requirement. Compare solutions for the following probability levels (some of which may be infeasible): 0.5, 0.6, 0.7, 0.8, 0.9, and 0.95. Discuss the impact of higher probabilities of satisfying the meat requirement. You may use the function NORMSINV(*probability*) to get the appropriate z-value from Excel. (As a check, the z-value for a probability of 0.6 is 0.253347).

22. The Hal Chase Investment Planning Agency is in business to help investors optimize their return from investment by including consideration of risk. Hal deals with three investment mediums: a stock fund, a bond fund, and his own Sports and Casino Investment Plan (SCIP). The stock fund is a mutual fund investing in openly traded stocks. The bond fund focuses on the bond market, which has a stable but lower expected return. SCIP is a high-risk scheme, often resulting in heavy losses, but occasionally coming through with spectacular gains. Average returns, their variances, and covariances, are as follows:

	Stock	*Bond*	*SCIP*
Average return	0.148	0.060	0.152
Variance	0.014697	0.000155	0.160791
Covariance with stock		0.000468	−0.002222
Covariance with bond			−0.000227

Negative covariance indicates that SCIP tends to move in the opposite direction as stocks or bonds. The objective function to be minimized is:

$$0.014697 \text{ Stock}^2 + 0.000155 \text{ Bond}^2 + 0.160791 \text{ SCIP}^2$$
$$+ 2 \times \text{Stock} \times \text{Bond} \times 0.000468$$
$$- 2 \times \text{Stock} \times \text{SCIP} \times 0.002222$$
$$- 2 \times \text{Bond} \times \text{SCIP} \times 0.000227$$

Develop a nonlinear optimization model to minimize this function subject to achieving an average return of at least 10 percent, and a budget limit of $1,000.

23. Refer to the hotel pricing problem in chapter 8 (problem 22). Suppose that the hotel wishes to determine the optimal prices of each type of room to maximize revenue. The owners want to keep the price of a standard room between $70 and $90; a gold room between $90 and $110; and a platinum room between $120 and $149. Although the rooms may be renovated and reconfigured, there are no plans to expand beyond the current 450-room capacity. Develop a spreadsheet optimization model and solve using *OptQuest*.

References

Charnes, A., and Cooper, W. W., *Management Models and Industrial Applications of Linear Programming,* New York: Wiley, 1961.

Dantzig, G. B., *Linear Programming and Extensions,* Princeton, NJ: Princeton University, 1963.

Fylstra, Daniel, Lasdon, Leon, Watson, John, and Warren, Allan, "Design and use of the Microsoft Excel Solver," *Interfaces,* 28, 5, 1998, 29–55.

Gass, Saul I., *Linear Programming,* 5th ed., New York: McGraw-Hill, 1985.

Hillier, F. S. and Lieberman, G. J., *Introduction to Operations Research,* 5th ed., New York: McGraw-Hill, 1990.

Sheel, Atul, "Monte Carlo simulations and scenario analysis: decision-making tools for hoteliers," *Cornell Hotel and Restaurant Administration Quarterly,* 36, 5, 1995, 18–26.

Williams, H., *Model Building in Mathematical Programming,* 2d ed., New York: Wiley, 1985.

Appendix

Table A.1   The Standardized Normal Distribution
Table A.2   The Cumulative Standard Normal Distribution
Table A.3   Critical Values of t
Table A.4   Critical Values of F

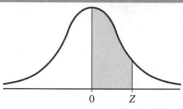

Entry represents area under the standardized normal distribution from the mean to z

z	.00	.01	.02	.03	.04	.05	.06	.07	.08	.09
0.0	.0000	.0040	.0080	.0120	.0160	.0199	.0239	.0279	.0319	.0359
0.1	.0398	.0438	.0478	.0517	.0557	.0596	.0636	.0675	.0714	.0753
0.2	.0793	.0832	.0871	.0910	.0948	.0987	.1026	.1064	.1103	.1141
0.3	.1179	.1217	.1255	.1293	.1331	.1368	.1406	.1443	.1480	.1517
0.4	.1554	.1591	.1628	.1664	.1700	.1736	.1772	.1808	.1844	.1879
0.5	.1915	.1950	.1985	.2019	.2054	.2088	.2123	.2157	.2190	.2224
0.6	.2257	.2291	.2324	.2357	.2389	.2422	.2454	.2486	.2518	.2549
0.7	.2580	.2612	.2642	.2673	.2704	.2734	.2764	.2794	.2823	.2852
0.8	.2881	.2910	.2939	.2967	.2995	.3023	.3051	.3078	.3106	.3133
0.9	.3159	.3186	.3212	.3238	.3264	.3289	.3315	.3340	.3365	.3389
1.0	.3413	.3438	.3461	.3485	.3508	.3531	.3554	.3577	.3599	.3621
1.1	.3643	.3665	.3686	.3708	.3729	.3749	.3770	.3790	.3810	.3830
1.2	.3849	.3869	.3888	.3907	.3925	.3944	.3962	.3980	.3997	.4015
1.3	.4032	.4049	.4066	.4082	.4099	.4115	.4131	.4147	.4162	.4177
1.4	.4192	.4207	.4222	.4236	.4251	.4265	.4279	.4292	.4306	.4319
1.5	.4332	.4345	.4357	.4370	.4382	.4394	.4406	.4418	.4429	.4441
1.6	.4452	.4463	.4474	.4484	.4495	.4505	.4515	.4525	.4535	.4545
1.7	.4554	.4564	.4573	.4582	.4591	.4599	.4608	.4616	.4625	.4633
1.8	.4641	.4649	.4656	.4664	.4671	.4678	.4686	.4693	.4699	.4706
1.9	.4713	.4719	.4726	.4732	.4738	.4744	.4750	.4756	.4761	.4767
2.0	.4772	.4778	.4783	.4788	.4793	.4798	.4803	.4808	.4812	.4817
2.1	.4821	.4826	.4830	.4834	.4838	.4842	.4846	.4850	.4854	.4857
2.2	.4861	.4864	.4868	.4871	.4875	.4878	.4881	.4884	.4887	.4890
2.3	.4893	.4896	.4898	.4901	.4904	.4906	.4909	.4911	.4913	.4916
2.4	.4918	.4920	.4922	.4925	.4927	.4929	.4931	.4932	.4934	.4936
2.5	.4938	.4940	.4941	.4943	.4945	.4946	.4948	.4949	.4951	.4952
2.6	.4953	.4955	.4956	.4957	.4959	.4960	.4961	.4962	.4963	.4964
2.7	.4965	.4966	.4967	.4968	.4969	.4970	.4971	.4972	.4973	.4974
2.8	.4974	.4975	.4976	.4977	.4977	.4978	.4979	.4979	.4980	.4981
2.9	.4981	.4982	.4982	.4983	.4984	.4984	.4985	.4985	.4986	.4986
3.0	.49865	.49869	.49874	.49878	.49882	.49886	.49889	.49893	.49897	.49900
3.1	.49903	.49906	.49910	.49913	.49916	.49918	.49921	.49924	.49926	.49929
3.2	.49931	.49934	.49936	.49938	.49940	.49942	.49944	.49946	.49948	.49950
3.3	.49952	.49953	.49955	.49957	.49958	.49960	.49961	.49962	.49964	.49965
3.4	.49966	.49968	.49969	.49970	.49971	.49972	.49973	.49974	.49975	.49976
3.5	.49977	.49978	.49978	.49979	.49980	.49981	.49981	.49982	.49983	.49983
3.6	.49984	.49985	.49985	.49986	.49986	.49987	.49987	.49988	.49988	.49989
3.7	.49989	.49990	.49990	.49990	.49991	.49991	.49992	.49992	.49992	.49992
3.8	.49993	.49993	.49993	.49994	.49994	.49994	.49994	.49995	.49995	.49995
3.9	.49995	.49995	.49996	.49996	.49996	.49996	.49996	.49996	.49997	.49997

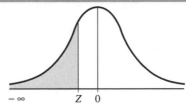

Entry represents area under the cumulative standardized normal distribution from $-\infty$ to z

z	.00	.01	.02	.03	.04	.05	.06	.07	.08	.09
−3.9	.00005	.00005	.00004	.00004	.00004	.00004	.00004	.00004	.00003	.00003
−3.8	.00007	.00007	.00007	.00006	.00006	.00006	.00006	.00005	.00005	.00005
−3.7	.00011	.00010	.00010	.00010	.00009	.00009	.00008	.00008	.00008	.00008
−3.6	.00016	.00015	.00015	.00014	.00014	.00013	.00013	.00012	.00012	.00011
−3.5	.00023	.00022	.00022	.00021	.00020	.00019	.00019	.00018	.00017	.00017
−3.4	.00034	.00032	.00031	.00030	.00029	.00028	.00027	.00026	.00025	.00024
−3.3	.00048	.00047	.00045	.00043	.00042	.00040	.00039	.00038	.00036	.00035
−3.2	.00069	.00066	.00064	.00062	.00060	.00058	.00056	.00054	.00052	.00050
−3.1	.00097	.00094	.00090	.00087	.00084	.00082	.00079	.00076	.00074	.00071
−3.0	.00135	.00131	.00126	.00122	.00118	.00114	.00111	.00107	.00103	.00100
−2.9	.0019	.0018	.0018	.0017	.0016	.0016	.0015	.0015	.0014	.0014
−2.8	.0026	.0025	.0024	.0023	.0023	.0022	.0021	.0021	.0020	.0019
−2.7	.0035	.0034	.0033	.0032	.0031	.0030	.0029	.0028	.0027	.0026
−2.6	.0047	.0045	.0044	.0043	.0041	.0040	.0039	.0038	.0037	.0036
−2.5	.0062	.0060	.0059	.0057	.0055	.0054	.0052	.0051	.0049	.0048
−2.4	.0082	.0080	.0078	.0075	.0073	.0071	.0069	.0068	.0066	.0064
−2.3	.0107	.0104	.0102	.0099	.0096	.0094	.0091	.0089	.0087	.0084
−2.2	.0139	.0136	.0132	.0129	.0125	.0122	.0119	.0116	.0113	.0110
−2.1	.0179	.0174	.0170	.0166	.0162	.0158	.0154	.0150	.0146	.0143
−2.0	.0228	.0222	.0217	.0212	.0207	.0202	.0197	.0192	.0188	.0183
−1.9	.0287	.0281	.0274	.0268	.0262	.0256	.0250	.0244	.0239	.0233
−1.8	.0359	.0351	.0344	.0336	.0329	.0322	.0314	.0307	.0301	.0294
−1.7	.0446	.0436	.0427	.0418	.0409	.0401	.0392	.0384	.0375	.0367
−1.6	.0548	.0537	.0526	.0516	.0505	.0495	.0485	.0475	.0465	.0455
−1.5	.0668	.0655	.0643	.0630	.0618	.0606	.0594	.0582	.0571	.0559
−1.4	.0808	.0793	.0778	.0764	.0749	.0735	.0721	.0708	.0694	.0681
−1.3	.0968	.0951	.0934	.0918	.0901	.0885	.0869	.0853	.0838	.0823
−1.2	.1151	.1131	.1112	.1093	.1075	.1056	.1038	.1020	.1003	.0985
−1.1	.1357	.1335	.1314	.1292	.1271	.1251	.1230	.1210	.1190	.1170
−1.0	.1587	.1562	.1539	.1515	.1492	.1469	.1446	.1423	.1401	.1379
−0.9	.1841	.1814	.1788	.1762	.1736	.1711	.1685	.1660	.1635	.1611
−0.8	.2119	.2090	.2061	.2033	.2005	.1977	.1949	.1922	.1894	.1867
−0.7	.2420	.2388	.2358	.2327	.2296	.2266	.2236	.2006	.2177	.2148
−0.6	.2743	.2709	.2676	.2643	.2611	.2578	.2546	.2514	.2482	.2451
−0.5	.3085	.3050	.3015	.2981	.2946	.2912	.2877	.2843	.2810	.2776
−0.4	.3446	.3409	.3372	.3336	.3300	.3264	.3228	.3192	.3156	.3121
−0.3	.3821	.3783	.3745	.3707	.3669	.3632	.3594	.3557	.3520	.3483
−0.2	.4207	.4168	.4129	.4090	.4052	.4013	.3974	.3936	.3897	.3859
−0.1	.4602	.4562	.4522	.4483	.4443	.4404	.4364	.4325	.4286	.4247
−0.0	.5000	.4960	.4920	.4880	.4840	.4801	.4761	.4721	.4681	.4641

(continued)

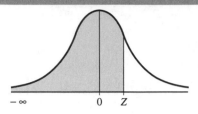

Entry represents area under the cumulative standardized normal distribution from −∞ to z

z	.00	.01	.02	.03	.04	.05	.06	.07	.08	.09
0.0	.5000	.5040	.5080	.5120	.5160	.5199	.5239	.5279	.5319	.5359
0.1	.5398	.5438	.5478	.5517	.5557	.5596	.5636	.5675	.5714	.5753
0.2	.5793	.5832	.5871	.5910	.5948	.5987	.6026	.6064	.6103	.6141
0.3	.6179	.6217	.6255	.6293	.6331	.6368	.6406	.6443	.6480	.6517
0.4	.6554	.6591	.6628	.6664	.6700	.6736	.6772	.6808	.6844	.6879
0.5	.6915	.6950	.6985	.7019	.7054	.7088	.7123	.7157	.7190	.7224
0.6	.7257	.7291	.7324	.7357	.7389	.7422	.7454	.7486	.7518	7549
0.7	.7580	.7612	.7642	.7673	.7704	.7734	.7764	.7794	.7823	.7852
0.8	.7881	.7910	.7939	.7967	.7995	.8023	.8051	.8078	.8106	.8133
0.9	.8159	.8186	.8212	.8238	.8264	.8289	.8315	.8340	.8365	.8389
1.0	.8413	.8438	.8461	.8485	.8508	.8531	.8554	.8577	.8599	.8621
1.1	.8643	.8665	.8686	.8708	.8729	.8749	.8770	.8790	.8810	.8830
1.2	.8849	.8869	.8888	.8907	.8925	.8944	.8962	.8980	.8997	.9015
1.3	.9032	.9089	.9066	.9082	.9099	.9115	.9131	.9147	.9162	.9177
1.4	.9192	.9207	.9222	.9236	.9251	.9265	.9279	.9292	.9306	.9319
1.5	.9332	.9345	.9357	.9370	.9382	.9394	.9406	.9418	.9429	.9441
1.6	.9452	.9463	.9474	.9484	.9495	.9505	.9515	.9525	.9535	.9545
1.7	.9554	.9564	.9573	.9582	.9591	.9599	.9608	.9616	.9625	.9633
1.8	.9641	.9649	.9656	.9664	.9671	.9678	.9686	.9693	.9699	.9706
1.9	.9713	.9719	.9726	.9732	.9738	.9744	.9750	.9756	.9761	.9767
2.0	.9772	.9778	.9783	.9788	.9793	.9798	.9803	.9808	.9812	.9817
2.1	.9821	.9826	.9830	.9834	.9838	.9842	.9846	.9850	.9854	.9857
2.2	.9861	.9864	.9868	.9871	.9875	.9878	.9881	.9884	.9887	.9890
2.3	.9893	.9896	.9898	.9901	.9904	.9906	.9909	.9911	.9913	.9916
2.4	.9918	.9920	.9922	.9925	.9927	.9929	.9931	.9932	.9934	.9936
2.5	.9938	.9940	.9941	.9943	.9945	.9946	.9948	.9949	.9951	.9952
2.6	.9953	.9955	.9956	.9957	.9959	.9960	.9961	.9962	.9963	.9964
2.7	.9965	.9966	.9967	.9968	.9969	.9970	.9971	.9972	.9973	.9974
2.8	.9974	.9975	.9976	.9977	.9977	.9978	.9979	.9979	.9980	.9981
2.9	.9981	.9982	.9982	.9983	.9984	.9984	.9985	.9985	.9986	.9986
3.0	.99865	.99869	.99874	.99878	.99882	.99886	.99889	.99893	.99897	.99900
3.1	.99903	.99906	.99910	.99913	.99916	.99918	.99921	.99924	.99926	.99929
3.2	.99931	.99934	.99936	.99938	.99940	.99942	.99944	.99946	.99948	.99950
3.3	.99952	.99953	.99955	.99957	.99958	.99960	.99961	.99962	.99964	.99965
3.4	.99966	.99968	.99969	.99970	.99971	.99972	.99973	.99974	.99975	.99976
3.5	.99977	.99978	.99978	.99979	.99980	.99981	.99981	.99982	.99983	.99983
3.6	.99984	.99985	.99985	.99986	.99986	.99987	.99987	.99988	.99988	.99989
3.7	.99989	.99990	.99990	.99990	.99991	.99991	.99992	.99992	.99992	.99992
3.8	.99993	.99993	.99993	.99994	.99994	.99994	.99994	.99995	.99995	.99995
3.9	.99995	.99995	.99996	.99996	.99996	.99996	.99996	.99996	.99997	.99997

Table A.3 Critical Values of *t*

For particular number of degrees of freedom, entry represents the critical value of t *corresponding to a specified upper tail area (α)*

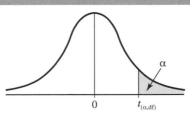

Degrees of Freedom	Upper Tail Areas					
	.25	.10	.05	.025	.01	.005
1	1.0000	3.0777	6.3138	12.7062	31.8207	63.6574
2	0.8165	1.8856	2.9200	4.3027	6.9646	9.9248
3	0.7649	1.6377	2.3534	3.1824	4.5407	5.8409
4	0.7407	1.5332	2.1318	2.7764	3.7469	4.6041
5	0.7267	1.4759	2.0150	2.5706	3.3649	4.0322
6	0.7176	1.4398	1.9432	2.4469	3.1427	3.7074
7	0.7111	1.4149	1.8946	2.3646	2.9980	3.4995
8	0.7064	1.3968	1.8595	2.3060	2.8965	3.3554
9	0.7027	1.3830	1.8331	2.2622	2.8214	3.2498
10	0.6998	1.3722	1.8125	2.2281	2.7638	3.1693
11	0.6974	1.3634	1.7959	2.2010	2.7181	3.1058
12	0.6955	1.3562	1.7823	2.1788	2.6810	3.0545
13	0.6938	1.3502	1.7709	2.1604	2.6503	3.0123
14	0.6924	1.3450	1.7613	2.1448	2.6245	2.9768
15	0.6912	1.3406	1.7531	2.1315	2.6025	2.9467
16	0.6901	1.3368	1.7459	2.1199	2.5835	2.9208
17	0.6892	1.3334	1.7396	2.1098	2.5669	2.8982
18	0.6884	1.3304	1.7341	2.1009	2.5524	2.8784
19	0.6876	1.3277	1.7291	2.0930	2.5395	2.8609
20	0.6870	1.3253	1.7247	2.0860	2.5280	2.8453
21	0.6864	1.3232	1.7207	2.0796	2.5177	2.8314
22	0.6858	1.3212	1.7171	2.0739	2.5083	2.8188
23	0.6853	1.3195	1.7139	2.0687	2.4999	2.8073
24	0.6848	1.3178	1.7109	2.0639	2.4922	2.7969
25	0.6844	1.3163	1.7081	2.0595	2.4851	2.7874
26	0.6840	1.3150	1.7056	2.0555	2.4786	2.7787
27	0.6837	1.3137	1.7033	2.0518	2.4727	2.7707
28	0.6834	1.3125	1.7011	2.0484	2.4671	2.7633
29	0.6830	1.3114	1.6991	2.0452	2.4620	2.7564
30	0.6828	1.3104	1.6973	2.0423	2.4573	2.7500
31	0.6825	1.3095	1.6955	2.0395	2.4528	2.7440
32	0.6822	1.3086	1.6939	2.0369	2.4487	2.7385
33	0.6820	1.3077	1.6924	2.0345	2.4448	2.7333
34	0.6818	1.3070	1.6909	2.0322	2.4411	2.7284
35	0.6816	1.3062	1.6896	2.0301	2.4377	2.7238
36	0.6814	1.3055	1.6883	2.0281	2.4345	2.1795
37	0.6812	1.3049	1.6871	2.0262	2.4314	2.7154
38	0.6810	1.3042	1.6860	2.0244	2.4286	2.7116
39	0.6808	1.3036	1.6849	2.0227	2.4258	2.7079
40	0.6807	1.3031	1.6839	2.0211	2.4233	2.7045
41	0.6805	1.3025	1.6829	2.0195	2.4208	2.7012
42	0.6804	1.3020	1.6820	2.0181	2.4185	2.6981
43	0.6802	1.3016	1.6811	2.0167	2.4163	2.6951
44	0.6801	1.3011	1.6802	2.0154	2.4141	2.6923
45	0.6800	1.3006	1.6794	2.0141	2.4121	2.6896
46	0.6799	1.3002	1.6787	2.0129	2.4102	2.6870
47	0.6797	1.2998	1.6779	2.0117	2.4083	2.6846
48	0.6796	1.2994	1.6772	2.0106	2.4066	2.6822
49	0.6795	1.2991	1.6766	2.0096	2.4049	2.6800
50	0.6794	1.2987	1.6759	2.0086	2.4033	2.6778

(continued)

Degrees of Freedom	Upper Tail Areas					
	.25	.10	.05	.025	.01	.005
51	0.6793	1.2984	1.6753	2.0076	2.4017	2.6757
52	0.6792	1.2980	1.6747	2.0066	2.4002	2.6737
53	0.6791	1.2977	1.6741	2.0057	2.3988	2.6718
54	0.6791	1.2974	1.6736	2.0049	2.3974	2.6700
55	0.6790	1.2971	1.6730	2.0040	2.3961	2.6682
56	0.6789	1.2969	1.6725	2.0032	2.3948	2.6665
57	0.6788	1.2966	1.6720	2.0025	2.3936	2.6649
58	0.6787	1.2963	1.6716	2.0017	2.3924	2.6633
59	0.6787	1.2961	1.6711	2.0010	2.3912	2.6618
60	0.6786	1.2958	1.6706	2.0003	2.3901	2.6603
61	0.6785	1.2956	1.6702	1.9996	2.3890	2.6589
62	0.6785	1.2954	1.6698	1.9990	2.3880	2.6575
63	0.6784	1.2951	1.6694	1.9983	2.3870	2.6561
64	0.6783	1.2949	1.6690	1.9977	2.3860	2.6549
65	0.6783	1.2947	1.6686	1.9971	2.3851	2.6536
66	0.6782	1.2945	1.6683	1.9966	2.3842	2.6524
67	0.6782	1.2943	1.6679	1.9960	2.3833	2.6512
68	0.6781	1.2941	1.6676	1.9955	2.3824	2.6501
69	0.6781	1.2939	1.6672	1.9949	2.3816	2.6490
70	0.6780	1.2938	1.6669	1.9944	2.3808	2.6479
71	0.6780	1.2936	1.6666	1.9939	2.3800	2.6469
72	0.6779	1.2934	1.6663	1.9935	2.3793	2.6459
73	0.6779	1.2933	1.6660	1.9930	2.3785	2.6449
74	0.6778	1.4931	1.6657	1.9925	2.3778	2.6439
75	0.6778	1.2929	1.6654	1.9921	2.3771	2.6430
76	0.6777	1.2928	1.6652	1.9917	2.3764	2.6421
77	0.6777	1.2926	1.6649	1.9913	2.3758	2.6412
78	0.6776	1.2925	1.6646	1.9908	2.3751	2.6403
79	0.6776	1.2924	1.6644	1.9905	2.3745	2.6395
80	0.6776	1.2922	1.6641	1.9901	2.3739	2.6387
81	0.6775	1.2921	1.6639	1.9897	2.3733	2.6379
82	0.6775	1.2920	1.6636	1.9893	2.3727	2.6371
83	0.6775	1.2918	1.6634	1.9890	2.3721	2.6364
84	0.6774	1.2917	1.6632	1.9886	2.3716	2.6356
85	0.6774	1.2916	1.6630	1.9883	2.3710	2.6349
86	0.6774	1.2915	1.6628	1.9879	2.3705	2.6342
87	0.6773	1.2914	1.6626	1.9876	2.3700	2.6335
88	0.6773	1.2912	1.6624	1.9873	2.3695	2.6329
89	0.6773	1.2911	1.6622	1.9870	2.3690	2.6322
90	0.6772	1.2910	1.6620	1.9867	2.3685	2.6316
91	0.6772	1.2909	1.6618	1.9864	2.3680	2.6309
92	0.6772	1.2908	1.6616	1.9861	2.3676	2.6303
93	0.6771	1.2907	1.6614	1.9858	2.3671	2.6297
94	0.6771	1.2906	1.6612	1.9855	2.3667	2.6291
95	0.6771	1.2905	1.6611	1.9853	2.3662	2.6286
96	0.6771	1.2904	1.6609	1.9850	2.3658	2.6280
97	0.6770	1.2903	1.6607	1.9847	2.3654	2.6275
98	0.6770	1.2902	1.6606	1.9845	2.3650	2.6269
99	0.6770	1.2902	1.6604	1.9842	2.3646	2.6264
100	0.6770	1.2901	1.6602	1.9840	2.3642	2.6259
110	0.6767	1.2893	1.6588	1.9818	2.3607	2.6213
120	0.6765	1.2886	1.6577	1.9799	2.3578	2.6174
∞	0.6745	1.2816	1.6449	1.9600	2.3263	2.5758

Table A.4 Critical Values of F

For a particular combination of numerator and denominator degrees of freedom, entry represents the critical values of F corresponding to a specified upper tail area (α)

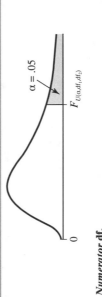

$\alpha = .05$

$F_{U(\alpha, df_1, df_2)}$

Numerator df_1

Denominator df_2	1	2	3	4	5	6	7	8	9	10	12	15	20	24	30	40	60	120	∞
1	161.4	199.5	215.7	224.6	230.2	234.0	236.8	238.9	240.5	241.9	243.9	245.9	248.0	249.1	250.1	251.1	252.2	253.3	254.3
2	18.51	19.00	19.16	19.25	19.30	19.33	19.35	19.37	19.38	19.40	19.41	19.43	19.45	19.45	19.46	19.47	19.48	19.49	19.50
3	10.13	9.55	9.28	9.12	9.01	8.94	8.89	8.85	8.81	8.79	8.74	8.70	8.66	8.64	8.62	8.59	8.57	8.55	8.53
4	7.71	6.94	6.59	6.39	6.26	6.16	6.09	6.04	6.00	5.96	5.91	5.86	5.80	5.77	5.75	5.72	5.69	5.66	5.63
5	6.61	5.79	5.41	5.19	5.05	4.95	4.88	4.82	4.77	4.74	4.68	4.62	4.56	4.53	4.50	4.46	4.43	4.40	4.36
6	5.99	5.14	4.76	4.53	4.39	4.28	4.21	4.15	4.10	4.06	4.00	3.94	3.87	3.84	3.81	3.77	3.74	3.70	3.67
7	5.59	4.74	4.35	4.12	3.97	3.87	3.79	3.73	3.68	3.64	3.57	3.51	3.44	3.41	3.38	3.34	3.30	3.27	3.23
8	5.32	4.46	4.07	3.84	3.69	3.58	3.50	3.44	3.39	3.35	3.28	3.22	3.15	3.12	3.08	3.04	3.01	2.97	2.93
9	5.12	4.26	3.86	3.63	3.48	3.37	3.29	3.23	3.18	3.14	3.07	3.01	2.94	2.90	2.86	2.83	2.79	2.75	2.71
10	4.96	4.10	3.71	3.48	3.33	3.22	3.14	3.07	3.02	2.98	2.91	2.85	2.77	2.74	2.70	2.66	2.62	2.58	2.54
11	4.84	3.98	3.59	3.36	3.20	3.09	3.01	2.95	2.90	2.85	2.79	2.72	2.65	2.61	2.57	2.53	2.49	2.45	2.40
12	4.75	3.89	3.49	3.26	3.11	3.00	2.91	2.85	2.80	2.75	2.69	2.62	2.54	2.51	2.47	2.43	2.38	2.34	2.30
13	4.67	3.81	3.41	3.18	3.03	2.92	2.83	2.77	2.71	2.67	2.60	2.53	2.46	2.42	2.38	2.34	2.30	2.25	2.21
14	4.60	3.74	3.34	3.11	2.96	2.85	2.76	2.70	2.65	2.60	2.53	2.46	2.39	2.35	2.31	2.27	2.22	2.18	2.13
15	4.54	3.68	3.29	3.06	2.90	2.79	2.71	2.64	2.59	2.54	2.48	2.40	2.33	2.29	2.25	2.20	2.16	2.11	2.07
16	4.49	3.63	3.24	3.01	2.85	2.74	2.66	2.59	2.54	2.49	2.42	2.35	2.28	2.24	2.19	2.15	2.11	2.06	2.01
17	4.45	3.59	3.20	2.96	2.81	2.70	2.61	2.55	2.49	2.45	2.38	2.31	2.23	2.19	2.15	2.10	2.06	2.01	1.96
18	4.41	3.55	3.16	2.93	2.77	2.66	2.58	2.51	2.46	2.41	2.34	2.27	2.19	2.15	2.11	2.06	2.02	1.97	1.92
19	4.38	3.52	3.13	2.90	2.74	2.63	2.54	2.48	2.42	2.38	2.31	2.23	2.16	2.11	2.07	2.03	1.98	1.93	1.88
20	4.35	3.49	3.10	2.87	2.71	2.60	2.51	2.45	2.39	2.35	2.28	2.20	2.12	2.08	2.04	1.99	1.95	1.90	1.84
21	4.32	3.47	3.07	2.84	2.68	2.57	2.49	2.42	2.37	2.32	2.25	2.18	2.10	2.05	2.01	1.96	1.92	1.87	1.81
22	4.30	3.44	3.05	2.82	2.66	2.55	2.46	2.40	2.34	2.30	2.23	2.15	2.07	2.03	1.98	1.94	1.89	1.84	1.78
23	4.28	3.42	3.03	2.80	2.64	2.53	2.44	2.37	2.32	2.27	2.20	2.13	2.05	2.01	1.96	1.91	1.86	1.81	1.76
24	4.26	3.40	3.01	2.78	2.62	2.51	2.42	2.36	2.30	2.25	2.18	2.11	2.03	1.98	1.94	1.89	1.84	1.79	1.73
25	4.24	3.39	2.99	2.76	2.60	2.49	2.40	2.34	2.28	2.24	2.16	2.09	2.01	1.96	1.92	1.87	1.82	1.77	1.71
26	4.23	3.37	2.98	2.74	2.59	2.47	2.39	2.32	2.27	2.22	2.15	2.07	1.99	1.95	1.90	1.85	1.80	1.75	1.69
27	4.21	3.35	2.96	2.73	2.57	2.46	2.37	2.31	2.25	2.20	2.13	2.06	1.97	1.93	1.88	1.84	1.79	1.73	1.67
28	4.20	3.34	2.95	2.71	2.56	2.45	2.36	2.29	2.24	2.19	2.12	2.04	1.96	1.91	1.87	1.82	1.77	1.71	1.65
29	4.18	3.33	2.93	2.70	2.55	2.43	2.35	2.28	2.22	2.18	2.10	2.03	1.94	1.90	1.85	1.81	1.75	1.70	1.64
30	4.17	3.32	2.92	2.69	2.53	2.42	2.33	2.27	2.21	2.16	2.09	2.01	1.93	1.89	1.84	1.79	1.74	1.68	1.62
40	4.08	3.23	2.84	2.61	2.45	2.34	2.25	2.18	2.12	2.08	2.00	1.92	1.84	1.79	1.74	1.69	1.64	1.58	1.51
60	4.00	3.15	2.76	2.53	2.37	2.25	2.17	2.10	2.04	1.99	1.92	1.84	1.75	1.70	1.65	1.59	1.53	1.47	1.39
120	3.92	3.07	2.68	2.45	2.29	2.17	2.09	2.02	1.96	1.91	1.83	1.75	1.66	1.61	1.55	1.50	1.43	1.35	1.25
∞	3.84	3.00	2.60	2.37	2.21	2.10	2.01	1.94	1.88	1.83	1.75	1.67	1.57	1.52	1.46	1.39	1.32	1.22	1.00

(continued)

Table A.4 *(continued)*

$\alpha = .025$

$F_{U(\alpha, df_1, df_2)}$

Numerator df_1

Denominator df_2	1	2	3	4	5	6	7	8	9	10	12	15	20	24	30	40	60	120	∞
1	647.8	799.5	864.2	899.6	921.8	937.1	948.2	956.7	963.3	968.6	976.7	984.9	993.1	997.2	1001	1006	1010	1014	1018
2	38.51	39.00	39.17	39.25	39.30	39.33	39.36	39.37	39.39	39.40	39.41	39.43	39.45	39.46	39.46	39.47	39.48	39.49	39.50
3	17.44	16.04	15.44	15.10	14.88	14.73	14.62	14.54	14.47	14.42	14.34	14.25	14.17	14.12	14.08	14.04	13.99	13.95	13.90
4	12.22	10.65	9.98	9.60	9.36	9.20	9.07	8.98	8.90	8.84	8.75	8.66	8.56	8.51	8.46	8.41	8.36	8.31	8.26
5	10.01	8.43	7.76	7.39	7.15	6.98	6.85	6.76	6.68	6.62	6.52	6.43	6.33	6.28	6.23	6.18	6.12	6.07	6.02
6	8.81	7.26	6.60	6.23	5.99	5.82	5.70	5.60	5.52	5.46	5.37	5.27	5.17	5.12	5.07	5.01	4.96	4.90	4.85
7	8.07	6.54	5.89	5.52	5.29	5.12	4.99	4.90	4.82	4.76	4.67	4.57	4.47	4.42	4.36	4.31	4.25	4.20	4.14
8	7.57	6.06	5.42	5.05	4.82	4.65	4.53	4.43	4.36	4.30	4.20	4.10	4.00	3.95	3.89	3.84	3.78	3.73	3.67
9	7.21	5.71	5.08	4.72	4.48	4.32	4.20	4.10	4.03	3.96	3.87	3.77	3.67	3.61	3.56	3.51	3.45	3.39	3.33
10	6.94	5.46	4.83	4.47	4.24	4.07	3.95	3.85	3.78	3.72	3.62	3.52	3.42	3.37	3.31	3.26	3.20	3.14	3.08
11	6.72	5.26	4.63	4.28	4.04	3.88	3.76	3.66	3.59	3.53	3.43	3.33	3.23	3.17	3.12	3.06	3.00	2.94	2.88
12	6.55	5.10	4.47	4.12	3.89	3.73	3.61	3.51	3.44	3.37	3.28	3.18	3.07	3.02	2.96	2.91	2.85	2.79	2.72
13	6.41	4.97	4.36	4.00	3.77	3.60	3.48	3.39	3.31	3.25	3.15	3.05	2.95	2.89	2.84	2.78	2.72	2.66	2.60
14	6.30	4.86	4.24	3.89	3.66	3.50	3.38	3.29	3.21	3.15	3.05	2.95	2.84	2.79	2.73	2.67	2.61	2.55	2.49
15	6.20	4.77	4.15	3.80	3.58	3.41	3.29	3.20	3.12	3.06	2.96	2.86	2.76	2.70	2.64	2.59	2.52	2.46	2.40
16	6.12	4.69	4.08	3.73	3.50	3.34	3.22	3.12	3.05	2.99	2.89	2.79	2.68	2.63	2.57	2.51	2.45	2.38	2.32
17	6.04	4.62	4.01	3.66	3.44	3.28	3.16	3.06	2.98	2.92	2.82	2.72	2.62	2.56	2.50	2.44	2.38	2.32	2.25
18	5.98	4.56	3.95	3.61	3.38	3.22	3.10	3.01	2.93	2.87	2.77	2.67	2.56	2.50	2.44	2.38	2.32	2.26	2.19
19	5.92	4.51	3.90	3.56	3.33	3.17	3.05	2.96	2.88	2.82	2.72	2.62	2.51	2.45	2.39	2.33	2.27	2.20	2.13
20	5.87	4.46	3.86	3.51	3.29	3.13	3.01	2.91	2.84	2.77	2.68	2.57	2.46	2.41	2.35	2.29	2.22	2.16	2.09
21	5.83	4.42	3.82	3.48	3.25	3.09	2.97	2.87	2.80	2.73	2.64	2.53	2.42	2.37	2.31	2.25	2.18	2.11	2.04
22	5.79	4.38	3.78	3.44	3.22	3.05	2.93	2.84	2.76	2.70	2.60	2.50	2.39	2.33	2.27	2.21	2.14	2.08	2.00
23	5.75	4.35	3.75	3.41	3.18	3.02	2.90	2.81	2.73	2.67	2.57	2.47	2.36	2.30	2.24	2.18	2.11	2.04	1.97
24	5.72	4.32	3.72	3.38	3.15	2.99	2.87	2.78	2.70	2.64	2.54	2.44	2.33	2.27	2.21	2.15	2.08	2.01	1.94
25	5.69	4.29	3.69	3.35	3.13	2.97	2.85	2.75	2.68	2.61	2.51	2.41	2.30	2.24	2.18	2.12	2.05	1.98	1.91
26	5.66	4.27	3.67	3.33	3.10	2.94	2.82	2.73	2.65	2.59	2.49	2.39	2.28	2.22	2.16	2.09	2.03	1.95	1.88
27	5.63	4.24	3.65	3.31	3.08	2.92	2.80	2.71	2.63	2.57	2.47	2.36	2.25	2.19	2.13	2.07	2.00	1.93	1.85
28	5.61	4.22	3.63	3.29	3.06	2.90	2.78	2.69	2.61	2.55	2.45	2.34	2.23	2.17	2.11	2.05	1.98	1.91	1.83
29	5.59	4.20	3.61	3.27	3.04	2.88	2.76	2.67	2.59	2.53	2.43	2.32	2.21	2.15	2.09	2.03	1.96	1.89	1.81
30	5.57	4.18	3.59	3.25	3.03	2.87	2.75	2.65	2.57	2.51	2.41	2.31	2.20	2.14	2.07	2.01	1.94	1.87	1.79
40	5.42	4.05	3.46	3.13	2.90	2.74	2.62	2.53	2.45	2.39	2.29	2.18	2.07	2.01	1.94	1.88	1.80	1.72	1.64
60	5.29	3.93	3.34	3.01	2.79	2.63	2.51	2.41	2.33	2.27	2.17	2.06	1.94	1.88	1.82	1.74	1.67	1.58	1.48
120	5.15	3.80	3.23	2.89	2.67	2.52	2.39	2.30	2.22	2.16	2.05	1.94	1.82	1.76	1.69	1.61	1.53	1.43	1.31
∞	5.02	3.69	3.12	2.79	2.57	2.41	2.29	2.19	2.11	2.05	1.94	1.83	1.71	1.64	1.57	1.48	1.39	1.27	1.00

(continued)

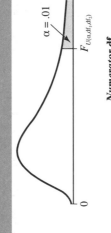

$\alpha = .01$

$F_{U(\alpha, df_1, df_2)}$

Numerator df_1

Denominator df_2	1	2	3	4	5	6	7	8	9	10	12	15	20	24	30	40	60	120	∞
1	4052	4999.5	5403	5625	5764	5859	5928	5982	6022	6056	6106	6157	6209	6235	6261	6287	6313	6339	6366
2	98.50	99.00	99.17	99.25	99.30	99.33	99.36	99.37	99.39	99.40	99.42	99.43	99.45	99.46	99.47	99.47	99.48	99.49	99.50
3	34.12	30.82	29.46	28.71	28.24	27.91	27.67	27.49	27.35	27.23	27.05	26.87	26.69	26.60	26.50	26.41	26.32	26.22	26.13
4	21.20	18.00	16.69	15.98	15.52	15.21	14.98	14.80	14.66	14.55	14.37	14.20	14.02	13.93	13.84	13.75	13.65	13.56	13.46
5	16.26	13.27	12.06	11.39	10.97	10.67	10.46	10.29	10.16	10.05	9.89	9.72	9.55	9.47	9.38	9.29	9.20	9.11	9.02
6	13.75	10.92	9.78	9.15	8.75	8.47	8.26	8.10	7.98	7.87	7.72	7.56	7.40	7.31	7.23	7.14	7.06	6.97	6.88
7	12.25	9.55	8.45	7.85	7.46	7.19	6.99	6.84	6.72	6.62	6.47	6.31	6.16	6.07	5.99	5.91	5.82	5.74	5.65
8	11.26	8.65	7.59	7.01	6.63	6.37	6.18	6.03	5.91	5.81	5.67	5.52	5.36	5.28	5.20	5.12	5.03	4.95	4.86
9	10.56	8.02	6.99	6.42	6.06	5.80	5.61	5.47	5.35	5.26	5.11	4.96	4.81	4.73	4.65	4.57	4.48	4.40	4.31
10	10.04	7.56	6.55	5.99	5.64	5.39	5.20	5.06	4.94	4.85	4.71	4.56	4.41	4.33	4.25	4.17	4.08	4.00	3.91
11	9.65	7.21	6.22	5.67	5.32	5.07	4.89	4.74	4.63	4.54	4.40	4.25	4.10	4.02	3.94	3.86	3.78	3.69	3.60
12	9.33	6.93	5.95	5.41	5.06	4.82	4.64	4.50	4.39	4.30	4.16	4.01	3.86	3.78	3.70	3.62	3.54	3.45	3.36
13	9.07	6.70	5.74	5.21	4.86	4.62	4.44	4.30	4.19	4.10	3.96	3.82	3.66	3.59	3.51	3.43	3.34	3.25	3.17
14	8.86	6.51	5.56	5.04	4.69	4.46	4.28	4.14	4.03	3.94	3.80	3.66	3.51	3.43	3.35	3.27	3.18	3.09	3.00
15	8.68	6.36	5.42	4.89	4.56	4.32	4.14	4.00	3.89	3.80	3.67	3.52	3.37	3.29	3.21	3.13	3.05	2.96	2.87
16	8.53	6.23	5.29	4.77	4.44	4.20	4.03	3.89	3.78	3.69	3.55	3.41	3.26	3.18	3.10	3.02	2.93	2.84	2.75
17	8.40	6.11	5.18	4.67	4.34	4.10	3.93	3.79	3.68	3.59	3.46	3.31	3.16	3.08	3.00	2.92	2.83	2.75	2.65
18	8.29	6.01	5.09	4.58	4.25	4.01	3.84	3.71	3.60	3.51	3.37	3.23	3.08	3.00	2.92	2.84	2.75	2.66	2.57
19	8.18	5.93	5.01	4.50	4.17	3.94	3.77	3.63	3.52	3.43	3.30	3.15	3.00	2.92	2.84	2.76	2.67	2.58	2.49
20	8.10	5.85	4.94	4.43	4.10	3.87	3.70	3.56	3.46	3.37	3.23	3.09	2.94	2.86	2.78	2.69	2.61	2.52	2.42
21	8.02	5.78	4.87	4.37	4.04	3.81	3.64	3.51	3.40	3.31	3.17	3.03	2.88	2.80	2.72	2.64	2.55	2.46	2.36
22	7.95	5.72	4.82	4.31	3.99	3.76	3.59	3.45	3.35	3.26	3.12	2.98	2.83	2.75	2.67	2.58	2.50	2.40	2.31
23	7.88	5.66	4.76	4.26	3.94	3.71	3.54	3.41	3.30	3.21	3.07	2.93	2.78	2.70	2.62	2.54	2.45	2.35	2.26
24	7.82	5.61	4.72	4.22	3.90	3.67	3.50	3.36	3.26	3.17	3.03	2.89	2.74	2.66	2.58	2.49	2.40	2.31	2.21
25	7.77	5.57	4.68	4.18	3.85	3.63	3.46	3.32	3.22	3.13	2.99	2.85	2.70	2.62	2.54	2.45	2.36	2.27	2.17
26	7.72	5.53	4.64	4.14	3.82	3.59	3.42	3.29	3.18	3.09	2.96	2.81	2.66	2.58	2.50	2.42	2.33	2.23	2.13
27	7.68	5.49	4.60	4.11	3.78	3.56	3.39	3.26	3.15	3.06	2.93	2.78	2.63	2.55	2.47	2.38	2.29	2.20	2.10
28	7.64	5.45	4.57	4.07	3.75	3.53	3.36	3.23	3.12	3.03	2.90	2.75	2.60	2.52	2.44	2.35	2.26	2.17	2.06
29	7.60	5.42	4.54	4.04	3.73	3.50	3.33	3.20	3.09	3.00	2.87	2.73	2.57	2.49	2.41	2.33	2.23	2.14	2.03
30	7.56	5.39	4.51	4.02	3.70	3.47	3.30	3.17	3.07	2.98	2.84	2.70	2.55	2.47	2.39	2.30	2.21	2.11	2.01
40	7.31	5.18	4.31	3.83	3.51	3.29	3.12	2.99	2.89	2.80	2.66	2.52	2.37	2.29	2.20	2.11	2.02	1.92	1.80
60	7.08	4.98	4.13	3.65	3.34	3.12	2.95	2.82	2.72	2.63	2.50	2.35	2.20	2.12	2.03	1.94	1.84	1.73	1.60
120	6.85	4.79	3.95	3.48	3.17	2.96	2.79	2.66	2.56	2.47	2.34	2.19	2.03	1.95	1.86	1.76	1.66	1.53	1.38
∞	6.63	4.61	3.78	3.32	3.02	2.80	2.64	2.51	2.41	2.32	2.18	2.04	1.88	1.79	1.70	1.59	1.47	1.32	1.00

(continued)

Table A.4 (continued)

$\alpha = .005$

$F_{U(\alpha, df_1, df_2)}$

Numerator df_1

Denominator df_2	1	2	3	4	5	6	7	8	9	10	12	15	20	24	30	40	60	120	∞
1	16211	20000	21615	22500	23056	23437	23715	23925	24091	24224	24426	24630	24836	24940	25044	25148	25253	25359	25465
2	198.5	199.0	199.2	199.2	199.3	199.3	199.4	199.4	199.4	199.4	199.4	199.4	199.4	199.5	199.5	199.5	199.5	199.5	199.5
3	55.55	49.80	47.47	46.19	45.39	44.84	44.43	44.13	43.88	43.69	43.39	43.08	42.78	42.62	42.47	42.31	42.15	41.99	41.83
4	31.33	26.28	24.26	23.15	22.46	21.97	21.62	21.35	21.14	20.97	20.70	20.44	20.17	20.03	19.89	19.75	19.61	19.47	19.32
5	22.78	18.31	16.53	15.56	14.94	14.51	14.20	13.96	13.77	13.62	13.38	13.15	12.90	12.78	12.66	12.53	12.40	12.27	12.14
6	18.63	14.54	12.92	12.03	11.46	11.07	10.79	10.57	10.39	10.25	10.03	9.81	9.59	9.47	9.36	9.24	9.12	9.00	8.88
7	16.24	12.40	10.88	10.05	9.52	9.16	8.89	8.68	8.51	8.38	8.18	7.97	7.75	7.65	7.53	7.42	7.31	7.19	7.08
8	14.69	11.04	9.60	8.81	8.30	7.95	7.69	7.50	7.34	7.21	7.01	6.81	6.61	6.50	6.40	6.29	6.18	6.06	5.95
9	13.61	10.11	8.72	7.96	7.47	7.13	6.88	6.69	6.54	6.42	6.23	6.03	5.83	5.73	5.62	5.52	5.41	5.30	5.19
10	12.83	9.43	8.08	7.34	6.87	6.54	6.30	6.12	5.97	5.85	5.66	5.47	5.27	5.17	5.07	4.97	4.86	4.75	4.64
11	12.23	8.91	7.60	6.88	6.42	6.10	5.86	5.68	5.54	5.42	5.24	5.05	4.86	4.76	4.65	4.55	4.44	4.34	4.23
12	11.75	8.51	7.23	6.52	6.07	5.76	5.52	5.35	5.20	5.09	4.91	4.72	4.53	4.43	4.33	4.23	4.12	4.01	3.90
13	11.37	8.19	6.93	6.23	5.79	5.48	5.25	5.08	4.94	4.82	4.64	4.46	4.27	4.17	4.07	3.97	3.87	3.76	3.65
14	11.06	7.92	6.68	6.00	5.56	5.26	5.03	4.86	4.72	4.60	4.43	4.25	4.06	3.96	3.86	3.76	3.66	3.55	3.44
15	10.80	7.70	6.48	5.80	5.37	5.07	4.85	4.67	4.54	4.42	4.25	4.07	3.88	3.79	3.69	3.58	3.48	3.37	3.26
16	10.58	7.51	6.30	5.64	5.21	4.91	4.69	4.52	4.38	4.27	4.10	3.92	3.73	3.64	3.54	3.44	3.33	3.22	3.11
17	10.38	7.35	6.16	5.50	5.07	4.78	4.56	4.39	4.25	4.14	3.97	3.79	3.61	3.51	3.41	3.31	3.21	3.10	2.98
18	10.22	7.21	6.03	5.37	4.96	4.66	4.44	4.28	4.14	4.03	3.86	3.68	3.50	3.40	3.30	3.20	3.10	2.99	2.87
19	10.07	7.09	5.92	5.27	4.85	4.56	4.34	4.18	4.04	3.93	3.76	3.59	3.40	3.31	3.21	3.11	3.00	2.89	2.78
20	9.94	6.99	5.82	5.17	4.76	4.47	4.26	4.09	3.96	3.85	3.68	3.50	3.32	3.22	3.12	3.02	2.92	2.81	2.69
21	9.83	6.89	5.73	5.09	4.68	4.39	4.18	4.01	3.88	3.77	3.60	3.43	3.24	3.15	3.05	2.95	2.84	2.73	2.61
22	9.73	6.81	5.65	5.02	4.61	4.32	4.11	3.94	3.81	3.70	3.54	3.36	3.18	3.08	2.98	2.88	2.77	2.66	2.55
23	9.63	6.73	5.58	4.95	4.54	4.26	4.05	3.88	3.75	3.64	3.47	3.30	3.12	3.02	2.92	2.82	2.71	2.60	2.48
24	9.55	6.66	5.52	4.89	4.49	4.20	3.99	3.83	3.69	3.59	3.42	3.25	3.06	2.97	2.87	2.77	2.66	2.55	2.43
25	9.48	6.60	5.46	4.84	4.43	4.15	3.94	3.78	3.64	3.54	3.37	3.20	3.01	2.92	2.82	2.72	2.61	2.50	2.38
26	9.41	6.54	5.41	4.79	4.38	4.10	3.89	3.73	3.60	3.49	3.33	3.15	2.97	2.87	2.77	2.67	2.56	2.45	2.33
27	9.34	6.49	5.36	4.74	4.34	4.06	3.85	3.69	3.56	3.45	3.28	3.11	2.93	2.83	2.73	2.63	2.52	2.41	2.29
28	9.28	6.44	5.32	4.70	4.30	4.02	3.81	3.65	3.52	3.41	3.25	3.07	2.89	2.79	2.69	2.59	2.48	2.37	2.25
29	9.23	6.40	5.28	4.66	4.26	3.98	3.77	3.61	3.48	3.38	3.21	3.04	2.86	2.76	2.66	2.56	2.45	2.33	2.21
30	9.18	6.35	5.24	4.62	4.23	3.95	3.74	3.58	3.45	3.34	3.18	3.01	2.82	2.73	2.63	2.52	2.42	2.30	2.18
40	8.83	6.07	4.98	4.37	3.99	3.71	3.51	3.35	3.22	3.12	2.95	2.78	2.60	2.50	2.40	2.30	2.18	2.06	1.93
60	8.49	5.79	4.73	4.14	3.76	3.49	3.29	3.13	3.01	2.90	2.74	2.57	2.39	2.29	2.19	2.08	1.96	1.83	1.69
120	8.18	5.54	4.50	3.92	3.55	3.28	3.09	2.93	2.81	2.71	2.54	2.37	2.19	2.09	1.98	1.87	1.75	1.61	1.43
∞	7.88	5.30	4.28	3.72	3.35	3.09	2.90	2.74	2.62	2.52	2.36	2.19	2.00	1.90	1.79	1.67	1.53	1.36	1.00

Source: Reprinted from E. S. Pearson and H. O. Hartley, eds., Biometrika Tables for Statisticians, 3d ed., 1966, by permission of the Biometrika Trustees.

324

Index

Activity times, 253
Alternative hypothesis, 112
Analysis, defined, 2
Analysis of variance (ANOVA), 125–127,
   130, 178, 179, 180
Anderson-Darling test, 136
Arithmetic mean (average), 34
Assumption cell, 84
Attributes, control charts for, 152–154
Attributes data, 10, 142, 157
Autocorrelation, 181
Average (arithmetic mean), 34

Balanced scorecard of business
   performance, 3–4
Bar charts, 23, 24, 25
Benefit/cost analysis, 263
Bernoulli distribution, 63
Best practices benchmarks, 3
Best subsets regression, 190–191
Beta distribution, 76, 77
Biased estimator, 105
Binder constraint, 288
Binomial distribution, 63–65
Box-and-whisker plots, 43–46
Branches, of decision trees, 246
Budget-constrained product selection,
   257–259
Business data, types and sources of, 3–10
Business decisions, 1–18
Business performance
   balanced scorecard of, 3
   measure of, 3–4

Categorical (nominal) data, 10–11
CB Predictor, 229–233
Central limit theorem, 85
Central tendency, measures of, 34–36
Charts and graphs
   area, 29
   bar, 23, 24
   benefits and drawbacks of, 30
   Chart Wizard, 22
   column, 23–24
   control, 143
   line, 25–28
   pie, 28–29
   run, 143
   scatter diagrams, 29–30
   stacked column, 25–26

Chi-square for independence, 127–130
Chi-square statistic, 128
Choice node, of decision tree, 246
Cluster sampling, 101, 102
Coefficient of determination, 176
Coefficient of multiple determination, 187
Coefficient of skewness, 39
Coefficient of variation, 38, 243
Column charts, 23–24
Conditional probabilities, 60–61
Confidence bands, 176–177
Confidence coefficient, hypothesis testing
   and, 113
Confidence intervals (CI), 105–106
   mean, 106–109
   population parameters, 103
   proportions, 110
   rationale for, 106
   sample size, 110–111
Confidence, level of, 105–106
Constraints, 278
Constraints function, 278
Contingency table, 127
   chi-square test, 128
Continuous data, 10
Continuous probability distributions
   exponential distribution, 72–74
   normal distribution, 68–71
   parameters, 66–67
   probability distributions in *PhStat,*
      74–75
   triangular distribution, 71–72
   uniform distribution, 67–68
Continuous random variables, 59
   examples, 61
Control charts
   analyzing, 148
   attributes, 152–154
   center line, hugging, 150–151
   control limits, hugging, 151–152
   cycles, 149–150
   design issues, 154–155
   process average shift, 148
   trends, 150
Convenience sampling, 100
Correlation, 49, 167
Correlation coefficient, 49, 176
Covariance, 49
Crystal Ball, 15, 17, 80, 82, 83, 86, 136,
   249–263

correlated assumptions, 271
distribution fitting and, 137–139
freezing assumptions, 271–272
Monte Carlo simulation, 89
output, 94–96
overlay charts, 272
sampling from a normal distribution, 84
sensitivity charts, 272–275
specifying input information, 90–94
spreadsheet model, 297–298
steps in using, 89
trend charts, 272
Cumulative distribution function, 59–60
Cumulative frequency, 33
Customer satisfaction data, 4
Customer satisfaction measures, 3, 8
Cyclical effects, 209

Data
   classifying by measurement scale, 10–11
   continuous (variables), 10
   discrete (attributes), 10
   purpose of, 54
   working with, 15–17
   See also Displaying data
Data analysis, 2, 17
   importance of, 2–3
Data, business, 3–10
Data measurement scales
   categorical (nominal), 10–11
   interval, 11
   ordinal, 11
   ratio, 11
Data profiles (fractiles), 41–43
Data visualization, 20
Deciles, 41, 43
Decision criteria and selection
   decision trees, 246–249
   expected monetary value and risk
      (EMV), 243–245
   expected value of perfect information
      (EVPI), 246
   mutually exclusive alternative decisions,
      239–241
   nonmutually exclusive alternatives,
      241–242
   opportunity loss, 245–246
   sensitivity analysis, 237–239
   single alternative decisions, 236–237
   uncertainty decisions, 242–249

Decision modeling
  example, 6–17
  importance of, 2–3
Decision models, 13, 17
  defined, 3
  types, 14
Decision trees, 246, 248–249
  disadvantage of, 263
  symbols, 247
Decision variables, defining, 298
Decisions
  business and data, 1–18
  categories of business, 235
Degrees of freedom (df), 107
Delphi method, 205, 226
  applying, 206
  conclusions, 207–208
  rounds of, 206–207
Deming W. Edwards, 141, 198, 226
Descriptive statistics
  central tendency, 34–36
  coefficient of skewness, 38, 39
  coefficient of variation, 38
  data profiles (fractiles), 41–43
  defined, 12, 30
  dispersion, 36–38
  frequency distribution and histograms,
    32–34
  Microsoft Excel support of, 30, 32
  proportion, 43
Discount rate, 236
Discrete data, 10
Discrete probability distributions, 79
  Bernoulli, 63
  binomial, 63, 64–65
  Poisson distribution, 65–66
Discrete random variables, 59
Dispersion, measures of, 36–38
Displaying data
  area charts, 29
  benefits and drawbacks of, 30
  column and bar charts, 23–25
  line charts, 25–28
  pie charts, 28–29
  scatter diagrams, 29–30
  stacked column charts, 25–26
Distribution fitting, 130, 133–136
  Crystal Ball and, 137–139
Distributions. *See* Continuous probability
  distributions; Discrete probability
  distributions
Durbin-Watson statistic, 182, 183

Erlang distribution, 76
Errors in sampling, 102
Estimation
  defined, 103
  interval estimates, 105–106
  point estimates, 103–105
  See also Confidence intervals
Event node, of decision tree, 246
Excel notes
  add trendline option, 174
  ANOVA analysis tool, 126
  CB Predictor, 229–233
  Chart Wizard, 22

column chart, 24
correlation tool, 50
F-test for equality of variances tool, 121
forecasting with exponential
  smoothing, 218
forecasting with moving averages, 213
histogram, 33
NPV and IRR functions, 236
paste function button, 65
regression tool, 179
sampling from probability
  distributions, 81
sampling tool, 101
two-sample *t*-test with unequal variances, 120
Expected monetary value and risk
  (EMV), 243–245
Expected value, 263
  random variable, 62–63
Expected value of perfect information
  (EVPI), 246
Explanatory/causal models, 204
Exponential distribution, 72–74
Exponential smoothing models, 216–217
External data, 4
Estimation of population parameters, 103
Extreme value distribution, 78

F-test for testing variances, 119–122
Factor, 125
Feasible solution, 279
Financial and market performance mea-
  sures, 3–4, 9
Financial decision model, 13
Finite populations, sampling from, 103
Fitzsimmons, J. A., 193
Forecast cell, 84
Forecasting, 168
  categories of, 203–204
  CB Predictor, 229–233
  models, 14
  practice of, 223–226
  qualitative and judgmental methods,
    204–209
  regression models, 220–223
  statistical forecasting models, 209–220
  time series, 204
  See also Qualitative and judgmental
    methods; Regression models in fore-
    casting; Statistical forecasting models
Fractiles (data profiles), 41–43
Frequency distributions, 32–34
  probability distribution contrasted with,
    61–62

Gamma distribution, 76, 77
Generated data, 4
Geometric distribution, 76, 77
Goodness-of-fit tests, 135
Graphs and charts. *See* Charts and graphs

Histograms, 32–34, 38, 39
Holt, C. C., 217
Holt-Winters model, 217, 221
Homoscedasticity, 181

Human resources measures, 4, 9
Hypergeometric distribution, 78
Hypothesis testing, 103, 130
  decision rules, 114–116
  defined, 111
  drawbacks, 125
  F-test for variances, 119–122
  hypothesis formulation, 112–113
  one-tailed test, 115
  outcomes (significance level), 113–114
  p-values, 116–118
  power of the test and, 114
  proportions, tests for, 122–124
  steps in, 112
  two-sample tests for means, 119
  two-tailed test, 114
  Type I error, 113
  Type II error, 113
  types of, 118

Independent variables, 60
Index of Leading Indicators, 203, 208
Indexes, 208–209
Indicators, 208–209
Infeasible optimization problem, 279
Information, defined, 2
Integer linear optimization problem,
  279, 304
Integer optimization models, solving,
  291–292
Internal data, 4
Internal rate of return (IRR), 236, 263
Interquartile range, 45
Interval data, 11
Interval estimates, 103

Joint probability distribution, 60
Judgment sampling, 100
Juran, Joseph M., 141

Kimes, S. E., 193
Kolmogorov-Smirnov test, 136, 137
kth percentile, 41

Lagging indicators, 208
Leading indicators, 208
Least-squares estimation, 170–173
Level of significance, hypothesis testing
  and, 113
Linear optimization models (linear
  program), 279, 280–281, 304
  difficulties with Solver, 290–291
  interpreting Solver reports, 288–290
  solving, 286–291
Location parameter, 66–67
Logistic distribution, 78
Lognormal distribution, 76, 77

Management by fact, 1–2
Marginal probabilities, 60
Mean absolute deviation (MAD), 215
Mean absolute percentage error
  (MAPE), 215
Mean square error (MSE), 215

Measurement and statistics, 10–11
  populations and samples, 12
Measurement scales for classifying data
  categorical (nominal), 10–11
  interval, 11
  ordinal, 11
  ratio, 11
Measures
  business performance, 3–4
  customer satisfaction, 3, 8
  financial and market performance, 3–4, 9
  human resources, 4, 9
  organizational effectiveness, 4, 10
  quality process, 10
  supplier and partner performance, 4, 9–10
Measures of shape, 38
Median, 35
Microsoft Excel, 2, 17, 20
  Analysis Toolpak, 14–15, 38
  Chart Wizard, 22
  descriptive statistics and, 30, 32
  using, 14–17
  See also Excel notes
Midrange, 36
Midspread, 45
Mixed integer linear optimization problem, 279
Mode, 35–36
Monte Carlo simulation, 89, 263
  budget-constrained product selection, 257–259
  project management and, 253–257
  risk analysis, 249–252
Multicollinearity, 190, 199
Multiple correlation coefficient, 187
Multiple linear regression, 169
  coefficient of multiple determination, 187
  interpreting results from, 187–188
  models, 185–186
  multiple correlation coefficient, 187
  partial regression coefficients, 186
Multiple linear regression model, 185
Multiple regression, 168, 193
Multiple regression model, 185, 198
Multistage decision trees, 248–249
Mutually exclusive alternatives decisions, 239–241

Negative binomial distribution, 76, 77
Net present value (NPV), 236, 263
Nodes, of decision trees, 246
Nominal (categorical) data, 10–11
Nomininal specification, 144
Nonlinear optimization models, solving, 292–294
Nonlinear optimization problem, 279, 304
Nonlinear terms, 194–198
Nonmutually exclusive alternatives decisions, 241–242
Nonsampling error, 102
Normal distribution, 68–71
Null hypothesis, 112

Objective function, 276
One-sample hypothesis tests, 113

Opportunity loss, 245–246
Optimal solution, 276
Optimization, 277
  constrained, 278–279
  defined, 276
  integer optimization models, solving, 291–292
  linear optimization models, solving, 286–291
  nonlinear optimization models, solving, 292–294
  problems, types of, 279–286
  risk analysis of results, 294–295
  simulation combined with, 296–304
  See also Linear optimization models; Optimization and simulation, combining; Optimization problems, types of; Spreadsheet optimization
Optimization and simulation, combining
  adding a requirement, 303–304
  constraints, specifying, 299–300
  creating new file, 298–299
  Crystal Ball spreadsheet model, 297–298
  decision variables, 298–299
  forecast, selecting, 300
  OptQuest, 297–304
  portfolio allocation model, 296–297
  results, interpreting, 303
  saving a file, 301–302
  solving problem, 301
Optimization models, 14
Optimization problems, types of
  integer optimization models, 282–283
  linear optimization, 280–281
  nonlinear optimization, 283–284
Optimization results, risk analysis of, 294–295
OptQuest, 297–304
Ordinal data, 11
Organizational effectiveness measures, 4, 10
Outliers, 36

p-charts, 152, 157
p-values, hypothesis testing, 116–118
Parameters, continuous probability distributions and, 66–67
Pareto distribution, 77, 78
Partial regression coefficients, 186
Performance of business. *See* Business performance
PHStat, 15, 17, 32, 86
  probability distributions in, 74–75
PHStat notes
  best subsets regression, 191
  binomial probabilities, 74–75
  box-and-whisker plots, 43
  chi-square test for independence, 129
  confidence intervals for the mean, 109
  expected monetary value tool, 244
  p-charts, 154
  probability plot, normal, 136
  random sample generator, 102
  sample size, determining, 112
  sampling distributions simulation, 82
  simple linear regression, 183
  stack data and unstack data tools, 16

stem-and-leaf displays, 47
  testing hypothesis for the mean, sigma unknown, 117
  $\bar{x}$- and R-charts, 147
  z-tests for proportions, 124
Point estimates, 103
  biased estimator, 105
  common, 104
  unbiased estimator, 105
Poisson distribution, 65–66
Population, defined, 12
Populations, finite, 103
Portfolio allocation model, 296–297
Predictive statistics, defined, 12
Probabilistic sampling methods, 100
Probability
  approaches, 58
  defined, 58
Probability density function, 61
Probability distribution support for Excel, 62
Probability distributions, 86
  beta, 76, 77
  conditional probabilities, 60–61
  cumulative distribution function, 59–60
  defined, 59
  Erlang distribution, 76
  expected value and variance of a random variable, 62–63
  extreme value, 78
  frequency distributions contrasted with, 61–62
  gamma, 76, 77
  geometric, 76, 77
  hypergeometric, 78
  importance of, 58
  independent variables, 60
  joint probability distribution, 60
  key concepts and tools, 58
  logistic, 78
  lognormal, 76, 77
  marginal probabilities, 60
  negative binomial, 76, 77
  Pareto, 77, 78
  probability density function, 61
  probability mass function, 59
  theoretical probability, 62
  Weibull, 76, 77
Probability mass function, 59
Probability plot, 134
Process average shift, 148
Process capability, 157
  analysis, 155–157
  index, 156
Product selection, budget-constrained, 257–259
Project Evaluation and Review Technique (PERT), 253
Proportion, 43

Qualitative and judgmental methods in forecasting, 204
  Delphi method, 205–208
  historical analogy, 205
  indicators and indexes, 208–209

Quality control
  attributes, control charts for, 152–154
  common causes of variation and, 140
  control charts design issues, 154–155
  necessity of, 140
  process capability analysis, 155–157
  special causes of variation and, 140–141
  statistical process control (SPC),
    141–142
  statistics and data analysis, 141–142
Quality process measures, 10
Quartiles, 41, 43

R-chart, 144–147
Random numbers, 78–79
Random sampling from probability distri-
    butions, 79–80
  Crystal Ball, 80, 82
  Excel and, 80–83
  random numbers, 78–79
  sampling distributions and sampling er-
    ror, 83–86
  simulation, 78
Random variables
  continuous, 59
  defined, 59
  discrete, 59
  expected value and variance of, 62–63
  importance of, 58
  key concepts and tools, 58
  standard deviation and, 63
Random variate, 80
Range, 36
Ratio data, 11
Rational subgroups, 154–155
Regression, 167–169
  analysis of variance, regression as,
    178–180
  assumptions, of analysis, 181–182
  building models, 188–191
  investment risk, applications to, 182–185
  linear, multiple, 185–188
  linear, simple, 170–173
  nonlinear models, 194–198
  ordinal and nominal independent vari-
    ables, 191–193
  variation, measuring of regression line,
    173–177
Regression analysis, 3, 167
  assumptions of, 181–182
  investment risk and, 182–185
  objective of, 173
Regression line, 170
Regression line, measuring variation,
    173–177
  coefficient of determination, 176
  confidence bands, 176–177
  correlation coefficient, 176
  standard error of estimate, 176–177
  sum of squares of the errors (SSE), 175
  sums of squares of variation explained
    by regression (SSR), 175
  total sum of squares (SST), 173, 175
Regression models, 3, 14, 198, 226
  categories of, 167–168
  developing, 169

Regression models, building
  best subsets regression, 190–191
  correlation, 189–190
  evaluate fit with adjusted R_2, 188–189
  multicollinearity, 189–190
Regression models in forecasting, 220–221
  seasonality and, 222–223
Regression models with nonlinear terms,
    194–198
Regression with ordinal and nominal inde-
    pendent variables, 191–193
Relative frequency, 33
Relative frequency definition of proba-
    bility, 58
Return-to-risk ratio, 244–245
Risk, 243
  specific, 182
  systematic, 182
Risk analysis of optimization results,
    294–295

Sample, defined, 12
Sample design, 99–100
Sampling
  probability distributions and, 79–80
  probability distributions and Excel,
    80–83
  purpose of, 102
  See also Statistical sampling
Sampling distribution of the mean, 83, 85
Sampling distributions, 83–86
Sampling error, 83–86
Sampling methods
  cluster, 101, 102
  probabilistic, 100
  stratified, 101
  subjective, 100
  systematic, 100, 102
Sampling plan
  defined, 99
  objectives, 99
Sampling (statistical error), 102
Sampling with and without
    replacement, 100
Scale parameter, 66
Seasonal effects, 209
Selection models, 14
Selection models and risk analysis
  decision criteria and selection, 235–249
  Monte Carlo simulation, applications of,
    253–259
  Monte Carlo simulation for risk analy-
    sis, 249–252
Sensitivity, 273
Sensitivity analysis, 237–239
Shape parameter, 66
Shewhart, Walter, Dr., 142
Significance of regression, 178
Simple exponential smoothing, 216
Simple linear regression, 169, 198
  defined, 170
  least-squares estimation, 170–173
Simple moving average, 210–212
Simple random sampling, 100
Simple regression, 168
Simulation, 78

Simulation models, 14
Single-stage decision tree, 248
Smoothing constant, 216
Solver, 304
Specific risk, 182
Spreadsheet optimization
  how to use, 284–285
  optimal pricing problem, solving,
    285–286
Spreadsheet software, 20
Standard deviation, 36–38
  of random variables, 63
Standard error of the estimate, 176–177
Standard error of the mean, 85
Standard normal distribution, 68–69
Statistical analysis, example, 6–17
Statistical analysis of sample data, 103
Statistical forecasting models
  error metrics and forecast accuracy,
    212, 215
  exponential smoothing models,
    216–220
  moving average model, 210–212
  time series, 209
  trend, 209
  weighted moving averages, 211–212
Statistical inference, defined, 12
Statistical measures, visual display of
  box-and-whisker plots, 43–46
  stem-and-leaf displays, 46–48
Statistical methodology, 12
Statistical process control, 157
  analyzing control charts, 148
  control charts, 143–144
  $\bar{x}$- and R-charts, 144–147
Statistical process control (SPC)
  defined, 142–143
Statistical quality control, 157
  See also Quality control
Statistical relationships, 20, 48–51
Statistical sampling, 98–99
  errors in, 102
  finite populations and, 103
  sample design, 99–100
  methods, 100–102
Statistical summaries, 20
Statistical thinking, 1–2
Statistics
  defined, 2, 12
  descriptive, 12, 20
  predictive, 12
Statistics and data analysis. *See* Quality
    control
Statistics, descriptive. *See* Descriptive
    statistics
Stem-and-leaf displays, 46–48
Stratified sampling, 101
Subjective method of probability, 58
Subjective sampling methods, 100
Sums of squares of the errors (SSE), 175
Sums of squares of variation explained by
    regression (SSR), 175
Supplier and partner performance mea-
    sures, 4, 9–10
Systematic risk, 182
Systematic sampling, 100, 102

t-distribution, 107
t-tests, 130
Theoretical probability distributions, 62
Time series, 226
    cyclical effects, 209
    forecasting and, 204
    forecasting methods used, 210
    seasonal effects, 209
Time series regression, 168
Tolerance, 144
Total sum of squares (SST), 173, 175
Triangular distribution, 71–72

Two-sample hypothesis tests, 113
Two-sample hypothesis tests for
    means, 119

Unbiased estimator, 105
Uncertainty decisions, 242–249
Uniform distribution, 67–68

Variables data, 10, 142
Variance, 36
Variance of random variables, 62–63

Variation, 157
    common causes of, 140, 141
    special causes of, 140–141
Visual data display, examples of, 20

Weibull distribution, 76, 77
Weighted moving averages, 211–212
Winters, P. R., 217

$\bar{x}$-chart, 144–147

LICENSE AGREEMENT

READ THIS LICENSE CAREFULLY BEFORE OPENING THIS PACKAGE. BY OPENING THIS PACKAGE, YOU ARE AGREEING TO THE TERMS AND CONDITIONS OF THIS LICENSE. IF YOU DO NOT AGREE, DO NOT OPEN THE PACKAGE. PROMPTLY RETURN THE UNOPENED PACKAGE AND ALL ACCOMPANYING ITEMS TO THE PLACE YOU OBTAINED THEM. THESE TERMS APPLY TO ALL LICENSED SOFTWARE ON THE DISK EXCEPT THAT THE TERMS FOR USE OF ANY SHAREWARE OR FREEWARE ON THE DISKETTES ARE AS SET FORTH IN THE ELECTRONIC LICENSE LOCATED ON THE DISK.

1. GRANT OF LICENSE and OWNERSHIP: The enclosed computer programs and data files ("Software") are licensed, not sold, to you by Prentice-Hall, Inc. ("We" or the "Company") in consideration of your purchase or adoption of the accompanying Company textbook, and your agreement to these terms. We reserve any rights not granted to you. You own only the disk(s) but we and/or licensors own the Software itself. This license allows you to use and display the enclosed copy of the Software on an unlimited number of computers at a single campus or branch or geographic location of an educational institution, for academic use only, so long as you comply with the terms of this Agreement. You may make one copy for back up only.

2. RESTRICTIONS ON USE AND TRANSFER: You may not transfer, distribute or make available the Software or the Documentation, except to instructors and students in your school in connection with the Course. You may not reverse engineer, disassemble, decompile, modify, adapt, translate or create derivative works based on the Software or the Documentation. You may be held legally responsible for any copying or copyright infringement which is caused by your failure to abide by the terms of these restrictions.

3. TERMINATION: This license is effective until terminated. This license will terminate automatically without notice from the Company if you fail to comply with any provisions or limitations of this license. Upon termination, you shall destroy the Documentation and all copies of the Software. All provisions of this Agreement as to limitation and disclaimer of warranties, limitation of liability, remedies or damages, and our ownership rights shall survive termination.

4. LIMITED WARRANTY AND DISCLAIMER OF WARRANTY: Company warrants that for a period of 60 days from the date you purchase this Software (or purchase or adopt the accompanying textbook), the Software, when properly installed and used in accordance with the Documentation, will operate in substantial conformity with the description of the Software set forth in the Documentation, and that for a period of 30 days the disk(s) on which the Software is delivered shall be free from defects in materials and workmanship under normal use. The Company does not warrant that the Software will meet your requirements or that the operation of the Software will be uninterrupted or error-free. Your only remedy and the Company's only obligation under these limited warranties is, at the Company's option, return of the disk for a refund of any amounts paid for it by you or replacement of the disk. THIS LIMITED WARRANTY IS THE ONLY WARRANTY PROVIDED BY THE COMPANY AND ITS LICENSORS, AND THE COMPANY AND ITS LICENSORS DISCLAIM ALL OTHER WARRANTIES, EXPRESS OR IMPLIED, INCLUDING WITHOUT LIMITATION, THE IMPLIED WARRANTIES OF MERCHANTABILITY AND FITNESS FOR A PARTICULAR PURPOSE. THE COMPANY DOES NOT WARRANT, GUARANTEE OR MAKE ANY REPRESENTATION REGARDING THE ACCURACY, RELIABILITY, CURRENTNESS, USE, OR RESULTS OF USE, OF THE SOFTWARE.

5. LIMITATION OF REMEDIES AND DAMAGES: IN NO EVENT, SHALL THE COMPANY OR ITS EMPLOYEES, AGENTS, LICENSORS, OR CONTRACTORS BE LIABLE FOR ANY INCIDENTAL, INDIRECT, SPECIAL, OR CONSEQUENTIAL DAMAGES ARISING OUT OF OR IN CONNECTION WITH THIS LICENSE OR THE SOFTWARE, INCLUDING FOR LOSS OF USE, LOSS OF DATA, LOSS OF INCOME OR PROFIT, OR OTHER LOSSES, SUSTAINED AS A RESULT OF INJURY TO ANY PERSON, OR LOSS OF OR DAMAGE TO PROPERTY, OR CLAIMS OF THIRD PARTIES, EVEN IF THE COMPANY OR AN AUTHORIZED REPRESENTATIVE OF THE COMPANY HAS BEEN ADVISED OF THE POSSIBILITY OF SUCH DAMAGES. IN NO EVENT SHALL THE LIABILITY OF THE COMPANY FOR DAMAGES WITH RESPECT TO THE SOFTWARE EXCEED THE AMOUNTS ACTUALLY PAID BY YOU, IF ANY, FOR THE SOFTWARE OR THE ACCOMPANYING TEXTBOOK. SOME JURISDICTIONS DO NOT ALLOW THE LIMITATION OF LIABILITY IN CERTAIN CIRCUMSTANCES, THE ABOVE LIMITATIONS MAY NOT ALWAYS APPLY.

6. GENERAL: THIS AGREEMENT SHALL BE CONSTRUED IN ACCORDANCE WITH THE LAWS OF THE UNITED STATES OF AMERICA AND THE STATE OF NEW YORK, APPLICABLE TO CONTRACTS MADE IN NEW YORK, AND SHALL BENEFIT THE COMPANY, ITS AFFILIATES AND ASSIGNEES. This Agreement is the complete and exclusive statement of the agreement between you and the Company and supersedes all proposals, prior agreements, oral or written, and any other communications between you and the company or any of its representatives relating to the subject matter. If you are a U.S. Government user, this Software is licensed with "restricted rights" as set forth in subparagraphs (a)-(d) of the Commercial Computer-Restricted Rights clause at FAR 52.227-19 or in subparagraphs (c)(1)(ii) of the Rights in Technical Data and Computer Software clause at DFARS 252.227-7013, and similar clauses, as applicable.

Should you have any questions concerning this agreement or if you wish to contact the Company for any reason, please contact in writing: Prentice Hall, Inc., Higher Education Division, Business Publishing—Media Technology Group, One Lake Street, Upper Saddle River, NJ 07458.